Studies in Regional and Local History

General Editor Nigel Goose

Previous titles in this series

Volume 1: *A Hertfordshire demesne of Westminster Abbey: Profits, productivity and weather*
by Derek Vincent Stern (edited and with an introduction by Christopher Thornton)
(ISBN 0-900458-92-5, £29.99 hb)

Volume 2: *From Hellgill to Bridge End: Aspects of economic and social change in the Upper Eden Valley, 1840–95*
by Margaret Shepherd
(ISBN 1-902806-27-1, £35.00 hb
ISBN 1-902806-32-8, £18.95 pb)

Volume 3: *Cambridge and its Economic Region, 1450–1560*
by John S. Lee
(ISBN 1-902806-47-6, £35.00 hb
ISBN 1-902806-52-2, £18.99 pb)

Volume 4: *Cultural Transition in the Chilterns and Essex Region, 350 AD to 650 AD*
by John T. Baker
(ISBN 1-902806-46-8, £35.00 hb
ISBN 1-902806-53-0, £18.99 pb)

Volume 5: *A Pleasing Prospect: Society and culture in eighteenth-century Colchester*
by Shani D'Cruze
(ISBN 1-902806-72-7 hb
ISBN 1-902806-73-5 pb)

Agriculture and Rural Society after the Black Death

Common themes and regional variations

Edited by
Ben Dodds and Richard Britnell

University of Hertfordshire Press
Studies in Regional and Local History

Volume 6

First published in Great Britain in 2008 by
University of Hertfordshire Press
Learning and Information Services
University of Hertfordshire
College Lane
Hatfield
Hertfordshire AL10 9AB

British Library Cataloguing in Publication Data
A catalogue record for this book is available from the British Library

ISBN 978-1-902806-78-5 hardback
ISBN 978-1-902806-79-2 paperback

Design by Geoff Green Book Design, CB4 5RA
Cover design by John Robertshaw, Harpenden, AL5 2JB
Printed in Great Britain by H. Charlesworth & Co. Ltd., Wakefield, WF2 9LP

Contents

List of figures vii
List of tables ix
General Editor's preface xi
Preface xiii
Abbreviations xv

Part 1: MARKETS, INCENTIVES AND THE ROLE OF PRICES

1 Markets and incentives: common themes and regional variations 3
Richard Britnell
2 English agricultural output and prices, 1350–1450: national trends and regional divergences 20
Richard Britnell
3 Regional price differentials and local economies in north-east England, *c*. 1350–*c*.1520 40
Phillipp Schofield
4 Town and region: the corn market in Aberdeen, *c*. 1398–*c*. 1468 56
Elizabeth Gemmill

Part 2: OUTPUT, PRODUCTIVITY AND THE EVIDENCE OF TITHES

5 Output and productivity: common themes and regional variations 73
Ben Dodds
6 A universal levy: tithes and economic agency 89
Robert N. Swanson
7 Patterns of decline: arable production in England, France and Castile, 1370–1450 113
Ben Dodds
8 Lord, tenant and the market: some tithe evidence from the Wessex region 132
John Hare

Part 3: LAND, LORDSHIP AND PEASANT COMMUNITIES

9 Land and lordship: common themes and regional variations 149
Richard Britnell
10 Changing land use in a moorland region: Spennymoor in the fourteenth and fifteenth centuries 168
Simon J. Harris
11 Accumulation and polarisation in two bailiwicks of the Winchester bishopric estates, 1350–1410: regional similarities and contrasts 179
John Mullan

12 Rural transformation in northern England: village communities of Durham, 1340–1400 199
Peter L. Larson

Part 4: CONCLUSION

13 Common themes and regional variations 217
Ben Dodds and Richard Britnell

Bibliography 231
Index 255

Figures

3.1a	Wheat prices compared, 1330–1500 (Durham)	45
3.1b	Wheat prices compared, 1330—1500 (Rogers)	45
3.1c	Wheat prices compared, 1330–1500 (Farmer)	46
3.2	Wheat price differentials, 1350–1500	46
7.1	Tithe receipts from between Tyne and Tees deflated to indicate arable output	116
7.2a	Estimated output in Shincliffe	118
7.2b	Estimated output in Old Durham	118
7.2c	Estimated output in 'Wastes'	118
7.2d	Estimated output in Newton	119
7.3	Percentage of San Clodio do Ribeiro (Galicia) documents mentioning newly cultivated or populated land	126
8.1	Downton grain tithe receipts, 1384–1454	135
8.2	Alton Priors grain tithe receipts, 1303–1316	136
10.1	Settlements, town lands and moorland farms of the townships around Spennymoor, showing the extent of the moor in the later Middle Ages	169
11.1	Number of land transactions on the Taunton manors, 1350–1410	182
11.2	Number of land transactions in the East Meon bailiwick, 1350–1410	182
11.3	Percentage of augmented virgates on the Taunton manors, 1350–1410	188
11.4	Percentage of augmented half virgates on the Taunton manors, 1350–1410	188
11.5	Percentage of augmented quarter virgates on the Taunton manors, 1350–1410	189
11.6	Percentage of augmented virgates in the East Meon bailiwick, 1350–1410	189
11.7	Percentage of augmented half virgates in the East Meon bailiwick, 1350–1410	190
11.8	Transfer of cottages and quarter virgates (ferlings) as a percentage of total transfers: Taunton bailiwick	191

Tables

2.1 Price movements (five year averages), 1350–79 22
2.2 Price movements (five year averages), 1370–1414 26
2.3 Price movements (five year averages), 1405–39 32
2.4 Price movements (five year averages), 1430–54 35
2.5 Indices of sown acreages and total livestock units at Wisbech Barton (Cambridgeshire) (five year averages), 1350–1429 36
2.6 Index of numbers of ewes and wethers at Crawley (Hampshire) (five year averages), 1350–1449 37
2.7 Numbers of sheep and dairy cattle at Wisbech Barton (Cambridgeshire) (five year averages), 1350–1429 37
2.8 Population index for Great Waltham and High Easter (Essex) (five year averages), 1350–1454 38
3.1 Harvest classifications compared (Durham wheat prices with national price series) 47
3.2a Frequency of runs of low price years, 1350–1500 (wheat) 48
3.2b Frequency of runs of high price years, 1350–1500 (wheat) 48
3.3 Decennial correlations of regional wheat prices with a national series (Thorold Rogers) 49
3.4 Durham Priory: decennial correlations of wheat prices with barley and oats, 1330–1500 50
3.5 Decennial correlations of wheat and rye prices, 1460–1500 51
4.1 Assized prices of wheat and malt in Aberdeen, 1398–1462 58
7.1 Arable production in the Cambrésis (after Neveux) 121
8.1 Parish tithes and demesne crops of five manors, 1270–1338 133
8.2 Parish tithes and demesne crops, 1350–1450 141
8.3 Tithe production at Meon Church, 1348–1436 144
9.1 The distribution of land in the territory of Chieri (Piedmont) in 1327 and 1437 159
10.1 Arable acres attached to two manors and nine townships around Spennymoor, 1340–1 173
10.2 Arable acres attached to two manors and nine townships around Spennymoor, 1396–7 173
10.3 Arable attached to five townships (excluding land 'in Spennymoor'), 1340–1 and 1396–7 174
11.1 The largest accumulated holdings in the Taunton bailiwick, 1350–1410 181
11.2 The largest accumulated holdings in the East Meon bailiwick, 1350–1410 183
11.3 Standard holdings with engrossments in the Taunton bailiwick, 1350–1410 185
11.4 Standard holdings with engrossments in the East Meon bailiwick, 1350–1410 186
11.5 Transfer of augmented virgates inside and outside the family in Taunton bailiwick 194
11.6 Transfer of augmented half virgates inside and outside the family in Taunton bailiwick 194

Publication grant

Publication has been made possible by a generous grant
from the Marc Fitch Fund

Studies in Regional and Local History

General Editor's preface

Each of the preceding volumes in this series have focused upon a particular geographical location as the object of study: the manor of Kinsbourne in Hertfordshire, the Upper Eden Valley in Cumbria, the town and hinterland of Cambridge, the broad region that stretched from the Chilterns to Essex and the town of Colchester in the eighteenth century. They are all monographs, and each originated in a PhD thesis. In all of these respects the current volume, the sixth in the series, is different. *Agriculture and Rural Society after the Black Death* is not a study of a particular place or region, although it does have a north-eastern England bias due to its genesis in a conference held at the University of Durham in September 2002, and where its two co-editors are based. It is also a collection of essays rather than a monograph, and includes contributions from established scholars as well as chapters that are developments of PhD research. The book's coherence, therefore, is not geographical: rather, it is thematic, and that theme is what might be called the 'problem' of the fourteenth and fifteenth centuries.

The economy and society of late medieval England is a fascinating subject of study. The fourteenth century was tremulous with change, witnessing the start of the major transformation of the later medieval period, the decline of serfdom and commutation of labour services. It is replete with economic disaster and human tragedy in the form of the famines and murrains of 1315–22 and the Black Death and subsequent plagues of 1348/9 and beyond, and it has been the focus of some of the most stimulating debates about cause and effect that medieval scholarship has produced. The fifteenth century saw the playing out of the consequences of these fourteenth-century developments, and has itself been the subject of intense scholarly controversy, both with regard to the relative importance of human agency and demographic determinism as causal influences, and with regard to the degree to which that economy and society, and the various social groups within it, witnessed economic vitality or depression. What is quite clear is that the economy and society that emerged in the early sixteenth century was a very different one to that existing at the height of demesne agriculture in the thirteenth century. The turning point remains controversial, but few would doubt that the loss of possibly one-third of the population and the subsequent paring back of numbers that the Black Death produced had a profound and long-term effect.

Historians continue to argue about the exact nature of the disease that the Black Death represented, and also about the relative importance of disease and climate change in causing the major economic disjunctures of the fourteenth century, but its impact is undeniable. With regard to that impact, however, there is considerable scope for further exploration of both the short and long-term effects, and how these manifested themselves in the various localities and regions that constituted the British Isles. This is the key contribution of the present volume. Through a series of case studies, many of which are based upon new evidence that has barely been explored to date, it offers local and regional perspectives upon the rural economy and society of later medieval Britain that demonstrate the variety that location, climate, resources and institutions could produce. These case studies are firmly bound together by editorial contributions at the start of each of the three sections of the book, as well as by a conclusion that re-emphasises the relationship between locality, region and nation, and reasserts the profound contribution to national history that local and regional studies can make.

Nigel Goose
University of Hertfordshire
May 2008

Preface

The fourteenth and fifteenth centuries were a turbulent period that has attracted the close attentions of economic historians ever since the possibility of medieval economic studies was first contemplated. The Black Death has always stood out as a disaster, although its significance as a cause of change, both in short-term and longer-term analysis, has been much discussed and disputed. Notwithstanding its severity, some analyses place a more critical turning point in economic development earlier, around 1315–30, and others place it later, around 1385–1400. One great advantage of these discussions has been to increase our awareness of the complexity and multi-causal determination of economic trends, and of the need to approach the later Middle Ages with a sharper eye to evidence of variations of experience from place to place and from time to time. The chapters in this volume have been inspired by the need to sharpen up these perceptions, both with the help of new data and by the closer analysis of what is already known.

One source of new data of general relevance derives from evidence of ecclesiastical tithe receipts, which in principle relate to peasant output as well as that of better recorded manorial demesnes. The three chapters in the volume that make use of such data were originally prepared for a conference held at the College of St Hild and St Bede in Durham in September 2002. At that time Ben Dodds was engaged in a novel and at times disconcertingly experimental research programme using evidence from the tithe receipts of Durham Priory, and there was a pressing need to have this work discussed in a wider context. John Hare kindly offered a chapter evaluating tithe evidence from the other end of England, and Robert Swanson agreed to cast a critical eye over the whole question of tithe management and the value of tithe data. These three chapters represent a new initiative in the economic history of the Middle Ages, and one which has now been advanced both by the publication of Ben Dodds' findings and by an ESRC research project to explore tithe data from southern England. The results of this work will be published over the next few years. Richard Britnell's chapter was presented at the conference as an attempt to summarise what could be said about fluctuations in the rural economy during the century after the Black Death using evidence already published. The chapters by Phillipp Schofield, Simon Harris, Elizabeth Gemmill and John Mullan were also prepared for this conference, which aimed broadly to advance our knowledge of economic and social developments in the later Middle Ages.[1] These have since been supplemented, for the purposes of this volume, with a new chapter from Peter Larson to illustrate an aspect of rural development that was not represented in the original collection.

---

1 Another paper prepared for this conference was David Stone's 'The productivity and management of sheep in late medieval England'. This was subsequently awarded the Agricultural History Society's Golden Jubilee Essay Prize, and was published in the *Agricultural History Review* 51 (2003), pp. 1–22.

The editors are committed to the view that regional studies are of greatest value when they contribute to an understanding of widespread historical changes, and to that end have contributed three introductory chapters, and a conclusion, to place the more specialised chapters in context. There is no good reason why that context should be narrowly English, since many of the changes experienced in England during the fourteenth and fifteenth centuries were closely linked to developments in much of Europe. The availability of several recent general surveys of English agrarian change in this period has persuaded us all the more that it would be useful to adopt a more broadly based approach. The northern English origins of the volume will nevertheless be apparent from the titles of the chapters; three out of the nine relate to north-eastern England and one to eastern Scotland.

Abbreviations

ACC	Aberdeen City Council
AHEW, III	E. Miller (ed.), *The agrarian history of England and Wales, III: 1348–1500* (Cambridge,1991)
AHEW, IV	J. Thirsk (ed.), *The agrarian history of England and Wales, IV: 1500–1640* (Cambridge, 1967)
Annales ESC	*Annales Économies. Sociétés. Civilisations*
AHR	*Agricultural History Review*
Bodley	Bodleian Library, Oxford
CA	Cathedral Archives
CUL	Cambridge University Library
DCM	Durham Cathedral Muniments, Durham
EcHR	*Economic History Review*
HRO	Hampshire Record Office
JEH	*Journal of Economic History*
KCA	King's College Archive, Cambridge
Lincs. AO	Lincolnshire Archives Office, Lincoln
PP	*Past and Present*
PRO	The National Archive, Public Record Office, London
RC	Record Commission
RO	Record Office
SGCA	St George's Chapel Archive, Windsor
VCH	*Victoria History of the Counties of England*
WCM	Winchester College Muniments, Winchester

Part 1

Markets, Incentives and the Role of Prices

Chapter 1

Markets and incentives: common themes and regional variations

Richard Britnell

However locally varied the commercial incentives that operated in Europe during the fourteenth and fifteenth centuries, many aspects of production and consumption were experienced almost everywhere. Agriculture was still largely the business of peasant families who used their own produce to supply much of their food and clothing; production for the market was combined with subsistence farming.[1] This was particularly true of the vegetables and fruit grown in cottage gardens, and of the poultry that scrabbled about in enclosed tofts, but much of the grain grown in village fields was also consumed by its growers, since bread remained the staple part of the normal diet. The largest units of farming, the demesne lands of kings and lords, lay and ecclesiastical, were either cultivated directly for the benefit of their owners or, more commonly, leased to others, but even these were subject to management for subsistence. Large estates had many mouths to feed and often preferred to supply themselves rather than depend upon bought produce. In addition to those resident in the central community or household, who needed to be fed daily, estate workers often received much of their wages in doles of grain. Another restriction on the amount available for sale was the amount of each year's output that growers had held back for the following year's farming operations. The proportion was much higher in the fourteenth and fifteenth centuries than now because of lower levels of productivity. In England it was usually necessary to retain a third or a quarter of the wheat harvest for seedcorn.[2]

English landlords at the time of the Black Death, and for a generation or so afterwards, generally preferred to supervise the management of their own properties rather than lease them, and it is possible from their accounts to assess how much they marketed. It turns out that even in south-eastern England they sold less than half the grain they grew each year.[3] The consumption of produce by landowners and their dependants was particularly characteristic of monasteries, colleges and hospitals.[4]

---

1 M. Aymard, 'Monnaie et économie paysanne', in V. B. Bagnoli (ed.), *La moneta nell' economia europea, secoli XIII–XVIII* (Florence, 1981), pp. 553–4; M. le Mené, *Les Campagnes angevines à la fin du moyen âge* (Nantes, 1982), pp. 292–7.

2 B. M. S. Campbell, *English seigniorial agriculture 1250–1450* (Cambridge, 2000), pp. 317-21.

3 B. M. S. Campbell, 'Measuring the commercialisation of seigneurial agriculture c. 1300', in R. H. Britnell and B. M. S. Campbell (eds), *A commercialising economy: England 1086 to c. 1300* (Manchester, 1995), pp. 154–63.

4 S. R. Epstein, *Alle origini della fattoria toscana: l'ospedale della Scala di Siena et le sue terre (metà'200 – metà '400)* (Florence, 1986), pp. 199–220; R. H. Hilton, *The economic development of some Leicestershire estates in the 14th and 15th centuries* (Oxford, 1947), pp. 79 and 131–3; R. C. Hoffmann, *Land, liberties and lordship in a late medieval countryside: agrarian structures and change in the duchy of Wrōclaw* (Philadelphia, 1989), p. 103; A. Plaisse, *La Baronie de Neubourg* (Paris, 1961), pp. 175–7.

Even commercial rents might be negotiated to ensure produce rather than cash for landlords. As the rural economy of northern Italy became more commercialised in the thirteenth century, for example, lords swung strongly into managing their estates by leasing them out, but they still exacted a large part of the rent in kind, either as fixed rents or as a fixed share of harvest. Although some of this produce was sold in city markets and elsewhere, some was used to supply their own needs.[5]

The volume of trade in agricultural produce

There were many regions like the Limousin in France where there were no large towns, and where the evidence for local trade is less than impressive, even if some aspect of farming, pastoral in this case, was relatively more commercialised than others. Regional differences in the extent of trade remain to be systematically explored by standardised criteria, since comparisons are likely to mislead without closer controls than historians currently have over their terminology. The results of such a survey are nevertheless likely to show that, despite strong contrasts between regions, some kind of local commercial infrastructure existed over most of Europe. Even in the Limousin there were numerous markets and fairs.[6] Some areas had so little trade that it is difficult to identify trading institutions of any kind, as in much of Scandinavia, western Ireland and western Scotland, but money rents were quite common even there by the fifteenth century.[7]

Despite the continuing weight of self-supply, and the existence of wide variations in the degree and character of commercial development, the multiplication of local markets across Europe implies that the marketing of surplus agricultural produce affected rural producers in almost every part of the Continent.[8] The most widespread evidence for the volume of demand at the time of the Black Death is the extent of town life and manufacturing industry. Europe had few large cities, but numerous small towns were significant centres of demand for food, fuel and raw materials because a large proportion of their inhabitants were landless and lived by manufacturing, trade or services rather than agriculture.[9] In Saxony at the start of the fourteenth century there

5 P. Jones, *Economia e società nell'Italia medievale* (Turin, 1980), pp. 234–6; L. A. Kotel'nikova, *Mondo contadino e città in Italia dall' XI al XIV secolo* (Bologna, 1975), pp. 59–60 and 68–79; D. J. Osheim, *An Italian lordship: the bishopric of Lucca in the late middle ages* (Berkeley, 1977), pp. 101–4 and 152–3.

6 J. Tricard, *Les Campagnes limousines du XIVe au XVIe siècle: originalité et limites d'une reconstruction rurale* (Paris, 1996), pp. 147–52.

7 R. H. Britnell, *Britain and Ireland, 1050–1530: economy and society* (Oxford, 2004), pp. 401–2, 512–13 and 517; S. Gissel, 'Rents and other indicators', in *idem et al. Desertion and land colonization in the nordic countries, c. 1300–1600* (Stockholm, 1981), pp. 145–53.

8 R. H. Britnell, 'Local trade, remote trade: institutions, information and market integration, 1270–1330', in S. Cavaciocchi (ed.), *Fieri e mercati nella integrazione delle economie europee, secc. XIII–XVIII* (Florence, 2001), pp. 185–203; C. Desplat (ed.), *Foires et marchés dans les campagnes de l'Europe médiévale et moderne* (Toulouse, 1996), pp. 15–103; Hoffmann, *Land, liberties and lordship*, pp. 259–60.

9 W. Abel, *Geschichte der deutschen Landwirtshaft* (Stuttgart, 1962), pp. 49–51; R. H. Britnell, 'Urban demand in the English economy, 1300–1600', in J. A. Galloway (ed.), *Trade, urban hinterlands and market integration c.1300–1600* (London, 2000), pp. 4–9 and 1–21; G. Cherubini, 'Foires et marchés

were about 103 towns of which almost half had fewer than 500 inhabitants, and none more than 5,000, but together they are estimated to have accommodated a fifth of the population of the province.[10] Many larger villages, too, contained poor families, who needed to buy their food because they had too little land to grow it themselves. Wool for textiles, hides for leatherware, and timber for carpentry and construction, were all vital to the functioning of everyday life, and these products were supplied in the countryside to meet market demand as well as family subsistence. Wool and hides were probably the most heavily commercialised of all agricultural products, since few of the households that supplied them needed more than a small fraction of what they could produce.

The volume of local trade varied across Europe chiefly according to the size of towns and the number of households dependent upon wages and profits for their livelihood. The larger a town, the larger the share of its population whose livelihood derived from manufacturing, trade or services, and the more dependent it was on trade in food and fuel.[11] Because their agrarian hinterlands were poor, some of Europe's largest cities, notably Venice and Genoa, had grown up dependent on farm produce imported from distant regions.[12] The most heavily urbanised region was northern Italy, with the four major cities of Milan, Venice, Florence and Genoa. Before the Black Death, on a conservative estimate, there were between 32 and 39 towns with more than 10,000 inhabitants in Italy between Rome and the Alps.[13] There was a secondary concentration of urban development in north-western Europe, including Paris, London, Ghent and Cologne. A similarly conservative estimate implies at least 19 towns of over 10,000 people in the triangle of territory between Paris, Cologne and London, all three included. To concentrate on larger towns even in these regions can be misleading, since there were also numerous smaller towns, industrial villages and marketing centres. Production and trade in agricultural produce was intensified by the overlapping demands of large cities and smaller centres of consumption within their supply region. Bonvesin de la Riva reports that the region subject to Milan's jurisdiction in 1288 contained 'fifty pleasant smaller towns (*borghi*), amongst which Monza, ten miles distant from Milan, deserves to be called a city rather than a

---

9 *cont.*

dans les campagnes italiennes au moyen âge', in C. Desplat (ed.), *Foires et marchés*, pp. 79–80; C. Dyer, 'Market towns and the countryside in late medieval England', in *Canadian Journal of History* 31 (1996), pp. 18–35; H. R. Oliva Herrer, *La Tierra de Campos a fines de la Edad Media: economía, sociedad y acción politica campesina* (Valladolid, 2002), pp. 17–50; D. Poppe, *Économie et société d'un bourg provençal au XIVe siècle: Reillanne en Haute Provence* (Wrocław, 1980), pp. 129–31 and 171–80.

10 K. Blaschke, *Geschichte Sachsens im Mittelalter* (Munich, 1990), pp. 225–6.

11 D. Herlihy and C. Klapisch-Zuber, *Les Toscans et leurs familles* (Paris, 1978), p. 295.

12 D. Abulafia, *The two Italies: economic relations between the Norman kingdom of Sicily and the northern communes* (Cambridge, 1977), pp. 71–3 and 76–91; G. Cherubini, *L'Italia rurale del basso medioevo* (Rome, 1984), pp. 107–8; F. C. Lane, *Venice: a maritime republic* (Baltimore, 1973), pp. 58–9, 132 and 305–6; C. M. de la Roncière, 'L'Approvisionnement des villes italiennes au moyen âge (XIVe–XVe siècles)', in Centre Culturel de l'Abbaye de Flaran, *L'Approvisionnement des villes de l'Europe occidentale au moyen âges et aux temps modernes* (Auch, 1985), pp. 38–40.

13 J. K. Hyde, *Society and politics in medieval Italy: the evolution of civil life, 1000–1350* (London, 1973), p. xxiii; J. C. Russell, *Medieval regions and their cities* (Newton Abbot, 1972), p. 41.

grain.[24] Such rules remained in force, and were often extended, during the fourteenth and fifteenth centuries. Meanwhile, as a principle of good government, secular rulers at all levels had devised practical rules to be enforced in secular courts, and these too contributed to ideals of fair trading dear to the heart of urban consumers.

Yet in spite of many internationally recognised principles of economic justice, local practice varied both from kingdom to kingdom in obedience to royal laws, and from place to place in accordance with local custom and bylaws. Market regulations were invariably a principal concern of urban officials. In public markets and fairs, more than in any other trading institutions, the interests of consumers were formally protected by regulations designed to ensure just prices. Such regulations also extended to the workshops, inns, alehouses and taverns that were a common feature of even the smallest towns by the fourteenth century, although these were more likely to be preparing and selling processed goods than retailing agricultural produce.[25] The sorts of regulation enforced in Aberdeen market, discussed by Elizabeth Gemmill in Chapter 4, illustrate well the range of devices by which urban authorities sought to protect consumers, and demonstrate the extent to which livelihoods, in even quite a small town by European standards, were thought to depend upon fair prices.[26] The fixed location and distinctive physical lay-out of market places, often surrounded by shops and merchants' houses, and often used for other occasions of public importance, made them the most visible signs of the commercial life in medieval Europe.[27] Their commercial role is liable to be overestimated for that reason. They were chiefly adapted to supply households with their needs from week to week, and they were often bypassed by considerable volumes of wholesale trade negotiated elsewhere.

Mercantile activity

Smaller communities could make do with the supplies brought in by producers from nearby villages, and often buyers went out into the countryside to buy produce directly from producers.[28] In these circumstances, foodstuffs and raw materials were unlikely to engage the attentions of a merchant class. But such face-to-face trading between buyer and consumer was inadequate to meet the needs of larger urban populations,

---

24 J. Davis, 'Baking for the common good: a reassessment of the assize of bread in medieval England', *EcHR* 57 (2004), pp. 465–502; F. Desportes, *Le Pain au moyen âge* (Paris, 1987), pp. 145–70; H. R. Oliva Herrer, *Ordenanzas de la villa de Becerril de Campos (c. 1492): transcripción y estudio* (Palencia, 2003), pp. 38 and 112–13; F. Lütge, 'Die Preispolitik in München im hohen Mittelalter. Ein Beitrag zum Streit über das Problem "Nahrungsprinzip "oder "Erwerbsstreben"', in *idem, Studien zur Sozial- und Wirtschaftsgeshichte* (Stuttgart, 1963), pp. 229–30; L. Zylbergeld, 'Les Régulations du marché du pain au XIIIe siècle en Occident et l'"assize of bread" de 1266–1267 pour l'Angleterre', in J.-M. Duvosquel and A. Dierkens (eds), *Villes et campagnes au moyen âge. Mélanges Georges Despy* (Liège, 1991), pp. 791–814.

25 J. M. Bennett, *Ale, beer and brewsters in England* (Oxford, 1996), pp. 98–121; H. Swanson, *Medieval artisans* (Oxford, 1989), pp. 11–18, 20–2, 54–7 and 116–18.

26 Chapter 4, pp. 60–5.

27 J. Masschaele, 'The public space of the marketplace in medieval England', *Speculum* 77 (2002), pp. 383–421.

28 D. L. Farmer, 'Marketing the produce of the countryside, 1200–1500', in *AHEW*, III, pp. 361–7.

which depended on merchants who contracted for the purchase of produce in bulk and had it transported, often over considerable distances. Inter-regional and international transactions often involved intermediaries between producer and ultimate user or consumer. Merchants in turn built up complex institutional structures of transport services, credit provision, mercantile jurisdiction, education and occupational training that far outstripped the needs of local traders. There is abundant evidence for these developments from long before 1350 in the Mediterranean world. England, too, had developed native mercantile traditions and institutions by the fourteenth century. Complex mercantile forms of trading affected many local producers in the later Middle Ages, particularly in the wool trade. In the 1470s and 1480s, for example, the Cely family of merchants acquired much of their wool in bulk from a 'woolman' called William Midwinter of Northleach, who in turn acquired it from those who had produced it.[29]

Such deals were commonly achieved by private negotiation rather than through markets or fairs. Private sale agreements and credit arrangements were a common feature of trade between rural producers and merchants, or other middlemen. This can be illustrated from the fifteenth-century accounts of King's College, Cambridge, which record hundreds of contracts made with farmers and middlemen in Cambridgeshire and the Isle of Ely for the supply of grain and fuel, and other contracts for acquiring building materials over an even more extensive region.[30] It can be illustrated by the purchases of hundreds of elms for use as piles by the wardens of Rochester Bridge in the earlier fifteenth century; they were purchased from many locations by agreement with the owners of woodland, as well as from one site that seems to have been a timber yard. Negotiations to buy timber are recorded, on several occasions, as having taken place in a tavern.[31] This type of informal trade is important for the study of regional development because it was the means by which commercial relations spread into some of the less urbanised parts of Europe. Even in the absence of strong local textile industries, for example, wool production was encouraged by mercantile enterprise in parts of northern England, southern Scotland and Ireland.[32] Christopher Dyer has termed such trade 'hidden', because it was conducted away from public markets and fairs, and its quantitative importance can hardly be exaggerated.[33]

In both the Mediterranean and Baltic regions mercantile trade in grain and other agrarian produce accounted for a large part of the shipping tonnage in use. Florentine exports of Apulian grain in 1311, amounting to about 45,000 tons, were enough to fill

---

29 A. Hanham, *The Celys and their world: an English merchant family of the fifteenth century* (Cambridge, 1985), p. 112.

30 A. B. Cobban, *The King's Hall within the university of Cambridge in the later middle ages* (Cambridge, 1969), pp. 212–17; J. S. Lee, *Cambridge and its economic region, 1450–1560* (Hatfield, 2005), pp. 155–60.

31 M. J. Becker, *Rochester Bridge, 1387–1856: a history of its early years* (London, 1930), pp. 68–9; R. H. Britnell, 'Rochester Bridge, 1381–1530', in N. Yates and J. M. Gibson (eds), *Traffic and politics: the construction and management of Rochester Bridge, AD 43–1993* (Woodbridge, 1994), pp. 61–4.

32 Britnell, *Britain and Ireland*, pp. 213–16.

33 C. Dyer, 'The hidden trade of the middle ages: evidence from the west midlands of England', *Journal of Historical Geography* 18 (1992), pp. 141–57.

about 225 standard bulk cargo-carriers of the period.[34] Although Italian merchants were known in Europe chiefly as a source of loans, and as suppliers of exotic goods from Asia and Africa, in fact by the early fourteenth century long-distance trade in cereals and livestock was a normal feature of their business. In 1329 Domenico Lenzi of Florence estimated that the city's own region could normally supply its grain requirements for only five months of the year.[35] Deficits of foodstuffs in northern Italy encouraged trade with the less urbanised parts of the South. Apulia and Sicily within the kingdoms of Naples and Sicily were specialised regions of primary production without parallel elsewhere in medieval Europe. From Naples, Barletta, Manfredonia and Salerno, the great ports of the kingdom of Naples, wheat, oil and wood were transported to northern consumers by sea. The biggest Italian business concerns of the period – which means the biggest in Europe – were involved in this trade in basic provisions.[36] In Paris, the largest city in western Europe, the food trade was again a major source of income for the merchant class. The rivers Rhine, Oise and Seine were major routes for carrying wheat and wine, although supplies also regularly came in by road over distances of 30–40 miles.[37] In London bulky produce came down-river along the Thames and the Lea, but also arrived by the Thames estuary from regions of the south-eastern English coast as well as from across the Channel. The group of London cornmongers, known as bladers, was large, organised and influential before the mid fourteenth century.[38] As urban populations declined after the Black Death, merchants in some victualling trades – notably in cereals – lost ground relative to others,[39] but Europe's principal cities nevertheless remained large enough to require a mercantile infrastructure for their supply.[40] Like the currency system, then, the institutional structure had evolved to accommodate trade at all levels from local retailing to international wholesale transactions.

Market integration and prices

As these observations imply, marketing institutions had matured by the fourteenth century to the point that commodity markets were well integrated across wide

---

34 D. Abulafia, 'Southern Italy and the Florentine economy, 1265–1370', *EcHR*, 2nd series 33 (1981), pp. 381–2; Lane, *Venice*, p. 46.

35 G. Pinto (ed.), *Il Libro del biadaiolo: carestie e annona a Firenze dalla metà del' 200 al 1348* (Florence, 1978), pp. 73 and 317.

36 Abulafia, 'Southern Italy', p. 381; E. S. Hunt, *The medieval super-companies: a study of the Peruzzi Company of Florence* (Cambridge, 1994), pp. 45–56.

37 R. Cazelles, *Nouvelle Histoire de Paris: de la fin du règne de Philippe Auguste à la mort de Charles V, 1223–1380* (Paris, 1972), pp. 383–5; D. Nicholas, *The growth of the medieval city: from late antiquity to the early fourteenth century* (London, 1997), pp. 287–9; Volk, *Wirtschaft und Gesellschaft*, p. 428–82.

38 B. M. S. Campbell, J. A. Galloway, D. Keene and M. Murphy, *A medieval capital and its grain supply: agrarian production and distribution in the London region c. 1300* (London, 1993), pp. 81–4.

39 Abulafia, 'Southern Italy', p. 386; Campbell *et al. Medieval capital*, p. 82.

40 J. Favier, *Nouvelle Historie de Paris: Paris au XVe siècle, 1380–1500* (Paris, 1974), pp. 289–94; J. Heers, *Gênes au XVe siècle* (Paris, 1971), pp. 34 and 234–47.

distances.[41] In other words, over extensive regions traders were normally sufficiently well-informed, and alert to profit opportunities, to transfer goods from places where prices were low to places where they were high, with the result that prices tended to converge towards a common level rather than varying erratically from market to market. In these circumstances, although there were procedures for determining prices in each local market, these necessarily responded to more general circumstances of supply and demand.[42] If prices were exceptionally high in a particular market, it would be favoured with increased supplies, and so the market price would fall; if prices were seen as low in a particular market, suppliers would avoid it, and so cause prices to rise. Prices in nearby markets could be expected to be about the same, which explains why the English government in 1349 supposed that fair prices for foodstuffs could be assessed for any particular market by reference to 'the price for which such victuals are sold in nearby places'. Producers selling in the countryside were able to trust the prices established in their local markets when they came to negotiate either small retail sales to their neighbours and dependants or sales in bulk to middlemen.[43] The growing urban demand for meat, although satisfied through regional networks of supply rather than through long-distance international transactions, was large and predictable enough to allow specialisation by local centres of supply. Diest, for example, gathered steers from a wide area of the southern Netherlands to supply to middlemen from the major towns of Brabant.[44] Some major wine-producing regions, like the Bordelais and central Rhineland, were so specialised that they depended upon grain imports from elsewhere.[45] The evidence from northern Italy and Flanders implies that markets for foodstuffs were even to some extent integrated internationally through mercantile activity. Regional and international markets were particularly responsive to commercial opportunity if they were connected by river or sea transport. River transport facilitated, for example, the expansion of Rhenish viticulture as the demand for cereals contracted.[46] Much of Britain was well served by waterways even in the absence of canals. There was a well-established coastal trade in grain, and the Thames, the Severn, the Trent and the Yorkshire Ouse all permitted important trading networks for the distribution of grain and other bulky goods.[47]

---

41 A. Derville, *L'Agriculture du Nord au moyen âge (Artois, Cambrésis, Flandre wallonne)* (Villeneuve-d'Ascq, 1999), p. 64; J. A. Galloway, 'One market or many? London and the grain trade of England', in *idem* (ed.), *Trade*, pp. 23–42.

42 For England, see R. H. Britnell, 'Price-setting in English borough markets, 1349–1500', *Canadian Journal of History* 31 (1996), pp. 2–15; Seabourne, *Royal regulation*, pp. 73–124.

43 Britnell, *Commercialisation*, p. 100.

44 I. Blanchard, 'The continental European cattle trades, 1400–1600', *EcHR*, 2nd series 39 (1986), pp. 428–9.

45 R. Boutruche, *La Crise d'une société. Seigneurs et paysans du Bordelais pendant la Guerre de Cent Ans* (Paris, 1963), pp. 16–19; Volk, *Wirtschaft und Gesellschaft*, pp. 728–30.

46 W. Abel, 'Landwirtschaft, 1350–1500', in H. Aubin and W. Zorn (eds.), *Handbuch der deutschen Wirtschafts- und Sozialgeschichte* (2 vols, Stuttgart, 1971), I, p. 320.

47 Campbell *et al. Medieval capital*, pp. 60–3; Farmer, 'Marketing', pp. 353–6; R. H. Hilton, *A medieval society: the west midlands at the end of the thirteenth century*, 2nd edition (Cambridge, 1983), pp. 181–2; M. Kowaleski, *Local markets and regional trade* (Cambridge, 1995), pp. 224–32; S. H. Rigby, *Medieval Grimsby: growth and decline* (Hull, 1993), pp. 28 and 57–61.

The mercantile supply of larger centres of population served to integrate markets over long distances. In the Mediterranean, Black Sea and Baltic regions trade in grain, other comestibles and raw materials, accounted for a large part of the shipping tonnage in use. England benefited from the cheapness with which grain could be imported from abroad, particularly from northern Germany.[48] Yet even England, despite its abundance of sea routes and rivers, was not thoroughly integrated as a single market, as Phillipp Schofield shows in Chapter 3 by comparing north-eastern prices with those of the rest of the kingdom. High long-distance overland transport costs meant that prices were more volatile in inland markets because it was less likely that deficiencies would be made good from a distance, or that surpluses would be disposed of.[49] Consequently some regions were less able than others to benefit from trade in periods of dearth or abundance.

However well integrated particular regional markets may have been, prices of agricultural products fluctuated much more from year to year than in the twenty-first century. Because of prohibitive transport costs, interdependent regions were smaller in the Middle Ages than they are now, and the benefits of market integration were correspondingly smaller. There was little exchange of cereals even across Europe, so that the two major urban complexes of the Continent did little to remedy each other's deficiencies in years of bad harvest.[50] Since good and bad weather alike were often general across large regions of the Continent, supplying and consuming regions were likely to suffer together from bad harvests, and in some years shortages were widespread and acute. This was most disastrously demonstrated in the great European famine of 1315–18, when mortality rates were exceptionally high in much of western Europe.[51]

By the fourteenth century the widespread availability of coin had encouraged the creation of credit arrangements to cope with all possible types of commerce. But these systems had widely different degrees of formality and legal elaboration. When credit was involved in face-to-face transactions between neighbours, as it often was, it usually operated upon trust rather than written contracts.[52] In local market places goods were purchased by retail for cash down with a minimum of legal formality; the rules of the market determined what was fair trade.[53] Bulk-purchasing on credit, which was more characteristic of heavily urbanised regions, was more likely to involve

---

48 M. Kowaleski, 'The grain trade in fourteenth-century Exeter', in E. B. DeWindt (ed.), *The salt of common life: individuality and choice in the medieval town, countryside and Church* (Kalamazoo, 1995), pp. 1–52; N. Hybel, 'The grain trade of northern Europe before 1350', *EcHR* 55 (2002), pp. 229–45.

49 Galloway, 'One market or many?', pp. 34–5 and 42.

50 P. Spufford, *Power and profit: the merchant in medieval Europe* (London, 2002), p. 288.

51 W. C. Jordan, *The great famine: northern Europe in the early fourteenth century* (Princeton, N.J., 1996).

52 Farmer, 'Marketing', pp. 360–1. For an analysis of the reasons for rural indebtedness, see E. Clark, 'Debt litigation in a late medieval English vill', in J. A. Raftis (ed.), *Pathways to medieval peasants* (Toronto, 1981), pp. 247–79.

53 Chapter 4 (below), pp. 56–69 ; R. H. Britnell, 'Markets, shops, inns, taverns and private houses in medieval English trade', in B. Blondé, P. Stabel, J. Stobart and I. Van Damme (eds), *Buyers and sellers: retail circuits and practices in medieval and early modern Europe* (Turnhout, 2006), pp. 109–23.

a written contract specifying the terms of payment. At a yet higher level of formality, an elaborate international system of credit allowed merchants to transfer money, at least along the busiest trade routes, by means of bills of exchange, which during the fourteenth and fifteenth centuries permitted the development of a sophisticated system of credit that was to be the foundation of merchant banking.[54] Of course, the development of credit systems ultimately depended upon public courts for legal redress against defaulters, and much of our knowledge of them is derived from recorded litigation. These mercantile developments could not have occurred, however, unless those concerned normally fulfilled their obligations.

Demand, supply and fluctuations

It is difficult to determine whether, as some historians assume, the scope of informal trade was broadening during the later Middle Ages, or whether in fact it had been for centuries the normal way of acquiring produce in bulk from rural producers. This question seems the more pressing because of the evident weakening of some public structures of local trade during the hundred years after the Black Death. In England many rural markets established in the thirteenth century were later abandoned as not worth maintaining, and similar decline of smaller marketing centres can be documented elsewhere.[55] This may represent a growth of private trade to the detriment of former market places, or a decline in the total volume of trade, or both.

It is likely that the total volume of rural trade in fact contracted in many parts of Europe. England's population declined after the Black Death from 4.5–6.0 million in 1300 (estimates vary considerably) to only 1.8–2.3 million in the 1520s; the figure was probably even lower in the 1450s. The number of landless families dependent on the purchase of food declined even more sharply than the total population. Since formal markets had been established chiefly to supply individual households which had not produced their own food, a reduction in their number in rural areas between 1350 and 1450 could be a response to falling total rural market demand, and does not constitute adequate grounds for supposing that other institutions of trade had increased sufficiently to compensate. Although the number of large peasant holdings undoubtedly increased, so that peasant producers had an even larger share in the supply of agricultural produce than before 1350, it is uncertain that the total increase in peasant sales was enough to offset reduced sales by manorial lords and their officers, so that this, too, is inadequate as an argument in favour of overall stability.

The strongest argument in favour of a general decline in the total household demand for agrarian produce between 1350 and 1450 must begin with the evidence of coinage in circulation, whose trends we should expect to follow that of the total

54 T. W. Blomquist, 'The dawn of banking in an Italian commune: thirteenth century Lucca', in Centre for Medieval and Renaissance Studies, University of California, Los Angeles, *The dawn of modern banking* (New Haven, 1979), pp. 68–75; K. L. Reyerson, *Business, banking and finance in medieval Montpellier* (Toronto, 1985), pp. 107–26; R. de Roover, *L'Évolution de la lettre de change* (Paris, 1953), pp. 23–64.

55 Britnell, *Commercialisation*, pp. 156–60; J.-L. Fray, *Villes et bourgs de Lorraine: réseaux urbains et centralité au moyen âge* (Clermont-Ferrand, 2006), pp. 256–63, 266; M. Mate, 'The rise and fall of markets in southeast England', *Canadian Journal of History* 31 (1996), pp. 67–74.

volume of trade in the absence of the invention of new types of money. This period was one of recurrent European monetary crises in the course of which silver-mining declined. The decline was experienced particularly in the silver coinage that was used for everyday local trade by most of Europe's inhabitants and so of particular relevance for purchases of food, fuel and clothing. In the absence of adequate new sources of bullion, European stocks of silver bullion dwindled through exports to other parts of the world, through wear and tear to the existing currency, through the conversion of coined bullion to silver and gold plate to satisfy the aspirations of status-conscious magnates, and through hoarding exacerbated by political and economic uncertainty.[56] The last of these considerations, in particular, explains why even in the short term it was unlikely that monetary problems could be resolved by the extension of credit; credit tended to contract, not expand, when potential borrowers were less confident of being repaid.[57] The result was a series of general, Europe-wide bullion famines during which circulating coinages contracted severely. The first, beginning in the 1370s, was at its most severe between about 1395 and 1415. Then after a period of recovery, there was a second crisis of even more serious proportions from about the mid-1430s, which was at its worst from about 1440 to 1460.[58] Such monetary problems had widespread effects upon prices and business activity. Shortages of currency often had a long-term deflationary effect in Europe; prices were particularly low in these two twenty-year periods.[59] Marketing the produce of the countryside inevitably became more problematic in periods of recession, particularly for producers who had large quantities to dispose of to merchants.[60]

Historians disagree about the relative importance of fluctuations and long-term trends in the history of money and prices. Many claim to have identified a Europe-wide long-term depressive tendency between a high point in 1350–75 and a trough in 1450–75,[61] while others have described the price level as comparatively stable but with dramatic swings induced by monetary crises.[62] Neither view is compatible with a sustained household demand for agrarian produce. The changing composition of the money stock towards currency of large denominations implies that household demand for locally produced foodstuffs contracted, particularly if there was no unsatisfied demand for small coinage.[63] And since there is good reason to suppose that trade in

56 M. C. Bailly-Maître and P. Benoit, 'Les Mines d'argent de la France médiévale', in Société des Historiens Médiévistes de l'Enseignement Supérieur Public, *L'Argent au moyen âge* (Paris, 1998), pp. 38–45; I. Blanchard, *Mining, metallurgy and minting in the middle ages* (3 vols, Stuttgart, 2001–5), III, pp. 934 and 1064–8; J. Day, *The medieval market economy* (Oxford, 1987), pp. 33–5 and 111; Spufford, *Money*, pp. 343–62.

57 P. Nightingale, 'Monetary contraction and mercantile credit in later medieval England', *EcHR*, 2nd series 43 (1990), pp. 560–75; Spufford, *Money*, pp. 347–8.

58 Day, *Medieval market economy*, pp. 1–54; Spufford, *Money*, pp. 349–62.

59 W. C. Robinson, 'Money, population and economic change in late medieval Europe', *EcHR*, 2nd series 12 (1959), pp. 63–76; Day, *Medieval market economy*, pp. 94–7, 102 and 113–14.

60 R. H. Britnell, 'The Pastons and their Norfolk', *AHR* 36 (1988), pp. 137–9.

61 Genicot, 'Crisis', pp. 682–3; Rösener, *Peasants*, p. 258.

62 Day, *Medieval market economy*, p. 102.

63 J. H. Munro, 'Deflation and the petty coinage problem in the late-medieval economy: the case of Flanders, 1334–1484', *Explorations in Economic History* 25 (1988), pp. 387–423.

manufactured goods and services increased relative to trade in primary produce between 1350 and 1450, chiefly as a result of higher incomes per capita for the majority of the population, the case for an overall expansion of trade in agricultural produce is weak.

Britain was not isolated from the general monetary experience of Europe during these hundred years, although the kingdom was spared the worst of government-induced crises induced by destabilising minting policies.[64] Unfortunately there is no available estimate of money stocks during the trough of depression of the mid fifteenth century, but the most recent estimates suggest that the total English currency in circulation declined from a peak of £2,100,000 (± £200,000) in 1319 to £950,000 (± £150,000) in 1351 and £850,000 (± £100,000) in 1470. What happened to the silver stock is more significant for the development of retail trade than these aggregate totals. It halved from about £800,000 (± £100,000) in 1351 to only £400,000 (± £50,000) in 1470.[65] Comparative details for Scotland are unavailable, although there is reason to suppose that the currency in circulation declined from a peak of £155,000 (± £25,000) in 1280.[66] It is hardly surprising that some of the established institutions of retail trade failed to survive through this period.

Prices, incentives and change

Such changes do not imply any declining evidence of commercial awareness on the part of rural producers. Price movements were critically important in deciding what farmers produced. In a market economy, commodity prices, taken in conjunction with production costs, indicate to producers what their most profitable option might be, but being able to use such information depends upon having reasonably confident expectations about the future. The uncertainty of harvests made such confidence problematic for medieval farmers. When recorded on a graph, the movement of late medieval prices from year to year shows as a jagged line, which indicates well the limited advantages of market integration for price stability in this period. This is well illustrated by graphs 3.1a–c in Phillipp Schofield's discussion of regional price variations.[67] It might be thought that farmers would find it impossible to be guided by such volatile prices, governed as they were by unpredictable weather conditions.[68] Yet this is not in fact the case. The time between investment (sowing) and pay-off

---

64 E.g. F. and W. P. Blockmans, 'Devaluation, coinage and seignorage under Louis de Nevers and Louis de Male, counts of Flanders, 1330–84', in N. J. Mayhew (ed.), *Coinage in the Low Countries (880–1500)* (Oxford, 1979), pp. 69–94; P. Lardin, 'La Crise monétaire de 1420–1422 en Normandie', in Société des Historiens Médiévistes de l'Enseignement Supérieur Public, *L'Argent*, pp. 101–43; J. H. Munro, *Wool, cloth and gold: the struggle for bullion in Anglo-Burgundian trade, 1340–1478* (Toronto, 1972).

65 M. Allen, 'The volume of the English currency, 1158–1470', *EcHR* 54 (2001), p. 607.

66 E. Gemmill and N. Mayhew, *Changing values in medieval Scotland: a study of prices, money, and weights and measures* (Cambridge, 1995), pp. 140–2.

67 Chapter 3, pp. 45–6.

68 J. Z. Titow, 'Evidence of weather in the account rolls of the bishopric of Winchester, 1209–1350', *EcHR*, 2nd series 12 (1960), pp. 360–407; *idem*, 'Le Climat à travers les rôles de comptabilité de l'évêché de Winchester (1350–1458)', *Annales ESC* 25 (1970), pp. 312–50.

(reaping) in cereals farming was sufficiently short for farmers to be able to make good guesses. David Stone has shown that cropping on the demesne lands at Hinderclay (Suffolk) and Wisbech Barton (Cambridgeshire) fluctuated from year to year in the fourteenth century, and that the quantity of each grain sown was strongly affected by price levels and relative prices. This strategy depended on a high level of managerial competence and responsibility.[69] But if farm managers, who were chosen from peasant communities, could follow market indicators in this way, it is to be expected that other commercially minded peasant farmers could do the same, and perhaps with more incentive to do so, since the anticipated profits in question were their own rather than those of their employer. That this was indeed the case can be demonstrated from the evidence of fluctuating tithe receipts. At Hambledon (Hampshire) the evidence for peasant responsiveness to price changes is particularly strong for the period 1345–81, suggesting that the social changes consequent upon the Black Death encouraged a more commercial attitude to wheat cultivation, in particular. Tithe evidence from the parish of Billingham (Co. Durham) implies positive relationships between fluctuations in peasant production of wheat and barley cultivation and prices during the fourteenth and fifteenth centuries; indeed on some occasions peasant farmers responded more energetically than the managers of Durham Priory's demesne lands.[70]

Because of this price awareness, even in outlying parts of the countryside, local variations in demand and supply conditions meant that farmers responded differently to market opportunities. We should think of farmers being nudged into particular directions only bit by bit, and not even consistently, as a result of persistent tendencies in the movement of prices. For these reasons the chronological shape of agrarian trends in the period 1350–1450 can often be indicated only very approximately, for want of aggregated data. The long-term direction of change after the Black Death, by lords and tenants alike, was governed by price movements, which encouraged restructuring agrarian output in line with changed conditions of supply and demand. Almost everywhere the area under crops contracted during the fourteenth and fifteenth centuries, but the extent of the decline varied according to the quality of the soil, vicinity to markets, and other relevant variables. In other respects it is more difficult to generalise about output, except to observe that the relative importance of non-arable to arable husbandry increased. Over long periods, changing prices of goods and labour had the power to reshape the character of production profoundly; some of the ways in which these changes affected England are examined in Chapter 2.

We can but speculate on the effects of depopulation in the absence of a market for goods, labour and land. The alternatives open to tenants would have been significantly fewer in the absence of paid employment; perhaps lords would have competed to capture tenants from each other by force or by guile, or maybe they would have had more success in increasing the burdens and restricting the liberties of such tenants as they retained. But in fact by 1350 the rural economy was heavily dependent on paid

---

69 D. Stone, *Decision-making in medieval agriculture* (Oxford, 2005), pp. 51–6, 89–94, 127–33 and 163–71; *idem*, 'Medieval farm management and technological mentalities: Hinderclay before the Black Death', *EcHR* 54 (2001), pp. 619–23.

70 B. Dodds, *Peasants and production in the medieval North-East: the evidence from tithes, 1270–1536* (Woodbridge, 2007), chapter 6.

workers, even if the labour market had severe imperfections. To varying degrees in different parts of Europe, competition for labour amongst landowners drove up wages relative to the price of agricultural produce after 1348–9.[71] It was this, rather than long-term price movements, that squeezed the profits of farming, and encouraged producers to reshape both the quantity and the composition of their output. It has long been recognised that one of the most rapid effects of labour scarcities all over Europe was to encourage farmers to take arable land out of cultivation because the resulting revenues no longer justified the financial outlay.[72] Even small producers who did not need hired labour might have had some incentive to modify their farming strategy if they could themselves be earning good money rather than working on their own land; they would have the same incentive to save labour on their own lands as the employing landlord had on his. There is no reason to suppose, then, that the effects of higher wages on agricultural output were confined to estates that depended on hired labour, even if they were felt more acutely there. Although abandoning cropland was not necessarily accompanied by any positive inducement to use it for livestock, it is true that lower labour costs struck at the profits of pastoral farming less heavily than at those of crop husbandry. The long-term shift into a more pastoral husbandry was also encouraged by movements of commodity prices that were generally, although not consistently, more favourable to pastoral products. This was partly because, in many parts of Europe, higher living standards after the Black Death allowed consumers to choose more meat and dairy produce at the expense of grain products.[73]

Britain's experience between 1350 and 1450 is not out of line with what was happening in many parts of Europe. Benefiting from shortages of labour after 1349, wage-earners were able to improve their lot by negotiation. Indeed, the experience of the generations after the Black Death, by encouraging a higher degree of mobility on the part of wage-earners, encouraged the freeing of the labour market from customary constraints. Despite widespread legislation to restrict their growth, wages rose relative to the price of agrarian produce.[74] The period of labour scarcity in England was more prolonged than in much of Europe; real wages peaked only in the 1470s. This implied continuing pressure on the profitability of farming, given the absence of any

---

71 G. Duby, *Rural economy and country life in the medieval West,* trans. C. Postan (London, 1962), pp. 304–5, 309 and 321; L. Genicot, 'Crisis: from the middle ages to modern times', in M. M. Postan, (eds), *The Cambridge economic history of Europe, I: the agrarian life of the middle ages,* 2nd edition (Cambridge, 1966), pp. 688–91; D. Nicholas, *Medieval Flanders* (London, 1992), p. 358; W. Rösener, *Peasants in the middle ages,* trans. A. Stützer (Oxford, 1994), pp. 259 and 261.

72 Abel, *Geschichte,* pp. 109–11; Britnell, *Britain and Ireland,* pp. 389–95; Cherubini, *L'Italia rurale,* pp. 36–9; Duby, *Rural economy,* pp. 301–2; H. Neveux, 'Déclin et reprise: la fluctuation biséculaire, 1340–1560', in G. Duby and A. Wallon (eds), *Historie de la France rurale, 2. De 1340 à 1789* (Paris, 1975), pp. 60–2. See also the observations in this volume by Ben Dodds (Chapter 7) and Simon Harris (Chapter 10).

73 S. Jenks, 'Von den archaischen Grundlagen bis zur Schwelle der moderne (ca. 1000–1450)', in M. North (ed.), *Deutsche Wirtschaftsgschichte; ein Jahrtausend im Überblick* (Munich, 2000), p. 51; M. Montanari, *Campagne medievali: strutture produttive, raporto di lavoro, sistemi alimentari* (Turin, 1984), p. 209; Rösener, *Peasants,* pp. 103–4 and 259.

74 D. L. Farmer, 'Prices and wages, 1350–1500', in *AHEW,* III, pp. 467–83; J. Hatcher, 'England in the aftermath of the Black Death', *PP* 144 (1994), pp. 3–35.

comparable secular rise in commodity prices. [75] Employers' problems could not be solved by the use of labour services. Even in southern England and the Midlands, where servile labour services were managed conservatively, their contribution to the total labour force had already dwindled to probably less than 3 per cent by the later thirteenth century.[76] Their importance waned even further after 1350, as lords were obliged to abandon them, or modify their number, in order to retain or acquire tenants. As elsewhere in Europe, too, rising standards of living encouraged an increase in per capita demand for meat and dairy produce more than in the demand for cereal-based products.[77] The output of pastoral products per capita after the Black Death also benefited more than in many parts of Europe from an export demand for wool and woollen cloth, particularly up to the 1370s.

Besides influencing the balance between arable and pasture, the prices of commodities and labour influenced the distribution of activity within these broad categories. Such shifts in production were inevitably subject to considerable regional variation.[78] Across Europe, a growing demand for meat stimulated the keeping of cattle in some parts and of sheep in others. In England, the main emphasis of pasture farming in the later fourteenth century was in sheep flocks and wool production, but in the period *c.* 1410–35 it was chiefly in dairy farming.[79] Not everywhere had the same opportunity as England to develop the commercial production of wool as a raw material for manufacturers, but some regions were able to profit from other industrial crops such as flax, madder or woad.[80] There was a widespread shift into foodstuffs of higher quality. Not only did wheat cultivation expand relative to that of inferior grains, but in parts of Europe (although not in England) there was also more emphasis on vegetables, fruit, olives and nuts.[81] The cultivation of vines and making of wine expanded in Germany, France and Italy.[82]

The old notion that there is something particularly modern about market incentives, sometimes coupled with the view that these came into operation only in the Renaissance period or later, is wide of the mark, given the evidence that even peasant society in places far from the great cities was heavily geared to producing for the market by the fourteenth century, and responded to price changes in order to do so

75 Farmer, 'Prices and wages', pp. 437 and 492–3.

76 R. H. Britnell, 'Commerce and capitalism in late medieval England: problems of description and theory', *Journal of Historical Sociology* 6 (1993), pp. 364 and 374.

77 C. Dyer, *Standards of living in the later middle ages: social change in England c. 1200–1520* (Cambridge, 1989), pp. 157–9, 199 and 202.

78 B. M. S. Campbell, 'Matching supply to demand: crop production and disposal by English demesnes in the century of the Black Death', *JEH* 57 (1997), pp. 827–58.

79 Chapter 2, pp. 31, 39.

80 Abel, 'Landwirtschaft', pp. 320–1; Derville, *Agriculture du Nord,* pp. 277 and 295–6; Neveux, 'Déclin et reprise', pp. 60–3.

81 Abel, *Geschichte,* pp. 117–19; C. Dyer, 'Gardens and orchards in medieval England', in *idem, Everyday life in medieval England* (London and Rio Grande, 1994), pp. 126–7 and 130–1; Jenks, 'Von den archaischen Grundlagen', pp. 49–50; G. Pinto, *La Toscana nel tardo medio evo* (Florence, 1982), pp. 166–95.

82 Abel, 'Landwirtschaft', p. 320; Neveux, 'Déclin et reprise', p. 62; Pinto, *Toscana,* pp. 175–88.

most profitably. Indeed, we cannot understand the regional variations observable in this period without reference to commercial incentives. The historical study of habits of thought often concentrates on the different forms of visual and literary symbolism associated with religion, power, and social rank, many of which serve to distance past societies from those of the present day. The symbolic world of relative value – using various concepts of money and prices – has just as valid a claim to a place in the study of past *mentalités*, and one that is increasingly important in the agenda of historians of the countryside. It enables us to appreciate ways in which late medieval people had habits of mind, and modes of everyday practice, that we recognise as still current.

Chapters 2–4

The argument of the first of the following three chapters is rooted in the view that prices mattered to the farming community at all levels, and that the study of agricultural output in England between 1350 and 1450 needs to be considered against a background of changing marketing opportunities. Of course, population movements were an important source of change in the commercial environment. So, however, were other things, such as changes in *per capita* income, and changes in the overseas demand for English wool. Rather than analysing this hundred years as a single period of late medieval crisis, the study aims to identify the principal sub-periods within it. By looking more closely at the nature of commercial opportunities available in different contexts, it also goes some way to identifying regional differences of commercial opportunity and response.

Chapter 3 takes seriously the idea that, although prices moved in much the same way across England, regional experiences were sufficiently divergent to carry implications for productivity and welfare. Phillipp Schofield takes advantage of the fortunate availability of price data from Durham, in north-eastern England, to make systematic comparisons with series from the southern part of the kingdom. He suggests that, despite low population densities, households were here more vulnerable to periods of dearth than those further south, partly because of the population was more heavily market-dependent as a result of a strong regional swing against arable farming. This meant that the North-East perhaps depended more than southern regions on imported grain in years of local shortage, and was correspondingly more vulnerable to fluctuations in price.

In Chapter 4, Elizabeth Gemmill looks more closely at the operation of markets and prices in a yet more localised context. She shows from the records of Aberdeen how the urban authorities in even quite small towns felt obliged to take active measures to defend the interests of market-dependent townsmen. The chapter illustrates, in a Scottish context, many principles and procedures familiar to urban administrations in different legal contexts across Europe. It demonstrates well, too, the extent to which urban supplies by the fifteenth century had become dependent upon commercial exchange from afar. Aberdeen was one of the most remote towns on the eastern coast of Britain from the London–Paris–Bruges triangle, and yet its supplies of many products depended upon shipments from England and the Continent. Even the diet of Aberdonians was affected by the growing availability of rye from the Baltic.

Chapter 2

English agricultural output and prices, 1350–1450: national trends and regional divergences

Richard Britnell

Analysis of agrarian change between 1350 and 1450 does not amount to a history of aggregate income or population, but it is closely related to these topics both because of the size of the agrarian sector in the total economy, and because of its importance in providing the basic necessities of life. In these respects the record of changes in land use, and in the volume and composition of agrarian output, is central to debates about the fourteenth and fifteenth centuries. We have many more quantitative indices of agrarian change than we have demographic statistics. On the other hand, much of our understanding of what happened to output after 1350 is poorly defined, partly because historians have concentrated on other things. They have unanimously rejected any simple model of agrarian contraction between 1350 and 1450, but it is unclear what to put in its place. We can define this as a twofold problem, first to define any general agrarian trends, as indicated by changes in prices and aggregate output, and second to account for the local variations that are so apparent in our records.

Two developments over the last few decades, in particular, have fostered discontent with older general models of late medieval agrarian performance. One is the perception that trends in agrarian prosperity were not all one way. Although doubtless the size of the English population decreased between 1350 and 1450, short-term economic fluctuations are an important aspect of any narrative of this hundred years. Hatcher has commented that 'instead of constituting an era of either economic decline or economic growth, closer examination reveals that the fourteenth and fifteenth centuries experienced a succession of sub-periods each with its own distinctive characteristics.'[1] This theme is now prominent in our literature. Bridbury's article on the 'Indian Summer' of 1350–*c.*1377, originally published in 1973, indicates one important discontinuity.[2] Hatcher's study of the mid-fifteenth-century slump demonstrates another, which has to be set against, and distinguished from, any earlier fifteenth-century malaise. Articles by Pollard on the North-East, Mate on the South-East and by Hare on Wiltshire, to be cited later in this paper, have demonstrated the instability that could shape the history of regional economies. Historians are now, in fact, committed to perceiving the period 1350–1450 as one in which fluctuations and regional variations mattered, and it would be greatly to our advantage to have a more coherent view of what those fluctuations and variations were.

---

1 J. Hatcher, 'The great slump of the mid-fifteenth century', in R. H. Britnell and J. Hatcher (eds), *Problems and progress in medieval England: essays in honour of Edward Miller* (Cambridge, 1996), pp. 237 and 239.

2 A. R. Bridbury, 'The Black Death', reprinted in *idem, The English economy from Bede to the Reformation* (Woodbridge, 1992), p. 202.

A second reason for redefining the later fourteenth and fifteenth centuries arises from doubts about an earlier emphasis on arable husbandry as the prime index of agrarian dynamism. Much older literature assumes that landlords and tenants retreated into pasture farming as a second-best option, and that expanding flocks and herds may consequently be read as a depression phenomenon. That argument is not wholly misguided. In some phases of the period 1350–1450 regions rich in pasture seem to have benefited more than more arable regions from the growth of domestic or overseas demand. But it is demonstrable, too, that farmers unable to grow crops profitably under pressure of rising labour costs often converted arable to alternative uses for which labour costs were less pressing, even if profit rates were low. In either casethese benefits could last only so long as demand conditions remained favourable, or until an expanding supply of pastoral produce drove prices down to the point that profits disappeared. To interpret the period 1350–1450 as one of continuous growth in the output of pastoral products would be at least as misleading as to classify it as one of continuous decline in cereals. None of the evidence relating to pasture farming has established that there was a steady increase in the output of sheep and cattle, or even that the profits of pasture farming were able to compensate for losses of profits in arable husbandry. On this point too, then, there is a need for greater clarity concerning both intertemporal and regional differences of experience.

Evidence currently available permits no more than a crude approximation to the reality of fluctuations, since only estimated statistics of aggregate output would enable us to discuss the chronological course of change with any refinement. Nor has the research been done that would enable us to present estimates of income from agriculture at different times, embracing all the different aspects of the rural economy. Such a project, which would have to include evidence of output and incomes from a wider range of agrarian activities, such as woodland management, gardening, and poultry-keeping, would depend upon extensive data collection and *a priori* assumptions so elaborate as to invite eternal scepticism. The major fluctuations so far identified, to be surveyed here, relate to the price movements and changes in land use in a few major branches of agriculture. The price movements in question are identified by Farmer's national series; although some features of regional variation would doubtless be illuminated by local price series, that represents a degree of refinement beyond the scope of the present study; this is a topic for the next chapter, in which Phillipp Schofield demonstrates some aberrant features of the price history of the North-East of England. The focus of attention here will be on arable husbandry, wool production and cattle farming; evidence from these activities implies a division of the period into four, whose uncertain boundaries need discussion. Despite the limitations of the exercise, an analysis in terms of these branches of agriculture and these sub-periods can be justified because it pays greater respect to the evidence than a simple story of decline, although doubtless a more sophisticated process of modelling might add nuance and precision to the analysis presented here.

After the Black Death, *c.* 1349–76

Much of the discussion of the period following the Black Death has related only loosely to levels of output. Historians have been impressed by the high prices obtainable for agrarian produce, while nevertheless being aware of the higher labour costs that offset them. Table 2.1 shows clearly an impressively rising price level for

Table 2.1
Price movements (five year averages), 1350–79

	Grain	*Wool*	*Cows*	*Cheese*	*Agricultural wages*
1350–4	100	100	100	100	100
1355–9	113	105	107	105	90
1360–4	125	110	117	98	96
1365–9	120	145	136	67	110
1370–4	146	165	140	81	109
1375–9	108	178	116	77	119

Source: D. L. Farmer, 'Prices and wages, 1350–1500', in *AHEW*, III, pp. 495–525.

some principal commodities up to the mid 1370s; cheese prices, representing those of dairy products, lag behind, which is interesting in the light of their quite different behaviour from the 1370s onwards. Historians have also been struck by the institutional continuity of manorial institutions in England, and the capacity of landlords to recover rent losses following the crisis of 1348–9. High prices and institutional continuity are themes discussed together by Bridbury in 1973, when he argued that everything rapidly returned to normal between 1350 and 1376. However, his argument is framed largely in institutional terms and shows little concern with levels of production, except to imply that institutional recovery indicates some measure of growth.

There is some justification for this inference in the early years of this period, even if the reoccupation of tenancies proceeded to a differing degree, and with differing speed, in different contexts. To the extent that holdings were not immediately taken up by new tenants in 1348 and 1349, there had been some loss of agricultural output, and the reduction of output caused by the death and migration of tenants was locally compounded by drought in some of the most highly commercialised parts of England.[3] However, by the mid 1350s the drought was over and there had been widespread re-tenanting of land in many parts of England, including some far from the more commercialised shires of the South-East. In some places, as on the St Albans manor of Abbots Langley, new tenants came forward so quickly that there was scarcely any discontinuity of occupation.[4] Raftis observes a rapid take-up of tenements on the estates at Ramsey Abbey, as does Hatcher on those of the Duchy of Cornwall.[5] Similar recovery, whether complete or partial, has been reported in greater detail in studies of individual manors and in regional studies. At Cuxham (Oxfordshire), by May 1355 new tenants had been found for all the land that had come into the lord's hands in 1349.[6] At Holywell (now in Cambridgeshire, but formerly in Huntingdonshire) there were only three untenanted crofts in 1356, and all these had

3 M. Mate, 'Agrarian economy after the Black Death: the manors of Canterbury Cathedral Priory, 1348–91', *EcHR*, 2nd series 37 (1984), pp. 342–3.

4 A. E. Levett, *Studies in manorial history* (Oxford, 1938), pp. 253–4.

5 J. A. Raftis, *The estates of Ramsey Abbey: a study in economic growth and organization* (Toronto, 1957), p. 252; J. Hatcher, *Rural economy and society in the duchy of Cornwall, 1300–1500* (Cambridge, 1970), pp. 104–20.

6 P. D. A. Harvey, *A medieval Oxfordshire village: Cuxham, 1240 to 1400* (London, 1965), p. 44.

been rented by 1363.[7] In the Breckland, Bailey comments on 'the relatively complete uptake of land in the 1350s'.[8] We can deduce, with some confidence, that tenant output rose during the 1350s from the low level to which it had dropped as a result of the disruption caused by the Black Death. A period of rapid growth of tenant husbandry in the early 1350s was followed by slower recovery once the immediate demand for holdings was satisfied. On the bishop of Durham's estates a brief period of rapid voluntary reoccupation of vacant holdings in the months following the retreat of the Black Death was followed by a more gradual take-up that was partly involuntary.[9]

The level and composition of output as agriculture recovered is less easily discussed, since evidence of tenures does not usually carry with it evidence of land use. After the immediate disruption caused by the Black Death, cereals cultivation surely increased. The Durham tithe data even suggests that between 1350 and the early 1360s grain output revived to a level approaching that of the 1340s. Given the heavy loss of population in the palatinate in 1348–9, this clearly implies an increased consumption of cereals per head of the population.[10] Recovery to this extent was probably unusual, though, and it was not universal. Because of rising costs, land was less intensively cultivated in the 1350s than earlier, so that a larger portion of both demesne land and tenant holdings lay uncultivated.[11]

A better known feature of the 1350s is the expansion of demesne flocks, which has traditionally been interpreted as a response to a crisis in the profitability of arable husbandry. Increasing numbers of demesne sheep, to levels higher than in the 1340s, implies some restructuring of land use out of arable into pasture, perhaps facilitated by the existence of large demesne units. There are many known instances, as for example on the manors of Ramsey Abbey and Canterbury Cathedral Priory.[12] It seems that a surge in wool production, in response to declining arable acreages, temporarily restrained price increases and made English wool exceptionally attractive in international markets. The evidence for this was already apparent to economic historians of the nineteenth century.

The take-up of vacant land slowed down well before the end of the 1350s, and the circumstances that briefly favoured the recovery of cereals output no longer operated so strongly during the 1360s and 1370s. There were recurring plague epidemics in 1361–2, 1368–9 and 1375. At Halesowen the population of adult males was reduced

---

7 E. B. DeWindt, *Land and people in Holywell-cum-Needingworth* (Toronto, 1971), p. 65.

8 M. Bailey, *A marginal economy? East Anglian Breckland in the later middle ages* (Cambridge, 1989), p. 225.

9 R. H. Britnell, 'Feudal reaction after the Black Death in the palatinate of Durham', *PP* 128 (1990), p. 31.

10 B. Dodds, 'Durham Priory tithes and the Black Death between Tyne and Tees', *Northern History* 39 (2002), pp. 15 and 17–20; *idem*, 'Estimating arable output using Durham Priory tithe receipts, 1341–1450', *EcHR* 57 (2004), p. 270.

11 For tithe evidence to this effect, see R. H. Britnell, *Growth and decline in Colchester, 1300–1525* (Cambridge, 1986), pp. 150–1.

12 Mate, 'Agrarian economy', p. 344; Raftis, *Estates*, pp. 147–51.

what landlords expected.[42] But the falling general price level from the later 1370s, combined with rising wage rates, faced both landlords and their servants with an altogether different set of problems; it was difficult to decide what to do for the best. It took some time for landlords to realise that marginal adjustments to relative prices, within static administrative systems, were not the best solution, and that fundamental changes in methods of management were called for. The severe problems of the 1390s were decisive, and from then onwards the leasing of demesnes eventually became well nigh universal.

The greater responsiveness to crisis from 1389 implied by the study of manorial organisation extended to movement in the level and composition of output, although many indices of crisis during the 1390s, as of the 1350s, leave us poorly informed about the details. Most available data comes from the dwindling number of demesnes still in direct cultivation. Amongst larger grain producers, low prices and rising wages often induced some measure of retrenchment in arable well before 1390. On the estates of Norwich Cathedral Priory, sown acreages dropped during the 1380s after three decades of stability; on that estate, indeed, the 1380s were the low point of arable activity, measured by sown acreage, since activity subsequently increased in the 1390s and again after 1400.[43] On the Derbyshire estates of the Duchy of Lancaster, too, output was reduced in the 1380s.[44] In his study of production on the Westminster demesnes, Farmer chooses 1380 as the relevant breakpoint for the later fourteenth century.[45] Some estates, too, responded rapidly to falling wool prices. On Westminster Abbey's demesne at Kinsbourne falling prices and profits for wool were smartly matched by a reduction in the sheep flocks during the late 1370s and early 1380s.[46] However, as with estate management, swift changes of output in response to changed profit levels were far from universal. There is little sign of reduction in sown acreages on the estates of Ramsey Abbey between 1379 and 1390. Nor did pastoral output on demesnes always follow falling prices, since the constraints of high labour costs were so much lower; Ramsey Abbey not only maintained but in some cases expanded its herds of cows and flocks of sheep, perhaps in an effort to maintain income levels.[47] The maintenance of demesne output during the 1380s, where it occurred, was not simply reluctance to face reality. Some landlords had increasing amounts of untenanted land, which they chose to cultivate in demesne rather than abandon to waste.

In the last decades of the fourteenth century, however, evidence of agrarian contraction, as of institutional crisis, is more universal. On various north-eastern Essex

---

42 D. Stone, 'Medieval farm management and technological mentalities: Hinderclay before the Black Death', *EcHR* 54 (2001), pp. 619–23.

43 Campbell, *Seigniorial agriculture*, p. 235.

44 C. Dyer, 'The occupation of the land: the west midlands', in *AHEW*, III, p. 83 (citing unpublished work by Blanchard).

45 D. Farmer, 'Grain yields on Westminster Abbey manors, 1271–1410', *Canadian Journal of History* 18 (1983), p. 339.

46 Stern, *Hertfordshire demesne*, pp. 138 and 140.

47 Raftis, *Estates*, pp. 138–40, 146–51 and 187–9.

demesnes, the movement of output was downwards, especially in the later 1390s.[48] Farmer's calculations for the Winchester episcopal estates between 1395–7 and 1419–22 show a contraction of the sown acreage on 20 out of the 22 demesnes for which figures are available. Except perhaps at Taunton, this represents a genuine abandonment of arable acres rather than merely the leasing out of parcels of demesne.[49] It is more difficult to be certain of the movement of animal numbers after 1390. Even now some estates built up their sheep flocks, despite low prices, rather than leave land idle.[50] The discontinuous evidence from nine demesnes of Ramsey manors suggests continuing high numbers; in six instances (Abbots Ripton, Wistow, Upwood, Elton, Broughton, Warboys) the number of sheep between 1390 and 1410 exceeded that of the 1350s and 1360s, although the size of these flocks was volatile. Evidence of contraction on demesne lands is nevertheless widespread. On the Westminster demesnes (15 manors) the total number of animal units fell by 8.5 per cent between 1350–80 and 1381–1410.[51] The sheep flocks on Westminster Abbey's Essex manors were reduced after *c.* 1390 at Kelvedon and after *c.* 1399 at Feering.[52]

It must be assumed that one of the reasons for the widespread leasing of these years was that lessees, with lower administration costs and better local knowledge, expected to be able to generate larger net incomes from demesne lands than their landlords had been able to do. Unfortunately, though, lessees did not need to render accounts, and the 180 years or so when our knowledge of demesne agriculture is dominated by the records of large and centrally administered estates is succeeded by a period of equivalent length when such information is rare from estates of any kind. Other data needs to be called in to play. Broader evidence for changing output levels falls into two main categories, one relating to the occupancy of the land by tenants, the other to the level of tithe receipts. Both these sources, which will be examined in turn, in fact support the idea of a widespread reduction of arable acreages from at least the 1380s in response to changed conditions, although it is less clear what happened to pasture farming, particularly since tenant flocks and herds often made use of common pastures for which, by definition, there is no tenurial evidence.

Just as evidence of the take-up of land in the 1350s implies expanding production, so in the period 1390–1410 mounting evidence of abandoned and untenanted tenures implies declining output from peasant farming. One of the reasons why lords were no longer able to maintain manorial structures was the ease with which tenants could get their way by migrating or threatening to migrate to vacant tenements elsewhere. This implies that an increased percentage of available tenant land was uncultivated. Evidence for an accelerated abandonment of tenures in this period is widespread, if not voluminous; it could be speedily augmented if made the object of a particular research exercise. In the east Midlands it is found on the estates at Ramsey Abbey.[53]

---

48 R. H. Britnell,'The occupation of the land: eastern England', in *AHEW*, III, p. 58.

49. D. L. Farmer,'Grain yields on Winchester manors in the later middle ages'. *EcHR* 2nd series 30 (1977), p. 562.

50 Britnell, *Growth and decline*, p. 155.

51 This is calculated from Farmer,'Grain yields on Westminster Abbey manors', pp. 339 and 341.

52 Britnell, *Growth and decline*, p. 156.

53 Raftis, *Estates*, p. 152.

At Kibworth Harcourt clandestine departures and abandoned land are more in evidence from 1400.[54] On Crowland Abbey estates difficulty in finding tenants was a characteristic of the 1390s; Page noted it as a problem from 1391.[55] The characteristic manifestation of deserted tenant land is an increase in the number of court-roll entries instructing manorial officials to summon defaulting tenants to return, or to fine tenants for holdings that had recently become empty. In manorial accounts, where they exist, it is represented by an increase in the number of unpaid rents. Because the historical agenda for this period tends to be the decline of the manor rather than the level of output, few historians have commented on the relevance of the abandonment of peasant holdings as evidence for the quantitative history of agriculture.

The available tithe data provide striking evidence of crisis as far as arable husbandry is concerned. Essex evidence, from the Westminster Abbey rectories of Feering and Kelvedon, is decisively in support of a severe recession.[56] The Durham evidence, too, show unambiguous evidence of a late-fourteenth-century reduction in cereals output, with particularly low values between 1394 and 1400. Evidence of the composition of grain tithes from townships in the parish of Billingham shows that the decline in wheat production was exceptionally severe, suggesting that contraction of the demand for bread grain was a prominent feature of the immediate crisis.[57] There can be little doubt, therefore, of a widespread reduction in arable acreages between the late 1370s and the early fifteenth century, although its magnitude is bound to be problematic. Across 16 Westminster demesnes, the sown acreage declined by 6 per cent, between 1350–80 and 1381–1410, even if this contraction of sowing was to some extent offset by rising yields per acre.[58]

The history of pastoral farming is more problematic. None of the evidence supplies very reliable data relating to its fortunes. The price history of the period suggests that pastoral output would have held up better than arable output, both because prices of wool, cattle and cheese fell less and because their costs of production were less affected by wage increases. The recession of 1376–1410 accordingly placed farmers under pressure to change the composition of their output. Some innovation and entrepreneurial originality can be identified as recession phenomena, although to some extent these were the continuation of trends already established in the third quarter of the fourteenth century. The likeliest area for expanding output was in meat and dairy produce from cattle; ewes' milk and cheese were losing favour.[59] Dyer's evidence on diet suggests that animal products, especially meat, were more prominent in rural diets from the 1360s onwards.[60] Despite the tendency to substitute

---

54 C. Howell, *Land, family and inheritance in transition: Kibworth Harcourt, 1280–1700* (Cambridge, 1983), p. 54.

55 F. Page, *The estates of Crowland Abbey: a study in manorial organisation* (Cambridge, 1934), pp. 152–3.

56 Britnell, *Growth and decline*, p. 155.

57 B. Dodds,'Estimating arable output', pp. 248–9, 260 and 270.

58 Farmer,'Grain yields on Westminster Abbey manors', pp. 338–9.

59 D. Stone,'The productivity and management of sheep in late medieval England', *AHR* 51 (2003), p. 15.

60 C. Dyer,'Changes in diet in the late middle ages : the case of harvest workers', reprinted in *idem*, *Everyday life in medieval England* (London and Rio Grande, 1994), pp. 82 and 91.

meat for dairy produce in harvest workers' remuneration, the price history summarised in Table 2.2 suggests that dairy farming was one of the most attractive areas of agricultural investment in the late fourteenth century. Some landlords simultaneously increased their commitment to forms of compensating activity such as mines, fisheries and saltworks, according to the resources at their disposal.[61] The 1380s saw greatly increased investment in the commercial rearing of rabbits in East Anglia.[62] Some of these new ventures were to have lasting implications for the structure of rural activity, even when they failed to make up the shortfall in income from traditional sources.

The movement of wool and dairy prices from the later 1390s suggests that the pastoral sector led the agrarian economy out of the depths of the depression of the early-1390s. However, wool prices need interpreting with some caution. They fell badly after 1380 to a trough that bottomed in 1388–91 and then only partially and slowly recovered. This perhaps encouraged some restoration of sheep flocks, although total wool exports, whether in the form of raw wool or in the wool content of cloth exports, never regained the level of the 1350s and 1360s. The decline in exports was temporarily reversed in the 1380s, but this did not coincide with a surge in prices and profits in that decade, and probably represents a diversion of surpluses from domestic industry to overseas markets at a time of low prices and an exceptionally disadvantageous balance of trade. In the first decade of the fifteenth century cloth exports fell seriously, and it is most unlikely that the home market was growing sufficiently rapidly to convert this slump into a general textile boom.[63] Evidence concerning standards of flock management suggests that investment in quality fell throughout this period.[64] In other words, we should be cautious about reading too much prosperity into the modest increase in wool prices during the period 1395–1414.

Early-fifteenth-century recovery, *c.* 1410–35

The next period is by far and away the most difficult to define or date, but what happened then matters for our interpretation of the fifteenth century. If agricultural output remained at the lower level to which it had been driven in the 1390s, or continued to decline, only to be driven even lower by the mid-fifteenth-century slump, our view of the century is bound to be more gloomy than if there was stabilisation, or even significant recovery, in an intervening period. Price history (Table 2.3) suggests a brief improvement in profits during the second decade of the century followed by a lengthy period of relative stability, when prices for wheat and wool were low by historical standards but showed no great propensity to fall and the upward movement of agricultural wages was arrested. The grounds for optimism here are in the movement of prices for grain and for cheese rather than for wool. Current historical

---

61 B. Dodds, *Peasants and production in the medieval North-East: the evidence from tithes, 1270–1536* (Woodbridge, 2007), pp. 85–93.

62 M. Bailey,'The rabbit and the medieval East Anglian economy', *AHR* 36 (1988), pp. 6 and 10.

63 Bridbury, *Medieval English clothmaking*, p. 116; Britnell, *Britain and Ireland*, p. 417.

64 Stone,'Productivity and management', pp. 7–8, 11 and 13–14.

Table 2.3
Price movements (five year averages), 1405–39

	Grain	*Wool*	*Cows*	*Cheese*	*Agricultural wages*
1405–9	100	100	100	100	100
1410–4	116	112	105	108	96
1415–9	119	82	89	103	99
1420–4	103	83	80	102	96
1425–9	100	81	89	113	92
1430–4	125	98	85	122	91
1435–9	132	84	80	118	103

Source: D. L. Farmer, 'Prices and wages, 1350–1500', in *AHEW*, III, pp. 495–525.

writing, although lacking quantitative precision, suggests that these features of the period were of particular importance for the way farmers behaved, and invites a more optimistic picture than the overall price level would have implied. The resulting stability or recovery was not universal, however, and may not have benefited regions more remote from major marketing centres.

Pollard's account of the North-East describes the years 1410–35 as a period when lowland arable changed little, as far as seigniorial incomes from rent are an indicator, but when pasture farming in the Pennine dales became more profitable. Pasture rents rose in Teesdale, Arkengarthdale and on Bowes Moor. The agricultural prosperity of these regions was closely associated with cattle-raising.[65] Further north the sacrist of Durham Cathedral Priory expanded his flocks and herds sometime between 1425 and 1438 by developing a stock farm, probably for sheep, at Ayhope Shield near Wolsingham in Weardale, as well as a vaccary nearer home at Sacriston.[66] Any recovery of cereals husbandry in this region was more muted. Output levels in Durham Priory's parishes recovered from the late-fourteenth-century crisis after about 1405. The 1420s were a period of stability at a level around half the grain output of the 1340s, but the 1430s were a decade of renewed crisis in which the estimated output of cereals repeatedly fell below this level.[67] Schofield's analysis of regional prices suggests that by the 1430s the rural economy of Durham had moved so heavily away from arable farming that the region was exceptionally dependent on external supplies in years of poor harvests.[68] The present analysis adopts Pollard's periodisation for this phase, together with his emphasis on the significance of the pastoral sector, although with no great confidence that the north-eastern chronology will fit the rest of England closely. Some of the southern evidence suggests a recovery of pastoral farming that began earlier, about 1405, and finished earlier, about 1430.

Mate comments on the difficulty of defining national trends in pastoral farming on current evidence, but identifies war in France as a stimulus to pasture farming in the

65 A. J. Pollard, 'The north-eastern economy and the agrarian crisis of 1438–1440', *Northern History* 25 (1989), pp. 91–3; *idem*, *North-eastern England during the Wars of the Roses: lay society, war and politics, 1450–1500* (Oxford, 1990), pp. 49–50.

66 Lomas, 'Priory of Durham', pp. 350–1.

67 Dodds, 'Estimating arable output', p. 271; *idem*, *Peasants and production*, pp. 98–100.

68 Chapter 3, pp. 52–5. See also Dodds, *Peasants and production*, pp. 84–94.

South-East, and observes a surge of exports to supply troops on Henry V's campaigns, as well as the growth of domestic sales to meet rising urban demand in the same region. She identifies the 1420s as the peak of a pastoral boom in which peasants, townsmen and landlords all stood to benefit, and comments that almost every manor on the duchy of Lancaster estate experienced a steady demand for pasture through the first quarter of the fifteenth century.[69] There may have been local expansion of arable husbandry as well to judge from the tithe evidence from Eastry, which shows particularly large receipts of wheat and barley in the late 1420s.[70] Mate identifies the 1430s as a period of downturn in pasture farming in the South-East, something that could not be predicted from the price data.

In the Breckland, again, Bailey records agrarian recovery based on pastoral farming. After a short-lived slump in the 1390s the first quarter of the fifteenth century saw investment in sheep to the point that by the 1420s flocks were back to the numbers of the 1320s. This boom in sheep farming involved peasant producers as well as manorial demesnes. Meanwhile demesne arable cultivation contracted on the few Breckland manors for which there is evidence. A contrast between pastoral and arable husbandry is implicit in Bailey's comment that at Hilborough 'the expansion of sheep farming in the early fifteenth century was certainly enough to compensate for the contraction in arable production'. However, he sees the profitability of sheep as undermined by falling prices in the 1420s, so that the period of pastoral expansion was short-lived. The declining fortunes of Breckland sheep farming seem not to have been offset by opportunities in cattle raising, partly because of the poor quality of pastures.[71]

This period was also apparently one in which cattle grazing became a more distinctive feature of farming in parts of the west Midlands, although there seems in fact to be little direct evidence of expansion in the 1410s and 1420s. Most of the discussion about this branch of agriculture relates to a slightly later period, but demonstrably specialised vaccaries had already been created in the Forest of Arden by the 1430s and 1440s.[72]

The evidence from the estates of the bishopric of Winchester, one of the few estates still able to supply a coherent body of statistics for demesne agriculture, is partially in support of this representation of the period. Farmer produces data relevant to cereals output for the three periods 1409–11, 1420–22 and 1433–5. The arable acreage on the 13 demesnes with evidence for all three remained fairly stable, declining by only 3 per cent. This decline had already happened by 1419–22, implying considerable stability during the 1420s and early 1430s. There was a slight decline in mean gross yield ratios across this period, confirming that the level of output was slightly down. The difficulties of generalising about arable farming in this period are nevertheless demonstrated by the experience of Downton and other Wiltshire

69 M. Mate, 'Pastoral farming in south-east England in the fifteenth century', *EcHR*, 2nd series 40 (1987), pp. 524–5; *idem*, 'The occupation of the land: Kent and Sussex', in *AHEW*, III, p. 120.

70 Mate, 'Occupation of the land', p. 133.

71 Bailey, *Marginal economy?* pp. 209–13, 289–91 and 294–5.

72 A. Watkins, 'Peasants in Arden', in R.H. Britnell (ed.), *Daily life in the late middle ages* (Stroud, 1998), p. 85.

villages, where barley production contracted sharply during the 1420s.[73] Meanwhile, on the 11 Winchester demesnes for which there are data, the number of livestock units rose by 3 per cent in the earlier part of the period, between 1409–11 and 1420–2, although they then fell. By 1433–5 numbers were 6 per cent lower than at the beginning of the period.[74] The timing of this decline needs further definition, but it is in line with Mate's observation that any livestock boom was over by the 1430s.

We have enough evidence to speak with some confidence of a phase of profitable and expanding pastoral husbandry in many parts of England during the early fifteenth century, based to greater or lesser degrees on sheep or cattle. In some localities such as western Wiltshire, it was boosted by an expanding textile industry.[75] In eastern Cornwall textiles and tin-mining supported a remarkable increase in land values that was strongest between 1406 and 1427, although it continued in some places until the 1440s.[76] To the extent that pastoral farming increased we may suppose that there was a net increase in agricultural output, associated with rising domestic consumption rather than with exports. Some producers took advantage of the movement of prices to increase their incomes from wheat.[77] However, the aggregate arable acreage is unlikely to have experienced any growth comparable to the expansion in pastoral activity. Since wage levels were relatively static, there would hardly be any rising demand for grain unless population was growing, and there is little reason to suppose that it was. The Essex tithing-penny data shows no demographic recovery associated with the upswing of 1410–35. There was no recovery in the number of mills; indeed, Langdon speaks of 'the collapse of milling from the 1390s to the middle of the fifteenth century'.[78] The Breckland was not the only region where arable farming declined. Durham evidence demonstrates some unprecedented low levels of cereals production between 1410 and 1435, and between 1419 and 1450 the calculated level of output never again exceeded 60 per cent of the 1340s average.[79] Regional variation depended greatly upon adaptations to the variable fortunes of urban and overseas economies.

The end of this mildly expansive phase was locally variable, like its beginning. In the Breckland the rising trend was over by the 1420s, and in Kent and Sussex it ended by 1430, partly because of bad weather.[80] At Wisbech Barton the expansion of a pastoral activities phase can be dated quite precisely; it began in 1413 with the construction of a new dairy and the purchase of cows, and ended about 1426 with the abandonment of the dairy; the whole demesne was leased out from 1429.[81] In the North-East, despite problems in arable husbandry from 1432 onwards, the pastoral economy

---

73 Chapter 8, pp. 143–5.

74 Farmer, 'Grain yields on the Winchester manors', pp. 562–3.

75 J. Hare, 'Growth and recession in the fifteenth-century economy: the Wiltshire textile industry and the countryside', *EcHR* 52 (1999), pp. 10–18.

76 Hatcher, *Rural economy and society*, pp. 151–4 and 262–4.

77 Stone, *Decision-making*, pp. 160–1.

78 Langdon, *Mills*, p. 30

79 Dodds, Tithe and agrarian output, p. 166; *idem*, 'Estimating arable output', pp. 269 and 271.

80 Mate, 'Pastoral farming', p. 525.

81 Stone, *Decision-making*, pp. 158 and 180.

Table 2.4
Price movements (five year averages), 1430–54

	Grain	*Wool*	*Cows*	*Cheese*	*Agricultural wages*
1430–4	100	100	100	100	100
1435–9	106	86	94	96	113
1440–4	75	87	110	n.a.	113
1445–9	72	81	88	89	108
1450–4	76	64	89	89	107

Source: D. L. Farmer, 'Prices and wages, 1350–1500', in *AHEW*, III, pp. 495–525.

shows little sign of a break in trend until the later 1430s, notably following the plague outbreak of 1438.[82] To assign the date 1435 to the end of this phase is therefore somewhat arbitrary. Perhaps it ended sooner to the extent that it depended on sheep (as in the Breckland) and later to the extent that it depended on cattle (as in Teesside and its surrounding parts, which implies an accelerated movement into cattle in this part of the country during the period 1425–35).

The mid-fifteenth-century slump, *c.* 1435–65

Finally, we reach the phase that Hatcher has christened the Great Slump of the mid fifteenth century. Subsequent general accounts of the phenomenon have been published by Nightingale and the late Edmund Fryde.[83] The main features of the record concerning agricultural prices, as illustrated in Table 2.4, are a steep fall in the price of cereals and wool, especially during the 1440s, and a slightly less steep drop in dairy prices, accompanied by a renewed upsurge in labour costs.

Most of the hard statistical evidence relating to the mid-fifteenth-century slump relates to prices, rents and the statistics of overseas trade rather than to output. This is simply the result of the rarity of good manorial or tithe accounts that would allow a year-by-year analysis of trends. The series from the Norfolk demesne of Ormesby St Margarets shows an unambiguous recession in arable farming, all the more significant because this was a demesne in one of the most commercialised parts of the kingdom.[84] The recession on the Paston estates in the same area, although mostly to be told in terms of marketing difficulties and problems with tenants, has some clear implications for output insofar as land was left untenanted and waste.[85] After the 1430s, the level of cereals output in Durham was more stable through the 1440s, settling at a level of output about half that of the 1340s.[86]

The pastoral sector is generally represented in a more optimistic light, and price history alone would suggest that dairy and meat production was less severely affected

82 Pollard, 'North-eastern economy', pp. 93–4.

83 P. Nightingale, 'England and the European depression of the mid-fifteenth century', *Journal of Economic History* 26 (1997), pp. 631–56; E. B. Fryde, *Peasants and landlords in later medieval England* (Stroud, 1996), pp. 145–68.

84 R. H. Britnell, 'The economic context', in A. J. Pollard (ed.), *The Wars of the Roses* (Basingstoke, 1995), p. 50.

85 R. H. Britnell, 'The Pastons and their Norfolk', *AHR* 36 (1988), p. 141.

86 Dodds, 'Estimating arable output', p. 271.

Table 2.5
Indices of sown acreages and total livestock units at Wisbech Barton (Cambridgeshire) (five year averages), 1350–1429

	Sown acres (100 ~ 341.1 acres)	*Livestock units* (100 ~ 132.8 units)
1350–4	100	100
1355–9	n.a.	n.a.
1360–4	79	78
1365–9	86	107
1370–4	82	86
1375–9	84*	109
1380–4	85*	112*
1385–9	85*	49*
1390–4	89*	116
1395–9	89	99
1400–4	80	92
1405–9	86	92
1410–4	85	112
1415–9	85	174
1420–4	85	187
1425–9	76	122

Source: D. Stone, The management of resources on the demesne farm of Wisbech Barton, 1314–1430 (unpublished Ph.D. thesis, University of Cambridge, 1998), appendices 1 and 4.
Note: An asterisk denotes an average of fewer than three years.

than that of cereals. This is likely to have brought some relative advantage to areas already specialised in sheep and cattle, which could take advantage of such opportunities as existed more cheaply than those which had to invest in change. There is little reason to suppose that wool production was unscathed, however, and there is anecdotal evidence, at least, to suggest that this was a period of crisis and contraction in sheep farming amongst larger and more commercial producers. Hatcher cites several examples of large wool growers who gave up between the 1440s and the 1460s: the duchy of Lancaster estate, the duke of Buckingham, Ralph Lord Cromwell, the earls of Warwick, the bishops of Worcester, Syon Abbey.[87] He is cautious, rightly, about the capacity of meat and dairy production to bale farmers out of the recession. In the west Midlands, it is true, there is evidence of stocking with cattle by John Dey around Drakenage from about 1440, and by John Brome of Baddesley Clinton from about 1442.[88] But some of the northern vaccaries, evidently dependent upon a long-distance trade, were clearly in difficulties, and contracted their operations during the second quarter of the fifteenth century.[89] It seems unlikely, on present showing, that any expansion of pasture farming outweighed declining output of grain and wool during these decades.

87 Hatcher, 'Great slump', p. 251.

88 C. Dyer, 'A small landowner in the fifteenth century', *Midland History* 1 (1972), pp. 6–8; A. Watkins, 'Cattle grazing in the Forest of Arden in the later middle ages', *AHR* 37 (1989), pp. 18–19 and 24.

89 Britnell, 'Economic context', p. 51; Hatcher, 'Great slump', p. 253. To the references cited in these studies, add J. McDonnell, 'Upland Pennine hamlets', *Northern History* 26 (1990), p. 27.

Table 2.6
Index of numbers of ewes and wethers at Crawley (Hampshire) (five year averages), 1350–1449

	Ewes	Wethers	Combined Total 100 ~ 849.8 sheep
1350–4	100	100	100
1355–9	106	140	122
1360–4	100	140	112
1365–9	103	141	121
1370–4	104	127	114
1375–9	100	139	118
1380–4	93	154	121
1385–9	93	135	112
1390–4	92	134	112
1395–9	93	125	108
1400–4	90	124	105
1405–9	78	125	100
1410–4	84	129	105
1415–9	85	128	105
1420–4	85	130	106
1425–9	85	122	102
1430–4	87	129	106
1435–9	82	112	96
1440–4	90	123	106
1445–9	92	131	110

Source: N. S. B. Gras and E. C. Gras, *The economic and social history of an English village (Crawley, Hampshire) A.D. 909–1928* (Cambridge, Mass., 1930), pp. 401–3 and 407–9.

Table 2.7
Numbers of sheep and dairy cattle at Wisbech Barton (Cambridgeshire) (five year averages), 1350–1429

	Sheep	Dairy cattle
1350–4	485.5	31.8
1355–9	n.a.	n.a.
1360–4	497.3	0.0
1365–9	524.2	5.0
1370–4	334.8	1.5
1375–9	580.7	0.0
1380–4	574.5*	0.0*
1385–9	0.0*	0.0*
1390–4	609.0	0.0
1395–9	487.0	0.8
1400–4	428.2	0.2
1405–9	456.6	0.0
1410–4	527.0	8.2
1415–9	586.2	53.4
1420–4	569.2	63.0
1425–9	545.5	16.8

Source: D. Stone, The management of resources on the demesne farm of Wisbech Barton, 1314–1430 (unpublished Ph.D. thesis, University of Cambridge, 1998), appendices 1 and 4.
Note: An asterisk denotes an average of fewer than three years.

Table 2.8
Population index for Great Waltham and High Easter (Essex) (five year averages), 1350–1454

	Great Waltham	*High Easter*	*Combined population Combined N = 290*
1350–4	[67]	[68]	[68]
1355–9	100	100	100
1360–4	108	106	107
1365–9	113	110	112
1370–4	118	104	112
1375–9	109	101	105
1380–4	101	102	102
1385–9	99	103	101
1390–4	88	104	95
1395–9	83	98	90
1400–4	92	101	96
1405–9	95	102	98
1410–4	88	92	90
1415–9	81	99	89
1420–4	82	98	89
1425–9	79	95	87
1430–4	78	100	88
1435–9	86	89	88
1440–4	89	93	91
1445–9	86	94	89
1450–4	86	92	89

Source: Tithing-penny data kindly supplied by Professor L. R. Poos. See also L. R. Poos, 'The rural population of Essex in the later middle ages', *EcHR* 38 (1985), pp. 515–30.

Conclusions

The question of agricultural output between 1350 and 1450 is a frustrating topic of research because of the many unknowns. For a conclusion, however, it may be useful to summarise a few points to be deduced from the evidence currently at our disposal.

First, the history of output may be better told as a series of fluctuations, or phases, than as one of continuous trend. Seen as a cyclical history, the period 1350–1450 may roughly be described as having troughs of output in the early 1350s, the early 1400s and the 1450s and peaks of output in the 1370s and 1420s.

Second, the changing composition of output towards a different mix of cereals and a greater weight on pastoral husbandry is a vital part of any study of agricultural output, difficult although it is to integrate the arable and the pastoral into any single index of performance. The upswing of 1350–1376 and 1410–35 were led by pastoral activity rather than arable. But in pastoral husbandry, as in arable husbandry, there were periods of expansion and periods of difficulty and contraction, and it is as misleading to think of a continuous expansion of pasture farming as to describe the period 1350–1450 as one of continuous decline. This instability is well illustrated by the evidence from Wisbech Barton (Table 2.5). The evidence of Crawley sheep numbers, chosen simply because of their easy availability and the exceptional length of the run, gives partial support to the cyclical character of production (Table 2.6). Sheep numbers at Crawley rose rapidly after the Black Death to a level they never subsequently surpassed. The number remained high into the mid 1380s, that is, for a full decade after prices had fallen in the late 1370s, although there was then a phase of marked recession from the later 1380s to a trough in 1405–9. Here, however, there was no sustained revival during the period up to the 1430s; sheep numbers remained below the level of the 1390s, and the Crawley demesne did not take up dairy farming.

Third, there seems to be some distinction to be made within pasture farming concerning the relative importance of sheep and cattle in different phases. The upswing of 1350–76 was led by sheep, that of 1410–35 by cattle. This is well illustrated by the evidence from Wisbech Barton (Table 2.7). It seems likely that the switch into greater dependence on cattle occurred in the context of the recession of 1376–1410.

Fourth, although the agrarian history of the period has a cyclical history it also has a trend. The upswing of 1410–35 was weaker, shorter and more narrowly based than that of 1350–76; the downswing of 1435–65 was more destructive than that of 1376–1410. The troughs of 1350, 1410 and 1465 represent successively lower levels of output.

Fifth, the underlying causes of agrarian fluctuation remain poorly understood. There is some evidence that particular agrarian crises corresponded to demographic crisis. This is obvious enough in 1348–9, less obvious in the late 1380s and the later 1430s. However, if demographic decline was the principal cause of contracting arable husbandry, over the whole period it is unlikely that the turning points defined here were uniquely determined by demographic events. The Essex tithing-penny data (Table 2.8) suggest that the upswing to 1376 is associated with population growth, and that the subsequent downswing with declining population to 1410–14. After that, however, the Essex data imply little fluctuation in population, so that neither the upswing of 1410–35 nor the mid-fifteenth-century crisis are related to demographic fluctuations. Changes in population are likely to relate more closely to the output of cereals than to that of products of pasture farming, but the relationship is stronger for the later fourteenth century than for the fifteenth.[90] Fluctuations in weather conditions are likely to account for periods of acute instability in levels of output, as in the years 1398–1403, although at present it is less easy to relate them to quasi-cyclical variations of the sort proposed in this overview.[91] It is difficult, too, to assess the extent to which monetary history is a dependent variable rather than an independent one, partly because monetary crises could derive from different causes. Some, like the 'shortage of money' in 1390 described by Knighton, derived from export failure and the consequent contraction of domestic spending. Others derived from a propensity to hoard cash and restrict credit in times of uncertainty and danger, as in the 1440s.[92] Although monetary contraction figures prominently in the crises of both the 1390s and the 1440s, even in these periods its role as an independent cause is unclear. Yet, although at present the fluctuations of agricultural output between 1350 and 1450 cannot be explained altogether satisfactorily, recent research has made historians much more aware of what needs to be explained.

---

90 Dodds, Tithe, pp. 219–21; *idem*, 'Estimating arable output', pp. 271–2.

91 Dodds, 'Estimating arable output', pp. 272–3.

92 Nightingale, 'England and the European depression', pp. 638–9.

Chapter 3

Regional price differentials and local economies in north-east England, *c.* 1350–*c.* 1520

Phillipp Schofield

The study of prices has numerous implications both for defining general economic trends and for the identification of regional variations, although the literature of price history pays more attention to the former concern than the latter. Comparison between good annual series from different locations can help to identify regions that were particularly vulnerable to harvest crises, or poorly integrated into wider commercial networks, or both. Price data, in fact, offer the best hope for identifying differences of this kind in medieval England. This chapter explores that possibility by using the prices series that, by good fortune, can be constructed from the accounting records of Durham Cathedral Priory in north-eastern England. It offers a test case of the way in which price history can be used to move from broad generalities towards a closer awareness of regional diversity.

Much depends upon the extent to which changes in price can be interpreted to indicate changes in the availability of commodities. 'Agricultural historians command far more evidence about prices in the past than about aggregate output or yield, so that their picture of harvest fluctuation is often based principally upon a knowledge of the behaviour of prices'.[1] E. A. Wrigley, in expressing this view of the relativities of historical material, also counselled caution in the use of price data as an alternative to yield data, a point to which we shall return, but acknowledged that historians and economists have long attempted to posit just such a relationship. As is well known, Gregory King established a relationship between the price of grain and the quality of the harvest, often referred to as 'King's Law'.[2] It is in its broadest sense, a basic assumption that yield and price are inversely related year on year, that historians of medieval and early modern England have explicitly and implicitly applied it, with price employed as a surrogate for implied yield. Hoskins, in particular, in two influential articles in 1964 and 1968, assumed a direct and largely consistent relationship between the two variables, writing that 'the yield of the harvest was the most fundamental fact of economic life in England. [...] When we look at the graph of the fluctuations in the average price of wheat from year to year we are looking at an electro-cardiagram of a living organism'.[3] Hoskins' analysis was subsequently criticised by Harrison who attempted to show, most especially, that the wheat price

---

1 E. A. Wrigley, 'Some reflections on corn yields and prices in pre-industrial economies', in J. Walter and R. Schofield (eds), *Famine, disease and the social order in early modern society* (Cambridge, 1989), p. 243.

2 B. H. Slicher van Bath, *The agrarian history of western Europe, A.D. 500–1850* (London, 1963), p. 119; Wrigley,'Reflections', pp. 237 and 239.

3 W. G. Hoskins,'Harvest fluctuations and English economic history, 1480–1619', *AHR* 12 (1964), p. 40; *idem*,'Harvest fluctuations and English economic history, 1620–1759', *AHR* 16 (1968).

did not adequately reflect the behaviour of other grains; he also, in a concluding section, pondered the relationship between price and yield but confined his comments to the inadequacies of aggregated national series. Like Hoskins, Harrison was generally content to allow a direct and generally consistent relationship between price and yield.[4]

The fundamental premise of King's Law has, however, been questioned by more than one commentator. Wrigley, in also casting some doubt on Hoskins' earlier assertion that runs of high or low prices within the data indicated the knock-on effect of a single bad harvest on subsequent sowings – in other words that runs of prices were also matched by runs of yield, seed sown being the significant variable – suggested that, given this lack of an apparent relationship between price and yield in 'price runs', it was the scale of the 'carry-over' from one harvest to the next which determined price runs. The year after a very good harvest, perhaps itself an average year, might still see a surplus of grain on the market, hence continued lower prices; the reverse, of course, was true where the first harvest was poor.[5] For Wrigley, then, price did not necessarily reflect production.[6] Fogel has also recently considered the relationship between price and yield. In exploring the relationship between price and implied yield, applying the formulation of King and later economists, notably Jevons and Bouniatian, for the years 1555 and 1556, when the price of wheat moved from 51 per cent above the average to 105 per cent above the average, Fogel calculated that the consequent lower-class consumption was 1180 calories per individual, a sum far below 'basal metabolism'.[7] Since, as Fogel notes, there was no evident mortality peak in that year consistent with such shortage, the interpretative problem lies within assumptions associated with King's Law and, in particular, to return to Wrigley, a failure to recognise the influence of carried over grain. Fogel estimated that 'even the worst pair of years identified by Hoskins (1555 and 1556) would still have left more than 10 per cent of the normal carry-over inventory as a buffer without encroaching on feed, seed, or human consumption in either year' and that King's Law, applied to food prices as an index of supply, greatly exaggerates the variability of that supply.[8] Both Wrigley and Fogel offer a series of important insights on the range of influences, in addition to harvest yield, which may have influenced year-on-year behaviour of grain prices and, in particular, discuss the important relationship between institutional structures and the protection of the needy in years of limited supply. Further to this, both stress the relationship between grain prices and those whose income was significantly affected by their need to buy food. The existence of a significant cohort of the population receiving low or relatively low wages with little in the way of surplus will have a determining effect upon grain price movements, but only up to the point where price is so high that the poor are excluded from the market.[9]

---

4 C. J. Harrison,'Grain price analysis and harvest qualities, 1465–1634', *AHR* 19 (1971), pp. 156–7.

5 Wrigley,'Reflections', pp. 243–5 and 265–6.

6 *Ibid.*, p. 278.

7 R.W. Fogel,'Some thoughts on the European escape from hunger: famines, chronic malnutrition and mortality rates', in S. R. Osmani (ed.), *Nutrition and poverty* (Oxford, 1992), p. 250.

8 *Ibid.*, p. 254.

9 Wrigley,'Reflections', pp. 242–3; Fogel,'Thoughts', pp. 257–61.

Close exploration of such issues for the Middle Ages, and especially for the fifteenth century, is far from straightforward. While we can certainly investigate the relationship between yield and price for the thirteenth and early fourteenth centuries in a number of local and regional contexts, such endeavours become more difficult from the late fourteenth century as our sources respond to a changed agrarian economy and shifts in institutional expectations. While we lose a good deal of information on yield by the early fifteenth century through a seigneurial retreat from direct management, and the greater propensity to lease estates, we retain, and perhaps even gain, price data, as landlords were forced increasingly into a closer acquaintance with a market economy. In such a context, the willingness of historians to employ price data as a substitute for yield data, or output, is understandable but, as the representation of the views of Wrigley and of Fogel outlined above has been intended to show, problematic. In what follows, I wish to test the relevance of price differences for variations in the supply of food by looking at the Durham Priory price data for the late fourteenth and fifteenth centuries. In such an investigation the message of Wrigley and Fogel, a counter-blast to the pioneering investigations of Hoskins, is vitally important. If we are to risk an assumption that price of grain is in some way directly equivalent to yield, then we also place ourselves open to an inaccurate characterisation of the medieval economy and of those whose lives were interwoven with it.

Historiography

Medieval historians have, from the earliest work of Thorold Rogers through Beveridge to Farmer, exploited grain price material, gathering national price series which have provided a central component of historical narratives of change and development in the medieval economy.[10] Farmer's work on grain prices comes closest to offering a systematic analysis of this data; like his predecessors he remarks on the relatively stable long-term price levels of the late fourteenth and fifteenth centuries, a condition to be compared with their variability during the thirteenth and fourteenth centuries. As Farmer also notes, grain prices were also susceptible to quite wide short-term fluctuations in the post-plague period. While such fluctuations were, as he explains in the context of the Winchester estates, undoubtedly a consequence of variations in crop yields, other factors also impacted upon them. The proximity of major urban centres, changing standard of living *vis à vis* population movement, estate management and land use, and so on, may all have affected the behaviour of grain prices.[11] Further, while Farmer acknowledged a degree of regional variation in this behaviour of prices, he was keen not to exaggerate its impact. He identifies certain anomalies in grain price movements but does not appear to have pushed his analysis of such variation beyond *c.* 1420.[12] If Farmer was very much aware of the influences

---

10 W. Beveridge, *Prices and wages in England from the twelfth to the nineteenth century*, I (London, 1939); J. E. T. Rogers, *A history of agriculture and prices in England* (7 vols, Oxford, 1866–1902); D. L. Farmer,'Price and wages, 1350–1500', in *AHEW*, III, pp. 431–525.

11 See Farmer,'Price and wages', pp. 443–55.

12 *Ibid*,'Price and wages', pp. 446–9.

on price that could challenge any simple association with yield, others have been less chary, influenced in no small part by Hoskins' alluring model of wheat prices from the late Middle Ages.

Earlier consideration of the price data from the Durham Priory estates has posited a direct relationship between price and production in ways not entirely dissimilar to those employed by Hoskins. Lomas and Dobson both make reference to the behaviour of grain prices as part of their particular studies of the local and regional economies. Dobson, in his study of Durham Priory in the first half of the fifteenth century, suggests that, aside from certain years of evident crisis (notably 1438), it is the relative stagnation and general consistency of behaviour with national series that is most striking, and he characterises the economic problems faced by the monks at Durham as 'representative rather than unique'.[13] Lomas also remarks on the apparent similarity between the behaviour of the Durham price data and that found in national price series but notes that, in certain years, 'the area did not suffer the poor harvests recorded elsewhere'. While Lomas does not elaborate his assessment of the message of this Durham price data, he does suggest that two out of every five harvests were better than average, whilst only 20 per cent were in significant excess of the average, a situation which, if correct, encouraged favourable comparison with Thorold Rogers' estimates of the proportion of good years (10 per cent) and bad years (33 per cent) for this period.[14] Both of these works imply that the agrarian economy of Durham tended to follow national trends in the fifteenth century and that, where it did not, it behaved in a manner that was less disadvantaged than was typical for the country. It is not entirely clear how either Dobson or Lomas explored their data in order to reach the conclusions set out in their work. In what follows, I wish to offer a limited statistical analysis of the price data from Durham Priory to test these basic assumptions, and to offer some further reflections on the regional economy and its vulnerability in this period.

Price data: sources and analysis

In order to test the usefulness of price data as a viable indicator of the regional experience of the North-East, a number of price series have been employed here. The most important of these, essentially the ones that permit any discussion of regionality and the contextualisation of price behaviour, issue from the muniments of Durham Priory and, in particular, the bursar's rolls (for all grains) and an aggregate of the rolls of all obedientiaries (for wheat prices). Some relatively thin data for individual cells of the priory have also been examined. The price data from Durham, as employed here, is part of the vast collection of price and wage material gathered by Beveridge and his team between 1923 and 1963, now stored at the London School of Economics.[15] This data, for the purposes of this paper, has been cross-referenced with published and unpublished accounts. In addition to the Durham price series, use has been made of

13 R. B. Dobson, *Durham Priory, 1400–1450* (Oxford, 1973), pp. 266–8.

14 T. Lomas, 'Southeast Durham: late fourteenth and fifteenth centuries', in P. D. A. Harvey (ed.), *The peasant land market in medieval England* (Oxford, 1984), pp. 319–20.

15 London School of Economics, Lord Beveridge Price History Archive, Box C8.

the more familiar national aggregated series compiled by Thorold Rogers and by Farmer, as well as, for the end of our period, the series of Bowden and of Hoskins.[16] Finally, in order to introduce a further regional dimension into the discussion, the Exeter wheat price series, first published by Beveridge in 1929, has also been employed as a point of comparative reference.[17]

The Durham price series can comfortably claim a place next to these other price series for the period. The bulk of the Durham material comes from the bursar's accounts for the priory, an office which was remarkable for the extent of its business.[18] A process of leasing of demesnes from the end of the fourteenth century, which accelerated in the early fifteenth century, meant that the priory was obliged to purchase much of its grain, principally from its own tenants in the villages and manors within the palatinate. While, as Dobson has shown, not all of the business of the priory passed through the office of the bursar, the office received two-thirds of the income of the house and represents the best guide to the economic fortunes of the priory in the late Middle Ages. Moreover, its accounts number amongst 'the longest non-governmental accounts ever produced in England'. The accounts of the other obedientiaries, the granator, almoner, hostillar and cellarer, are generally less forthcoming, not least because the role of these obedientiaries was so closely tied to that of the bursar. The granator, although responsible for the management of grain supplies in the fifteenth century, was not charged with the purchase of the grain, which was the responsibility of the bursar. Therefore, the granator's accounts contain relatively little in the way of price data but it is interesting to note that, in those years when the bursar's accounts are lacking price data, the granator's accounts appear to take up the story.[19] In addition to the obedientiary accounts, individual manorial accounts survive sporadically from the estates of the priory and some very limited use of data from these has also been made.

Further, while the material drawn from the bursar's accounts is not complete for all years of the series, a mean calculated for wheat alone by Beveridge and his team from all of the obedientary accounts – although, in fact, the available data was often limited to that of the bursars' accounts – allows a more complete run of data to be employed. While no other run of obedientary accounts matches those compiled by the bursar, data from these other offices has filled most of the gaps in the series. This composite series of obedientary accounts has been employed for those calculations particularly demanding of complete series, notably calculation of moving averages for wheat.

Overall, the Durham records produce a range of price data which, in terms of incidence of individual prices, is comparable in scale with previously compiled aggregate series. For certain years in the mid fifteenth century, the range of prices

16 Rogers, *History*, I, pp. 230–4; IV, pp. 282–9; Farmer, 'Price and wages', pp. 502–5; Hoskins, 'Harvest fluctuations, 1480–1619', pp. 44–6; P. Bowden, 'Statistical appendix', in *AHEW*, IV, pp. 815–17.

17 B. R. Mitchell, *British historical statistics* (Cambridge, 1988), pp. 752–3, taken from W. Beveridge, 'A statistical crime of the seventeenth century', *Journal of Economic and Business History* 1 (1929).

18 For this and what follows, Dobson, *Durham Priory*, pp. 257–61.

19 Dobson, *Durham Priory*, pp. 263–4; see, for instance, 1439. For an explanation of this in terms of the changing administration of the priory, see *ibid.*, pp. 287–8.

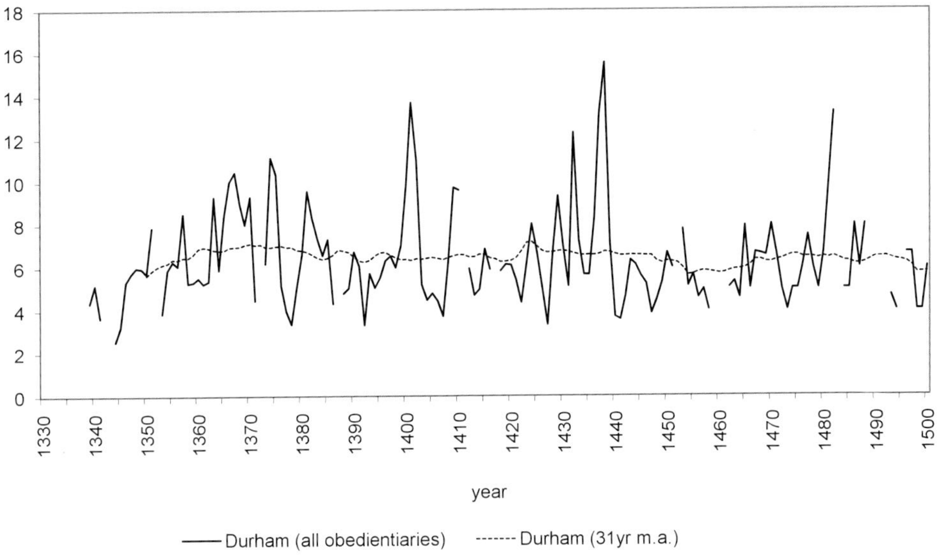

Figure 3.1a Wheat prices compared, 1330–1500 (Durham)

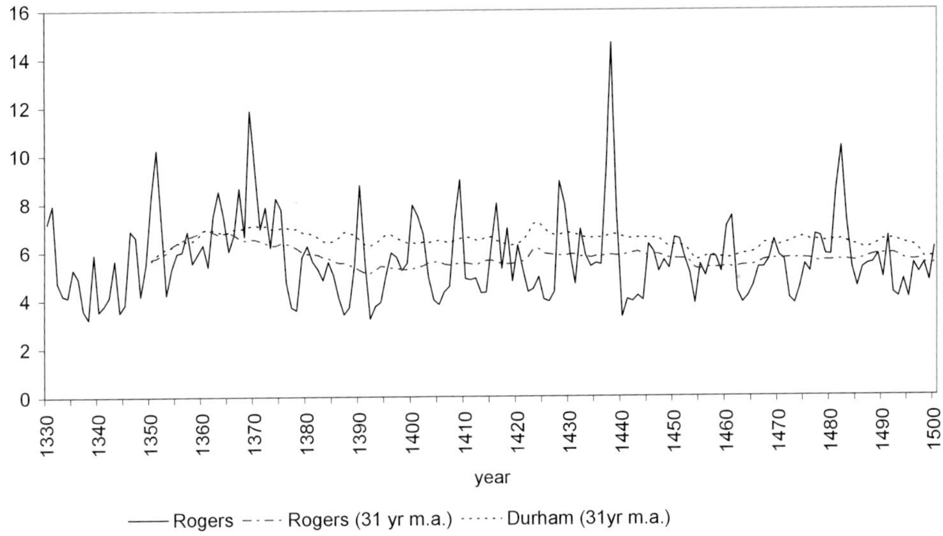

Figure 3.1b Wheat prices compared, 1330–1500 (Rogers)

employed in the construction of the Durham wheat averages includes more than 50 (1445) or 60 (1437) observations in a single year. While some years are weakly represented in the series, or not represented at all, the series does appear sufficiently robust, drawing as it does on price data from around the priory's estate and beyond, to permit a degree of confidence in attempting comparison with other series.

There are a number of approaches which can be employed in order to test the behaviour of prices on Durham manors both in comparison with price data drawn from national series and as a discrete series. We can begin with a simple observation of annual and average grain price movements, including identification of runs of high- and

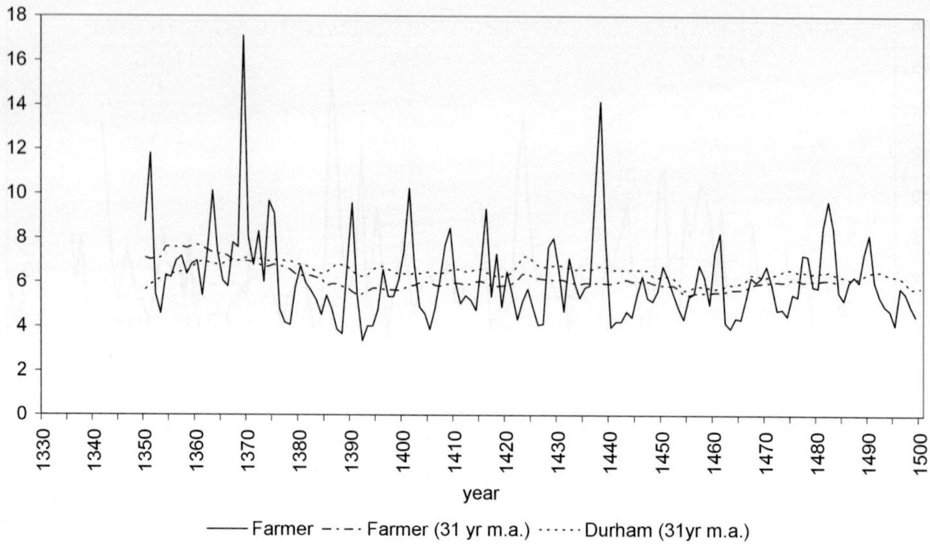

Figure 3.1c Wheat prices compared, 1330–1500 (Farmer)

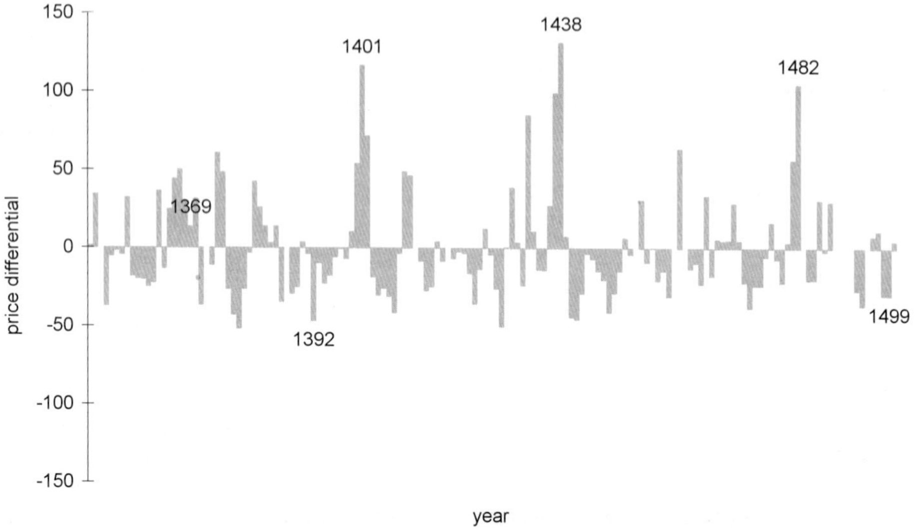

Figure 3.2 Wheat price differentials, 1350–1500

low-price years; we can also correlate grain price movements within the Durham grain price series and in relation to single grains across one or more series from elsewhere.

To begin, a simple presentation of the grain price data is broadly instructive. Figures 3.1a–c plot wheat prices from Durham from 1330–1500 and compares them with two national series. A centred 31-year moving average for each has also been included, a choice of average determined by earlier work by Beveridge, Hoskins and Harrison. Hoskins reasoned that this represents a sufficiently long time-span (one generation) to produce 'the price at which wheat would have sold after a harvest of average quantity and after eliminating non-harvest factors [here identified as monetary changes and

Table 3.1
Harvest classifications compared (Durham wheat prices with national price series)

	1350–99			*1400–1449*			*1450–79*		
	D	*R*	*F*	*D*	*R*	*F*	*D*	*R*	*F*
>50	2	3	2	5	5	4	1		
25 to 50	9	5	5	4	6	6	3	2	2
10 to 24	4	4	5	3	4	6	1	6	6
+/-10	13	22	15	14	11	12	11	11	12
-11 to -30	12	11	17	14	16	14	8	10	9
<-30	7	5	6	8	8	8	2	1	1
Total	47	50	50	48	50	50	27	30	30

Sources: D = Lord Beveridge Price History Archive, Box C8, London School of Economics; R = Rogers, I, pp. 230–4; IV, pp. 282–9; F = Farmer, 'Prices', pp. 502–5.

population movement]'.[20] Beyond a simple identification of peaks and troughs in the actual price data, we can also attempt limited analyses of fluctuation and of volatility through both the comparison of price in any one year with the moving average, and a year-on-year calculation of volatility, with price in one year calculated as a percentage of price in the next. The frequency of volatility by some arbitrary measure, such as quartiles, can then be presented.

In comparing the price of wheat at Durham against the moving average, as in Figure 3.2, the same categorisation of variance employed by Hoskins in 1964 has been used. If we were to follow his lead and terminology, then, in years where the price was 30 per cent or more below the average, the harvest should be classified as 'abundant' and between 10 and 30 per cent below as 'good'. A price that was within 10 per cent above or below the average was identified by Hoskins as just that, 'average'. Distinctions were also made between 'deficient' harvests, where the price was 10–25 per cent above, 'bad', 25–50 per cent, and 'dearth', over 50 per cent above the average price.[21]

As can be seen from Figures 3.1a–c and Table 3.1, the behaviour of wheat prices on the Durham estates is, in general terms, largely consistent with that calculated for national price series, an observation already made by Lomas and by Dobson, with a concentration relatively close to the moving average. And yet, despite this reasonably close association, we can observe significant differences. Notable, at this first stage of analysis, are the inconsistencies in the peaks and troughs, an observation that is not without its problems since it is unclear whether a uniform measure was applied to all grains recorded here. That said, there is clear volatility exhibited by this price data, with significant peaks in years already identified as problematic in other price series, especially in the late 1430s and early 1480s.[22] However, as Lomas also noted, there is some significant mismatch in peaks, with certain national high-price years not

20 Hoskins,'Harvest fluctuations', p. 43.

21 *Ibid.*

22 C. Dyer, *Standards of living in the later middle ages. social change in England, c. 1200–1520* (Cambridge, 1989) , pp. 262–3 and 267–8.

Table 3.2a

Frequency of runs of low price years, 1350–1500 (wheat)

Duration of price run (years)	*1350–99*			*1400–49*			*1450–79 (B=1465–79)*		
	D	*R*	*F*	*D*	*R*	*F*	*D*	*B*	*F*
1	2	2		2	3	3	3	1	2
2	1	1	4	1			1	1	
3				3	2	2	2		
4	1	3	1			2			1
5	2		1		3		1	1	1
6				1		1			1
7	1				1	1			
8		2	1						
9									
10			1	1					

Source: D = Lord Beveridge Price History Archive, Box C8, London School of Economics; R = Rogers, I, pp. 230–4; IV, pp. 282–9; F = Farmer, 'Prices', pp. 502–5; B = P. Bowden, 'Statistical appendix', in *AHEW*, IV, pp. 815–17.

Table 3.2b

Frequency of runs of high price years, 1350–1500 (wheat)

Duration of price run (years)	*1350–99*			*1400–49*			*1450–79 (B = 1465–79)*		
	D	*R*	*F*	*D*	*R*	*F*	*D*	*B*	*F*
1	4	4	3	2	3	3	6		
2	2	4	3	2	2	3	1	1	3
3			2	2	3	3	1		1
4		1		1	1			1	1
5	1						1		
6	1		1						
7									
8									
9									
10									

Source: D = Lord Beveridge Price History Archive, Box C8, London School of Economics; R = Rogers, I, pp. 230–4; IV, pp. 282–9; F = Farmer, 'Prices', pp. 502–5; B = P. Bowden, 'Statistical appendix', in *AHEW*, IV, pp. 815–17.

reflected in the Durham data, as in 1351, 1369, 1390, the late 1400s and 1410s.[23]

We can also make the further simple observation that prices at Durham tended to move in runs higher and lower than the moving average (Tables 3.2a and 3.2b). In making this observation, we should note only minor distinctions to be drawn with other contemporary grain price series. If a subtle distinction were to be made in relation to the national price series, it would be that runs of lower-priced years were

23 Lomas, 'Southeast Durham', p. 320.

Table 3.3

Decennial correlations of regional wheat prices with a national series (Thorold Rogers)

Decade	*Correlation (Durham)*	*Correlation (Farmer)*	*Correlation (Exeter)*
1350–9	0.63163	0.89836	0.73780
1360–9	0.15511	0.94011	0.59146
1370–9	0.93901	0.91910	0.93092
1380–9	0.31299	0.83412	0.69938
1390–9	0.70013	0.97873	0.78811
1400–9	0.83719	0.86933	0.61694
1410–9	0.12428	0.95926	0.96921
1420–9	0.76920	0.94419	0.74338
1430–9	0.87837	0.99333	0.92975
1440–9	0.29083	0.90842	0.67634
1450–9	-0.16848	0.84990	0.77388
1460–9	0.66126	0.96669	0.92545
1470–9	0.76625	0.92767	0.70963
1480–9	0.93803	0.94311	0.51345
1490–9	0.93781	0.33903	0.24695

Source: Durham = Lord Beveridge Price History Archive, Box C8, London School of Economics; Farmer = Farmer, 'Prices', pp. 502–5; Exeter = B. R. Mitchell, *British historical statistics* (Cambridge, 1988), pp. 752–3, taken from W. Beveridge, 'A statistical crime of the seventeenth century', *Journal of Economic and Business History* 1 (1929), pp. 503–33.

generally weaker in the Durham price series than in the national series. This is most notable for the second half of the fourteenth century but also evident for the first decades of the fifteenth century. This seems to be largely consistent with the message of the Durham tithe receipts, analysis of which has indicated a period of instability in the last decades of the fourteenth century and some periods of significant crisis in the first decades of the fifteenth century.[24]

There is also a weak correlation between the wheat price data for Durham and those gathered by Thorold Rogers and by Farmer. Intriguingly, if we also compare another regional wheat price, from Exeter, we find that the Exeter series displays a stronger correlation with the national series than does the Durham data (see Table 3.3). As is also evident, although earlier caveats regarding measures clearly apply also in this respect, the moving average is higher for the Durham material than it is for the other series (see Figures 3.1a–c).

Further analysis of the grain price movements within the Durham series, an analysis which removes potential errors of comparability across series – especially the correlation of price-movement between grain types – indicates that an impression of similarity between the Durham series and other series is open to question.[25] Appleby, in exploring the relationship between the French and English experiences of famine in the early modern period, showed how, through an investigation of correlations between the prices of cereals, trading down to poorer quality grains was evident in

24 B. Dodds, 'Estimating arable output using Durham Priory tithe receipts, 1341–1450', *EcHR* 57 (2004), pp. 270–1.

25 On correlation of grain price movements and contrasting views of the same, see Dobson, *Durham Priory*, p. 266; Lomas, 'Southeast Durham', pp. 319–20.

Table 3.4

Durham Priory: decennial correlations of wheat prices with barley and oats, 1330–1500

Decade	*Correlation (barley)*	*Correlation (oats)*
1330–9	0.991507	0.952656
1340–9	-1.000000	0.733522
1350–9	0.287311	0.907414
1360–9	0.892708	0.675702
1370–9	0.942236	0.855537
1380–9	0.761484	0.920236
1390–9	0.093249	0.725410
1400–9	0.989787	0.918552
1410–9	0.401776	0.412529
1420–9	0.725403	0.396336
1430–9	0.773113	0.892210
1440–9		0.748455
1450–9	0.977100	-0.409680
1460–9	0.250006	0.347599
1470–9	0.267341	0.341433
1480–9	0.825070	0.661985
1490–9	0.747192	0.689908

Source: Lord Beveridge Price History Archive, Box C8, London School of Economics.

France in the eighteenth century, by which time it had disappeared from England.[26] In fact, in fifteenth-century England, all published grain price series display some indication that prices moved together, and movement of grain prices at Durham also suggests some fairly strong if inconsistent positive correlation across the fifteenth century (Table 3.4). The correlation between Durham grains, in particular wheat and the cheaper food grains, notably rye, is especially strong. In fact, this stands in some contrast to the behaviour of wheat and rye in the national series, as Table 3.5 shows. It is, of course, possible that, as with our discussion of differentiation of the price series, the correlation of price within a single series is more precise and not subject to the smoothing of data likely to be encountered in composite series of the kinds constructed by Farmer and by Thorold Rogers.[27]

What are the implications of this data? While the behaviour of the Durham price data is in many ways entirely consistent with that observed in general price series for England as a whole in the fifteenth century, there are clearly some indications that a different regime may have operated there. Close examination of the Durham data encourages us to think that, aside from the traditional 'crisis years' of the fifteenth century, there are also muted indications of some pressure on food resources in the North-East.

26 A. B. Appleby, 'Grain prices and subsistence crises in England and France, 1590–1740', *JEH* 39 (1979), pp. 877–81.

27 To this end, although it has not been possible to attempt this here, it would also be potentially instructive to compare the correlation of individual grains against wheat both in terms of national series but also in terms of other good regional series, such as the Exeter material. If such regional data reveal a better correlation between grains than the national series does, in other words in the same way as is found for Durham, we might suspect either that composite series simply hide such relationships or that this other regional economy was as distinctive as that of the North-East.

Table 3.5

Decennial correlations of wheat and rye prices, 1460–1500

Decade	*Correlation (Durham)*	*Correlation (Thorold Rogers)*	*Correlation (Farmer)*
1460–9	0.990249	0.188895	0.552246
1470–9	0.915525	0.414792	0.497228
1480–9	0.932699	-0.053570	0.414721
1490–9	0.915837	0.768252	0.693385

Sources: Lord Beveridge Price History Archive, Box C8, London School of Economics; Rogers, I, pp. 230–4; IV, pp. 282–9; Farmer, 'Prices', pp. 502–5.

We can identify this pressure in a number of ways, including the frequency of fluctuation, the high prices above the mean, and, above all, the correlation of grain price movements. All of these, to follow Bouniatian's formula of implied yield, might suggest a limited agricultural output or, as an alternative, some failure of supply or of entitlement which had a particular, although not always consistent, effect upon grain prices. Of course, there are a whole series of variables to be taken into account before we can, with any confidence, conclude that the Durham price data is equivalent to low yields for certain years, and that those yields implied conditions of dearth for a proportion of that regional population. In particular, the extent of specialisation and land use within the region, as well as the market integration and the socio-economic profile of the population have to be taken into account.

Finally, and most importantly but also most intractably, we have to confront the vexing problem that high prices do not necessarily imply famine conditions any more than low prices spell general security and well-being. While the high price years of 1438–9 can be characterised, for instance, as years of real distress, marked by evidence of mortality in the North-East (at Scarborough), it is also recognised that a rise in grain prices might indicate the existence of a security device, protecting the needy; in the same way, low prices could augur badly for the most needy, who, through lack of entitlement, failed to gain resources. Thus, for London in 1390–1, Henry Knighton records prices sometimes in excess of 10s per quarter for wheat and the national price series record significant increases in 1390, with differentials of 67.21 (Thorold Rogers) and 71.97 (Farmer).[28] This stands in some contrast to the 3.96 differential calculated for Durham which might indicate that the dearth was not experienced there. However, given that the indications are of national shortage (with prices also high at Exeter and Leicester in this year), that there were deaths from apparently famine-related illness (dysentery) at York, and also given what we know of the institutional support within London and its region, we might be tempted to speculate that the rise in prices there reflected, indeed was a response to, that

28 G. H. Martin (ed.), *Knighton's Chronicle, 1337–1396* (Oxford, 1995), pp. 538–9.

29 Knighton records that in 1390 the citizens of London paid 2,000 marks (£1,333 6s 8d) to purchase food from the orphans' common chest and that the alderman arranged food for the indigents, sufficient that they could sustain themselves and their families during the period of the shortage. Ships also sailed from London to various parts of the realm in relief of the people there. Knighton also notes that, although the price of grain rose, it did not rise in proportion to the shortage: 'and yet although the scarcity was great the price of grain was not excessively high', Martin (ed.), *Knighton's Chronicle*, pp. 538–9.

support.[29] A relatively low price of grain at Durham might, in fact, indicate a relative failure or paucity of institutional safeguards.[30] In addition, we have also to recognise the potential distorting effect of independent variables, including the money supply and the amount of specie in circulation.[31]

Durham Priory price data and the north-eastern economy

Undoubtedly, in certain measure, the price data reflect the exogenous factors, including the shocks familiar throughout late medieval England, but it is in the particular and discrete response that the influence of a range of additional, largely endogenous, variables may also be suggested. This section reviews a series of features which are suggestive of the particularities of the economy of south-east Durham and its wider region. These features are the nature of the rural economy, the region's population structure, and the institutional and marketing structures. While rather intractable, they may offer particularities which, in turn, encourage us to contemplate a slightly more subtle reading of the Durham price data, one that perhaps reflects its wider regional context.

Contemporaries certainly appear to have been alive to the vulnerability of the region. Chroniclers, perhaps employing familiar literary devices, were keen to suggest that famine conditions hit the north of the country harder than they did the south. The Brut chronicler, as more than one historian has noted, draws attention to the famine of 1438 and remarks that deaths from the famine were especially evident in the 'north cuntre'[32] while earlier accounts of mortality in 1391 also single out the north as especially vulnerable.[33]

Historical discussion of the development of the agrarian economy in the North-East in the fifteenth century has followed two particular strands. Dobson, in his discussion of the monastic economy of Durham Priory, with clear justification, dismissed suggestions that there was a significant shift from arable to pasture on the priory estates during this period. Other commentators, however, notably Pollard and Tuck, discussing the whole region, from Northumbria to North Yorkshire, rather than the immediate vicinity of the priory and its estates in south-eastern Durham, have been more prepared to stress the decline in arable in favour of pasture and livestock

30 See also Wrigley, 'Reflections', pp. 247–8.

31 A. J. Pollard, *North-eastern England during the Wars of the Roses: lay society, war and politics, 1450–1500* (Oxford, 1990), pp. 77ff.

32 F. W. D. Brie (ed.), *The Brut, or the Chronicles of England,* Early English Text Society, original series 131 and 146 (2 parts, London, 1906–8), II, pp. 472–4, cited in Dyer, *Standards of living,* p. 268; also P. J. P. Goldberg, 'Mortality and economic change in the diocese of York, 1390–1514', *Northern History* 24 (1988), pp. 45–6. For a much earlier reference to the 'North' as particularly exposed to famine see, for instance, W. Childs (ed.), *Vita Edwardi Secundi* (Oxford, 2005), pp. 120–1.

33 Goldberg, 'Mortality', pp. 44–5 and references cited there.

34 Dobson, of course, was fully aware of these distinctions and recognised the potential significance of them beyond the county of Durham. 'The transformation of large numbers of Northumberland villages into predominantly pastoral communities had more severe consequences for the Durham chapter than any comparable development in their own country': Dobson, *Durham Priory,* p. 276.

husbandry.[34] Thus Tuck has described a process of abandonment of arable in much of the region in the fifteenth century and notes that on the estates of Tynemouth Priory almost all arable demesne had been turned into pasture by the early sixteenth century; the same was also true of the acquired freehold and the bondland *in manu domini*.[35] Similar processes can be detected between the Tyne and the Tees. At Easington, the land of 16 cottagers was converted to pasture by the early 1380s.[36] Pollard, while accepting Dobson's characterisation of the south-eastern Durham economy at the beginning of the fifteenth century, argues for general decline in the region and a depression in agriculture from the late 1430s, one which, he also suggests, was far more acute than elsewhere in England.[37] While certain decades in the second half of the fifteenth century saw improvement, this was not sustained and, according to Pollard, an irreversible conversion of arable into pasture led to further contraction of the agrarian economy and a further swathe of abandonments of arable in the last years of the fifteenth century.[38] The region contained good arable, capable of returning high yields by the standards of the Middle Ages.[39] It nevertheless appears that, with the exception of home farms such as Elvet Hall, which was retained by the Durham monks for purposes of consumption, the move was firmly away from arable production during this period.[40] Most recently Dodds has employed tithe data from the Durham estates to posit an overall reduction of approximately 53 per cent in arable output in the century after the Black Death.[41]

We know relatively little of the size of the population of the region that faced these changes during this period.[42] While the consensus among historians appears to be one of a general decline of the North-East population during the fifteenth century, Lomas has suggested, on the basis of estimates from villein lists attached to the records of priory courts, that at least one section of the region's population was greater in the later Middle Ages than it was in the early nineteenth century.[43] As to indicators of mortality and some sense of a regionally distinct demographic regime, one more or less responsive to failures of food supply, we can agree with Walter and Schofield that medievalists are far from blessed when it comes to meaningful data which will allow any investigation of famine-related dislocation, especially famine-related mortality in this period. The majority of key indicators of mortality in the

---

35 J. A. Tuck, 'The occupation of the land: the northern borders', in *AHEW*, III, pp. 40–1.

36 *Ibid.*, p. 40.

37 Pollard, *North-eastern England*, pp. 48–52; *idem*, 'The north-eastern economy and the agrarian crisis of 1438–40', *Northern History* 25 (1989), especially pp. 103–4.

38 Pollard, *North-eastern England*, pp. 56–8. For a further assessment of the stagnation of the regional agrarian economy, see C. M. Newman, 'Darlington and Northallerton in the later middle ages', in C. D. Liddy and R. H. Britnell (eds), *North-east England in the later middle ages* (Woodbridge, 2005), pp. 127–40.

39 J. A. Tuck, 'Farming practice and techniques: the northern borders', in *AHEW*, III, p. 179.

40 Pollard, *North-eastern England*, pp. 59–60.

41 B. Dodds, 'Tithe receipts', p. 261.

42 Lomas, 'Southeast Durham', p. 257.

43 *Ibid.*, p. 259. Here the argument is confined to south-eastern Durham. Note also, Dodds, 'Tithe receipts', pp. 263–4.

fifteenth century, notably wills and the internal records of monastic houses, are generally unlikely to reflect the status of those most susceptible to a downturn in food availability.[44] Some few pieces of mortality data do survive for more general populations for this period, notably tithing-penny payments, burial records in churchwardens' accounts and records of mortuary payments, such as those at Scarborough which indicate an upsurge of mortality in the late 1430s.[45] However, the extent of such data is thin and historians have frequently been thrown back on the information of the chronicles to support or confound arguments of heightened or particular mortality and dislocation.

Furthermore, while we have information on tenants, there appears to be far less information on the landless and those employed in local proto-industry and mining. While we also know that while certain towns within the region, for instance Newcastle, suffered some considerable hardship in the fifteenth century, others, such as North Shields, appear to have enjoyed some relative success.[46] Mining in the region also created employment opportunities of fluctuating importance.[47] More important than mining, in terms of employment opportunities, was the textile industry.[48] Cloth making, and the urban and marketing centres associated with it, underwent severe decline in the second half of the fifteenth century. At the same time, York, the principal trading centre for the region, suffered contraction in its share of overseas trade, losing out to London in the North Sea trade.[49] Importantly also, Dobson has observed a stagnation of wages on the priory's demesnes in the fifteenth century.[50]

It is possible, therefore, that the region was home to a mobile population that was, to a fairly enhanced degree, market dependent. Given the move towards pastoral husbandry, it is also conceivable, therefore, that a process of specialisation increased both the market dependency of the region and its vulnerability in the face of volatile political, economic or climatic environments. If a substantial and possibly increasing proportion of the population was market dependent, were the institutional supports of that market structure sufficiently sophisticated to cope? Especially given the proximity of much of the region to the coast and to important ports, we might imagine that the North-East, even in the Middle Ages, was sufficiently integrated with other markets to avoid the worst of calamities.[51] Galloway's recent exploration of the relationship between Exeter and London in terms of the grain trade may be revealing here, suggesting as it does that while a developed integrated market existed in the early

---

44 R. S. Gottfried, *Epidemic disease in fifteenth-century England; the medical response and the demographic consequences* (New Brunswick, 1978); Goldberg, 'Mortality', pp. 38–55; B. F. Harvey, *Living and dying in England, 1100–1540: the monastic experience* (Oxford, 1993), pp. 122–7; J. Hatcher, 'Mortality in the fifteenth century: some new evidence', *EcHR*, 2nd series 39 (1986).

45 L. R. Poos, *A rural society after the Black Death: Essex 1350–1525* (Cambridge, 1991); P. Heath, 'North Sea fishing in the fifteenth century: the Scarborough fleet', *Northern History* 3 (1968), pp. 53–68; G. Rosser, *Medieval Westminster, 1200–1540* (Oxford, 1989), pp. 177–9.

46 Pollard, *North-eastern England*, p. 51

47 *Ibid.*, pp. 74–6.

48 *Ibid.*, pp. 39–40.

49 *Ibid.*, p. 71 ff.

50 Dobson, *Durham Priory*, p. 267, n. 4. But note Dodds, 'Tithe receipts', p. 264.

51 But note the comments of Dodds, 'Tithe receipts', p. 266.

fourteenth century, one that was capable of responding to major agrarian crises, the extent of integration may have declined in the second half of the fourteenth century. A decline in the volatility of the Exeter price series in the mid to late fifteenth century suggests, according to Galloway, the existence once again of 'a well-functioning grain market', a revival which he explains in terms of the good performance of the rural and urban economy of Devon in this period.[52] In its suggestion that market integration, where it existed in the Middle Ages, was dependent upon entitlement, as we might expect, and that the prosperity of the region and its current fortune effected a positive relationship with other markets, the earlier observations regarding the relative poverty and stagnation of the north-eastern economy in the fifteenth century may be telling.[53]

Conclusion

John Walter and Roger Schofield raise some important, yet frustrating, issues for the medievalist. In reflecting upon the chronology of famine in the pre-modern period, they review briefly the evidence for famine in medieval England and conclude that 'after the savage mid-fourteenth century losses of population associated with the Black Death and subsequent plagues, the general economic context would suggest that famine should not have been a problem, at least on a national scale'.[54] With more than half an eye on Appleby's work on early modern Cumbria and Westmorland, they speculate that the 'corn-poor and remote pastoral-highland communities' may have been more exposed to famine but their overall assessment is one that, 'in the light of the highly unsatisfactory state of the medieval evidence', plays down the likelihood that harvest shortfalls in the period created famine conditions 'over much of the country'.[55] As we have seen, historians working on the North-East have been generally prepared to consider shortage in the fifteenth century as confined to certain problem years and, indeed, have used the grain price data from Durham Priory to support their case for a fairly secure regional economy.[56] While the grain price material from Durham Priory does not of itself undermine any such thesis – in fact, as we have seen, it has more than once been employed to support it – there are sufficient inconsistencies with the general message of 'national' series to encourage some further investigation of the potential vulnerabilities of the wider region in the late Middle Ages, both in terms of supply and of entitlement.

---

52 J. A. Galloway, 'One market or many? London and the grain trade of England', in *idem* (ed.), *Trade, urban hinterlands and market integration, c. 1300–1600* (London, 2000), pp. 39–41.

53 Note, for instance, the recent comments of Threlfall-Holmes regarding the regional focus of trade, at least in relation to Durham Priory, which suggest 'a regional economy which was afloat, if not positively buoyant': M. Threlfall-Holmes, 'Newcastle trade and Durham Priory, 1460–1520', in Liddy and Britnell (eds), *North-east England*, p. 152.

54 J. Walter and R. Schofield, 'Famine, disease and crisis mortality in early modern society', in *idem* (eds), *Famine, disease and the social order in early modern society* (Cambridge, 1989), p. 29.

55 *Ibid.*, p. 30.

56 The notable exception is Dodds, Tithe receipts, although in his analysis he cautions against any simple identification of discrete regional experiences in the later Middle Ages and suggests instead that 'the exceptional quality of the land in the Durham Priory's appropriated parishes…may be more representative of patterns in southern and midland England' (p. 276).

Chapter 4

Town and region: the corn market in Aberdeen, c. 1398–c. 1468

Elizabeth Gemmill

An important factor in the survival and prosperity of any medieval town was its relationship with the surrounding countryside. As a place characterised by its pursuit of commerce and manufacture, a town needed to have a supply of food and raw materials to support those activities and to feed those who carried them on.[1] Such regular regional patterns of supply, with their necessary institutional support, constitute the smallest identifiable structures of medieval commerce. It is true that medieval towns were more rural than their modern counterparts, being agricultural producers as well as consumers, and Aberdeen was no exception. Even so, the major part of the food and raw materials consumed in the burgh came from its hinterland, with other parts of Scotland and even other countries providing supplies as well. The amount of the goods coming from the countryside to Aberdeen depended on the amount of produce available for sale, as well as on the level of demand for it in the town. This paper aims to examine the nature of the evidence relating to the corn market in Aberdeen, to explore the regulations governing the sale and handling of corn in the burgh, and to consider the provenance of Aberdeen's grain supply, especially in the context of her wider trading connections. It illustrates matters of concern and forms of trading organisation that were characteristic of urban communities all over Europe.

The period which this paper covers reflects that of the particular volumes of the Aberdeen Council Registers which are the main source of information about the corn market in the burgh.[2] The first surviving volume of the series known as the Council Registers starts in 1398, and they continue to the present day. After the period covered by the second volume, up to September 1414, there is a gap in the records until January 1434, and there is at least one, and possibly three, volumes missing.[3] The next two volumes cover the period 1434 to the late 1460s. There are also guild

1 See D. M. Palliser, 'Introduction', in *idem* (ed.), *The Cambridge urban history of Britain: I, 600–1540* (Cambridge, 2000), p. 5, where Susan Reynolds' functional and social definitions of the town are adopted for towns in the high and later Middle Ages.

2 I first studied these records while working at Oxford University on an ESRC-funded project directed by Nicholas Mayhew. The main outcome of the project was the book on Scottish prices, E. Gemmill and N. Mayhew, *Changing values in medieval Scotland: a study of prices, money, and weights and measures* (Cambridge, 1995).

3 This is the most notable of the gaps in the series of Council Registers. The current archivist, Judith Cripps, undertook a search for the missing volume or volumes in 1980–1 and concluded that the missing volumes had decayed rather than had been mislaid. Another significant break in the material is in the first volume, between 1402 and 1405.

court records for this later period.[4] Thus, the period under study is divided into two, with a gap of about 20 years in between.

The Aberdeen Council Registers document the proceedings of the burgh's council and of its head, bailie and guild courts. Because of the extreme scarcity of material relating to Scottish urban history in the medieval period, and because the Aberdeen records begin much earlier than equivalent evidence from any other Scottish burgh, they are a most important source for our understanding of the medieval Scottish town.[5] Of course, it is important to resist using the Aberdeen evidence to make claims about conditions and practices in other burghs, but it is true that Aberdeen was well placed to know what those conditions and practices were. As a royal burgh, Aberdeen was visited by the king's chamberlain, or chief financial officer, in the court known as his ayre, and such visits were occasions on which the town's customs and their enforcement were inspected and, presumably, brought into line with best practice.[6] In cases of uncertainty over burghal custom the chamberlain and the burgh courts themselves could ask for guidance from the special advisory body known as 'the four burghs'. There must have been debate and interchange when Aberdeen sent its representatives to parliament, and when its officers, the bailies and customs collectors, went to render account at the royal exchequer. Sometimes, indeed, burghs actively consulted one another in complex cases: in early 1467, in a case involving the rights of the daughters and sons of a man who had married twice, the authorities at Aberdeen consulted their counterparts in Edinburgh, Perth, and Dundee, each of which replied offering advice, citing law and precedent.[7]

It is, however, dangerous to use the more copious evidence in the later records from Aberdeen as a guide to earlier practices, because policies and procedures were changing during the first half of the fifteenth century, as indeed was the process of record keeping. Experimentation with record keeping is especially true of the guild court records. There are no such records in the first two volumes; perhaps at this stage they were kept separately and have disintegrated or have been lost. For the later period, there are guild records in the volume which opens in 1434, but these are kept

---

4 Aberdeen Council Registers, volumes I (1398–1407), II (1408–14), IV (1434–48), V.i (1448–68) and V.ii (Guild Court records, 1441–67). These volumes are in the possession of Aberdeen City Council, and are housed in the Town House, Aberdeen. The material for 1398 to 1400, a court roll for 1317 and extracts from 1401 to 1407 were published in W. C. Dickinson (ed.), *Extracts from the early records of Aberdeen, 1317, 1398–1407*, Scottish History Society, 3rd series 49 (1957). An earlier edition of extracts is J. Stuart (ed.), *Extracts from the council register of the burgh of Aberdeen, I: 1398–1570*, Spalding Club 12 (Aberdeen, 1844).

5 I. Flett and J. Cripps, 'Documentary sources', in M. Lynch, M. Spearman and G. Stell (eds), *The Scottish medieval town* (Edinburgh, 1988), pp. 18–41 (p. 25).

6 For the articles which the chamberlain was supposed to cover in his ayre see 'Articuli inquirendi in itinere camerarii' and 'Modus procedendi in itinere camerarii', in C. Innes (ed.), *Ancient laws and customs of the burghs of Scotland, I: A.D. 1154–1424*, Scottish Burgh Record Society 1 (Edinburgh, 1868), pp. 114–26 and 132–54. See also R. Nicholson, *Scotland: the later middle ages* (Edinburgh, 1974), p. 17.

7 ACC Council Register (hereafter CR), V.i, pp. 593–4 and 602–3.

separately for the period 1441–67. Thereafter the guild records are, again, found among those for other burgh courts.[8]

The material in the registers is judicial, administrative, and legislative. There are disputes between individuals about real and moveable property, rents, fishing rights and debts. There are records of the appointment of officials, regulations about urban security and sanitation and the conduct of manufacturing, trade, and commerce, as well as prosecution of offenders against the burgh statutes. There are lists of taxpayers, admissions of burgesses and guildsmen, leases of urban property, valuations of moveable goods, inquisitions *post mortem* on people's lands and rents, accounts of burgh officials and copies of royal charters granting privileges. In short, no document of public interest in Aberdeen would be out of place here. The records are, ostensibly, divided into the sessions of the burgh courts of Aberdeen, but there are other entries, often unheaded, sometimes dated and sometimes not, suggesting that the Council Register was used as a convenient way of recording business which did not form part of the actual court sessions.

The information about urban transactions in grain, or victual as it was called, is in a number of different forms. There are reports about the market prices of grain. There are cases where the rules about conduct in the market place are broken, which enable us to infer, at least to some degree, what the rules were. There are ordinances regulating the conduct of trade in the town. There are lawsuits between individuals concerning debts in agricultural produce. There are leases of town offices relating to grain, and there are, finally, details of incoming ships' cargoes.

The most direct and copious information is in reports made by sworn jurors or assize members about the prices of wheat and malt in the town's market, made for the purpose of regulating the prices of bread and ale (see Table 4.1).[9] In the earlier fifteenth century bakers were expected to base the weight of their loaves on the price of wheat and brewers to set the price of ale according to the cost of malt, with an allowance for their costs and profit.[10] Notices of assizes of bread and ale are most copious in the early period, and tend to be recorded in the registers in a more detailed way. Later on, they are found less frequently and the entries are more laconic, a brief marginal note being found sufficient. The reports in this form gradually dwindle, although they are still found occasionally in the sixteenth century. As this form of assize faded out, a new form came in: we find unequivocal instructions issued to bakers and brewers, and the assizes are recorded as the prescribed weight of penny and twopenny loaves and the price of gallons of ale. Perhaps the chamberlain's ayre of February 1435 helped to prompt this change, for it was then that the assize of ale in

8 The guild court records in volumes IV and V.ii are published in E. Gemmill (ed.), *Aberdeen guild records, 1437–1468*, Scottish History Society, 5th series 17 (2005).

9 The Latin text of the twelfth-century Burgh Laws tells us: 'Pistores qui faciunt panes ad vendendum faciant albos panes et bisos secundum consideracionem et probacionem proborum hominum ville prout tempus se habuerit. Et pistor habeat ad lucrum de qualibet celdra secundum quod videatur probis hominibus ville'. 'Leges Burgorum', in Innes (ed.), *Ancient laws*, p. 29. For a detailed discussion of the relationship between the prices of grain and those of bread and ale, see Gemmill and Mayhew, *Changing values*, pp. 30–41 and 48–53.

10 Chapter 1, pp. 7–8.

the new form is first found.[11] There are two further indications that a new system was being adopted. In November 1462 the assize confirmed that the bailies should ordain the measure for bakers according to the price of 6s per boll, which was notionally two English bushels.[12] Then, in July 1465, the authorities decided that bakers had to bake penny bread of 17 oz however wheat was sold.[13] There seems to have been a change in emphasis, perhaps reflecting a desire for greater control over the activities of bakers.[14]

These reports have certain limitations as a guide to price fluctuations. First, the shortest interval between valuations is a fortnight, and sometimes, especially when there are long gaps in the records, they appear much less frequently. We cannot, therefore, always compare prices in the same month from year to year, nor can we always track seasonal changes clearly. Another area of difficulty is in the figures themselves. Unless the assize distinguished different qualities of grain, it was usual for each cereal to be given a single price per boll. The figures given always have an even number of pence, and are for the most part divisible by four. Perhaps the bakers, for whom the assize was intended, were buying by the boll, but it will be argued below that, in fact, the boll was not the main unit of measure in the market place and that most people were buying by the firlot, which was one quarter of a boll. A further limitation is that these assizes only cover those grains to which it was licit to add value by baking or brewing for sale to townspeople, that is, wheat and malt. Thus, we do not (with one exception, from 29 November 1435) have prices for oats or oatmeal because townspeople were not allowed to make oatcakes for sale at this period.[15] That oatmeal was commonly grown in the Aberdeen hinterland, and was sold in the market, is clear from the copious evidence in these records of offences against the market regulations associated with meal buying. It was, after all, the Scottish cereal par excellence.

The assize sometimes glossed its reports of high prices with comments about quality. The sworn members of the assize were perhaps uncomfortable when prices soared too high, so they explained it in terms of higher intrinsic value. Thus, the assize of 21 October 1438, which gives an unusually high price of 9s per boll for wheat, indicated that this was the price of 'sufficient wheat' and that 9s was the maximum.[16] In the report of 1 October 1442 wheat that was good, dry, and sufficient for milling was valued at 5s, while good malt at 3s 6d the boll was distinguished from the best at 4s.[17] It is only occasionally that on any given day variations in the price (as opposed to

---

11 ACC CR, IV, p. 33.

12 ACC CR, V.i, p. 461. 'Assisa determinavit frumentum esse precii vj s. et quod ballivi facient mensuram pistoribus secundum precium sex solidorum.'

13 ACC CR, V.i, p. 541.

14 It may be noted in this connection that in the mid-fifteenth century bakers at Aberdeen were required to mark their loaves with a sign: see E. Gemmill, 'Signs and symbols in medieval Scottish trade', *Review of Scottish Culture* 13 (2000–1), pp. 7–17 (pp. 10–11).

15 See Gemmill and Mayhew, *Changing values*, p. 42. The exceptional case is in ACC CR, IV, p. 53: oatmeal was priced at 3s 8d per boll.

16 ACC CR, IV, p. 142.

17 ACC CR, IV, p. 281.

the quality of the product) were hinted at. On 4 February 1443 malt was said to have been found at 7s the boll 'and more'.[18] This implies at least that there was not one, fixed price on any given day which all townspeople paid.

That prices would fluctuate on any given market day seems a reasonable expectation. For one thing, people of all sorts were allowed into the market place, to judge from those involved in offences against the market regulations or mentioned in ordinances. In times of scarcity, the categories of people allowed into the market place to negotiate prices were restricted; in the notoriously bad year 1438, for example, it was ruled that only men were allowed to buy meal in the market.[19] Women were targeted because they were so often associated with spoiling the market. Retailers, known in Aberdeen as regrators or hucksters, whose presence in the market was restricted, were very commonly women. In the statutes made in the chamberlain's ayre in February 1435, for example, they were only allowed to buy anything for resale after 11 o'clock.[20] The scarcity ordinance of October 1438 also targeted female regraters; they were not allowed to operate in town unless their husbands were burgesses, and bakers were not to sell their loaves to them.

It is difficult to see clearly how the process of negotiation actually occurred in this period. Evidence from the sixteenth century, when the process of negotiation or 'making price' was on occasion confined to free people, and, on one occasion, to female representatives of each of the town's quarters, suggests that such negotiations were the norm.[21] Yet, there were limits. The practice of 'overbuying' – interfering with a bargain which had already been agreed by offering the vendor a better deal – was forbidden. Later evidence from Aberdeen suggests that, even when it was not a case of overbuying, offering more than the going rate amounted to spoiling the market and was forbidden.[22] Taken cumulatively, the evidence perhaps suggests that bargaining was allowed when its effect was to keep prices down, which was in everyone's interests, rather than to raise them, which was only in the interest of the dealer. If this is so, then the assize price might have real authority, representing the highest that responsible members of the community were prepared to tolerate.

Looking at the assize prices we can see a number of trends and patterns. The sensitivity of the prices of wheat and malt to seasonal fluctuations is most clearly seen in the early fifteenth century, when the assize valuations are most copious. Prices tended to be high in the spring and early summer, up until July. Wheat prices, for example, look particularly high in March 1401 and 1402. Prices started to fall in August, although not invariably. Particular years stand out as good or bad, such as the harvest year 1401–2 for wheat, early summer 1410 and January to July 1413 for wheat and malt. Above all, the prices of wheat and malt in the 1430s were significantly above earlier levels although the break in the records after 1414 makes it impossible to date this increase more precisely. A commonly found price level in the early period would be 4s for wheat and 3s for malt; by the 1440s wheat is never found

18 ACC CR, IV, p. 297.

19 ACC CR, IV, p. 143, printed in Gemmill and Mayhew, *Changing values*, p. 78.

20 ACC CR, IV, p. 33.

21 Gemmill and Mayhew, *Changing values*, pp. 59–60.

22 *Ibid.*, pp. 58–9.

below 5s and malt rarely below 4s. Wheat was usually more expensive than malt, and sometimes much more expensive, but it periodically sold at the same price and, on occasion, for less. Malt made in town was more expensive than wheat in February 1400, and was on several occasions either the same price as wheat or more in 1443.[23] If demand for wheat and malt was fairly constant in the town, then the changes in price and ratio reflect changes in source of supply as well as seasonal changes and good and bad harvest years.

A principle of paramount importance was that all grain coming to town had to be presented to the market cross, and the tolls paid at the tollbooth.[24] Outside dealers were not allowed to sell it privately before the market. In practice, both vendors and purchasers had something to gain by avoiding the market: the vendor avoided tolls levied in the market place and the buyer competition. In the early fifteenth century, this rule seems to have been broken quite frequently by townspeople buying and selling malt and meal privately in their homes. There is evidence that particular townsmen set up their own houses as private markets from which grain could be bought. In December 1399 Andrew Culane was given a day to prove that he had not made a market in his home, buying and measuring meal or malt with a common firlot.[25] On 12 February 1400 John Jameson and William Inverory explained the circumstances which had led to their being accused of having spoiled the market. John told the court that a countryman had come to his house with a sample of malt, saying that the remainder was as good. Having examined the sample, his wife bought a boll or more of the malt which she received in Hugh Plummar's house, and he said that everything had been done lawfully. William told the court that his wife had bought a load (*onus*) of malt in Hugh's house, in the same manner and for the same price that the rest was sold for, and he too claimed to have acted lawfully. That there was some sort of ambiguity over this is clear from the fact that the matter was referred to the town council.[26] Another doubtful practice was when a sample of grain was presented at the cross for townspeople to buy, while the main consignment was left at someone's house. The wife of John Wodman was accused of buying malt at the cross by sample (*per exemplarem*) from John Wyss' of Dornoch; the actual malt which she bought was in the house of Gilbert de Kynros and had not been presented to the cross and the market by the vendor.[27] The entry is struck through and the defendant was acquitted, but it is not clear whether this was because she had not done what she was accused of, or because it did not constitute an offence. In yet another case, the wife of John de Abernethy bought oats which came to her house in blankets and sheets, which was seen as a sign that they had been measured before they came there.[28]

---

23 The patterns of seasonal fluctuation and of the overall ratio of malt to wheat prices, as shown in these assize valuations, is discussed in Gemmill and Mayhew, *Changing values*, pp. 149 and 179–80.

24 *Ibid.*, p. 57 and note 167.

25 Dickinson (ed.), *Early records*, p. 118.

26 *Ibid.*, p. 127.

27 ACC CR, II, p. 20.

28 ACC CR, II, p. 20. These cases occur as part of a number of cases involving illicit purchases of grain, on pp. 20–1.

These private sales of grain in townspeople's homes show that there were contacts between individual rural suppliers and townspeople outside the market place. It is, however, rare to find evidence that townspeople went out into the countryside to forestall grain. There are some such instances, as the case of Simon 'palframan' (whose name, it is tempting to believe, does in this case indicate his craft), who in October 1408 admitted buying oats outside town and afterwards offering them for sale in the market as though they had not been purchased previously.[29] But this practice usually involved animal products intended for export rather than grain.

The council registers demonstrate amply and repeatedly that Aberdeen's authorities had a real problem with enforcing its monopoly on the export trade which it enjoyed in common with other 'cocket' burghs, namely, that only those merchants from burghs with such liberties had the right to engage in exporting. But Aberdeen found that wool, skins, and hides were being bought up in the countryside and sent via other ports, particularly those further south, for export abroad. Grain products, however, do not seem to have been much involved in this illicit trade, and this may have implications for the level of the grain supply in the surrounding countryside. If Aberdeen's hinterland had been producing enough surplus grain to supply both the domestic market in Aberdeen, and to export abroad, instances of such practices would include references to grain. Likewise, if malt or meal were being exported we might expect to find maximum prices for such products in the same entries as we find maximum prices at which merchants were allowed to buy wool and skins.[30]

Although the boundaries between legitimate and illicit practices are not always clear, and were not always clear to contemporaries, it is clear that private sales in people's homes before goods had come to the market were definitely forbidden. One reason for this was to ensure that what was available was on display so that there could be no unwarranted rumour or perception of shortage, which might in itself drive up prices. Another was to protect the town's dues in the market place. The job of clerk of the market is known variously as that of 'farmer of the firlot', 'tollar', or 'melemetstar' (this last term perhaps confirming the importance of meal in the Scottish cereal market). This was an office which was farmed out in the first part of the fifteenth century. As well as collecting tolls, the so-called farmers of the firlot seem to have taken a commission for making available measures and for measuring grain in the market place. Several people who had bought bark, wheat, and oats at home were fined in January 1410 for prejudicing the position of the 'farmers of the firlot' by not paying their tolls.[31] The council register records on 13 May 1450 the five-year lease of the tolls of the firlots and stallholders' rents to Alexander Rolland, for an annual farm of £24. The farm was again given to Alexander in February 1464 for a further five years for the same annual farm. The agreement on this occasion required him, when he left office, to leave 12 sufficient firlots in the booth for the alderman and bailies that were responsible for arranging the next lease. On this occasion the provost, bailies and council promised not to impose any 'scot or lot' burdens on Alexander.[32]

---

29 ACC CR, II, p. 20.

30 See Gemmill and Mayhew, *Changing values*, pp. 65–8.

31 ACC CR, II, p. 56.

32 ACC CR, V.ii, pp. 818 and V.i, p. 531.

The title of this office implies that the firlot was the chief measure used in the market place, at least for exacting tolls. The farmers of the firlot had the incentive of needing to make enough profit to recoup their farm, but they also seem to have been liable for any losses incurred by townspeople who had had to use an unofficial, or common, firlot in the market when they made their purchases of grain. Thus in December 1408 one John Atkynson was given a day to prove his losses from having had to buy wheat by a common firlot, for which the farmers of the firlot were to reimburse him.[33] At times of scarcity or high prices, extra checks on the measures were put into place. In October 1438, a series of ordinances about the purchase of meal, fish, and tallow provided that meal was to be measured by the half firlot as well as the peck and half peck.[34] The importance of the firlot, peck and half peck are confirmed later on, in 1505, when the toll collector was ordered to have these measures ready for everyone's use.[35]

The town's millers also profited from incoming grain brought to them by purchasers, who had to see to the grinding of their victual. The Council Registers show that the burgh authorities had the lease of four or more mills in their gift in the first part of the fifteenth century. In 1443 the Upper and Nether mills, the Justice mills and the Fuller's mill were each leased for a period of six years in return for a fixed annual payment. The three farmers of the Upper Mill had to maintain it, and to pay the expenses of the water conduit. Thus, they were under pressure to ensure that they did business in order to exact multure to cover these costs and make the venture a worthwhile undertaking.[36] By 1465 the alderman, bailies and council were able to lease the two Justice mills to their neighbour Matthew Couper and his helper Christy of Abirdour. The lease was for fifteen years, and the amount of the farm was calculated to allow for rebuilding one of the mills and both had to be sufficiently and profitably equipped by the end of the term. As in the 1443 leases, no rate of multure was specified but the farmers were under obligation to grind four chaldrons of victual per year free for the Blackfriars of Aberdeen.[37]

We are only occasionally told something about the sort of people who brought grain to Aberdeen to sell. When there were offences against the market rules, it was the townspeople who were in trouble rather than the countrymen, and sometimes the lawsuit did not even mention the name of the seller, but referred to them as 'a certain countryman' (*quidam ruralis*) or 'a certain man' (*quidam homo*) or 'a certain countrywoman' (*quedam mulier ruralis*). It is telling that the authorities distinguished some people by their rural origins, but it is possible too that when names were given there was no need also to mention that those involved were from the countryside. Country people whose names were not provided were likely to have been of fairly

33 ACC CR, II, p. 23.

34 ACC CR, IV, p. 143, printed in Gemmill and Mayhew, *Changing values*, p. 78.

35 ACC CR, VIII, pp. 518–19.

36 ACC CR, V.ii, p. 672.

37 ACC CR, V.i, p. 550. For the location of the Upper and Nether mills, see E. P. Dennison, D. Ditchburn and M. Lynch (eds), *Aberdeen before 1800: a new history* (East Linton, 2002), pp. 20 and 23.

humble status. Conversely, there is evidence that lords were important as suppliers of wool, fells, and hides.[38]

As to the extent to which townspeople themselves produced grain, the evidence is inconclusive, although it is suggestive. It was ruled, for example, in March 1401 that anyone buying or having malt or meal in the country should only sell it in town in the market.[39] Again, on 23 August 1441 it was ruled that if any neighbour had victual to sell he must sell it not in his house but in the market, plainly on the market day.[40] If there were townspeople who had malt or meal in the country that they had not bought, then the inference must be that it belonged to them already. Perhaps they had produced it themselves; or perhaps it was owing to them as rent or in return for some service they had provided. That townspeople were engaged in farming activities around Aberdeen cannot be doubted. On 5 May 1399 the wife of Henry Masoun, who was not a burgess, was given a day to answer for a number of offences including the charge that 'she should not spoil the market by buying flour unless she is acting for her husband in the matter of hiring out his oxen'. Henry, it seems, hired out his oxen, perhaps for ploughing, in return for a render of meal.[41] Another case which may involve urban farming activity came on in October 1443: a townsman claimed he had four bolls of meal at 10s the boll and 18 sheep with their produce owing to him for nine years.[42]

One rural aspect of Aberdeen's economy is evident from the number of occasions on which the authorities reiterated legislation to ensure that pigs did not wander about unchecked doing damage to urban property. In the chamberlain's ayre of 1465 four men were to be chosen to round up and present to the master of the kirkwork (St Nicholas Church, the parish church of Aberdeen) any swine they found wandering loose, damaging anyone's property, or going about the streets. They were either to get a fine of 6d per pig, or were to kill the pigs on the spot and keep the bodies as escheats.[43] The fact that the authorities had to reiterate warnings about stray pigs, and the fact that Aberdeen butchers never seem to have sold pork, suggest that keeping pigs was a common practice in Aberdeen. It was doubtless usual for people to keep their own poultry, too, as this would require little space. As far as beasts requiring pasture were concerned, the town's butchers, or fleshers as they were known, grazed cattle for slaughter on the town's common land, but they also purchased fodder.[44]

---

38 Gemmill and Mayhew, *Changing values*, pp. 65–6.

39 Dickinson (ed.), *Early records*, p. 179.

40 ACC CR, IV, p. 252, printed in Stuart (ed.), *Extracts*, p. 397.

41 The phrase cited, in the original Latin, is '[quod] non peiorat forum quoad empcionem farine nisi quod prouenit marito suo racione conduccionis bouium suorum': Dickinson (ed.), *Early records*, p. 41. On the use of seals and stamps to authorise standards, see Gemmill, 'Signs and symbols', p. 9.

42 ACC CR, IV, p. 323.

43 ACC CR, V.i, p. 549.

44 For example, in October 1408 James the butcher was accused of buying fodder before the market bell rang: ACC CR, II, p. 20. The entry is struck through, however, implying that he was acquitted. See also I. Blanchard, E. Gemmill, N. Mayhew and I. D. Whyte, 'The economy: town and country', in Dennison, Ditchburn and Lynch (eds.), *Aberdeen before 1800*, p. 140.

Evidence in these records about arable land use is, however, much more scarce. A rare example comes from 1437, when there was a case involving two townsmen over a horse which had been captured on the defendant's father's crops (*messes*) and which the defendant had failed to release even though the plaintiff had offered to pay for damages.[45] The inquisitions *post mortem* on burgesses' lands do not help very much with any estimate on produce; they indicate the location of the land, its value, the service by which it was held, any rent due, and the identity of the heir. But they do not provide any evidence of how the land was used. Nor are actions heard in the burgh courts for unpaid rents any more helpful; the usual procedure was that the plaintiff brought in a sample of earth and stones on the land as a symbolic testimony that there was nothing else to distrain. Such evidence may shed light on the extent of vacant tenements in fifteenth-century Aberdeen, but not on land use as such. Any arable land owned by burgesses outside the burgh itself would not be covered by inquisitions taken by the burgh authorities. In the early sixteenth century a statute provided that all corn grown in the freedom of the burgh must be brought for grinding at the town's mill.[46] We are told in the seventeenth century that the fields outside Aberdeen were fruitful in oats, bear (a form of barley), and wheat, and that there was plenty of pasture land.[47] Within Aberdeen the wealthier burgesses owned gardens which could be used for growing vegetables but, again, we do not know how much their produce contributed to the burgh economy.

Of course, Aberdeen did not have to rely wholly on corn coming from its rural hinterland for its supply of corn. Its coastal situation meant that it was favourably placed to receive cargoes of corn from other parts of eastern Scotland or, indeed, further afield. By the time the fourth volume of the Council Register, in the 1430s, there is a lot more evidence in the records of Aberdeen's overseas trade links, particularly with Flanders. There are lawsuits involving imports and exports from there, and there are many more references to debts in Flemish money. Aberdeen's wool, skins, hides and fish, particularly salmon, were by then being marketed in Flanders in exchange for imports of wine, salt, cloth, iron, soap, and woad. Imports were not confined to these items, but they are the ones which occur most frequently. It is in this context – a perceived increase in the amount of evidence of overseas trade – that we should look at the new evidence for imports of grain from abroad. In the later volumes of the period under study there is much evidence that large quantities of grain were being imported, not so much from Flanders, but from England and Prussia. Some goods came to Aberdeen via other Scottish or English ports. In a case of 1447 Thomas Forman bought a Prussian last of wheat from John Smot of Edinburgh. The agreement, according to Thomas, was that the delivery would be made wherever the ship happened to arrive and unload, whether Rattray, Aberdeen, or Leith. He had agreed to pay partly in money and partly in a horse valued at £4.[48] In another case a consignment of bear, shipped from Stralsund in Prussia, was bought at Inverness by

---

45 ACC CR, IV, p. 92.

46 ACC CR, VIII, p. 427.

47 J. Gordon, *Aberdoniae vtrivsque descriptio: a description of both touns of Aberdeen*, C. Innes (ed.), Spalding Club 5 (1842), p. 5.

48 ACC CR, IV, p. 498.

an Aberdeen burgess, Thomas Broissour. In a lawsuit of 1464 Thomas took upon himself to prove that the two vendors, Hans and Henry the Dutchmen, had agreed that he should only have to pay as much as the vendors were selling for in Inverness. Aberdeen merchants seem to have imported on behalf of merchants of other burghs too, like Andrew Broisour who in 1446 had English malt put in his ship at Berwick on Tweed for delivery to Henry Bonar, a citizen of St Andrews.[49]

At the end of volume V.i of the registers there is a section recording the cargoes of a number of ships arriving in Aberdeen from abroad. It is not clear whether they were deliberately grouped together, or whether it was simply a convenient place to record cargoes arriving in Aberdeen over a longer period. Some of the entries, it is true, have dates next to them – August 1465, November 1466 – so we at least know that they did not all arrive at the same time.[50] However this may be, it is clear that each ship carried a large amount of grain as part of its cargo. A ship from Dordrecht brought wheat, rye and maslin. The *Christopher*, whose master was from Delft, and the *Jacob*, whose master was from Veere, were both loaded with wheat, maslin, and bear. A ship from 'Armore' in Zeeland brought in rye; the *Christopher* from Antwerp brought bear; the *Katherine* from 'Hundfleit' brought malt. A ship of Robert Wormot, who was a burgess of Aberdeen, brought in malt by English measure. Clearly Aberdeen was not importing cereals only. The ships were bringing in other goods as well: timber, soap, lint, salt, apples, onions, iron, wine, cloth, rice, butter and cheese. Above all there was food in these cargoes, as well as other essential raw materials, some of which will have been sold to country men, like iron and salt.

Much imported grain was, however, destined for use in the town itself. That the town officers had some sort of a hand in the disposal of imported grain seems to be implied in one incident, in April 1438, where the guild court convicted John Lorymer of trying to buy victuals from a Prussian ship, both at sea and in port. He was reported to have said to all and sundry that he did not want to lose his own profit for the alderman and bailies.[51] A few years later on, a memorandum of November 1444 recorded that Matheus Crukin, master of a Stralsund ship, said that he had sold to the town all the rye and boards in his ship. The council, in return, agreed that the alderman would be responsible for delivering the rye (presumably to the townspeople) and collect the money for it in return for 1d per barrel and 6d per hundred boards, so the alderman was, on this occasion, responsible for collecting payment for these imported goods.[52]

The imported grain perhaps added to the range of cereals available in the market, as well as to its quantity. Rye and maslin (a mixture of wheat and rye) seem new. The assize of bread seemed to recognise the new grain which was arriving; for example, an assize of rye bread as well as of wheat bread was given for the first time in June 1455, while the assize of July 1461 distinguished white bread, bread of Scottish wheat, and rye bread.[53]

---

49 ACC CR, IV, pp. 461 and 490.

50 ACC CR, V.i, pp. 642–4. Ships' cargoes are itemised in the early part of Council Register, VI, esp. pp. 10, 16, 18, 30, 59, 60, 120. Cereals continue to feature prominently.

51 ACC CR, IV, p. 132.

52 ACC CR, V.ii, p. 687.

53 ACC CR, V.i, pp. 237 and 428.

It is difficult to say whether the import of grain from abroad was made possible by a larger volume of exports from Aberdeen, perhaps especially salmon, which was its speciality, or was driven by insufficient local supply. Transport by sea certainly involved risks; as noted above, it was not always possible to predict exactly where ships would come in to port. The Council Registers provide plenty of evidence that shipwreck was a common hazard and, especially when goods travelled over long distances, it was difficult for owners to trace what had happened. The stability of trade overseas was also subject to the state of international politics.[54] But it is clear that Aberdeen's coastal location opened up alternative sources of supply so that the burgh was not prey to every local difficulty. This must have been an advantage. Yet, the character of Aberdeen's overseas trade in grain, which was handled in the first place by merchants, was quite different from transactions with the hinterland, where we have the impression of direct contact between ordinary townspeople and ordinary countrymen. In this way, by the later fifteenth century Aberdeen was already embarked on a course of international interdependence that has become such an essential feature of later forms of urbanisation.[55]

Nevertheless, this chapter has sought to show above all that the supply of corn was always a matter of concern for the town authorities. The manifold regulations governing the corn market – those for controlling the prices of bread and ale in relation to the prices of wheat and malt, those concerned with the process of negotiation in the market place, those seeking to avoid private transactions in grain, those concerned with the duties of the clerks of the market and even the arrangements for leasing of the mills – were always about ensuring fair and even supply and avoiding individual profiteering out of a commodity essential for all. This principle seems to apply to imports of corn from abroad as well as to that brought in from the countryside. In this way, a study of the corn market shows that the burgh operated with a sense of the needs of the community as a whole.

---

54 Dickinson (ed.), *Early records*, p. 212. A study of Scotland's trade with England, France, and the Low Countries is A. Stevenson, 'Trade with the South, 1070–1513', in Dennison, Ditchburn and Lynch (eds).

55 Chapter 1, pp. 8–10, 19.

Part 2

Output, Productivity and the Evidence of Tithes

Chapter 5

Output and productivity: common themes and regional variations

Ben Dodds

The measurement of levels of agricultural output and productivity lies at the heart of the historiography of the economy of pre-industrial Europe, and of the late Middle Ages in particular. The pioneering work of Abel and Postan before and after the Second World War deployed the theories of classical economists Malthus and Ricardo to explain economic development.[1] They saw the relationship between population levels and available resources as the key to understanding long-term change. As population grew, the area of land under cultivation expanded and output rose. However, given that there was no revolution in agricultural technique to precipitate a rise in productivity, pressure on available resources grew. Poorer quality land was brought into cultivation, with the result that productivity per acre fell. The number of labourers working the land rose and the law of diminishing returns meant labour productivity also fell. Output continued to rise but not as quickly as population. Eventually, the pressure on resources reached crisis proportions. High famine- and disease-related mortality led to demographic collapse and the cycle started again. The model necessarily implies regional variation, since it assigns a determining importance to variations in the quality of agricultural land. Historians have sought to test these hypotheses by accumulating data on population and production levels and by examining variations in land and labour productivity.

Output: the varying impact of general crises

Some catastrophes were so widespread in Europe that they devastated the economies of all kinds of regions. A succession of harvest failures from 1315 to 1318 led to some of the highest grain prices on record and to high mortality. Many parts of Europe were affected and the chronicles are full of lurid descriptions of people's desperation to find food.[2] Just over thirty years later, the Black Death swept through Europe, leaving few areas untouched, and was accompanied by a collapse in output levels.[3] The heavy mortality led to an acute shortage of labour in the countryside.

---

1 M. M. Postan, 'Medieval agrarian society in its prime: England', in *idem* (ed.), *The Cambridge economic history of Europe, 1: the agrarian life of the middle ages*, 2nd edition (Cambridge, 1966), pp. 549–632; W. Abel, *Agricultural fluctuations in Europe from the thirteenth to the twentieth centuries*, trans. O. Ordish (London, 1980). For a recent discussion of this historiography see J. Hatcher and M. Bailey, *Modelling the middle ages: the history and theory of England's economic development* (Oxford, 2001), pp. 21–65.

2 W. C. Jordan, *The great famine: northern Europe in the early fourteenth century* (Princeton, N.J., 1996), pp. 24–5 and 51–2.

3 O. J. Benedictow, *The Black Death, 1346–1353: the complete history* (Woodbridge, 2004), pp. 381–4.

Henry Knighton in Leicester in England observed the 'great shortage of servants and labourers' and commented that 'many crops rotted unharvested in the fields'.[4] In the Tuscan countryside, Giovanni Boccaccio described animals 'driven away and allowed to roam freely through the fields, where the crops lay abandoned and had not even been reaped, let alone gathered in'.[5]

Despite the rarity of long and continuous series of indicators of output, historians in this tradition have interpreted the fourteenth-century crises as confirmation of their pessimistic conclusions concerning long-term development. If the crises did not affect all regions in exactly the same way, the same broad pattern is observable. Expressed in Malthusian terms, the famines of the 1310s and the pestilence of 1347–9 were the culmination of a long period of demographic growth, accompanied by rising output. Although caused by exogenous factors such as poor weather conditions and the mutation of the plague bacillus, the scarcity of food in an overpopulated countryside meant people were weakened and vulnerable and the impact of the crises was catastrophic.

Many historians still find the Malthusian model a useful tool for interpreting changing production and productivity in the late Middle Ages, but detailed documentary research has added much regional nuance to the picture. There are two main sources which provide direct information on medieval agricultural output: manorial accounts and tithe records. The former are documents presented to lords by agents responsible for the cultivation of demesne land under the lords' direct control.[6] Seigneurial agriculture was particularly well-developed in England during the thirteenth and fourteenth centuries and data from manorial accounts provide evidence from an important sector of the rural economy.[7] Manorial accounts are almost absent from continental European archives because fewer continental landlords cultivated demesne land directly, meaning historians of agricultural production outside England have had to rely on other sources.[8] Most abundant are records of receipts from tithe, an ecclesiastical tax levied on all types of production, usually at a rate of 10 per cent. Tithe data do not provide the detailed information on the day-to-day running of agricultural enterprises found in manorial accounts, but they do give an indication of production levels and fluctuations in output.[9] Unlike manorial accounts, tithe data

---

4 G. H. Martin (ed.), *Knighton's Chronicle, 1337–1396* (Oxford, 1995), pp. 100–1, extracted in R. Horrox (ed.), *The Black Death* (Manchester, 1994), p. 78.

5 Giovanni Boccaccio, extracted in Horrox (ed.), *Black Death*, p. 33.

6 For discussion of this source see P. D. A. Harvey, *Manorial records* (London, 1984) and M. Bailey (ed.), *The English manor, c. 1200–c. 1500* (Manchester, 2002), pp. 97–166.

7 B. M. S. Campbell, *English seigniorial agriculture, 1250–1450* (Cambridge, 2000), pp. 26–37.

8 For a study of continental documents comparable with English manorial accounts, see A. Derville, *L'Agriculture du Nord au moyen âge (Artois, Cambrésis, Flandre wallonne)* (Villeneuve-d'Ascq, 1999).

9 Major continental studies of medieval tithe data include: M. A. Ladero Quesada and M. González Jiménez, *Diezmo eclesiástico y producción de cereales en el reino de Sevilla (1408–1503)* (Seville, 1979); H. Neveux, *Les Grains du Cambrésis (fin du XIVe–début du XVIIe siècles). Vie et déclin d'une structure économique* (Paris, 1980); G. Bois, *The Crisis of feudalism: economy and society in eastern Normandy c. 1300–1550* (Cambridge, 1984). For discussions of tithe historiography see:

reflect changes in both the seigneurial and tenant sectors. Long series of tithe accounts are rare for the Middle Ages, much scarcer than surviving series of manorial accounts in England. As a result, many historians have had to rely on less direct sources to comment on changing production levels, including rental income and references to newly ploughed land.[10]

Evidence from most regions suggests falling arable output for much of the fourteenth and fifteenth centuries. The direct exploitation of manorial demesnes in England peaked around the turn of the fourteenth century and by the mid fifteenth century most had been leased. Although this does not necessarily mean aggregate production fell, as demesne land often continued to be cultivated, it does give an indication of the difficulties faced by cultivators, particularly from the late fourteenth century when prices fell and wages rose.[11] So far, few data on aggregate output have been made available for England but evidence from rents and vacant holdings suggests contraction in the cultivated area was widespread. The village of Elkington in Northamptonshire, for example, contained thirty taxpayers in 1377 but by 1412 seems to have been almost depopulated. In the early sixteenth century all the village's arable was used for pasture.[12] In north-eastern England, a region from which tithe data have been collected, the collapse in arable production levels was very marked. By the first decade of the fifteenth century, grain production levels between the Tyne and Tees appear to have been less than one-third their level of a century earlier.[13]

Many other parts of Europe suffered falls in output over the same period. In the region around Cambrai in north-east France, grain production fell by up to 50 per cent between 1320 and 1370, and had dropped by a further 25 per cent by the mid fifteenth century.[14] In Spain, depopulated villages and rising wages suggest that the area cultivated with cereals and vines fell in the aftermath of the Black Death. Cabrillana found several examples from the 1330s and 1340s of disputes between neighbouring communities in Tierra de Campos, in the Castilian diocese of Palencia, concerning the ploughing of pasture land, but observed that such disputes did not arise after the Black Death. He used this as evidence of falling output and a release of pressure on arable resources.[15] Evidence from Italy is even scarcer but, in the late

---

9 cont.

E. Le Roy Ladurie and J. Goy, *Tithe and agrarian history from the fourteenth to the nineteenth centuries: an essay in comparative history*, trans. S. Burke (Cambridge and Paris, 1982); B. Dodds, *Peasants and production in the medieval North-East: the evidence from tithes, 1270–1536* (Woodbridge, 2007), chapter 1.

10 For Spanish and French examples see M. Lucas Álvarez and P. Lucas Domínguez, *El monasterio de San Clodio do Ribeiro en la Edad Media: estudio y documentos* (La Coruña, 1996), p. 63; G. Fourquin, *Les Campagnes de la région parisienne à la fin du moyen age du milieu du XIIIe siècle au début du XVIe siècle* (Paris, 1964), pp. 212–4.

11 A. R. Bridbury, 'The Black Death', *EcHR* 26 (1973), reprinted in *idem*, *The English economy from Bede to the Reformation* (Woodbridge, 1992), pp. 200–17.

12 E. King, 'The occupation of the land: the east midlands', in *AHEW*, III, pp. 73–4.

13 Dodds, *Peasants and production*, figure 2.

14 Neveux, *Grains du Cambrésis*, pp. v, 66 and 75.

15 N. Cabrillana, 'La crisis del siglo XIV en Castilla: la Peste Negra en el obispado de Palencia', *Hispania* 109 (1968), pp. 249–50 and 257.

fourteenth century at least, it appears that there was some curtailment of cereal production.[16] Laws promulgated by Italian city communes imply that cultivators were curtailing the area sown following the Black Death, although, in northern Italy at least, this may have been restricted to marginal areas.[17] The evidence of some Piedmontese chatelains' accounts, relating chiefly to tithe and mill receipts, implies widespread and severe contraction of agricultural output during the thirty years after the Black Death; in the years 1363–80, the chatelain of Vigone, one of the most severely affected, accounted for only half the produce he had received in the 1340s. In this region, however, recovery was already in evidence from the 1380s.[18] In addition to the western European examples cited here, attempts have been made to comment on changing levels of output in other countries. One recent and unusual example is the study made by Borsch on Egyptian cadastral surveys which suggests a fall in agrarian output for the country as a whole of approximately 60 per cent between 1315 and 1517.[19]

Within this broad pattern of falling output, there were many exceptions and differences. Output of agricultural products other than cereals may have fallen less sharply, although it is difficult to measure with any consistency. For example, a series of agreements concerning saffron tithes in a number of parishes in Cambridgeshire in England indicates that cultivators began the commercial production of this high-value, labour-intensive crop in the mid fifteenth century.[20] In parts of the Italian countryside, land which had been used for cereal cultivation was given over to the production of fruit and wine.[21] Likewise, in La Rioja in northern Spain, the crises of the fourteenth century broke the monopoly held by the king and monasteries on wine production, permitting smaller producers to practise viticulture.[22] Land which had once been ploughed reverted to pasture, releasing the pressure on grazing land experienced in some densely populated areas, and meaning that flocks and herds may not have shrunk as much as arable output. In the east Midlands in England, for example, the fifteenth century saw the deliberate depopulation of some villages and conversion of arable land into pasture.[23] A comparison of grain tithe receipts and the stocking of demesne livestock centres in north-east England suggests that sheep and cattle operations were less badly affected than grain production in the late fourteenth

16 C. M. de La Roncière, *Prix et salaires à Florence au XIVe siècle (1280–1380)* (Rome, 1982), p. 761.

17 P. Jones, 'Medieval agrarian society in its prime: Italy', in Postan (ed.), *Cambridge economic history of Europe*, 1, pp. 362–3.

18 C. Rotelli, *Una campagna medievale. Storia agraria del Piemonte fra il 1250 e il 1450* (Turin, 1973), pp. 97–100 and 117–19.

19 S. J. Borsch, *The Black Death in Egypt and England: a comparative study* (Austin, 2005), pp. 67–84.

20 J. S. Lee, *Cambridge and its economic region, 1450–1560* (Hatfield, 2005), p. 108.

21 La Roncière, *Prix et salaires*, p. 761; Jones, 'Medieval agrarian society', p. 361.

22 J. A. Tirado Marínez, 'Los medios de vida: agricultura, ganadería y artesanía', in M. T. Sánchez Trujillano *et al.* (eds), *A la sombra del Castillo: la edad media en el museo de la Rioja* (Logroño, 2002), p. 73.

23 King, 'The occupation of the land: the east midlands', p. 76.

century.[24] Pastoral farming also flourished in parts of Italy and Spain.[25] The growth of seigneurial livestock numbers was particularly pronounced in Andalusia where severe depopulation following thirteenth-century reconquest, aggravated by the crises of the fourteenth century, permitted nobles to build up very extensive estates.[26]

If the output of all sectors of the rural economy did not follow the same trajectory in the late Middle Ages, there were also marked differences between regions. Hatcher's study of properties belonging to the Duchy of Cornwall in south-western England found some manors where rent levels recovered quickly after the Black Death and, in some cases, remained buoyant throughout the fifteenth century. He attributed this to the growth in industry which benefited local agriculture.[27] Regional data from France are scarce and it is difficult to distinguish the effects of demographic decline and warfare on patterns of settlement and output. However, studies of the desertion of villages and the extent of land under cultivation in northern France show marked variations in the period after the Black Death.[28] Regional contrasts abound in the agrarian history of Italy, most notably those between the north and south of the country. Whereas in Lombardy it appears that the expansion of cultivation continued, little affected by the crises of the fourteenth century, in Sardinia half the settlements were deserted during the fourteenth and fifteenth centuries.[29]

It is also important to recognise that the chronology of changing output levels was not simple and continuous but marked by phases of recovery, stagnation and renewed decline. The most famous English example of a sub-period in the agrarian history of the late Middle Ages is the temporary revival of demesne farming between 1349 to about 1376. Although there was some movement towards the leasing of manorial demesnes from around 1300, the main phase during which landlords curtailed direct management began at the end of the fourteenth century, and the Black Death itself was not immediately decisive in bringing about this important administrative change in the countryside.[30] The history of the direct management of manorial demesnes should not, of course, be regarded as a proxy for output levels: land may have become

---

24 B. Dodds, 'Peasants, landlords and production between the Tyne and Tees, 1349–1450', in R. H. Britnell and C. D. Liddy (eds), *North-east England in the later middle ages* (Woodbridge, 2005), pp. 191–5.

25 G. Duby, 'Medieval agriculture, 900–1500', in C. M. Cipolla (ed.), *The Fontana economic history of Europe: the middle ages* (London, 1972), p. 194; T. F. Ruiz, *Crisis and continuity: land and town in late medieval Castile* (Philadelphia, 1994), p. 297; J. A. García de Cortázar, *La sociedad rural en la España medieval* (Madrid, 1988), p. 218; J. M. López García, *La transición del feudalismo al capitalismo en un señorío monástico castellano. 'El Abadengo de la Santa Espina' (1147–1835)* (Valladolid, 1990), p. 46.

26 E. Cabrera, 'The medieval origins of the great landed estates of the Guadalquivir valley', *EcHR* 42 (1989), pp. 477–9.

27 J. Hatcher, *Rural economy and society in the duchy of Cornwall, 1300–1500* (Cambridge, 1970), pp. 148–73.

28 H. Neveux, 'Déclin et reprise: la fluctuation biséculaire, 1340–1560', in G. Duby and A. Wallon (eds), *Historie de la France rurale, 2. De 1340 à 1789* (Paris, 1975), pp. 75–6; N. J. G. Pounds, *An economic history of medieval Europe* (London, 1974), pp. 185–6.

29 Jones, 'Medieval agrarian society', pp. 363–4.

30 Bridbury, 'Black Death'.

more, not less, productive following leasing.[31] However, all those producing grain for the market, whether on demesne or tenant land, benefited from the high price of grain in the 1350s and 1360s. The Black Death inevitably caused serious disruption to agricultural production but the market provided sharp incentives to producers to maximise output in the succeeding years. Not until the price wage scissor movement began in the mid 1370s, with falling prices and continued rises in wages, did arable cultivation become sufficiently unattractive for landlords generally to abandon their demesnes to lessees.[32]

The question whether other European countries experienced any recovery of arable output accompanied by high prices in the aftermath of the Black Death has not been given much attention. The rarity of directly managed manorial demesnes outside England means the effects of any such period are much less visible to historians. However, Genicot was able to bring together evidence from France and Italy to suggest high grain prices between the Black Death and the mid 1370s.[33] Likewise, Castilian wheat prices appear to have been high between around 1350 and the final decades of the fourteenth century.[34] Nor can there be any doubt that wages rose in the second half of the fourteenth century outside England. Like Edward III's legislative attempts to prevent spiralling wages, Peter I tried to fix maximum payments for labour in the Cortes of Valladolid in 1351. Indeed, such legislation was common throughout Europe.[35] Without more direct production indicators it is difficult to be certain, but a period of recovering output levels after the Black Death in other European countries is quite possible.

Agrarian productivity: lords and peasants

Establishing changing levels of output is fundamental to the economic history of any period. For pre-industrial economies, this enquiry must centre on fluctuations in agricultural production, by far the most significant economic activity in almost all areas. Both the method employed and the results generated by medieval economic historians have been debated and criticised.[36] However, debate has focused less on

---

31 See the discussion of the productivity of peasant farming below.

32 Chapter 2, pp. 26–30.

33 L. Genicot, 'Crisis: from the middle ages to modern times', in Postan (ed.), *Cambridge economic history of Europe*, 1, pp. 681–2.

34 J. Valdeón Baruque, 'La crisis del siglo XIV en Castilla: revisión del problema', *Estudios de Historia Económica II, Revista de la Universidad de Madrid* 20 (1971), p. 173.

35 *Ibid*. Genicot, 'Crisis', p. 706. For a discussion of some French evidence, including that for local labour legislation, see: E. Perroy, 'Revisions in economic history, XVI: wage labour in France in the later middle ages', *EcHR* 8 (1955), pp. 232–9.

36 For critical comments on the use of continental tithe data, for example, see: J. Ruwet, 'La Mesure de la production agricole sous l'ancien régime: le blé en pays mosan', *Annales ESC* 4 (1964), pp. 636–40; A. Derville, 'Dîmes, rendements du blé et "révolution agricole" dans le nord de la France au moyen age', *Annales ESC* 42 (1987), pp. 1411–32; Derville, *L'Agriculture du Nord*, p. 200. For a detailed consideration of the potential and pitfalls of English medieval tithe evidence see Swanson's chapter (Chapter 6).

levels of aggregate output than on productivity. Underpinning Malthusian interpretations of pre-industrial rural economies is the notion that the productivity of land and labour was low and inflexible. In his study of the Languedoc during the fifteenth to eighteenth centuries, for example, Le Roy Ladurie suggested that low yields meant food supply was strictly limited and population growth constrained.[37]

Work on seigneurial agriculture in the Middle Ages has, to some extent, confirmed this hypothesis. Medieval grain yields were miserably low by modern standards, averaging as little as three or four times the seed sown.[38] Soil exhaustion may have been one causal factor in constraining productivity, especially following the expansion of the cultivated area onto less fertile land. Resources were too limited to employ techniques aimed at returning nutrients to the soil.[39] Others have criticised the evidence for soil exhaustion but blame instead poor husbandry techniques and the 'chronically dirty' medieval arable.[40] However, the picture is not one of unremitting gloom. High yields were possible, although rare. Some estates in northern France, for example, enjoyed returns of up to 16:1 on the seed sown.[41] Even if yields per seed remained low, it was possible to raise output per acre through dense sowing. Given the right incentives, demesne managers were capable of raising yields. Campbell has argued that productivity remained low because of '[s]tructural, institutional, and economic disincentives to greater specialisation and the wider adoption of available technology'.[42]

The difficulty with this evidence is that, even in England, the greater share of agricultural output always came from non-seigneurial holdings.[43] Both the resources available to non-seigneurial cultivators and their economic priorities differed from those of their seigneurial counterparts: it cannot be assumed that levels of productivity were the same on demesne and peasant land. The debate over the productivity of land and labour in the Middle Ages therefore turns on the differences between the seigneurial and peasant and tenant sectors.

The historiography of peasant yields has followed a similar course to the interpretation of yields on manorial demesnes, although actual data are so rare that they form a precarious basis for any conclusions. A handful of non-seigneurial yield data have been assembled. In 1367 the auditors of Westminster Abbey in England enquired into yields on land set aside for the salaried demesne workers known as *famuli*. On their own plots, the *famuli* realised grain yields double those on the

---

37 E. Le Roy Ladurie, *The peasants of Languedoc*, trans. J. Day (Urbana, 1974), pp. 289–97.

38 Campbell, *Seigniorial agriculture*, pp. 321–6.

39 M. M. Postan, 'The economic foundations of medieval society', reprinted in *idem*, *Essays on medieval agriculture and general problems of the medieval economy* (Cambridge, 1973), p. 14; J. Z. Titow, *Winchester yields: a study in medieval agricultural productivity* (Cambridge, 1972), pp. 25–9 and 32; M. M. Postan, *The medieval economy and society: an economic history of Britain in the middle ages* (Harmondsworth, 1972), pp. 62–9.

40 W. Harwood Long, 'The low yields of corn in medieval England', *EcHR* 32 (1979), pp. 459–69.

41 B. M. S. Campbell, 'Agricultural progress in medieval England: some evidence from eastern Norfolk', *EcHR* 36 (1983); Campbell, *Seigniorial agriculture*, pp. 316–34.

42 Campbell, *Seigniorial agriculture*, pp. 428–30.

43 *Ibid.*, pp. 55–60.

adjacent manorial demesne. The representativeness of this example is questionable, however, given that the *famuli* may have enjoyed access to tools, manure, and so on, beyond the reach of the majority of peasant cultivators. Tithe returns from individual peasant holdings in the same area suggest yields were only half those on the manorial demesne.[44] Elsewhere, yields on holdings which were transferred to the lord on the death of the tenant were sometimes higher and sometimes lower than those on the adjacent manorial demesnes.[45]

Productivity: modelling the peasant economy

In the absence of more complete data, historians have resorted to modelling the peasant economy. Traditionally, the emphasis has been on the supply-side restraints operating on peasant farmers. Postan argued that a long period of population expansion and the ploughing of land formerly used for pasture created a shortage of manure. If this affected seigneurial demesnes, then its impact was worse on peasant land where access to pasture was even more limited. Yields on peasant land were therefore likely to have been even lower than those on manorial demesnes.[46] Titow, who conducted a pioneering study of yields on manorial demesnes, considered that the matter of peasant yields 'need not occupy us long'. For him, it went without saying that peasant yields were at best equal to those on manorial demesnes and probably rather lower. The reason for this was the 'manifestly superior ability of the great landlords to maintain the productivity of their land, as against the peasants' ability to do so'.[47] Nor was the capacity of peasant farmers to maximise output constrained only by the lack of manure. They may also have been affected by other factors, including inadequate calorific intake, which has been shown to reduce the amount of labour an individual is able to perform.[48]

Alongside the material constraints operating on peasant productivity, such as the lack of available pasture, were other less tangible impediments. Central to the Malthusian interpretation of the medieval economy is the lack of technological progress, the persistent 'backwardness' of agriculture. Work on seigneurial agriculture demonstrates that techniques were available to raise yields but they were not adopted universally. It has been argued that lack of interest, as much as limited know-how, prevented peasant farmers from raising the productivity of their land. In his study of a

44 D. V. Stern, *A Hertfordshire demesne of Westminster Abbey: profits, productivity and weather*, ed. C. Thornton (Hatfield, 2000), pp. xxxix, 83–4, 129.

45 D. Stone, *Decision-making in medieval agriculture* (Oxford, 2005), p. 269; C. Dyer, *Standards of living in the later middle ages: social change in England c. 1200–1520* (Cambridge, 1998), p. 129.

46 Postan, 'Medieval agrarian society', p. 602.

47 Titow, *Winchester yields*; J. Z. Titow, *English rural society, 1200–1350* (London, 1969), pp. 80–1 and 95. For a summary of the implications of the work of Postan and Titow for peasant productivity see: E. Miller and J. Hatcher, *Medieval England: rural society and economic change, 1086–1348* (London, 1978), pp. 57–8 and 149.

48 E. A. Wrigley, 'Energy availability and agricultural productivity', in B. M. S. Campbell and M. Overton (eds), *Land, labour and livestock: historical studies in European agricultural productivity* (Manchester, 1991), p. 325; M. Bailey, 'Peasant welfare in England, 1290–1348', *EcHR* 51 (1998), p. 231.

fourteenth-century village in the Pyrenees, for example, Le Roy Ladurie described the peasants' indifference to the accumulation of wealth:

> The people of Montaillou were fond of having a nap, of taking it easy, of delousing one another in the sun or by the fire. Whenever they could, they tended to shorten the working day into half a day.[49]

In his earlier study of population and production in the Languedoc, Le Roy Ladurie had developed this idea as an explanation for the failure to improve yields over the long term, despite the pressure of increasing numbers of mouths to feed. In sixteenth- and seventeenth-century Languedoc, the peasants spent their energy on religious matters, not on maximising the productivity of their land.[50] It has been calculated that the English medieval peasant may have lost as many as one hundred working days each year through holidays and religious festivals.[51]

Some Marxist historians have also emphasised the constraints operating on the productivity of peasant holdings. Brenner considered that the 'serf-based agrarian economy' prevented peasants from employing innovative yield-raising techniques 'even under extreme market incentives'. It was impossible for peasant cultivators to invest in their holdings because of the heavy surplus extraction imposed by the lords and restrictions on their freedom to respond to incentives through the land market and mobility of labour. To Brenner's mind, a 'crisis of productivity' was precipitated by class relations which prevented peasants operating in a 'free and rational manner'.[52] Whether considered from a Malthusian or a Marxist perspective, Miller and Hatcher summed up the supply-side restraint view of peasant productivity, commenting that the 'medieval countryside ... lacked some of the capacities for self-improvement'.[53]

In the light of revisionist work by Campbell and others on seigneurial agriculture, however, a different view of the productivity of peasant agriculture has emerged. Campbell has demonstrated that the population maxima proposed by some historians would be unfeasible if arable productivity in the non-seigneurial sector was not significantly higher than that on manorial demesnes.[54] Although Campbell himself proposed a much lower population estimate, Stone has recently plumped for a high population figure, explicable in terms of the greater productivity of peasant holdings.[55] In a recent attempt to estimate aggregate English grain output in 1300, Wrigley assumed that yields were 10 per cent higher on peasant land than on demesne land.[56]

---

49 E. Le Roy Ladurie, *Montaillou: cathars and catholics in a French village, 1294–1324*, trans. B. Bray (Harmondsworth, 1980), p. 339.

50 Le Roy Ladurie, *Peasants of Languedoc*, pp. 289–311.

51 H. S. A. Fox, 'Exploitation of the landless by lords and tenants in early medieval England', in Z. Razi and R. M. Smith (eds), *Medieval society and the manor court* (Oxford, 1996), pp. 546–7.

52 R. Brenner, 'Agrarian class stucture and economic development in preindustrial Europe', *PP* 70 (1976), pp. 48–50.

53 Miller and Hatcher, *Rural society*, p. 62.

54 Campbell, *Seigniorial agriculture*, pp. 402–5.

55 Stone, *Decision-making*, pp. 271–2.

56 E. A. Wrigley, 'The transition to an advanced organic economy: half a millennium of English agriculture', *EcHR* 59 (2006), pp. 443–4.

Britnell made a related point concerning the capacity of producers to raise output, arguing that the growth in population between the end of the twelfth and early fourteenth centuries cannot have been sustained only by an expansion of the cultivated area since there was not enough available land: there must have been a rise in the output per unit of area.[57]

There is no consensus concerning the operation of supply-side restraints on peasant agriculture but the soil exhaustion thesis has come under particularly heavy fire. As long ago as 1922, Lennard pointed out that when wheat was grown continuously for over a hundred years in the Rothamsted experiment, without any manuring, yields fell initially but then remained stable. Postan disputed the validity of this comparison, pointing out the superiority of technology in the nineteenth and twentieth centuries when the Rothamsted experiment was conducted, and the invalidity of any comparison with the Middle Ages. In reviewing the debate, however, Harwood Long supported Lennard's conclusions and did not consider soil exhaustion to have been the cause of low yields in the Middle Ages.[58] Campbell's work on manorial demesnes has also questioned the relationship between the availability of manure and the productivity of the land. In east Norfolk he found examples of high yields per acre even on manors with low ratios of livestock to arable land.[59] Stone has questioned the connection between the supply of manure and supposed low peasant yields. He suggested peasant stocking densities may not have been as low as some of the evidence suggests. More importantly, he has emphasised the difference between the availability of manure and the use of manure. Even peasant households with very few beasts may have been able to fertilise their land, helped by the careful use of other sources of dung, including that of family members and poultry.[60]

Assuming peasants did not have reliable access to well-paid employment, they had to rely on their holdings for their subsistence. Depending on the size of the holding, the maintenance of high yields may have been less a question of market responsiveness and more a matter of survival. Fox pointed out that living standards would have been very low for many peasant landholders at Ditcheat (Somerset) in England if they obtained the same yields as the managers of the Glastonbury Abbey manorial demesne in the same village. He therefore suggested that peasant yields were higher than those on the adjacent demesne.[61] Derville made a forceful case for high yields on the small peasant holdings of north-eastern France on the grounds of the exceptionally high yields on manorial demesnes in the area and the food needs of the local population.[62] At certain times in the Middle Ages, and notably during the late-thirteenth century, there were large numbers of very small holdings. In England, for example, there were many areas in which over one-fifth of tenants holding directly

---

57 R. H. Britnell, *The commercialisation of English society, 1000–1500*, 2nd edition (Manchester, 1996), pp. 103–4.

58 R. V. Lennard, 'The alleged exhaustion of the soil in medieval England', *Economic Journal* 32 (1922), pp. 12–27; Postan, *Economy and society*, pp. 77–9; Harwood Long, 'Low yields'.

59 Campbell, 'Agricultural progress', pp. 29–30.

60 Stone, *Decision-making*, pp. 263–5.

61 Fox, 'Exploitation of the landless', p. 544.

62 Derville, *L'Agriculture du Nord*, pp. 65–9.

from the lord had one acre of land or less. It is likely that as many as a quarter of all tenants in England, excluding subtenants, held less than three acres of land. Other parts of Europe saw a similar profusion of *minifundia*.[63] Work on late-twentieth-century farming in the developing world has found an inverse proportionality between the size of holding and output per acre in many areas prior to the introduction of new technologies. The empirical data used to reach this conclusion must be treated cautiously but one important factor seems to have been the intensive application of inputs, especially labour.[64]

Modern-day peasants are capable of producing high yields per acre. One particularly famous study was conducted in Indonesia by Geertz who found peasants were able to raise productivity consistently and over a long period of time on flooded rice paddy fields in response to the demands of increasing population. This they achieved through what Geertz termed 'involution', that is the intensification of cultivation with the refinement of complex techniques.[65] On small peasant holdings in medieval Europe, there may have been a similar process of 'involution'. Prior to the introduction of chemical fertilisers and mechanisation to agriculture, there were many ways of improving yields. The tilth could be better prepared through more careful and more frequent ploughing, perhaps involving the use of draught animals or improved equipment. Time and resources could be spent improving the drainage of the land. The fertility of the soil could be restored through the cropping of legumes, which fixed nitrogen from the air in the soil, or through the application of manure and marl. The crops' access to resources could be improved with the removal of weeds by ploughing or weeding.

Some yield-raising techniques available to medieval cultivators required the injection of capital, including the purchase of different and stronger draught animals. However productive his land, the peasant smallholder's capital resources were extremely limited. Moreover, Harwood Long used evidence from twentieth-century India and Pakistan to show that some of the difficulties presented by weeds, drainage and so on were impossible to remedy using traditional methods.[66] Nevertheless, there is evidence that peasants did adopt many yield-raising techniques. For example, there are records of tenants purchasing manure and court entries referring to the illegal digging of marl.[67] Many of the techniques could be applied through the intense application of labour.[68] Some peasant holdings were very well supplied with labour, especially if the opportunities for work elsewhere were limited. Campbell estimated

---

63 Miller and Hatcher, *Rural society*, p. 149; Neveux, 'Déclin et reprise', p. 29.

64 G. A. Cornia, 'Farm size, land yields and the agricultural production function: an analysis for fifteen developing countries', *World Development* 13 (1985), pp. 514–25; G. Dyer, 'Output per acre and size of holding: the logic of peasant agriculture under semi-feudalism', *Journal of Peasant Studies* 24 (1996), pp. 103–5, 111–13 and 125–8.

65 C. Geertz, *Agricultural involution: the process of ecological change in Indonesia* (Berkeley and Los Angeles, 1963), pp. 29–36 and 80–2.

66 Harwood Long, 'Low yields', pp. 467–9.

67 Campbell, 'Agricultural progress', p. 40.

68 Stone, *Decision-making*, pp. 262–72; E. Karakacili, 'English agrarian labour productivity rates before the Black Death: a case study', *JEH* 64 (2004), pp. 32–7.

that the ratio of labour to land at Martham (Norfolk) in England was 'at least six times greater' on peasant holdings than on the demesne in 1292.[69] There were pools of family labour to draw on, as when women and children helped at harvest time.[70] Not only was labour more abundant on some peasant holdings, it is also likely to have been more energetic and enthusiastic than the servile labour often used on manorial demesnes.[71]

The issue of the application of labour by peasant farmers has been central to the debate on productivity for over a century because of the contribution of the Russian agronomist Chayanov. He argued that peasant families would continue to apply labour inputs to their farms until subsistence needs were met, even if this meant a fall in the marginal product of labour. In other words, even though each extra hour worked has less and less effect on output from the holding, the absence of any alternative means of meeting subsistence requirements makes it worthwhile and, indeed, essential for the family's survival.[72] In a situation of high population and small holdings, such a regime would lead to high output per acre and low output per worker. Even when there was little commercial incentive for a demesne manager to increase productivity, peasant farmers operating in the same local economy aiming to feed their families may well have done so. The Chayanovian model cannot automatically be applied to medieval European peasant economies. A number of doubts have been raised, particularly concerning the supposedly abundant labour resources of the peasant family. The loss of working days through holidays and religious festivals, bad weather and the payment of labour services could be very considerable. Nor should it be assumed that all members of the family were available to work when required, especially during busy periods of the year when waged labour was available.[73] Nevertheless, the possibility of high peasant yields through the intensive application of labour inputs should not be ruled out.

Nor are issues of peasant productivity confined to the output of cereals and legumes. Some smallholders may have grown crops used for industrial purposes and then used the proceeds of sale to buy cheaper foodstuffs.[74] Crops such as flax, hemp and madder required high labour inputs but produced a high unit value per acre. Moreover, the peasant cultivators themselves may have been involved in subsidiary industrial activities, adding value to their own output.[75] In densely settled parts of the countryside, where labour was abundant and holdings small, specialisation of this kind

---

69 B. M. S. Campbell, 'Arable productivity in medieval England: some evidence from Norfolk', *JEH* 43 (1983), p. 39.

70 B. Hanawalt, *The ties that bound: peasant families in medieval England* (Oxford, 1986), p. 126.

71 Bailey, 'Peasant welfare', p. 228; D. Stone, 'The productivity of hired and customary labour: evidence from Wisbech Barton in the fourteenth century', *EcHR* 50 (1997), pp. 640–56.

72 A. V. Chayanov, *The theory of peasant economy* (eds) D. Thorner, B. Kerblay, and R. E. F. Smith (Manchester, 1986), pp. 81–4 and 113.

73 Bailey, 'Peasant welfare', p. 231; Fox, 'Exploitation', pp. 546–68; J. Langdon, *Horses, oxen and technological innovation: the use of draught animals in English farming from 1066 to 1500* (Cambridge, 1986), p. 174.

74 Bailey, 'Peasant welfare', p. 228; Chayanov, *Theory*, pp. 113–4.

75 Campbell, 'Agricultural progress', p. 41.

may have made sense. Non-seigneurial pastoral producers were important suppliers of wool to the market. Given the importance of supervision and the careful observation of sheep in securing high wool yields, it may be that peasants with smaller flocks were best placed to maximise output.[76]

In contrast to the Marxist view, which attribute the lack of investment, and consequent low productivity, in the Middle Ages to the exploitation of the peasant by the lord, it could equally be argued that heavy surplus extraction meant peasants had little option but to raise yields.[77] A recent revisionist view has questioned the relevance of exploitation of peasants by landlords. Using evidence from Ramsey Abbey in England, Raftis has argued that it was in the landlord's interest to maintain and foster the prosperity of peasants on his estate. Far from extracting ever higher proportions of the peasants' output, Raftis tried to demonstrate that lords' estate management policies show the careful protection of peasant farming. Unfortunately, Raftis seems to confuse the notions of 'efficiency' and 'productivity' and the implications of his argument for peasant yields are not clear. Equally, his conclusions are based on Ramsey Abbey's customary tenants and he does not consider peasants with much smaller holdings.[78] The view that tenant farming was seriously damaged by the exactions of landlords is nevertheless open to other objections. It exaggerates the importance of unfree tenants relative to free tenants who were not liable to exploitative landlord exactions, and whose obligations were often fixed, particularly in eastern England. It also overlooks the extent to which manorial custom protected tenants in villeinage against the higher rent levels that contractual tenures would have implied at the height of thirteenth-century land hunger.[79]

The evidence indicates that the medieval peasant economy may have been characterised by high levels of output per acre, perhaps considerably higher than on adjacent manorial demesnes, although this may have been achieved at the expense of labour productivity. However, numerous though the smallholders were at certain times and in certain places, there were also many much larger peasant holdings which, because of their size, must have taken up a significant proportion of available arable land.[80] Nor was intense pressure on resources universal during the Middle Ages. In Castile, for example, land remained abundant throughout the period. Although data on productivity are very scarce, Clemente Ramos found little evidence of changing agricultural techniques from the eleventh to thirteenth centuries: the ox was not replaced by the horse as a working animal and crop rotations were not intensified.[81] The case of Castile is exceptional because of the unusual history of conquest and reconquest but, even in more densely populated and less disrupted societies, there

---

76 D. Stone, 'The productivity and management of sheep in late medieval England', *AHR* 51 (2003), pp. 1–22.

77 Dyer, 'Output per acre', pp. 122–3.

78 J. A. Raftis, *Peasant economic development within the English manorial system* (Montreal and Kingston, 1996), pp. 5, 118–19 and 131.

79 J. Hatcher, 'English serfdom and villeinage: towards a reassessment', *PP* 90 (1981), pp. 6–26.

80 Fox, 'Exploitation', p. 565.

81 J. Clemente Ramos, *La economía campesina en la Corona de Castilla (1000–1300)* (Barcelona, 2003), pp. 116–19

were regions where landed resources were never scarce. In Durham, for example, the colonisation of wasteland continued until the early fourteenth century and there was never a time in the Middle Ages when all available arable land was cultivated.[82] These various arguments reduce the significance of 'natural fertility of the soil' as a determining constraint in economic change, although they do so only by emphasising the wide range of different local responses that might be relevant to sustaining employment and income from the land.

The studies in this volume concentrate on the period after the crises of the mid fourteenth century when demographic collapse had, in many areas, created a relative abundance of land. How high was productivity on larger peasant holdings, especially those emerging after the Black Death? It has been suggested that the release of pressure on land would have permitted the abandonment of less fertile soils, therefore increasing the average output per acre.[83] There is some evidence from north-eastern England suggesting just such a retreat took place, accompanied by rising output, during the 1350s and 1360s.[84] The question of the incentives operating on peasant farmers suggests an alternative hypothesis, however. As the size of holdings grew, and lords found they could no longer increase surplus extraction, the pressure on peasant farmers to produce high yields fell. Miller and Hatcher considered that many peasants 'became less, and not more, commercial farmers; they became more, and not less, subsistence farmers'.[85] Other historians have questioned the dynamism of 'peasant entrepreneurship' in the fifteenth century, pointing out that the profits from arable holdings were small in a period of low grain prices. Instead of trying to maximise output under these conditions, producers may have showed 'a preference for greater leisure'.[86] The question of the comparative productivity of demesne and peasant land becomes less relevant from the end of the fourteenth century when, even in England, most manorial demesnes were leased. While fifteenth century peasant farmers enjoyed the use of fertile land, and often had more freedom to decide on crop rotations and methods of cultivation, it should be recognised that many of the incentives that had encouraged the achievement of high yields by their thirteenth-century predecessors no longer applied.

Debates over peasant productivity nevertheless underpin the understanding of changing agricultural output in the late Middle Ages. The long-term rise and then fall in grain output levels reflect both the influence of profound external shocks and the innumerable decisions made by different types of cultivator, with varying priorities. They also conceal different trends in other sectors of the rural economy including pastoral output, viticulture and the production of non-food crops. Whilst it seems that peasants, like the managers of manorial demesnes, enjoyed a range of options in the

---

82 H. M. Dunsford and S. J. Harris, 'Colonization of the wasteland in County Durham, 1100–1400', *EcHR* 56 (2003), pp. 34–56.

83 Postan, 'Economic foundations', p. 14; Neveux, 'Déclin et reprise', p. 76.

84 Dodds, 'Peasants, landlords and production', pp. 175–84.

85 Miller and Hatcher, *Rural society*, p. 164.

86 M. Bailey, 'Rural society', in R. Horrox (ed.), *Fifteenth-century attitudes: perceptions of society in late medieval England* (Cambridge, 1994), pp. 161–6; R. H. Britnell, *Britain and Ireland 1050–1530: economy and society* (Oxford, 2004), p. 403.

way they cultivated their holdings and may have been capable of producing high yields, having the capacity to raise productivity is not the same as actually doing so. The issues of the incentives operating on peasant producers in the Middle Ages, and their response to these incentives, is complex but of critical importance for an understanding, not only of the way in which economies grew or shrank, but also in explaining the transition from the medieval to the modern economy.

Chapters 6–8

The three papers in this section reflect new strands of research on the issues of output and productivity. In particular, all three contributions deploy the evidence of tithes, a source hitherto underused by historians of England as explained above. Swanson's article is included as an authoritative evaluation of a type of data that is vital for establishing accurately intertemporal and interregional changes in output. It draws on a wide range of documentary sources to explain the institutional aspects of this levy, including the distinction between parishes which were appropriated to ecclesiastical corporations and those in the hands of individual rectors. Swanson is concerned to point out the importance of a consideration of tithe for economic historians, not only as an indicator of levels of output but also for its commercial significance. Tithe represented a significant proportion of total output and large quantities of tithe produce were sold. The operation of the grain market, and the possibility of disposing of grain at a good price, which were crucial for peasant and seigneurial producers alike, are important and neglected aspects of the economic history of the Middle Ages.[87] Tithe data are likely to prove of exceptional value for identifying different trends in agricultural output across Europe, as well as between more restricted regions with different soil qualities and market opportunities. However, Swanson warns of the difficulties inherent in using tithe records as a source, considering both the survival of material and the often hidden pitfalls of sources such as accounts. In the light of the above discussion of the importance of estimating output and productivity levels outside the seigneurial demesnes, the further exploitation of ecclesiastical source material related to tithe is necessary, and Swanson's contribution provides a framework within which such research can be undertaken.

Dodds' paper attempts to use tithe data for broad comparisons between European countries. Unlike the evidence from manorial accounts, which is almost exclusively confined to England, tithe data survive from England and continental European countries. A number of series of tithe data have been selected and differences in the long-term changes in arable output in England, France and Castile in the late fourteenth and fifteenth centuries observed. These seem to reflect the varied timing of demographic recovery, and highlight the lateness of the English upturn in population by comparison with elsewhere in western Europe. This contrast has been observed using other sources but has received little detailed consideration by historians. There were very important regional differences in the economies from which tithe series were used, including the impact of different patterns of trading, topographical and

87 Bailey, 'Peasant welfare', pp. 234–8.

climatic conditions, and the disruption caused by warfare. However, significant differences in long-term patterns remain and Dodds points out that these are difficult to explain using the broad Malthusian framework described in this introduction.

Hare's work on late medieval Wessex is concerned with a comparison of output on manorial demesnes and non-seigneurial land in a region of southern England. He has chosen a number of manors from which both demesne accounting material and information on tithe receipts survive, permitting him to demonstrate the aggregate significance of tenant output in relation to that from the demesne, showing the importance of production outside the demesnes belonging to great landlords. There were also differences in the types of crops produced on demesne and tenant land, with the former producing more oats and the latter more barley. This is evidence for the different priorities of cultivators in the two sectors, an important aspect of the debate on productivity described above, and Hare is able to speculate on the relative impact of environment and the market on decision-making. By selecting manors and rectories with particularly long series of surviving data, Hare has examined change over time, finding evidence for recovery in the decades following the Black Death but a sharp downturn in output during the 1420s. The collapse in barley production was particularly severe, both on demesne and tenant land, and Hare attributes this to harsh weather conditions, a reminder that some important determinants of output affected the seigneurial and non-seigneurial sectors alike.

The historian of the medieval rural economy, and of output and productivity in particular, is in a fortunate position. The subject has been the focus of historians' interest for several decades and a wide and sophisticated historiography has emerged, reflected in the bibliography provided with this volume. However, there are some important puzzles which remain to be solved and, as these three papers show, new research on unfamiliar source material is shedding light on the shadowy issues of long- and short-term trends, differences between the seigneurial and peasant sectors, and comparative histories of European regions.

Chapter 6

A universal levy: tithes and economic agency

Robert N. Swanson

Economic and social historians regularly exploit the archives of medieval ecclesiastical institutions as raw material for their researches.[1] However, their discussions pay little attention to the church's specifically ecclesiastical qualities, especially its structure as a network of parochial benefices, each a distinct component of England's variable local, regional, and national economies. The analytical focus is usually on the estates, the temporalities, rather than the spiritualities: it seems indicative that no entry for 'tithes' appears in the index to the late-medieval volume of the *Agrarian History of England and Wales*.[2] There are good reasons for the bias; but the parish's economic role is arguably too important to ignore, and should be more fully integrated into analyses. Particularly significant here are tithes and their economic impact and implications, discussion of which forms the core of this chapter. Their derivation, administration, and disposal were obviously an essential component of ecclesiastical incomes. Their significance is not, however, confined to the ecclesiastical economy. They merit consideration for their broader economic role, especially their contribution to commercialisation and the genesis of capitalism. Surprisingly, such matters have received little attention from economic historians. In an attempt to establish their broader economic role, this chapter therefore considers tithes as agricultural outputs both deriving from producers, and channelled into the wider economy. The discussion is often speculative, yet if it affects the future research agenda on England's medieval economy it will have achieved its purpose.

Tithes and the economy

To say that tithes were important in the medieval economy is to state the obvious. In the agricultural sector, an annual 10 per cent levy on all agrarian produce, whether crops or livestock, was a considerable expropriation (even if the real rate of extraction was lower). The levy extended to other natural products gained via labour (including turves and wood), to wages received by servants and labourers, and to the profits of rural merchants.[3] Unfortunately, as little work has been done on tithing, its full complexities remain obscure. One incumbent wondered in the early sixteenth century

---

1 E.g. B. Harvey, *Westminster Abbey and its estates in the middle ages* (Oxford, 1977); C. Dyer, *Lords and peasants in a changing society: the estates of the bishopric of Worcester, 680–1540* (Cambridge, 1980).

2 *AHEW*, III, p. 976. Tithes are mentioned at various places in the text, chiefly in the description of patterns of cropping.

3 R. N. Swanson, *Church and society in late medieval England*, revised edition (Oxford, 1993), pp. 210–15, and references there.

whether wool which had already been tithed incurred a further charge when made up into cloth.[4] If so, the burden may have been incremental – as it was anyway from tithes on mills, on wages, and on trading profits – and therefore even more significant overall.

A tenth of rural produce seems hard to ignore, yet it often has been. The attitude of some commentators seems to be almost that tithes do not matter, or (more charitably) that no way has yet been devised to fit them into the picture. Traditional emphases on seigneurialism and peasants allow tithes to be treated as outgoings, and then effectively ignored. Once top-sliced out of the calculations, they become somebody else's problem.[5] Equally, their input is rarely noted. They may be cited among the income of a bishopric or monastery, but are often treated not as a specific type of income, but as a type of estate-holding, linked to a rectory which can then be treated almost manorially.[6] Being thus subsumed in the total resources, with their ecclesiastical character and peculiar origins airbrushed out, any distinctive contribution to the marketing operations resulting from estate management disappears.

Fortunately, recent work is beginning to address this long neglect.[7] The link with commercialisation is crucial. Unless consumed by their recipients, tithes were essentially worthless if not sold. Here two issues operated. First, the blunt fact that most rural tithes were consumables, either foodstuffs (especially grain), or raw materials for further processing (like fleeces). Some produce could be stored, such as grain and wool, but much had to be consumed speedily. Eggs are the most obvious example, yet surprisingly large quantities were collected. Of a total approaching 2,800 received by the Selby Abbey kitchener in 1416–17 (almost 2,000 from tithes), four

---

4 CUL MS Ll.2.2, f. 258r.

5 See, e.g., C. Dyer, *Standards of living in the later middle ages: social change in England, c.1200–1520* (Cambridge, 1989), pp. 110–17 and 148–9; S. H. Rigby, *English society in the later middle ages: class, status and gender* (Basingstoke, 1995), pp. 31–3. Both acknowledge tithes, but almost in passing. Other ecclesiastical dues receive little attention. The church is also ignored in J. A. Raftis, *Peasant economic development within the manorial system* (Montreal, 1997), even though his material derives from Ramsey Abbey archives. Tithes were only part of the total ecclesiastical demands which affected standards of living, which really ought to be considered overall. The detailed modelling of peasant budgets in H. Kitsikopolous, 'Standards of living and capital formation in pre-plague England: a peasant budget model', *EcHR* 53 (2000), pp. 237–61, incorporates grain tithes and some others (pp. 239–40), but makes insufficient allowance for the full ecclesiastical demands on his model budget. Other small tithes paid in cash (including the payments noted below, n. 47), plus regular annual offerings, would deplete the cash available. In addition to the regular outgoings, there would also be the immediate and potentially serious impact of mortuary payments at death, especially in conjunction with manorial heriots.

6 It is sometimes unclear whether discussion relates to formally manorial demesne, or to land which was really glebe. See, e.g., R. H. Hilton, *The economic development of some Leicestershire estates in the 14th and 15th centuries* (London, 1947), pp. 36–8 and 40–1.

7 B. Dodds, 'Managing tithes in the late Middle Ages', *AHR* 53 (2005), pp. 125–40; *idem*, *Peasants and production in the medieval North-East: the evidence from tithes, 1270–1536* (Woodbridge, 2007), pp. 162–71. Among more general surveys, see R. H. Britnell, *The commercialisation of English society, 1000–1500*, 2nd edition (Manchester, 1996), pp. 122–3 and 156, and *idem*, *Britain and Ireland, 1050–1530: economy and society* (Oxford, 2004), pp. 197–8, which discuss the commercial importance of tithes principally in a thirteenth-century context. For tithes and commercialisation, see also comments of B. M. S. Campbell cited below at n.62.

hundred went bad.[8] Storage merely accumulated stocks, and would not avert long-term decay. In one long-running lawsuit about a benefice in Lincoln diocese, the sequestered tithes (which technically belonged to the ultimate victor) had to be sold before they rotted.[9]

Perishability only becomes significant if the amounts obtained exceed those capable of being consumed before they decay. In most English rural parishes that would apply, because the incumbent also received similar produce from other sources. All rural parishes had their own landed endowment, the glebe, which might be a significant land-holding in itself, even a full-scale manor. The rectory complex was a home farm, with the appropriate buildings and implements. For most rectors, the glebe (if it was actually farmed) probably provided at least minimal agricultural subsistence.[10] Tithes were surplus to glebe production, and to the needs it supplied: again, they only had value if sold.

The sources for tithe history

The issue, and problem, is to integrate tithes into the economic processes of late medieval England. If tithing was essentially a transfer mechanism, extracting from producers and supplying the market, it becomes doubly important for any consideration of agricultural output. First, because (in theory) the tithing process provides access to the scale of rural production of such products, and by covering fiscal units rather than individual estates gives (again, in theory) evidence of such production at all levels in the agricultural sector. Second, because the processes of disposal supplied the economy's non-agricultural sector with both food and raw materials. Quantifying and assessing such collection and disposal, and their overall economic significance, therefore becomes highly important. It is also an extremely complex task, made more so by the nature of the available sources. As Ben Dodds has argued, some quantification is possible, even if only approximate, if the right sources exist in sufficient quantity and detail, but such ideal tranches of material are scarce.[11]

The sources require both preliminary general comment, and more detailed consideration. A basic problem is their frequent incompleteness and ambiguity: here historians confront with a vengeance the fact that medieval recorders did not write for

---

8 J. H. Tillotson (ed.), *Monastery and society in the late middle ages: selected account rolls from Selby Abbey, Yorkshire, 1398–1537* (Woodbridge and Wolfeboro, 1988), pp. 187–8.

9 Lincs. AO FOR.3, ff. 72v–73v.

10 The glebe and its management is another aspect of the church's contribution to agricultural outputs which needs much more analysis. See R. A. Lomas, *North-east England in the middle ages* (Edinburgh, 1992), p. 110. B. M. S. Campbell, *English seigniorial agriculture, 1250–1450* (Cambridge, 2000), p. 42, classifies glebe as 'quasi-seigniorial' rather than properly manorial. As a class of producers, rectors have largely been overlooked ... Like other single-enterprise producers, their priorities of production must have differed in many significant ways from those of the great multi-manorial estate complexes which have attracted a disproportionate amount of attention. Redressing this historiographic imbalance is likely to revise or at least qualify the verdict returned upon lords as a class of producer', *ibid.*, p. 62.

11 B. Dodds, 'Estimating arable output using Durham Priory tithe receipts, 1341–1450', *EcHR* 57 (2004), pp. 245–85.

modern historians. The fundamental distinction should be between statements of receipt and of disposal, but it is not so simple. Usually the record of receipt exists only because that produce was being disposed of: the record essentially demonstrates conversion into cash. The accounting process did not require details of quantities or payers when recording the income, abstraction reaching its peak in notes of payments of farms. Equally, with sales, there was no need to identify buyers, or places of sale; all that mattered was the monetary proceeds. We can therefore know – or, at least, assume – that, with some exceptions, valuations on the income side reflect sales, but moving beyond that often approaches speculation. However, full comprehension of the economic role of tithes requires analysis based on both sides of the balance sheet: information about derivation and destination. The former is reasonably clear, at the level of the parish, if not of the individual payer.[12] Destinations are often much more obscure.

An obvious starting point for assessing tithe records as records of agricultural output is the national surveys of church wealth. At first sight, such material exists in the *Taxatio* of 1291 and the *Valor ecclesiasticus* of 1535.[13] The information for 1291 can be refined from other statements, at the regional level in revaluations of the benefices of the northern province in the fourteenth century, or in other tax statements, like the Chester clerical poll tax returns of 1379, or a collection in Lincoln diocese in 1526.[14] The main control, originally national but now only fragmentary, is the *Nonarum inquisitiones*, supposedly based on agricultural production in 1340.[15]

Unfortunately, the surveys of 1291 and 1535 offer imperfect evidence for tithe receipts. The *Taxatio* evaluates the church as a whole, including the glebe and other

12 However, it cannot be assumed that a 'parochial' record covers the full parish. The fragmented geography of the late medieval church, with split rights even within a single parish, meant that not all of the tithes would necessarily go to that parish's rector. The medieval accounts of Dewsbury (Yorkshire) show grain tithes received from territories in several adjacent parishes. See, e.g., S. J. Chadwick, 'The Dewsbury moot hall', *Yorkshire Archaeological Journal* 21 (1911), pp. 354–5 and 368–9; W. R. B. Robinson, 'The *Valor ecclesiasticus* of 1535 as evidence of agrarian output: tithe data for the deanery of Abergavenny', *Bulletin of the Institute of Historical Research* 56 (1983), pp. 22–3.

13 T. Astle, S. Ayscough and J. Caley (eds.), *Taxatio ecclesiastica Angliæ et Walliæ, auctoritate P. Nicholai IV, circa A.D. 1291*, RC (London, 1802); J. Caley and J. Hunter (eds), *Valor ecclesiasticus*, RC (6 vols, London, 1810–34).

14 W. E. Lunt, 'The collectors of clerical subsidies', in W. A. Morris and J. R. Strayer (eds), *The English government at work, 1327–1336, II: fiscal administration* (Cambridge, Mass., 1947), pp. 241–2; J. H. Denton, 'The valuation of the ecclesiastical benefices of England and Wales, 1291–2', *Historical Research* 66 (1993), pp. 249–50; M. J. Bennett, 'The Lancashire and Cheshire clergy, 1379', *Transactions of the Historic Society of Lancashire and Cheshire* 124 (1972), pp. 23–4; H. E. Salter (ed.), *A subsidy collected in the diocese of Lincoln in 1526*, Oxford Historical Society 63 (1909).

15 G. Vanderzee (ed.), *Nonarum inquisitiones in curia scaccarii temp. regis Edwardi III*, RC (London, 1807); C. R. Elrington, 'Assessments of Gloucestershire: fiscal records in local history', *Transactions of the Bristol and Gloucestershire Archaeological Society* 103 (1985), pp. 7–13; see also comment on the surviving original material in J. Masschaele, *Peasants, merchants, and markets: inland trade in medieval England, 1150–1350* (New York, 1997), pp. 85, 91 and 100.

spiritual revenues.[16] Its figures can be tested against the *Inquisitiones*, which often permits adjustments to deduct glebe and spiritualities, as well as indicating the changed economic circumstances since 1291.[17] The *Valor* returns give detailed breakdowns of income for some individual incumbents, but again patchily; the survey's different imperatives, and the separation of vicarages and rectories, make full assessment difficult.[18] In some cases post-Dissolution accounts for benefices formerly held by religious houses and accounting at the Court of Augmentations might permit refinement; but the practicality and reliability of such an exercise is untested.[19] These national records – particularly the *Nonarum inquisitiones* and *Valor* – show the importance of the non-tithe elements to parochial incomes. Especially significant here is the potential contribution of the glebe to agricultural output, although historians perhaps may already tacitly include it in assessments where an institution held both manor and rectory, and glebe is effectively treated as demesne.[20]

Local factors are clearly central to any attempt to assess agricultural output, affecting tithe recipients as much as the producers. In the *Nonarum inquisitiones* there are numerous local complaints – of declining sheep farming and lack of cultivation in Yorkshire, of uncultivated lands and the impact of cold winters on the flocks and of dry summers on certain crops in Bedfordshire. Factors were variable even over a small area. In Shropshire tithes were reduced by illness among the sheep, as at St Mary, Shrewsbury, or Harley; storms had damaged crops at Wenlock and Stoke St Milburgh. Elsewhere lands lay uncultivated, reducing tithe receipts. Reductions might be due to a combination of factors, as at Montford where '6 carucates of land ... lie uncultivated ... and ... the greater part of the grain had been destroyed by flooding of the Severn'.[21]

Outputs would thus vary annually, but long-term trends also need consideration. Comparison of the figures from 1291 and 1535 reveals change over the intervening years, but allows little nuancing.[22] Yet changes in population levels, and consequent changes in rents, and regimes, fundamentally altered parish finances. Less arable

---

16 For the valuations, W. E. Lunt, *Financial relations of the Papacy with England, 1327–1534* (Cambridge, Mass., 1939), pp. 346–54; R. Graham, *English ecclesiastical studies; being some essays in research in medieval history* (London, 1929), pp. 280–301; Denton, 'Valuation of ecclesiastical benefices', pp. 231–50.

17 A. R. H. Baker, 'Evidence in the "Nonarum inquisitiones" of contracting arable lands in England in the early fourteenth century', *EcHR*, 2nd series 19 (1966), pp. 518–32.

18 For some consideration of the *Valor*'s utility, stressing the problems, Robinson, 'The *Valor*', pp. 16–33.

19 Information is scattered among the accounts in W. B. Bickley and W. F. Carter (eds), *Abstract of the bailiffs' accounts of monastic and other estates in the county of Warwick under the supervision of the Court of Augmentations for the year ending at Michaelmas, 1547*, Dugdale Society Publications 2 (London, 1923), pp. 13–143. Although usually farms of complete rectories, there is occasionally some detail, e.g. pp. 85–6 (Mancetter). See also Robinson, 'The *Valor*', p. 18.

20 Above, n.6.

21 Vanderzee (ed.), *Nonarum inquisitiones*, pp. 11–21, 182–94 and 220–43. See also Baker, 'Evidence'.

22 For one comparison, L. J. Proudfoot, 'Parochial benefices in late medieval Warwickshire: patterns of stability and change, 1291 to 1535', in T. R. Slater and P. J. Jarvis (eds), *Field and forest: an historical geography of Warwickshire and Worcestershire* (Norwich, 1982), pp. 203–31.

cultivation and more pastoral farming shifted the balance of the various types of tithe, especially that between grain (on the arable side) and wool and lambs (on the pastoral). This was often important, especially in appropriated parishes where the tithes were divided between recipients.[23] As much of the available tithe evidence relates to appropriated parishes, such division is significant. It is far too easy to be seduced by the omissions into examining only the grain receipts, and ignoring the other agricultural outputs whose tithes are more rarely recorded.

The distinction between types of tithes and their recipients affects both the nature and content of the records. Discounting the loss of virtually all detail when complete rectories were farmed out, the chief distinction must be between the institutional evidence for appropriated parishes, and the more personal records of individual incumbents of rectories and vicarages.

By 1535, some 3,500 of England's 9,000 or so parishes had been appropriated by assorted institutions, which took the bulk of the revenues.[24] Such institutionalisation, with its resultant inertia, might suggest that material would survive in relative abundance; but sources giving detailed information about tithes are surprisingly elusive. Receipts from appropriated rectories appear among the revenues of the major monastic and cathedral estates, sometimes in significant amounts, but the survival of material, and the information it provides, is often annoyingly sparse. This is, in part, testimony to the sophistication of medieval accounting techniques, with the surviving statements often reflecting only the final stage of a complex process from which most of the detail had earlier been eliminated. Partly, also, the lack of detail reflects the distribution of appropriations across institutions: often tithes made only a minor contribution to total income, with institutions holding just one or two benefices amongst a much larger accumulation of manors. The usual vagaries of survival, compounded by the effects of the Dissolutions of 1536–9, have also taken their toll, especially on the records of smaller religious houses for which tithe revenues possibly provided a substantial part of their total income. In consequence, the available useful evidence generally derives from institutions which survived the Reformation relatively unscathed – chiefly the cathedrals and Oxford and Cambridge colleges.

Where records survive, they may reflect any stage of the total accounting process, from individual bailiff's accounts through to the final summary statement. The records of St George's chapel, Windsor, accordingly contain a few bailliffs' statements for their appropriated rectory of Deddington (Oxfordshire), which give a reasonable amount of detail.[25] The corresponding entries in the central accounts usually provide only a rental figure for the rectory.[26]

The chief limitation affecting the records of appropriated parishes is that they usually relate only to that part of the parish income received by the appropriating

---

23 Swanson, *Church and society*, pp. 214–15

24 Swanson, *Church and society*, p. 44.

25 SGCA XV.53.34–5.

26 E.g. SGCA XV.34.1–28 and 48.

27 Trinity College Archives (Cambridge) Chesterton, Box 22, 45 [Gressom book], fo. 129r-v, for evidence that the vicar of Chesterton withheld grain tithes. See also below, n.116.

28 M. Page (ed.), *The pipe roll of the bishopric of Winchester, 1409–10*, Hampshire Record Series 16 (Winchester, 1999), pp. 273–4 and 277–9.

institution. The rest, with the pastoral responsibility, generally went to a vicar. Details of vicarial portions, subject to their own accounting processes, are only infrequently available, although the vicar might himself be liable to pay tithes on his own produce, and thus contribute to the funds which passed to the appropriator.[27] The distinction is clear in the pipe rolls of the bishopric of Winchester, which give information about the rectory of East Meon (Hampshire). In 1409–10 the roll records tithes received from a range of sources, including grain, lambs, wool, and apples.[28] However, the tithes which had been allocated to the vicarial portion in 1318 were omitted. Among other income, that division of the parochial revenues gave the vicar parcels of both great and small tithes from named places within the parish, and the parochial tithes from milk, cheese, calves, foals, piglets, geese, eggs, mills, honey, hay, dovecotes, flax, hemp, and curtilages. Normally tithes of wool, lambs, and apples would also have been vicarial, but here they were specifically excluded, as were all tithes from the episcopal demesnes and animals.[29] The later pipe roll entries are therefore incomplete statements of the parochial income, with the added complication that, as the bishop held both the manor and the rectory, his manorial demesnes were effectively tithe-free and make no discernible contribution to the rectorial receipts.[30]

Detailed tithe accounts survive from appropriated rectories in relative abundance in comparison with those available for the approximately 6,000 unappropriated parishes held as freeholds by individual incumbents. With these, very different considerations affect the records. Rural rectors should often have been well off, receiving all of their church's income, from the great tithes of sheaves down to the mere pence received for purifications, and able to exploit the glebe for their personal benefit. While the management of these resources would reflect the financial acumen of the individual incumbent, the sources revealing such management, and with it evidence on tithing and its economic exploitation, are decidedly meagre. For such parishes, with no long-term interest in archiving the accounts (assuming that they were actually maintained), very few rectorial statements exist. Not being subject to institutional hoarding, or likely to slip into family archives as estate papers, and maybe of only short-term interest to their compilers (marking just one stage of a longer career), such records were effectively ephemera, and have suffered accordingly. The accounts which do survive

---

29. F. J. Baigent (ed.), *The registers of Johan de Sandale and Rigaud de Asserio, bishops of Winchester (A.D. 1316–1323)*, Hampshire Record Society (1897, for 1893), pp. 103–4. The small tithes make an appearance in the printed pipe roll for 1301–2: M. Page (ed.), *The pipe roll of the bishopric of Winchester, 1301–2*, Hampshire Record Series 14 (Winchester, 1996), p. 291. Although vicars were often allocated tithes of wool and lambs, their exclusion from the vicarial portion was not uncommon: it occurred in the Derbyshire Peak District, and at Great Wolford (Warwickshire), where the vicar, unusually, was also liable for chancel repairs: R. N. Swanson, 'Economic change and spiritual profits: receipts from the peculiar jurisdiction of the Peak District in the fourteenth century', in N. Rogers (ed.), *Harlaxton medieval studies, III: England in the fourteenth century, proceedings of the 1991 colloquium* (Stamford, 1993), pp. 189–91; R. N. Swanson, 'Standards of livings: parochial revenues in pre-reformation England', in C. Harper-Bill (ed.), *Religious belief and ecclesiastical careers in late medieval England* (Woodbridge, 1991), p. 173.
30. Page (ed.), *Pipe roll (1409–10)*, pp. 262–72. Elsewhere in the accounts, grain receipts are evidently calculated after deduction of tithe. However, tithe payments for livestock and fleeces appear regularly, e.g. pp. 190–1, 302–3 and 368–9.

for unappropriated rectories tend to be late in date, and of limited use.[31] Similar considerations affect the records left by vicars, which are additionally limited by their receiving only part of the total parish income.

This haphazard survival of tithe evidence creates problems for any broad assessment of agricultural output. However, the surviving accounts can be supplemented by other sources which offer further insights. Chief among these are probably the valuations of rectories complied during the process of their appropriation. Such statements, like those for Harlow (Essex) in 1399, or Holme-next-the-Sea (Norfolk) in 1401, often give extremely detailed lists of the revenues and their worth, but valued in cash rather than measured quantities. Thus, at Harlow, the grain tithes were worth £20, with the hay tithe being split between the manor (6s 8d) and the other parishioners (£1). Also on the list are tithes of wool and lambs (£1 13s 4d each), calves and piglets (13s 4d each), geese (10s), and other products down to honey at 1s. At Holme the grain tithe dominates at £20, but there were also wool (13s 4d) and lambs (10s), eggs (2s 4d), honey and wax (5s), apples (6d), geese (8d), and other produce.[32] Such valuations give the overall value of a benefice, and its range of produce, but in isolation are merely snapshots. Other church sources, like tithe cases in the spiritual courts, or parochial visitations, may add to the picture, but not necessarily much.[33]

The formal analysis of tithe material to obtain information on production and the first stages of agricultural output clearly depends on its content. Unfortunately, the sources can rarely be taken at face value: most are incomplete. While they may appear to record outputs, accounts seldom give a full statement. Most are monetary records, not inventories of receipts in kind; they reflect sales (sometimes fictitious), not collection. The accounts for Lytham priory (Lancashire) show this clearly, and suggest the difficulties of dealing with such sources. Tithes are frequently noted, but without stating quantities.[34] Hay is mentioned, but in 1415–16 with a note that it brought in only 5s 3d because the rest had been used for the priory's animals. The evidence for grain tithes is particularly troublesome, especially those of Lytham itself.

---

31 E.g. N. H. Bennett (ed.), 'Blunham rectory accounts, 1520–1539', in J. S. Thompson (ed.), *Hundreds, manors, parishes and churches: a selection of early documents for Bedfordshire*, Bedfordshire Historical Record Society 69 (1990), pp. 124–69. The present discussion deals only with the records left by the actual incumbents of such benefices, or their representatives. During vacancies, which might be lengthy, the tithes and other revenues would be administered by sequestrators (sometimes on behalf of the executors of a deceased rector), who would draw up accounts and dispose of the produce. References to, and information about, such activities, including associated accounts and indications of marketing, are scarce. See e.g. PRO C1/19/4; Lincs. AO Add. Reg. 7, ff. 128v, 131v–132v and 135v–136v, and Bishops Accounts 7, ff. 31r–35r, 39r-v, 59v and 63r.

32 CUL MS Add. 6847, ff. 78v–79r; Bodleian Shropshire Charter 27B.

33 P. Heath, *Medieval clerical accounts*, St Anthony's Hall Publications 26 (York, 1964), pp. 19–20.

34 DCM Lytham accounts. (These are listed by year, as are the Holy Island accounts: footnotes will not be supplied where specific years are cited in the main text.) The Holy Island accounts are similar, sometimes quantifying lambs and wool sold (e.g. lambs 1466–77, wool 1463–79), but generally only giving the total sum for such receipts. Lambs are sometimes omitted, perhaps by accident, or because none were sold (in 1443–4 the receipt is formally entered as 'nil'). Sales of wool occur even when no lamb receipts are entered.

These were often consumed within the priory, their 'sale' in the receipts being purely fictitious, and matched by an equivalent 'payment' among expenses.[35] For some years, however, the income section offers only a comment that the tithes had been consumed in-house.[36] Some fifteenth-century accounts record grain tithe receipts (apparently those of Lytham) at only £2; but this is probably an arbitrary figure for a fictitious sale.[37] It is decidedly worrying that, in 1421–2, and with no mention of significant cereal tithes or other grain receipts in the preceding years, the house recorded sales of grain at £19 2s 10d, and of malt at £6 15s 6d.

At Lytham, and elsewhere, it appears that tithe accounts only record produce that was converted into cash. Such conversion, and its incomplete recording, is particularly important when trying to assess production of many of the lesser tithes. While tithe liability depended on production, and was in theory discharged in kind, cash payments and commutations became increasingly common in the later Middle Ages, especially for petty tithes. Information about the production of hemp, flax, and garden produce – to take a random selection – is often obscured behind a customary small cash payment. The limited role of such produce in the national economy may make this a minor point; but this cannot apply to the frequent failure to record hay receipts.[38] Such cash commutations particularly impact on the value of tithe accounts as indicators of livestock production. Ideally, accounts should be used in conjunction with full stock accounts, which may record produce collected but not sold, but unfortunately, such conjunctions are rare.[39]

Arrangements for the tithing of wool and lambs (and other items, like calves and the lactage of cows) had invoked the cash economy from the early thirteenth century. For fleeces and lambs (and possibly other animals), where five or fewer units were to be tithed, payment was made in cash; where six to nine units were liable, a whole lamb (or fleece) was delivered, with a cash refund for the overpayment.[40] The cash equivalents remained as decreed in the thirteenth century, regardless of changing

35 E.g. 1394–1401, all with £6 13s 4d on both sides of the account, suggesting that the figure is merely an accountant's invention.

36 E.g. 1373–94 and 1412–16. Similarly fictitious sales appear in the Holy Island accounts. In 1443–4 the total received from tithe grain amounted to £34 1s 4d, but note £11 paid under expenses for wheat and malt from tithes.

37 E.g. 1416–22. 1416–17 is a changeover year: in one version of the account (A) the entry for the grain tithes is altered from 'nil' to note consumption within the house; in the other (B) the tithes are identified as being from Lytham.

38 For commutation of hay tithes see e.g. Lichfield RO D30/4/10/3 (*c*.1346).

39 For a grain stock account identifying tithes, Canterbury CA DCc.Westerham 6 (1372–3); see also lists in the Ely sacrists' accounts: CUL EDC 5/10/35–6 (both from the reign of Edward IV: earlier accounts may contain similar information but are presently unfit for consultation). Stock accounts may also clarify the status of produce recorded as sold in the normal accounts. In the Dewsbury accounts, for instance, that wool recorded as sold derived from tithes only appears in the stock reckoning: see e.g. Chadwick, 'Dewsbury moot hall', pp. 370–1 and 374–5.

40 The arrangement set out in a mid-thirteenth-century ordinance ascribed to Archbishop Boniface of Canterbury: F. M. Powicke and C. R. Cheney (eds), *Councils and synods, with other documents relating to the English Church, II: A.D. 1205–1313* (2 vols, Oxford, 1964), II, pp. 794–5. For its continued validity into the sixteenth century, see proposed regulations on tithes in the abortive canons of 1535: G. Bray, *Tudor Church reform: the Henrician canons of 1535 and the* Reformatio legum ecclesiasticarum, Church of England Record Society 8 (2000), pp. 108–9.

market prices; but the key point is that cash was used, and that introduced complexities. While the quantities of wool and lambs and other produce received in kind may appear in the records, the cash commutations are only occasionally noted. Detailed records which indicate the scale and complexity of the operation exist for the Peak District in the early fourteenth century;[41] and less fully in the vicarial accounts of Hornsea (Yorkshire) in the 1480s.[42] Scattered references elsewhere reveal the practice incompletely, usually only noting the balance from the cash transactions, which permits no formal assessment of the overall output. At Topcliffe (Yorkshire), a total for such *decime fracte* appears in only a few accounts.[43] Similarly, at East Meon, the 'small tithes' of lambs appear in the accounts as a total figure.[44] At Dewsbury (Yorkshire), the cash balance for fleeces – nothing is entered for lambs – was always negative in surviving accounts.[45] At Woodbury (Devon), the records give the numbers of tithe lambs sold (not necessarily the same as those received), with no hint of any monetary exchange. There may have been none, with sophisticated recording allowing the proctor to wait until individual tithe-payers had accumulated sufficient liability to pay in kind. That this in fact happened at Woodbury seems unlikely from the recording of tithes of calves in the same accounts: there money payments are recorded in lieu of fractions, at 2d–3d per calf.[46]

Such complex cross-payments affect assessments of agricultural output and they also influenced producers' incomes.[47] Tithing of wool and lambs was further affected by the movement of flocks, and the length of time they spent in each parish. For this reason one finds occasional notes of payments made to compensate a neighbouring rector for his share, like those made at Topcliffe to a Ripon prebendary for tithes on flocks pastured in his jurisdiction.[48] Sometimes a named individual's liability is noted, as in the entry in the Woodbury account for 1433–4 of 1s 4d paid by John German of Bedale parish for his flocks pastured within Woodbury.[49] Such liabilities were hard to

41 For the decree in action, see Swanson, 'Economic change', pp. 188–9. One of these lists, now Lichfield RO D30/4/5/52, is printed in G. T. Wright (ed.), *Longstone records, Derbyshire* (Bakewell, 1906), pp. 334–8. I suspect that the Lenten itinerary reproduced in A. Henry, 'Silver and salvation: a late fifteenth-century confessor's itinerary throughout the parish of Bere Ferrers, Devon', *Report and Transactions of the Devonshire Association for the Advancement of Science* 133 (2001), pp. 22–3, relates to such a collecting drive, despite the argument of the article.

42 Heath, *Medieval clerical accounts*, pp. 36–7, 43–4, 48 and 50–1.

43 R. N. Swanson, 'An appropriate anomaly: Topcliffe parish and the fabric fund of York Minster in the later middle ages', in D. Wood (ed.), *Life and thought in the northern Church, c.1100–c.1700: essays in honour of Claire Cross*, Studies in Church History: Subsidia 12 (Woodbridge, 1999), p. 114.

44 Page (ed.), *Pipe roll (1301–2)*, p. 291; Page (ed.), *Pipe roll (1409–10)*, p. 273. See also U. Rees (ed.), *The cartulary of Haughmond Abbey* (Cardiff, 1985), nos 696, 958 and 1134.

45 Chadwick, 'Dewsbury moot hall', pp. 370–1, 378, 382, 387, 390 and 392.

46 Exeter CA VC 3364, although the names of individuals disappear in VC 3368.

47 Application of this cash-commutation arrangement to tithes of fleeces affects the calculation of income from wool in a recent model peasant budget (Kitsikopolous, 'Standards of Living', p. 240). From the estimate of seven fleeces a whole fleece should have been paid in tithe, leaving 0.9 lbs of wool for sale, worth 4¼d The producer would also receive 1½d to balance the overpaid fraction of the fleece. A cash liability would have arisen from the tithable fractions of lambs and calves in the figures at p. 241.

48 Swanson, 'Appropriate anomaly', p. 116.

49 Exeter CA VC 3364.

keep track of, but the early-sixteenth-century jottings of Richard Gosmer at Basingstoke meticulously record flocks and their movements.[50] The division of tithe rights in animals led to some tricky calculations. In a Norwich consistory court case of 1510, a witness reported that the 1½d he paid for tithes on a single calf was split between three different rectors.[51] Similarly, the Lytham priory accounts include small sums received for rights to animals pastured or born on the parochial borderlands (while firmly asserting that the territory was part of Lytham parish) which were shared with neighbouring incumbents.[52]

Tithe receipts do reflect changes in agricultural output, but to reveal them in any useful detail the records need to survive in bulk over a lengthy period, and to be consistent and detailed in their recording. Predictably, runs meeting these criteria are rare. For example, the available information on receipts from Deddington rectory consists almost entirely of annual statements of the farm in the accounts of St George's chapel, Windsor. Two bailiffs' accounts survive from the rectory, for 1431–2 and 1432–3.[53] These are more informative, but exemplify the difficulties in breaking through the records to the reality of output. Tithe grain is not quantified or identified as such among the receipts; that any of the rectory's grain derived from tithes is indicated only by the collecting costs which appear among the expenses, and a passing mention in the stock account of 1432–3. More detail is given about livestock, but it is still incomplete. There is a striking contrast between the two accounts, with tithe lambs absent from the first, but the sale of 54 recorded in the second. Only one tithe calf was received in 1431–2, and none in the following year; but this is a poor guide to the number of cattle in the parish. A list of tithe debts transferred to the farmer in 1433–4 gives sums due for tithes of cows and calves. Most of the debtors answered for between one and five, but John Blount answered for twelve; the total liability was for 77 calves.[54] There is nothing in the two bailiffs' accounts to hint at such production, but it is inconceivable that cattle rearing started only in 1433–4, with no equivalent tithes paid in the previous two years. It is equally unlikely that this list reflects lengthy arrears, although it may not reflect the calving of a single year.

Besides the problems of poor and incomplete sources for actual receipts, there is the strong possibility (indeed, often likelihood) of incomplete recording due to incomplete collection. Ignoring the possibility that some incumbents charitably did not always take their full due, tithe collection was not a straightforward operation. It required constant vigilance, and constant oversight of the parish. Crop tithes could be assessed fairly easily; but mobile flocks made life more complicated. Liability might be denied, and payment withheld. Disputes were common. One rector complained that a nunnery had refused tithes on sheep pastured in his parish, although there had been 300 in 1408, and 400 in 1413.[55] The sums and amounts involved could be significant:

---

50 CUL MS Ll.2.2, ff. 2v–3r.

51 E. D. Stone and B. Cozens-Hardy (eds), *Norwich consistory court depositions, 1499–1512 and 1518–1530,* Norfolk Record Society 10 (1938), no. 115.

52 E.g. DCM Lytham accounts, 1412–13 and 1427–52. In 1424–7 the equivalent entry refers only to tithes from a shared fishery.

53 SGCA XV.53.34–5.

54 SGCA XV.53.35 (second part).

55 Lincs. AO FOR.23, ff. 144v–145r.

the wool tithe of 340 sheep might well be worth £1.[56] The scale of evasion is impossible to estimate; unpaid tithes presumably found their way into the accounts only in particular circumstances.

With all the provisos which have to surround them, tithe records might by now seem a highly questionable source for assessing agricultural output in late medieval England. It is, however, easy to be negative and to understate the positive. If the conditions are right (as for instance with portions of the Durham Priory archive and the records of Exeter Cathedral) it is possible to use this material to get at least an approximation of output, and a sense of relative trends.[57] This is always going to be easiest for the grain tithes, and for appropriated benefices. For the rest – other tithes, and other parishes – the information is generally much less, the variables greater, and the amounts of produce smaller so less visible. Yet even these scattered, disordered, and incomplete records can indicate local production for isolated years, and most important of all illuminate production outside the manorial demesnes. Despite their problems, the available information about tithe receipts has much to offer for future research.

The disposal of tithes

So much, then, for one version of 'output' in relation to tithes: derivation and collection. While there were large-scale tithe-payers, most produce was handed over in small quantities. These, however, soon added up to considerable amounts, and would produce substantial final totals. A mid-fifteenth-century list for Bakewell parish (Derbyshire) records the collection of 3,365 tithe fleeces. Most of the named payers handed over fewer than ten, several only one or two.[58] The number of lambs collected would have been lower, but was still sufficiently large for the lamb tithes to be farmed separately.[59] At East Meon in 1409–10 there were 896 tithe fleeces, but only 240 lambs. In the same year, the tithe grain receipts totalled over 82 quarters of wheat, almost as much oats, and just over 43 quarters of barley. This was in addition to the glebe grain production, of just over 21 quarters of wheat, 32? quarters of oats, and nearly 14 quarters of barley.[60] Extrapolating receipts on this scale of production across the country, there were massive quantities of grain, wool, and livestock to be disposed of. There were also substantial, but less abundant, amounts of other produce which is less visible in the records – the cheeses, piglets, geese, eggs, honey, apples, and so on, often overlooked simply because they were the 'small tithes'.[61]

---

56 Lincs. AO FOR.23, f. 198r.

57 For Durham, see Dodds, 'Estimating arable output'; *idem, Peasants and production,* especially pp. 25–30; Lomas, *North-east England,* pp. 111–13.

58 Lichfield Cathedral Library Chapter Act Book II, ff. 46r–51v and 54r–55v. The date is torn at f. 46r.

59 E.g. Lichfield Cathedral Library Chapter Act Book II, f. 15 (1481).

60 Page (ed.), *Pipe roll (140–10),* pp. 273 and 277–9.

61 The Hornsea accounts give a usefully detailed record of the collection of such tithes: Heath, *Medieval clerical accounts,* pp. 30–4, 37–8, 40, 42 and 45–8. Many were probably recorded on lists of payers like that for Blunham in 1520: Bennett (ed.), 'Blunham rectory accounts', pp. 128–44. See also discussion of the Woodbury tithes in H. Fox, 'The people of Woodbury in the fifteenth century', *The Devon Historian* 56 (1998), pp. 1–6.

As already suggested, such accumulations of foodstuffs and raw materials were effectively worthless unless disposed of. With their varied sources, in bulk tithe receipts would be of variable quality, certainly not of the best – the wool would be *collecta*, and a term of similar meaning, if it existed, could be applied to the grain and other produce. Yet the loss in quality might be made up in quantity: tithes were 'an important element of total production and a major potential source of saleable surpluses', their 'commercial potential was considerable'.[62]

Here the emphasis moves to a second aspect of agricultural output: disposal and destinations. The output into the wider economy, the marketing, now needs attention. Tithes entailed no production costs for their recipients, but they were not entirely cost-free. Their collection had to be overseen and paid for, transport arranged, threshers hired for the grain, and tithe barns maintained.[63] Tithe lambs had to be collected, pastured, and cared for, as reflected in the Dewsbury accounts.[64] At Topsham (Devon), the vicarial accounts also include a payment of 4d to a man to collect the eggs.[65]

Much of this produce had to be sold on. This makes the disposal of tithes an important factor in local markets, for its scale, and for the economic activity which it encouraged and permitted. Tithe accumulations, and therefore the amount which a rector could market (possibly enhanced by glebe production), might exceed production for sale from the local seignorial demesne. That could cause difficulties if rector and lord were competitors in the same market.[66] While tithes and demesne production can be considered very similar – both effectively expropriating labour and its product from others – tithe-sellers arguably had the commercial advantage. The limited costs allowed a lower overall break-even selling price, as demesne production was itself tithable. Tithe exemption equally privileged glebe production. Accordingly, even when tithe-sellers were not driven by primarily commercial considerations, they could still undercut market rivals while (in theory) securing a higher profit margin through cost differentials. Whether this actually happened cannot yet be demonstrated, but awareness of the competition, and of the market rivalry, sometimes appears in the sources.[67] Something of the sort may also be reflected in the benefice accounts of Kirby Malham (Yorkshire) for 1454–5. These indicate a major upset there, probably a dispute over tithes with Thomas Malgham. He seemingly targeted the tithe granges, causing extensive and costly damage, perhaps as a form of commercial warfare.[68]

---

62 B. M. S. Campbell, J. A. Galloway, D. Keene and M. Murphy, *A medieval capital and its grain supply: agrarian production and distribution in the London region c.1300* (London, 1993), p. 41; Campbell, *Seignorial agriculture,* p. 204; see also B. M. S. Campbell, 'Measuring the commercialisation of seigneurial agriculture c.1300', in R. H. Britnell and B. M. S. Campbell (eds), *A commercialising economy: England 1086 to c.1300* (Manchester, 1995), pp. 154–5 and 185–6.

63 Swanson,'Appropriate anomaly', pp. 117–18; Dodds,'Managing tithes', pp. 128–33; D. Postles, 'The acquisition and administration of spiritualities by Oseney Abbey', *Oxoniensia* 51 (1986), pp. 74–6; Chadwick,'Dewsbury moot hall', pp. 358–9, 362–3 and 372–3.

64 Chadwick,'Dewsbury moot hall', pp. 358–9 and 374–5.

65 Exeter CA 4647, f. 12v.

66 Campbell *et al., Medieval capital,* p. 74, n.114; M. Haren, *Sin and society in fourteenth-century England: a study of the* Memoriale presbiterorum (Oxford, 2000), pp. 139 and 146.

67 Haren, *Sin and society,* p. 146.

68 British Library (London) Add roll 32957.

Disposing of the accumulated tithe produce would be a major undertaking, if done on the open market; but actual tithe sales are singularly ill-documented. Accounts give some references, but too few to construct a consistent picture. Carriage and other costs might sometimes make sales unattractive, but most of the produce would be disposed of, one way or another. Some of the grain was converted into malt to supply local brewers. At Lytham priory in 1398–1401 precisely that happened with the tithes of certain townships.[69] Richard Gosmer's Basingstoke jottings show him selling fairly large amounts of malt to local women, presumably ale-wives;[70] and the Blunham accounts of the 1530s also record malt in some quantity.[71]

Generally, however, it is impossible to construct a coherent and comprehensive record of sales through markets. There are odd references, like that to wheat marketed from Mortehoe (Devon) in 1454;[72] but as odd references their value is limited, especially if (as in the Mortehoe case) the market is not named. The tithe wool from Topcliffe was shipped down to York for sale, but to whom it is not noted.[73] With the detailed reconstruction of the marketing of tithe produce by incumbents being impossible (but perhaps with the assumption that much of it was marketed), other more visible forms of disposal dominate the picture, revealing alternative mechanisms for agricultural 'output'.

Usually cash dominates, perhaps dictates, the evidence for tithe transactions in late-medieval England. Quantities cannot be accurately determined if only a sale value is noted. Even so, the records may indicate the relative scale of production. This, however, depends on the territorial block: a single valuation for a complete rectory is simply a global figure, and effectively useless (especially if it covers glebe production as well). Yet where tithes were sold to individuals, especially back to the producers, hints may appear. The Exeter Cathedral records include extensive information about sales of grain tithes.[74] The lists rarely give quantities, or types of grain, but do offer valuations, often for small parcels. Exactly how they were dealt with is not revealed, but in general the tithes were probably sold off before the harvest.[75] Such pre-harvest sales were not always tolerated: Bishop Philip Repingdon of Lincoln actively opposed them, punishing at least one cleric for the offence.[76] However, not all Exeter sales occurred at that point; one entry notes that the tithes of 'Nortwerlond',

69 DCM Lytham accounts, 1398–1401. Malt sales are also noted in the accounts for 1374–6.

70 CUL MS Ll.2.2., ff. 3r–4r.

71 Bennett (ed.), 'Blunham rectory accounts', pp. 148 and 156-7. See also C. Oestmann, *Lordship and community: the Lestrange family and the village of Hunstanton, Norfolk, in the first half of the sixteenth century* (Woodbridge, 1994), p. 137.

72 N. Orme, 'A country parish in the 1450s', *Friends of Exeter Cathedral: seventy-second annual report* (Exeter, 2002), p. 22.

73 Swanson, 'Appropriate anomaly', p. 117.

74 Exeter CA 5235–52.

75 The context of a sale affects the use of such figures to develop 'output figures'. If sold in the fields or before the harvest, the grain would be in unthreshed sheaves, not measured quantities. The price was presumably then less than the full market price, which would have to cover the additional processing and carriage costs. However, the purchasers did acquire the straw, which was a commodity in itself and not totally without value. See the discussion of these and other issues in Dodds, 'Estimating arable output', pp. 252–7.

76 CUL MS Add. 7802, f. 19r.

'Medilwerlond', and 'Soudwerlond' in Asperton parish were actually collected (*colliguntur*), with a subsequent comment that they were sold from the barn in bulk to a single purchaser.[77] Occasionally, the local tithe collector was among those granted tithe rights – perhaps equating with the manorial practice of exempting officials from rent during their terms of office.[78]

While the usual practice at Exeter was to sell in parcels, by territory, individuals sometimes bought back their own grain tithes, or purchased tithes due from others. Such selling of tithes back to the producers (equivalent to the commutation of labour services) was perhaps not uncommon across the country as a whole.[79] At Staverton in 1455, several buyers bought their own tithes (*decima sua propria*).[80] Most paid under 10s, with sums ranging from 3s to 18s; the smallest parcel was Henry Hoggeman's purchase of Elinor Blakealler's tithes for 2s 8d. Some Staverton tithes were sold by territory, the largest payment being £2 13s 4d for those of Staverton barton. The buying of other people's tithe liabilities was not confined to Staverton: at Branscombe, for instance, John Hooke bought the tithes of John Trouns for 2s 8d, and Margery Boleford paid 16s for those of William Acreman and Michael Elyott.[81]

More structured selling could be done through formal leases. When assessing agricultural output, however, such leasing leads to imprecision, as management practices changed. Rectories and their tithes were leased fairly extensively even before the Black Death; the practice expanded further in its wake, but with variations.[82] One significant fourteenth-century factor was the granting of English benefices to cardinals and others at the papal court. These were generally leased, and the revenues shipped overseas.[83] Leasing eliminates all the detail, leaving only a statement of the annual rent in the accounts: concerns about derivation and destination were transferred to a third party, and disappear from sight. That, however, does not mean that they can slip out of the analysis.

One factor affecting tithe farming is the varied structural contexts for the transactions. There were significant differences between the strategies and imperatives for owners of appropriated rectories, and those for incumbent rectors. The former, generally holding only the rectorial part of the income, but in perpetuity, perhaps had more freedom of action. They did not have to provide parochial spiritual

---

77 Exeter CA 5238. See also *ibid.*, 5252, which includes sales by measure from the barns, after threshing. The Dewsbury accounts sometimes distinguish between sales 'ante intracionem' and 'post intracionem' (before or after being taken to the barn): Chadwick, 'Dewsbury moot hall', pp. 358–9, 383 and 386. Sales in the field obviously eliminated collection costs: see the comment *ibid.*, p. 385.

78 Exeter CA 5238.

79 This is implicit in the complaints against bailiffs cited by Haren, *Sin and society*, pp. 139 and 146.

80 Exeter CA 5251.

81 *Ibid.* Some 'territorial' sales might also reflect the return of produce to the producers. Mortehoe sales in 1456 were mostly 'territorial' (with one to three named people of 11s 6d, possibly a combination of individual sales), but the small sums, only a few shillings, could also mean they were sales to individuals: Orme, 'Country parish', p. 23.

82 R. A. R. Hartridge, *A history of vicarages in the middle ages* (Cambridge, 1930), pp. 201–3. At Topcliffe the farming seems to have been intermittent: Swanson, 'Appropriate anomaly', pp. 111–12.

83 See the account book for such activity in PRO E101/511/32.

provision, so could legitimately lease solely to laypeople, for relatively lengthy terms (although the vicar was frequently the lessee, compounding the complexity). Leasing to an individual, or to a consortium, was only one option: the tithes were not always leased as a whole; they might go by township or smaller unit, and for short periods.[84] If no formal lease survives, however, it is often difficult to know whether a recorded payment reflects a lease, or an annual sale.[85]

Incumbent rectors often adopted other practices, especially if leasing the whole benefice. An incumbent officially needed episcopal permission to lease, and this would be granted only for a set period. With some exceptions, a rector was probably absent only for a few years, and his tenure was itself terminable by death or movement. But he was responsible for the spiritual provision, being canonically required to ensure continuity of pastoral care, necessarily by a cleric.[86] Such preconditions dictated leasing arrangements: this was short-term privatisation, perhaps more speculative (at least for lay lessees) than the greater security of the leases of appropriated rectories.

A third variant must also be noted: what might be called passive leasing. Here the incumbent remained in residence, but effectively transferred economic responsibility for the benefice to a lessee. Examples are not prolific, perhaps mainly because leases of non-appropriated benefices rarely survive; but such arrangements probably occurred chiefly when rectors were growing old, and could no longer deal personally and fully with their responsibilities. One example is a lease of Ribchester (Lancashire) in 1440, for one year to Thomas Sedyll, priest, and Richard of Balderston.[87] The incumbent reserved parcels of glebe and tithes (including grain), transferring the rest for a total rent of 34 marks (£22 13s 4d). Provisions about tithes and payments if the rector died suggest that he was elderly, but renewal was also envisaged.

Leases were usually for cash rents, but payments in grain were not uncommon. This suited religious houses, which might otherwise have to purchase the grain from their farmers at full market prices.[88] However, the practice was not adopted by all religious houses, nor was it limited to them. Through leases of tithes, Hereford's dean and chapter received large amounts of grain which were processed through the common bakery.[89] Valuations of tithe farms payable to the bishops of Carlisle go one

84 Dodds, *Peasants and production*, pp. 24–7 and 166. Where portions of demesne were leased, the lease might also include tithes. See e.g. a lease for lives of demesne and tithes at Cotheridge (Worcestershire), from Westwood Priory (1460): Worcestershire RO (Worcester) BA 2309/17 (not individually numbered).

85 The Lichfield statements sometimes give the year of the farm being answered for (e.g. Lichfield RO D30/4/5/46); elsewhere stability in amounts received in successive years may indicate a lease, but with no clear statement in the account.

86 Characteristic is the licence for one year's absence granted in 1367 to William Cook, rector of Wichling: A. C. Wood (ed.), *Registrum Simonis Langham, Cantuariensis archiepiscopi*, Canterbury and York Society 53 (1956), pp. 134–5. This specifies that the farm should be granted *alicui viro ecclesiastico*, although lay farmers are regularly encountered later on, and insists on provision for the pastoral care. Sometimes the farming cleric is named in the licence, e.g. *ibid.*, p. 135.

87 Lancashire RO (Preston) DDTo K/S/60.

88 Harvey, *Westminster Abbey*, pp. 156–7; R. A. L. Smith, *Canterbury Cathedral Priory: a study in manorial administration* (Cambridge, 1943), pp. 193 and 200–1. For Selby Abbey buying grain from some of its own tithe farmers, Tillotson, *Monastery and society*, pp. 50 and 71–2.

better: the holders' liabilities were expressed in measures of oatmeal, so burdening the farmers with all the processing and delivery costs.[90] These agreements suggest a different, less cash-oriented, set of imperatives and priorities. The Carlisle statements translate the oatmeal into cash equivalents, but seemingly only notional equivalents, varying with the price of oatmeal in Carlisle market.[91] The bishop still received payment in kind, and the farmer could presumably play the market with the rest, the real cost of the lease fluctuating with the market price of the meal.

Any such contract was a delicate balance, especially given the variable contexts. Farmers sought to limit their liabilities, being sometimes excused from chancel repairs, or the payment of extraordinary taxes.[92] Particular local situations might require special clauses, like provisions on the Scottish border to abate a farm in case of war. Farmers also sought continuity, seeking assurances of first refusal at renewal, perhaps conditional on rivals not offering a higher rent.[93] Special care might be needed with respect to short leases of unappropriated rectories, with their potential insecurities. Rectors sometimes had to give bonds not to resign or exchange the benefice during the term – thus mirroring the bonds required from farmers to guarantee the rents of appropriated parishes.[94] When the prior of St James, Tiverton (Devon), leased his portion within the church for three years in 1400, it was agreed that if any of the rent had been paid in advance, and the prior then died or left, the lessees would have first claim as debtors before administration of his goods.[95] Here the prior seems to have been considered as acting in a private capacity, effectively as an incumbent.

Potentially, tithe farming was a good bet; but not all farmers were winners. Some absconded with rents unpaid; arrears were common.[96] Tithes, for all their scale, were vulnerable: a fire in a fully stocked tithe barn was a major catastrophe. One female tithe farmer in Lincoln diocese alleged that her losses and liabilities from such a mishap exceeded two hundred marks (£133 6s 8d), including her responsibility for rebuilding two barns.[97]

---

89 Hereford CA 1882 (1538), 2512 (1409), cf. 1846 (1378). See also lists of grain from tithes received for the bakery in e.g. R630 (1394–5).

90 E.g. Cumbria RO (Carlisle) DRC 2/10 (1461–2).

91 In Cumbria RO DRC 2/10 the valuation is 8s per *eskipp* (1461–2); 5s in 1478–9 (DRC 2/12); 6s 8d.in 1480–1 (DRC 2/14 – but noted as not being the actual market price). However, arrears may have been cleared in cash: DRC 2/15.

92 Northumberland RO (Newcastle upon Tyne) ZSW 1/86, 1/90.

93 Northumberland RO ZSW 1/86, 1/90 (farms of Simonburn rectory, 1392 and 1393). For the impact of war on tithes in the region, Lomas, *North-east England*, pp. 59–63.

94 One Workington (Cumberland) lease was to be voided if the lessee resigned, exchanged, or otherwise left the church: CUL EDR F5/32, f. 94r (1477). Incumbents are recorded giving bonds not to vacate their benefices in PRO C1/19/437, C1/60/172. For bonds to secure farms, e.g. Hereford CA 2513, 3183–4.

95 KCA SJP/82.

96 E.g. PRO C1/24/263 (1453). Cf. arrangements for clearing a debt of over £22 at £1 p.a. in Exeter CA 3350, f. 93r (1395, involving a butcher of Exeter).

97 Lincs. AO FOR 3, f. 54-v (1493).

Tithe farmers

Most tithe farmers are little more than names, if they can even be identified: they attract less attention than the lessees of demesnes.[98] The precautions to ensure their terms, or to deal with special circumstances, suggest canniness, even hardness, in their approach to the business. Some certainly exploited their position to asset-strip rectorial complexes and resources; some also took advantage of the financial and legal naivety of the incumbents from whom they farmed.[99]

For farmers of unappropriated benefices, the obligation to provide pastoral care meant that clerics were often involved in the enterprise. Lay-clerical partnerships often took out a joint lease; possibly the cleric was to assume the pastoral care.[100] Some lessees were explicitly required to provide a priest.[101] Clerics who appear as sole tenants may actually have been front men for lay exploiters, but that is beyond proof. One manoeuvre to secure priestly provision appears in a Tiverton lease of 1409. None of the prospective consortium was then in holy orders, but one of them, William Legh, was apparently considering the prospect. The lease stipulated that if he was ordained within three years the lease would be automatically renewed for five years.[102]

Leasing puts the farmers at the centre of attention: they became the effective agents in tithe disposal. They were probably persons of essentially the same quality as most demesne lessees, if not actually the same people. They certainly derived from a wide socio-economic range, from small-scale involvement by individual parishioners to gentry taking on complete parishes and integrating tithe farming into a grander economic strategy.

Gentry involvement was considerable, but great families are not prominent. The regular appearance of names like Foljambe, Curson, and Vernon among the lessees of tithes in the Peak District shows the steady appeal of tithes to gentry families.[103] At the other extreme, parishioners may have felt some pre-emptive right to lease their own tithes, and some clerics perhaps concurred. The practice of leasing complete rectories with all their appurtenances goes against such expectations; on the other

---

98 For some comments and identifications, Hilton, *Economic development*, pp. 93–4; T. A. R. Evans and R. J. Faith,'College estates and university finances, 1350–1500', in J. I. Catto and R. Evans (eds), *The history of the university of Oxford, II: late medieval Oxford* (Oxford, 1992), pp. 683–4, 686–7; A. J. Pollard, *North-eastern England during the Wars of the Roses: lay society, war, and politics, 1450–1500* (Oxford, 1990), p. 65.

99 PRO E135/24/46, C1/19/437 and C1/60/172; Cambridgeshire County RO (Cambridge) P50/3/1. m.12r (1471).

100 E.g. KCA SJP/82; Exeter CA 6046; Salisbury CA Chapter Act Book Newton, p. 40. In a projected lease at Swanscombe (Kent) in 1448/9, it appears that the priest involved was very much the junior partner: PRO, C1/19/437.

101 Lancashire RO DDTo K/S/60. Some tithe farms were precisely to support chapels and chaplains: KCA GBR/462 (of 1516) leases all the tithes of Little Finborough (Suffolk) to John Bagard of Great Finborough, gentleman, and his wife for ten years to sustain the chaplain celebrating there, giving them authority to engage the priest from year to year.

102 KCA SJP/83.

103 See the records of the Peak Jurisdiction in Lichfield RO. This material was not used by S. M. Wright, *The Derbyshire gentry in the fifteenth century*, Derbyshire Record Society 8 (Chesterfield, 1983).

hand there is the extensive evidence of small-scale sales. Some lessees may have been little more than middlemen, co-ordinating sales to parishioners to avoid the complexities of tithing, and more immediately anxious to exploit the glebe and its resources.[104] Some leases sought to control, if not actually prevent, sub-letting,[105] which suggests that many tithe farmers did so, effectively commuting with the payers, or maybe farming townships to local worthies. In 1513 the tithe farmer for Lewes priory in Yorkshire leased the tithes of his lands back to John Sayvile at Eland, at 4s for the grain, and 1s for the lambs and wool.[106] Some lessees clearly wanted the tithe produce for other business ventures, like brewing or inn-keeping:[107] for them, tithe farming promised a reduction in marginal costs of their raw materials. Others had different motivations. It has been suggested that the rectory account of Blunham (Bedfordshire) for 1534–5 was actually drawn up for Sir Henry Grey of Wrest as lessee (he was also patron); substantial amounts of the produce were sent to his household at Wrest.[108] From the lessees' perspective, their activity was only part of a broader enterprise, not detectable simply from the leases.[109]

Two groups of tithe farmers require particular mention. Because of the canonical requirements, clergy often appear among their ranks. Both before and after the Black Death, cathedral canons regularly took the leases of churches of their common fund, as they did the manors. Such men reacted immediately to the crisis of the Black Death: the canons of Lincoln refused to continue paying the pre-plague rents, forcing a revaluation of the leases.[110] Later, it was relatively common for a vicar to lease his parish's appropriated rectory, effectively reuniting the parish as a single economic entity (including access to the full glebe).[111] Such leasing may explain how many

104 In a lease of Kniveton chapelry granted by the dean and chapter of Lichfield in 1537, the local inhabitants were to be preferred over outsiders when tithes were sold, if they matched the external price: Derbyshire RO (Matlock) D258/16/14/1.

105 Hereford CA 2512 (1409); Lincs. AO NEL.5/7/3 (1410); CUL MS Ee.4.20, ff. 65r–66r; Merton College Archives (Oxford) 751 (although possibly a special case, given contemporary litigation); Wiltshire and Swindon RO (Chippenham) CC/Chapter 154/1.

106 Borthwick Institute for Archives (York) CP. G.3378.

107 M. Kowaleski, 'The grain trade in fourteenth-century Exeter', in E. B. DeWindt (ed.), *The salt of common life: individuality and choice in the medieval town, countryside, and Church. Essays presented to J. Ambrose Raftis* (Kalamazoo, 1995), pp. 35–7 and 47–8.

108 Bennett (ed.), 'Blunham', pp. 124–5, 148–55 and 158–60. The desire to use the produce elsewhere may explain stipulations like that sometimes found requiring all the tithe grain and other produce to be kept within the rectory site: CUL MS Ee.4.20, ff. 65r–v; Wiltshire and Swindon RO CC/Chapter 88/3. This limitation was sometimes imposed in the licence to farm in the first place: SGCA XI.J.22(11): *dum tamen fructus autumpnales ... in solo ecclesiastico reponantur* (1359). See also XI.J.18 (1485) – with a further provision that the farmer reside in the rectory, or ensure that someone else does.

109 E.g the suggestive combination of tithe grain leases with the stewardship of Hexham Abbey estates in the hands of George Swynburne of Nafferton in the early sixteenth century: Northumberland RO ZSW 168/14–16.

110 Lincs. AO A/2/26 f. 4v, see also 7v. For other evidence of the immediate impact of the plague on tithe receipts, Salisbury CA, Communars' rolls/4. See also comment on the hay harvest at Dewsbury in 1350: Chadwick, 'Dewsbury moot hall', pp. 368–9.

111 Kowaleski, 'Grain trade', pp. 37–8; Evans and Faith, 'College estates', pp. 675–6. This might be a means to augment the vicarage while avoiding the formal processes: see Hereford CA 2288.

apparently impoverished vicarages still managed to provide a viable living for their holders, or other lesser clergy. Access to rectorial leases probably explains the surprising wealth occasionally found among these lesser clergy, but not all leases were on a large scale, or of complete rectories. At Sidbury, in 1479, the tithes (except those of grain and hay) were leased to Master Richard Bradeley, the vicar, during his tenure of the post, at £1 4s a year.[112] Similarly, in the Peak District, clerics appear leasing their chapels, as at Chapel-en-le-Frith.[113] Others leased or bought parcels of tithes.[114] They also paid tithes, for their own lambs and wool; the vicar of Bakewell clearly possessed substantial flocks, presumably as private property.[115]

Also noteworthy is the evidence for female participation in tithe farming. This might be only at a low level, as with Margery Boleford at Branscombe (Devon).[116] Others, however, appear more fully involved, to a degree perhaps unexpected. Sometimes their role may have been accidental, as when a widow inherited the lease of Combe (Dorset). She was not widowed for long, the lease passing to her new husband, perhaps thereby attesting the attraction of tithes as an investment.[117] Moreover, it was a female tithe farmer whose enterprise turned sour when the barn was destroyed by fire shortly after the harvest.[118]

Tithe farming and commercialisation

Tithes had always been sold, and had had to be sold. Such sales meant that rural incumbents were of necessity intimately involved in the commercialisation of English society, although how much would depend on the local market structure and demand. Where tithe selling has been examined, it has been primarily in the thirteenth century, with one estimate that tithes provided between 15 and 27 per cent by value of the grain marketed in (southern) England around 1300.[119] Then, and later, rectors close to London and other major towns were among the leading grain suppliers, doubtless via tithes, sold in substantial quantities.[120]

In the new economic order of the late Middle Ages, the market significance of

---

112 Exeter CA 6050/1.

113 Lichfield RO D30/4/3/148, D30/4/5/36–7 and 51.

114 Lichfield RO D30/4/5/21, 26, 36–8, 48 and 51.

115 Lichfield RO D30/4/5/30 and 33–4, present three consecutive years of such records, in which the vicar offered successively 11, 13, and 12 lambs, with 44, 48, and 32 fleeces. These are among the highest individual payments recorded in these statements. See also reference to the sheep-farming activities of Master Hugh Evers at Thixendale (Yorkshire) in the early sixteenth century, although he was not the incumbent of the parish: J. S. Purvis (ed.), *Select XVI century causes in tithe from the York diocesan registry*, Yorkshire Archaeological Society Record Series 114 (1949, for 1947), pp. 25, 28 and 30–1.

116 Above, n.81.

117 SGCA XV.49.3, m.4 (Combe church, 1503–4), see also mm. 1, 5. For a similar transfer, XV.56.35, m.14r (Langley Marrers).

118 Above, n.97.

119 R. H. Britnell, 'La commercializzazione dei cereali in Inghilterra (1250–1350)', *Quaderni Storici* 32 (1997), p. 639.

120 Campbell *et al.*, *Medieval capital*, pp. 74 n.114 99. For tithe owners and the grain market around fourteenth-century Exeter, see Kowaleski, 'Grain trade', pp. 30–1, 37–8 and 49.

tithes may have changed. The collapse of seigneurialism reduced the burdens of lordship on peasants, and their need to sell produce to meet such exactions. This new situation, making marketing a matter of desire rather than need, potentially threatened commercialisation, and radically changed the economic motors. Tithes, however, were less affected. The rate of extraction did not change (at least, nominally), although the balance among the types of produce altered with the decline of arable and the growth of pastoralism. Nevertheless, everyone still owed their 10 per cent to the rector or appropriator and vicar, of both grain and livestock. Possibly, in the new economic environment, tithes became more important to the market than before 1350, perhaps constituting a larger percentage of the total amount sold.

Some benefice accounts show incumbents selling substantial amounts of produce to individuals or groups, but whether this derived from tithes or glebe is often unclear. In 1454–5, the vicar of Kirby Malham (Yorkshire) sold off 147 lambs at 8d each to John Wynsour and his associates, and a wool crop amounting to 54 stone and three fleeces, to Henry Robynson.[121] Sales were not always in such quantities. In 1461–2 at Almondbury (Yorkshire), six stones of wool and four calves were sold to one purchaser, for a total of £1 6s 8d.[122] In another transaction (or consolidated group of smaller deals) in January 1463, the rector of Fillingham apparently sold five quarters of wheat and two quarters of oats, for 17s 8d.[123] Animals were also sold, such as the 23 tithe lambs sold to William Bromesdon of 'Berwyke' by the Treasurer of Salisbury Cathedral in 1510.[124]

Even before 1350, some of this produce went to town via middlemen, and the people involved are revealing. A York case of 1333 is suggestive: a joint venture by several craftsmen paying £80 for the tithes of Riccall prebend, presumably to be sold in the city. How such speculations contributed to artisanal livelihoods awaits evaluation, but such activity is certainly noteworthy. Another case reveals similar involvement by no less a person than Richard Tunnok, bell-founder, mayor of York, and member of Parliament, and in 1327 among the wealthiest of York's inhabitants.[125]

The identification of the beneficiaries of tithe sales affects appreciation of their role in the market. There was a great difference between the impact of sales to speculative consortia, like the York cases, and the commutations by which individuals merely regained possession of their own produce – which might not end up on the market. The grain and foodstuffs might not be sold, but the fleeces and surplus livestock almost certainly would be. For such individuals, location and proximity to a thriving and demanding market would have influenced their marketing decisions as much as those of the speculators.

Unfortunately, the move to leasing blacks out marketing practices, unless they can be discovered elsewhere. Changing levels of rent may reflect changing prices or

---

121 British Library Add. roll 32957. Here the ultimate beneficiary was a religious house; secular clerics would have profited in person.

122 Lincs. AO Bj/5/15/19, fol. 1v.

123 Lincs. AO Bj/5/15/19, fol. 10v. The record is crossed through, but it is not clear just what that signifies. For other small sales, see Kowaleski, 'Grain trade', p. 38.

124 Wiltshire and Swindon RO D26/6/3, fo. 8v; see also fol. 24v.

125 York Minster Library M2(1)a, fols 17v and 45v; H. Swanson, *Medieval artisans: an urban class in late medieval England* (Oxford, 1989), pp. 75 and 136.

production, but how closely they mirrored either is unclear.[126] Different types of tithe might be treated differently: at Topcliffe (Yorkshire), the grain tithes were leased out, but the sheep tithes were kept in hand, and were directly marketed. The quantities were not large, but their value reflected market changes.[127]

Here again, it might be necessary to differentiate between the marketing impact of tithes owned by institutions ossified by tradition and renewed leases, and that of tithes owned by individual rectors, whose activity leaves much less evidence. It seems a logical assumption that such individuals were more anxious for their own financial situation, and more eager to drive a good bargain, although this probably violates Richard Britnell's strictures against making 'assumptions concerning the economic motivation of medieval landlords which probably ought not to be made'.[128] Possibly, then, the farms of individual rectories would be higher than those of appropriated benefices. Against this must be set the circumstances of such leases, and the economic awareness of the lessors. Individual rectory farms were generally only for one to three years, and were contingent on the lessor's continued tenure of the benefice. If a lease was voided when an incumbent died, this would also affect the rental value and leasing conditions of benefices held by elderly rectors.

The main consideration when assessing the commercial role of tithes is the marketing advantages enjoyed by a tithe-seller. While the effective elimination of production costs would be offset by those for collection and storage, even these were worthwhile. Storage in the tithe barns allowed a seller to exploit the grain market at critical points in the year. Just as foreign grain shippers apparently concentrated their exports to England in the critical months immediately before the harvest, so a tithe owner might release his stocks at that point, to gain from seasonally raised prices.[129] Moreover, the market advantage for tithes extended to all glebe produce. Glebe production costs were real, but mitigated by the tithing of wages. The economies of scale achieved by combining glebe produce with tithes gave a further cost benefit.[130] Possession of the tithe barns meant that glebe produce could also be stored pending favourable prices. Glebe exploitation accordingly becomes an important, if nebulous, element in the equations. It might mean that incumbents or appropriators had a distinctive cropping regime, to complement the anticipated receipts from tithes and possibly more tuned to production precisely for a market.[131] Alternatively, access to

---

126 Declining receipts from small parcels, with notes of former payments, sometimes appear in account rolls: Tillotson, *Monastery and society*, p. 229. If farmers undertook capital improvements, as at Burmington (Warwicks) in 1491 (Evans and Faith, 'College estates', p. 677), their rents were presumably reduced to compensate. Some farms were perhaps set low to encourage the farmer to develop the resources and recover lost rights: Northumberland RO, ZSW 168/15. For rectory rents as a crude indicator of changes in local output and consumption, see R. H. Britnell, *Growth and decline in Colchester, 1300–1525* (Cambridge, 1986), p. 254.

127 Swanson, 'Appropriate anomaly', pp. 112 and 114–16.

128 R. H. Britnell, 'Minor landlords in England and medieval agrarian capitalism', *PP* 89 (1980), p. 21.

129 For foreign grain shippers, see N. Hybel, 'The grain trade in northern Europe before 1350', *EcHR* 55 (2002), p. 235.

130 However, glebe and tithes might be separated: in 1388–9 the vicar of Melksham leased the tithes and other spiritual income from the dean and chapter of Salisbury for 21 marks, but the rectorial demesne went to Robert Reyner for 12. Salisbury CA, Chapter AB4/Dunham, p. 103/fol. 52r.

131 E.g. Hilton, *Economic development*, pp. 65–6.

the glebe released land for pasturage, and more effective management of the livestock obtained from tithes. All of this is, of course, speculation, but the possibilities cannot be entirely discounted.

Tithe-sellers were in a very different position in the market from every other supplier, including lords. Because the break-even point for selling tithes was (at least in theory) significantly lower than that of other producers, a tithe-seller could sell cheap in a glutted market with less risk of loss, or store pending higher prices. During dearth tithe-sellers could store to hold out for even higher prices, or could afford to sell at a lower price than others to secure sales. For some monastic appropriators, directly selling the tithes of their appropriated rectories, this market advantage might be disguised with a moral imperative. The Benedictine Rule warned its followers against being driven by a profit motive, and required them to accept less than market prices for their sales.[132] Given the different nature of the profit margins on tithes, the distinction between monks profiteering or undercutting to secure market share would be very fine indeed. With limited production costs, and cushioned by glebe production, receipts from tithe sales would be evened out over time, reflecting more simply the operation of laws of supply and demand, as cheapness in years of glut balanced high prices in those of dearth.[133]

Whether institutions adopted a commercially motivated policy of marketing is not clear. Individual tithe farmers, and perhaps individual incumbents who received tithes, may have had a clearer profit motive. This leads into a final aspect of the role of tithes and their disposal in the development of the late medieval English economy: their contribution to the early stages of capitalism.

Despite all the negative factors – rising labour costs, the burdens of maintenance, and the falling values of rectories – parishes in late medieval England still gave opportunities for profit, even profiteering and capital formation.[134] If the fifteenth century was an era of proto-capitalism, it seems a reasonable proposition that some tithe exploiters were among the proto-capitalists. Tithes supplied relatively large quantities of primary produce, mainly foodstuffs, with very little outlay.[135] Tithe farming was an effective way to increase market share significantly without major physical investment. Rectors and lessees could also sell the produce of glebe land, and any other lands they occupied, which would also be made effectively tithe free if within the parish whose tithes they owned or leased. Sellers of tithes were

132 J. McCann, trans., *The rule of St Benedict* (London, 1976), p. 62; Latin text in A. de Vogüé and J. Neufville (eds), *La règle de Saint Benoît, II (ch. VIII–LXXIII)*, Sources Chrétiennes 182 (Paris, 1972), p. 624.

133 See the discussion of tithes of Billingham (Durham) in the 1470s and 1480s in Pollard, *North-eastern England*, p. 54. Extraneous factors like war and epidemics obviously upset this balance: *ibid.*, p. 55.

134 For the falling value of rectories, see, for example, the record of changed values in Lincs. AO, D&C Bj/2/8, fol. 2r–v.

135 For proto-capitalists, see C. Dyer, 'Were there any capitalists in fifteenth-century England?', in J. Kermode (ed.), *Enterprise and individuals in fifteenth-century England* (Stroud, 1991), pp. 1–24, esp. 10–20; P. Glennie, 'In search of agrarian capitalism: manorial land markets and the acquisition of land in the Lea Valley, c.1450–c.1560', *Continuity and Change* 3 (1988), pp. 11–40. Rectors would certainly meet some of the requirements for agrarian capitalism listed in Glennie on p. 34.

accordingly in a position of market strength as bulk suppliers. A hint of the scale of clerical involvement in capitalistic enterprises may come from the Act of 1529 which restricted clerical involvement in benefice leasing, marketing, and enterprises like tanning and milling. Arguably, this shows the success of such activity, and the lay jealousy it provoked.[136] The one real obstacle to the rise of proto-capitalists among the secular rural clergy and tithe farmers was their short-term access to the resources: even incumbents had only temporary control. Continuity could not be guaranteed beyond a lifetime. Tithe farming was obviously limited by the terms of the lease, although continuity might be established through renewals. A recognition of the role of tithes in lay enterprise may again appear later, in the scramble for spoils of the Dissolution of the Monasteries, including appropriated rectories, and the economic advantages gained by tithe-owners as appropriation became impropriation.

Such enterprise need not be extensive to be rewarding. Economic strategies were matters of scale; for some families even limited ambitions could prove lucrative. A family which cornered the local economy by establishing one son as manorial bailiff or leading tenant and with another controlling the glebe and tithes (even if only to lease them to a relative) was in a very strong position.[137]

Concluding comment

Despite their complexity, and the difficulties in fully establishing their economic significance, tithes and tithe management had an impact on the English economy which merits more attention than it has yet received. Even if the real extraction rate was under 10 per cent, and not all of the produce was ultimately marketed, tithes clearly contribute to arguments about commercialisation in late medieval England.

The marketing of tithes is, however, only one element in their economic role. Alongside animals received as mortuaries, tithe livestock could have made a significant contribution to patterns of stock management, as an alternative to buying from specialist breeders, or importation over relatively long distances.[138] This is just one hint of how clerical fiscalism is a neglected feature of medieval peasant society, and of seigneurial economics. Even if less exploitative than secular lordship, tithes and other compulsory payments and offerings made the church a considerable, and constant, extractive force. Those demands ensured a constant transfer of agricultural produce from producers to consumers. The records of those transfers indicate the scale and nature of agricultural output in late medieval England, although an approximation rather than a full reconstruction. Equally important, tithe material offers evidence on the second aspect of output – marketing and destinations. Arguably, the collection and disposal of tithes were vital to England's commercial development after the Black Death; they merit closer attention to test the validity of that claim.

---

136 A. Luders *et al.* (eds), *Statutes of the realm* (11 vols, London, 1808–28), III, pp. 292–3 and 295–6.

137 R. N. Swanson, 'Clergy in manorial society in late medieval Staffordshire', *Staffordshire Studies* 5 (1993), p. 27.

138 This mechanism needs therefore to be added to the replacement methods discussed in Campbell, *Seignorial agriculture*, pp. 139–43. Calves received as tithes would fit perfectly into the pattern established at pp. 142–3, whether they were sold off to others or retained for fattening by the original clerical recipient.

Chapter 7

Patterns of decline: arable production in England, France and Castile, 1370–1450

Ben Dodds

Although there has long been argument about the causes and extent of arable contraction in the late Middle Ages, little has been done to establish interregional contrasts by means of comparative analysis. In some respects variation from place to place is all too obvious, but there is need of more investigation at levels intermediate between very local studies, whose representative status cannot be trusted, to excessively sweeping generalisations about Europe as a whole. The absence of such research is partly for want of appropriate statistical evidence. Tithe data, in this context, has the advantage that, in spite of vagaries of local custom, tithing was practised across Europe as a normal feature of parochial organisation, and there were some general principles regulating its assessment and collection. Historians of medieval England have hitherto largely ignored this source, but a recent study has been made of the abundant tithe data surviving in the Durham Priory accounting material.[1] The abundance of research undertaken elsewhere on tithe as an arable output indicator, especially in France, means it is a natural step to compare the Durham series with its continental counterparts.

Historians and tithes

Goy and Le Roy Ladurie long ago emphasised the potential of tithe records as indicators of agrarian production levels.[2] Attracted to the potential of tithe by early studies, Labrousse secured influential support in Paris for further work.[3] The result was an explosion of tithe studies, especially on French records but ranging as far as Hungary and Canada.[4] The large number of historians working on tithe material were

---

1 B. Dodds, *Peasants and production in the medieval North-East: the evidence from tithes, 1270–1536* (Woodbridge, 2007). For further discussions of the quantitative evidence see B. Dodds, 'Estimating arable output using Durham Priory tithe receipts, 1341–1450', *EcHR* 57 (2004), pp. 245–85 and B. Dodds, 'Peasants, landlords and production between the Tyne and Tees, 1349–1450', in C. D. Liddy and R. H. Britnell (eds), *North-east England in the later middle ages* (Woodbridge, 2005), pp. 173–96.

2 E. Le Roy Ladurie and J. Goy, *Tithe and agrarian history from the fourteenth to the nineteenth centuries: an essay in comparative history* (Cambridge, 1982), pp. 8–9.

3 E. Le Roy Ladurie and J. Goy, 'Présentation', in J. Goy and E. Le Roy Ladurie (eds), *Les Fluctuations du produit de la dîme. Conjoncture décimale et domaniale de la fin du Moyen Age au XVIIIe siècle* (Paris, 1972), p. 9. The first work to use series of tithe receipts as indicators of arable output was R. Baehrel, *Une Croissance: La Basse-Provence rurale (fin du XVIe siècle–1789): essai d'économie historique statistique* (Paris, 1961).

4 Goy and Ladurie (eds), *Fluctuations*; J. Goy and E. Le Roy Ladurie (eds), *Prestations paysannes dîmes, rente foncière et mouvement de la production agricole à l'époque préindustrielle* (Paris, 1982).

ambitious and hoped to use their new indicator 'so widespread in time and space ... to reconstitute trends in the gross and net product'.[5] After the presentation and publication of so much tithe data, especially at the Edinburgh conference of 1977, Goy described the enthusiasm of agrarian historians of all periods who regarded it as 'absolutely necessary' that the work continue.[6] It was envisaged that a central databank might be created in which tithe data could be stored and then manipulated to calculate national production averages.[7]

However, the French initiative began to founder following the publication of two major monographs which use tithe.[8] As Béaur comments, research on the rural economy is not in a healthy state across the Channel:

> Land productivity is no longer fashionable. The decay of economic history, the disarray of rural history, the mistrust of what we call quantitative history and more generally of numbers and statistics, could easily explain this neglect.[9]

Outside France, of course, agrarian history has flourished over the previous quarter century. Nevertheless, tithe has not attracted much interest or positive comment in circles of contemporary research activity. In a recent volume containing papers on land productivity in northern Europe from the Middle Ages to the twentieth century, a project which would have excited the French tithe historians of the 1970s, Dejongh and Thoen warned that 'tithe incomes are certainly not the ideal measure of the economic evolution of the rural world, as Le Roy Ladurie and Goy seemed to judge them'.[10] Although they did not completely dismiss tithe as a potential source of evidence, their own paper and the others in the volume use other indicators. There certainly are problems with using tithe as an indicator of production.[11] However, if treated with care, tithe can make a valuable contribution to our understanding of agrarian economic change, as is demonstrated by recent studies made by historians of

---

5 Ladurie and Goy, *Tithe and agrarian history*, p. 26.

6 *Ibid.*, p. 67.

7 E. Le Roy Ladurie, *The territory of the historian* (Hassocks, 1979), pp. 193–6.

8 G. Bois, *Crise du féodalisme. Economie rurale et démographie en Normandie orientale au début du XVIe siècle* (Paris, 1976), later published in English as G. Bois, *The crisis of feudalism: economy and society in eastern Normandy c. 1300–1550* (Cambridge, 1984); H. Neveux, *Les Grains du Cambrésis (fin du XIVe–début du XVIIe siècles). Vie et déclin d'une structure économique* (Paris, 1980).

9 G. Béaur, 'From the North Sea to Berry and Lorraine: land productivity in northern France, 13th–19th centuries', in B. J. P. van Bavel and E. Thoen (eds), *Land productivity and agro-systems in the North Sea area (middle ages–20th century). Elements for comparison,* Corn Publication Series 2 (Turnhout, 1999), p. 138. An example of a rare post-1980 French work on tithe is A. Derville, 'Dîmes, rendements du blé et "révolution agricole" dans le nord de la France au Moyen Age', *Annales ESC* 42 (1987), pp. 1411–32.

10 G. Dejongh and E. Thoen, 'Arable productivity in Flanders and the former territory of Belgium in a long-term perspective (from the middle ages to the end of the ancien régime)', in van Bavel and Thoen (eds), *Land productivity*, p. 33.

11 Dodds, 'Estimating arable output', pp. 254–7 and 276–8; Dodds, *Peasants and production*, pp. 6–8, 25, 27 and 29–30.

periods after the Middle Ages.[12] The most spectacular example of a post-Le Roy Ladurie and Goy tithe study is Leijonhufvud's work on Swedish tithes of the seventeenth and eighteenth centuries, in which tithe output data are compared with those from demesnes.[13]

This chapter does not aspire to resurrect 1970s dreams of the international quantification of agrarian production over several centuries. Instead, it aims to compare the first English aggregate production series with some of its continental counterparts. The Durham series is exceptional in its chronological continuity and detail; data survive for an almost complete run of tithe production indicators from around 1290 until the Dissolution. The first two decades after the Black Death have been excluded from this analysis because they are served by hardly any French tithe production estimates and no Castilian ones at all. Neveux and Bois produced reasonably continuous data from the beginning of the fifteenth century, although there are a few isolated figures from the 1370s, and Neveux has scattered data from before the Black Death. No study has yet been made of fourteenth-century Castilian tithe indicators but work by Ladero Quesada and González Jiménez, and a more recent article by Casado Alonso, present indicators comparable with the French and English material. Both these series begin in the first decade of the fifteenth century.[14] Even within the chronological limits imposed, evidence is often scant. For this reason, some data relating to the occupation of lands have also been considered.

The interpretation developed by French historians does not have the late-fourteenth-century detail bestowed on English historiography by the manorial accounts. In broad terms, however, the picture is a similar one: production levels were much lower in the mid-fifteenth century than prior to the Black Death.[15] Historians of Castile, enjoying neither the English abundance of manorial accounts nor the French proliferation of tithe studies, have painted a rather different picture. García de Cortázar presented a chronology of crisis and recovery, with hints of improvement between 1390–1410 which were followed by ever-increasing signs of growth during the fifteenth century.[16] It is the purpose of this paper to compare the scale and timing of production difficulties and recovery using statistical evidence from these three countries. The nature of the different trends in output will then be examined using population evidence, and that of other causal factors. It will then be possible to suggest reasons for similarities and differences, along with establishing useful directions for future research.

---

12 E.g. F. J. Cervantes Bello, 'Crisis agrícola y guerra de Independencia en el entorno de Puebla. El caso de San Martín y sus cercanías, 1800–1820', *Estudios de Historia Novohispana* 20 (1999), pp. 107–33, accessed at http://www.ejournal.unam.mx/historia_novo/ehn20/EHN02007.pdf (viewed July 2007).

13 L. Leijonhufvud, *Grain tithes and manorial yields in early modern Sweden: trends and patterns of production and productivity c. 1540–1680,* Acta Universitatis Agriculturae Sueciae Agraria 309 (Uppsala, 2001). For a fuller discussion of the historiography of tithe, see Dodds, *Peasants and production*, pp. 1–13.

14 M. A. Ladero Quesada and M. González Jiménez, *Diezmo eclesiástico y producción de cereales en el reino de Sevilla, (1408–1503)* (Seville, 1979); H. Casado Alonso, 'Producción agraria, precios y coyuntura económica en la diócesis de Burgos y Palencia a fines de la Edad Media', *Studia Historica Historia Medieval* 9 (1991), pp. 67–101.

15 Ladurie and Goy, *Tithe and agrarian history*, pp. 72–6 and 92.

16 J. A. García de Cortázar, *La sociedad rural en la España medieval* (Madrid, 1988), p. 194.

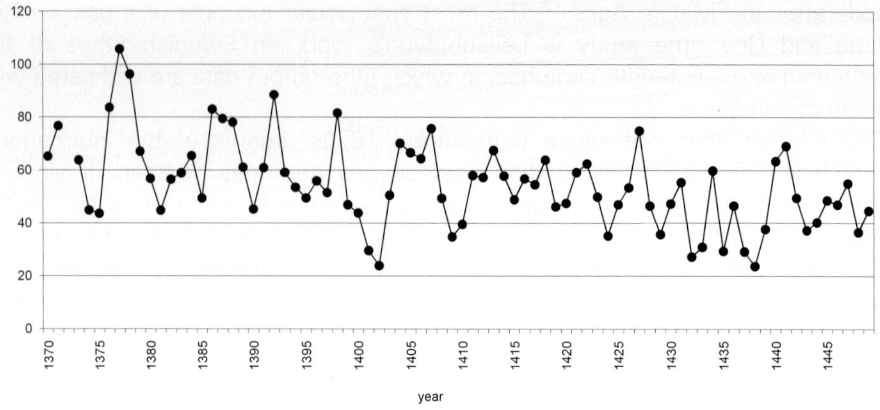

Figure 7.1 Tithe receipts from between Tyne and Tees deflated to indicate arable output
Source: For the data and method see B. Dodds, 'Estimating arable output using Durham Priory tithe receipts, 1341–1449', *EcHR* 57 (2004), 245-85.

England

'The Indian summer was struck by its first frost. And frost was followed by the swift onset of winter.'[17] With these words Bridbury described the new direction of the English seigneurial economy from the mid 1370s. Producers had been protected from rising wages after the Black Death by high prices but, following the bumper harvest of 1375, trends in prices and wages diverged. Prices slumped but wages continued to climb.[18] Some demesne managers, desperate to make good their losses, resorted to the draconian reinforcement of post-Black Death labour legislation, but to no avail.[19] The direct management of demesnes ceased to be a viable option. Although owners of large estates had nearly always leased some of their manors, and in increasing numbers from early in the fourteenth century, many seem to have finally renounced large-scale direct cultivation between 1370 and 1420.[20] The timing of the difficulties varied but the manorial evidence reflects a decline in demesne arable production levels from around 1370.[21]

17 A. R. Bridbury,'The Black Death', *EcHR* 26 (1973), p. 584.

18 D. L. Farmer,'Prices and wages, 1350–1500', in *AHEW*, III, p. 437.

19 E. B. Fryde, *Peasants and landlords in later medieval England* (Stroud, 1996), p. 118.

20 B. M. S. Campbell, *English seigniorial agriculture 1250–1450* (Cambridge, 2000), p. 59.

21 Chapter 2, pp. 26–30. Ramsey Abbey manors saw the beginnings of 'long-term agricultural depression during the 1390s': J. A. Raftis,'Peasants and the collapse of the manorial economy on some Ramsey Abbey estates', in R. H. Britnell and J. Hatcher (eds), *Progress and problems in medieval England: essays in honour of Edward Miller* (Cambridge, 1996), p. 196. Direct cultivation had been almost completely abandoned on the estates of the duchy of Lancaster by 1399: G. A. Holmes, *The estates of the higher nobility in fourteenth-century England* (Cambridge, 1957), p. 115. The number of demesnes directly cultivated by the bishop of Winchester only fell in the first decades of the fifteenth century: D. L. Farmer, 'Grain yields on the Winchester manors in the later middle ages', *EcHR* 30 (1977), p. 555.

At the end of the 1930s, Postan suggested that the fifteenth century was 'an age of recession, arrested economic development and declining national income'. One feature of the difficulties was 'a net contraction of the area under cultivation'.[22] Scholars have criticised Postan's overall interpretation, and quibbled with the scale of the decline in production, without being able to deny it. Peasant productivity may have increased, in part responding to vigorous urban life, but aggregate production levels still fell.[23] However, it is difficult to support these claims through manorial evidence alone. Demesnes only accounted for a fraction of overall production, especially from the late fourteenth century when landlords increasingly abandoned direct cultivation.[24] More importantly, the number of demesne accounts made, and therefore preserved, fell dramatically as landlords resorted to leases.

Tithe as a source for studying arable production levels suffers from neither deficiency: the tax was levied on all land, peasant and seigneurial alike, and many records continue throughout the fifteenth century. Figure 7.1 shows the results of a long series of calculations using tithe data, and presents estimates of average grain output in the dozens of townships which made up eleven of the parishes appropriated to Durham Priory between the Tyne and Tees.[25] The graph shows cash tithe receipts deflated by grain prices. This means of estimating arable output was devised by French historians during the 1960s and is based on recreating the calculations made by the tithe purchaser when he made his bid before the harvest. He would have based his bid on a multiplication of the volume of grain the tithe would produce and the price of the grain in the coming year. Deflation simply rearranges this equation to leave the predicted volume of tithe grain, roughly one-tenth of overall production.[26]

The most obvious fact about the production estimates in Figure 7.1 is that only once, in 1377, do they exceed the levels of the decade before the Black Death (that is, the index level of 100 on the *y*-axis).[27] The shape of the graph is one of overall decline. Grain output rarely exceeded 70 per cent of 1340s levels and fell below 40 per cent on 14 separate occasions. Within the context of overall decline – demonstrated by the

22 M. M. Postan, 'The fifteenth century', *EcHR* 9 (1938–9), p. 161.

23 E.g. A. R. Bridbury, *Economic growth: England in the later middle ages* (London, 1962), pp. 52–6 and 83–5.

24 Campbell estimates that, even when it was most common to cultivate demesnes directly around 1300, they produced between one-third and one-fifth of total output: Campbell, *Seigniorial agriculture*, pp. 55–60.

25 During the fourteenth and fifteenth centuries Durham Priory received tithe income from 35 parishes, although not all at the same time. This group of 11 was chosen because of the frequency of annual sale of tithes in parishes close to the mother house: annual sale receipts produce more accurate output indices. The method is described in Dodds, 'Estimating arable output'. The indices draw on around 500 individual accounts, inventories and sale of tithe lists contained in the D[urham] C[athedral] M[uniments]. Lists of these accounts are available on the Durham University Library Archives and Special Collections web pages at http://flambard.dur.ac.uk /dynaweb/handlist/ddc/dcdmaccs/ (viewed July 2007).

26 E. Le Roy Ladurie, *The peasants of Languedoc* (Urbana, 1974), pp. 77–8.

27 For a lengthier discussion of production around Durham between 1370 and 1450, see Dodds, *Peasants and production*, chapters 4 and 5.

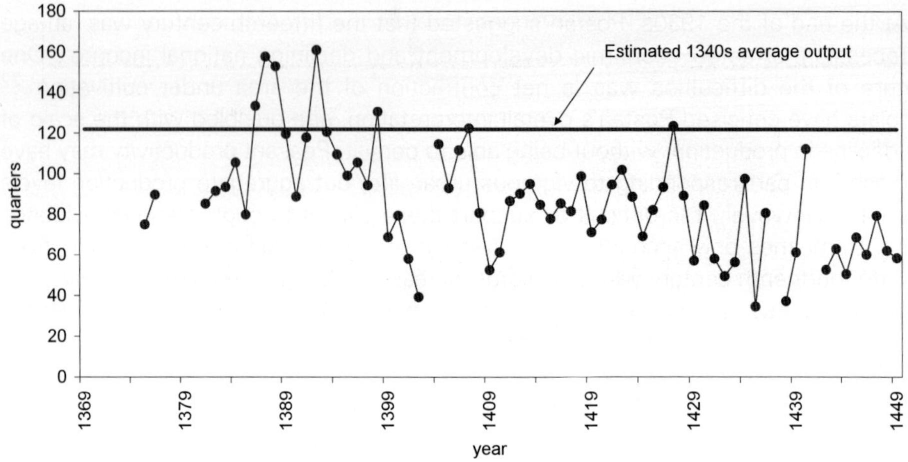

Figure 7.2a Estimated output in Shincliffe

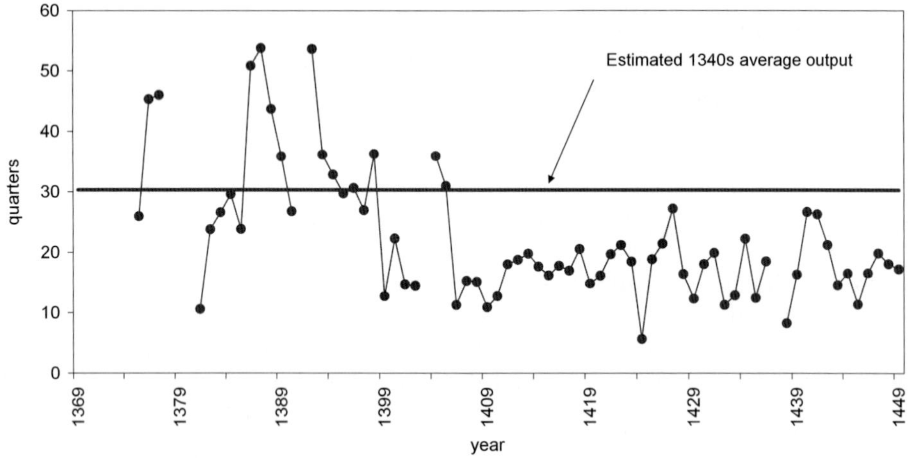

Figure 7.2b Estimated output in Old Durham

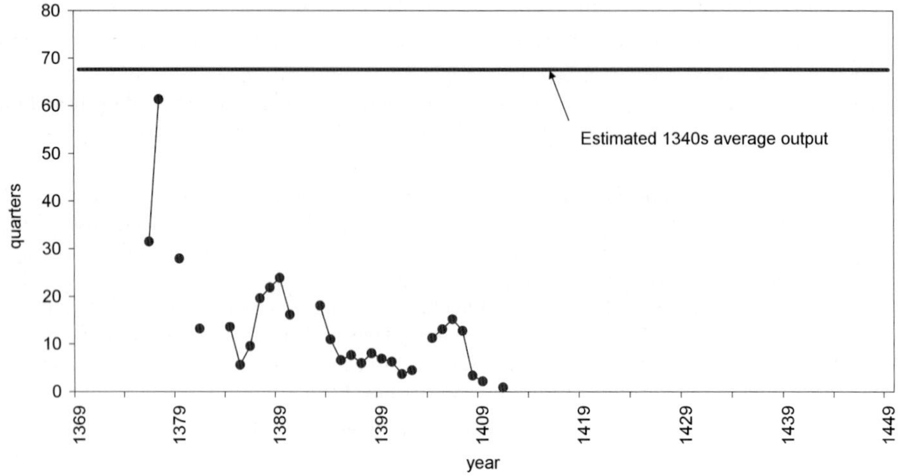

Figure 7.2c Estimated output in 'Wastes'

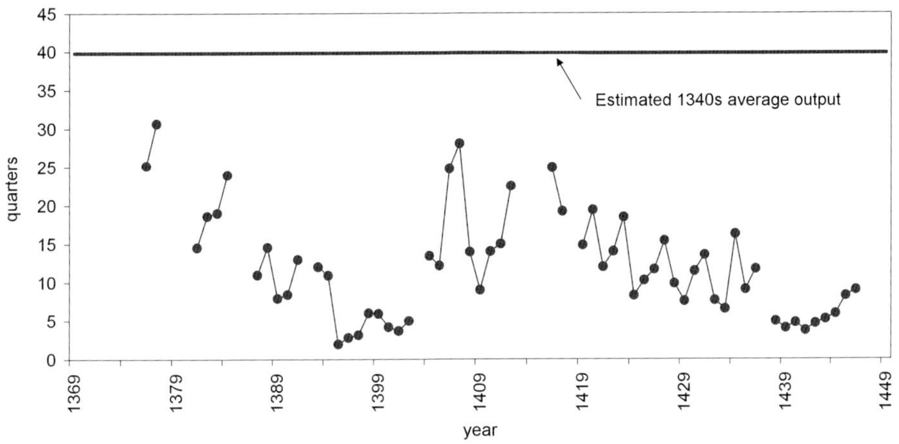

Figure 7.2d Estimated output in Newton

gradual fall in the peaks and troughs of the series – two periods of agrarian crisis are evident: at the turn of the century and in the 1430s. There was a steep fall in production during the 1390s followed by a moderate recovery and two decades of relative stability. This mini-recovery was at its strongest between 1411 and 1418 when the index does not fall below 49 per cent of 1340s levels. By contrast, grain production levels plunged to new depths during the 1430s: output fell below one-third of 1340s levels in five harvests.

Figures 7.2a–d demonstrate possible variations within the overall pattern established in Figure 7.1. Nevertheless, they confirm the pattern of overall and gradual decline. The individual township series are all taken from St Oswald's parish, which lay around Durham city. The tithes belonged to the hostiller, and the townships were chosen because of the good survival of accounts from this obedience for the turn of the century years. The four townships range from very large, in the case of Shincliffe, to fairly small, in the case of Newton. The St Oswald's data show that 1340s production levels were sometimes exceeded in individual townships, even if the overall indicators in Figure 7.1 fall far short of these levels. All the graphs show declining output in the final decade of the fourteenth century but Figures 7.2b and 7.2c suggest production levels were high during the 1380s in Old Durham and Shincliffe. Newton and 'Wastes', on the other hand, show steadily falling output from the end of the 1370s. The mini-recovery of the early fifteenth century is also in evidence, although to varying degrees. Newton and, to a lesser extent, Shincliffe recovered fairly substantially from the low output levels around the turn of the century. In Old Durham there was a gradual increase in production levels during the 1410s and 1420s. Although output showed signs of recovery at 'Wastes' from 1404–7, this township failed to produce any receipts at all from the second decade of the fifteenth century. These graphs are both a confirmation of the overall pattern observed and a warning that there could be significant variations, even within the same parish.

The fall in output in the Durham Priory parishes between 1370 and 1450 seems explicable in demographic terms. Judging by direct and indirect indicators it is likely the population of England had fallen to half its maximum pre-Black Death level, or lower, by the mid fifteenth century.[28] No long-term direct population indicators have been brought to light for the North-East of England and the indirect evidence has received little attention, although recent work has revealed a probable increase in mortality in the second half of the fifteenth century.[29] It is certain that the Black Death claimed as many lives around Durham as elsewhere in England: over 50 per cent of priory tenants died. Rental evidence suggests that in 1396 population may have stood at around half its 1347 level, indicating that if there had been any post-Black Death recovery, it was brief and subsequently reversed. Later evidence is less precise but Lomas thought it unlikely that population began to recover during the first half of the fifteenth century.[30] Steadily increasing wage rates in the area are suggestive of shrinkage of the available labour force into the mid fifteenth century.[31] Certainly the North in the late fourteenth and fifteenth centuries seems to have shared the high death rate resulting from endemic disease elsewhere in the country.[32] More specifically, the North may have been severely affected by renewed outbreaks of pestilence in the 1390s which did not affect all parts of the country.[33] The pattern of periodic high mortality rates throughout the fifteenth century is apparent in Goldberg's

---

28 E.g. Z. Razi, *Life, marriage and death in a medieval parish: economy, society and demography in Halesowen, 1270–1400* (Cambridge, 1980), p. 117; L. R. Poos, *A rural society after the Black Death: Essex 1350–1525* (Cambridge, 1991), pp. 90–6; J. Hatcher, *Plague, population and the English economy, 1348–1530* (London, 1977), pp. 68–9.

29 J. Hatcher, A. J. Piper and D. Stone, 'Monastic mortality: Durham Priory, 1395–1529', *EcHR* 59 (2006), pp. 667–87.

30 R. A. Lomas, 'The Black Death in County Durham', *Journal of Medieval History* 15 (1989), pp. 129–31 and 134–8. Lomas used samples of tithe receipts, along with court roll evidence, to argue that population declined around Durham into the mid fifteenth century. The pattern proposed here for Durham coincides with much more direct evidence for population change in Essex. Following a brief recovery during the 1360s, population fell and reached a fairly stable but very low level into and throughout the fifteenth century: Poos, *Rural society*, pp. 96 and 107–8.

31 B. Dodds, 'Workers on the Pittington demesne in the late middle ages', *Archaeologia Aeliana* 28 (2000), p. 152.

32 The reappearance of plague after the Black Death in the early 1360s is suggested by a payment of 12d made to a shepherd by the Durham Priory hostiller *a tempore pestilencie*: DCM, hostiller's account 1360–1, *Expense minute*. Around 1436 the Durham monks also blamed recurring pestilence for the reduction in their spiritual income: J. Raine (ed.), *Historiae Dunelmensis scriptores tres, Gaufridus de Coldingham, Robertus de Graystanes, et Willelmus de Chambre*, Surtees Society IX (London, 1839), p. ccl.

33 Chronicle evidence of severe outbreaks of plague in northern England during the 1390s can be found in C. Babington and J. R. Lumby (eds), *Polychronicon Ranulphi Higden monachi Cestrensis*, Rolls Series 41 (9 vols, London, 1865–86), IX, pp. 237–8 and 259; C. Creighton, *A history of epidemics in Britain from A.D. 664 to the extinction of the plague* (2 vols., Cambridge, 1891–4), I, p. 220. A complaint to the bishop of Durham made by the prior of Brinkburn (Northumberland) in the early 1390s argued that his convent's possessions had diminished because of frequently recurring plagues: W. Page (ed.), *The chartulary of Brinkburn*, Surtees Society XC (Durham, 1892), p. xi. Halesowen (West Midlands) does not appear to have suffered high mortality levels during this decade: Razi, *Life, marriage and death*, p. 125. For the importance of local outbreaks of various diseases on population change see Hatcher, *Plague*, pp. 57–8.

Table 7.1
Arable production in the Cambrésis (after Neveux)

	Wheat	*Oats*
1320	*c.* 100	*c.* 100
1370	70	60
1450	55	40

Note: These figures are a reworking of Neveux' estimates. His data series are not as continuous as those from Durham, especially for the mid-fourteenth century, so the values are very approximate. Neveux presented these figures indexed around the 1370s: Wheat – 1320: 140–150; 1370: 100; 1450: 80; Oats – 1320: 160–170; 1370: 100; 1450: 70–80. Neveux, *Les Grains*, 339. These estimates, in turn, derive from complex series of calculations based on several data series: *ibid.*, 29–111.

evidence using testamentary material from York.[34] The correlation is not necessarily precise, and statistics have not yet been produced to extend the comparison, but it seems likely that the falling grain production levels from around 1370 to 1450 were caused by declining and stagnant population levels.

What is more, the number of economically active members of the population may have fallen more rapidly than the population as a whole. There is a growing body of evidence to suggest that susceptibility to plague is strongly influenced by genetic immunity.[35] The result was a change in the age structure of the population. As a society was subjected to recurring outbreaks, wiping out those not immune to the disease, mortality would be highest among those younger generations who had not yet experienced the plague.[36] This would mean age pyramids would become increasingly top heavy: communities would contain more and more elderly people.[37] It is by no means certain what the impact of this change would have been on the productivity of communities. It is possible that the older surviving members continued to work and produce. Nevertheless, it seems likely that the removal of chunks of successive younger generations would have weakened overall productive capacity.

France

Arable production was at a low ebb in France in the mid-fifteenth century. Table 7.1 summarises the results of Neveux's analysis of production levels in the Cambrésis.

Comparison with Figure 7.1 suggests production fell by around 20 per cent in both Durham and the Cambrésis between 1370–1450, with the former suffering perhaps a

---

34 P. J. P. Goldberg, 'Mortality and economic change in the diocese of York, 1390–1514', *Northern History* 24 (1988), pp. 38–55.

35 This first became apparent in evidence from north Italian towns: D. Herlihy and C. Klapisch-Zuber, *Tuscans and their families: a study of the Florentine catasto of 1427* (New Haven, Conn., 1985), pp. 186–92. In the Benedictine community at Durham, those who survived one outbreak were more likely to survive the next: personal communication from Alan Piper.

36 J. C. Russell, *British medieval population* (Albuquerque, 1948), p. 60; Razi, *Life, marriage and death*, pp. 129 and 134–5.

little bit more. Although Durham data from around 1320 are poor, figures from the 1330s and 1340s, and the Cambrésis estimate for 1320, suggest the fall in production levels between the Black Death and the mid fifteenth century was also comparable in the two regions. Neveux' dataset is unmatched by other published French examples. Bois' Normandy data, for example, do not begin until the early fifteenth century, making this sort of comparison impossible. The only corroborative evidence from elsewhere in France comes from the area around Paris. Rental receipts suggest there was also a fall of around 60 per cent in the volume of grain production on the Ile-de-France between 1340 and 1450.[38]

Whilst the scale of the mid-fifteenth-century production crisis in the Cambrésis and in Durham was of comparable severity relative to mid- to late-fourteenth-century levels, the pattern of decline differed. Estimated production levels around Durham plunged into worsening crisis shortly before the turn of the century. In contrast, while there was a precipitous fall in output in north-east France in the mid fourteenth century, Neveux described the years 1370–1400 as 'thirty years of respite' after which crisis redoubled.[39] This pattern may have been repeated in Normandy. Bois' four rural parishes showed stability around the turn of the century followed by significant falls in output from 1410. On the basis of population and rent levels, Bois described the period 1364–1404 as 'forty years of economic and demographic growth'.[40] Since previously vacated lands were reoccupied, Bois suggested that production recovered during the same period.[41] Less direct production data from elsewhere in France add weight to the suggestion that there was a recovery in France towards the end of the fourteenth century. In the region around Paris a 35–40 per cent fall in grain production between 1356 and 1364 was followed by a period of recovery until further falls between 1410 and 1420.[42] Boutruche collected a large quantity of anecdotal evidence for recovery in the Bordelais during the same period, including the reconstruction of windmills and the extension of vineyards.[43]

---

37 Again, the first evidence for this was brought to light in northern Italy: e.g. D. Herlihy, *Medieval and renaissance Pistoia: the social history of an Italian town 1207–1430* (New Haven and London, 1967), p. 110. The same phenomenon is also documented for Halesowen: Razi, *Life, marriage and death*, p. 151.

38 H. Neveux, 'Déclin et reprise: la fluctuation biséculaire' in G. Duby and A. Wallon (eds), *Histoire de la France rurale, tome 2. L'âge classique des paysans 1340–1789* (Paris, 1975), p. 75. Neveux appears to have made this calculation on the basis of raw data, mostly from rents, presented in G. Fourquin, *Les Campagnes de la région parisienne à la fin du Moyen Age du milieu du XIIIe siècle au début du XVIe siècle* (Paris, 1964). Neveux does not specify which ones he used and there are various possibilities, e.g. Fourquin, *Les Campagnes*, pp. 212–4 and 484–8, and see also pp. 267–77. For Durham, see Dodds, *Peasants and production*, p. 28.

39 Neveux, *Les Grains*, p. 340.

40 Bois, *Crisis*, pp. 125 and 300.

41 *Ibid.*, p. 308.

42 Neveux, 'Déclin et reprise', pp. 75–6. Again, Neveux appears to have made these calculations using Fourquin's raw data. The receipts from windmills demonstrate a pattern similar to that described here: Fourquin, *Les Campagnes*, pp. 205 and 276.

43 R. Boutruche, *La Crise d'une société: seigneurs et paysans du Bordelais pendant la Guerre de Cent Ans* (Paris, 1947), pp. 217–18.

While arable production around Durham experienced its own brief 'respite' during the second and third decades of the fifteenth century, the French recovery was ending. Neveux described 'an almost uninterrupted avalanche of crises from 1400 to 1440'.[44] Both Durham and the Cambrésis experienced unprecedented disasters during the 1430s but very serious difficulties had begun in north-eastern France from 1400. Bois' evidence from Normandy presents a similar picture. For reasons associated with his method, Bois did not deflate tithe receipts on an annual basis. Aware of the usefulness of this technique, however, he did deflate average tithe receipts for 1425–32, indexing them against late-fourteenth-century levels.[45] In the rural parishes there was an average fall in production levels of just over 40 per cent between these two periods.

Not all parts of France experienced late-fourteenth-century recovery followed by renewed crisis. Lorcin's indirect production evidence from the Lyonnais shows a different pattern. She found widespread difficulties in rent collection around the turn of the fourteenth century. In spite of the renewed prosperity in the city of Lyon itself, there were increasing numbers of vacancies in the surrounding countryside. Marginal notes in the terriers of the Chapitre Primatial de Saint-Jean indicate 'a crisis of tenant recruitment' from 1375. In 1387–8, 99 out of 143 parcels of land changed hands and 21 of these were left vacant. By comparison, in the period 1356–75, 49 out of 207 parcels had been transferred of which none was left vacant. Not surprisingly, the Chapitre de Saint-Just found itself experiencing serious financial problems during the last third of the fourteenth century. Lorcin used the same rental evidence to show the beginnings of improvement at the very end of the fourteenth century. The Chapter Acts of the Chapitre de Saint-Just show that the canons were assessing vacant lands and discussing bringing them back into cultivation at this time. The terriers of the Chapitre Primatial de Saint-Jean suggest improvement began slightly later in 1414–15. Aside from localised renewed difficulties in the early 1420s, Lorcin places the turning point in rural land occupation between 1380 and 1417: after that the fortunes of the landlords started to improve.[46] Whilst recovery may have begun later in the Lyonnais than in the Cambrésis, and possibly earlier than in Durham, it appears to have been unaffected by the disasters of the first half of the fifteenth century.

Lorcin's evidence must be treated with caution, however, when making comparisons with estimated production levels based on tithe. Her indicators are much more scattered and anecdotal: the disappearance of references to vacant properties give only the loosest indicator of relative production levels. In particular, given the weight of evidence from elsewhere in France it seems unlikely the Lyonnais was enjoying agricultural prosperity in the middle years of the fifteenth century. Bearing in mind these notes of caution in interpreting Lorcin's data, a broad pattern of changing French output levels can be proposed. All parts of the country from which evidence is available experienced plummeting production levels in the mid fourteenth century.

44 Neveux, *Les Grains*, pp. 341–2. Again, Neveux' data are not as continuous as those from Durham but the difficulties of these years are clear in his graphs: *ibid.*, pp. 53, 54–5, 68, 74, 96 and 98.

45 Bois, *Crisis*, pp. 123–5.

46 M. –Th. Lorcin, *Les Campagnes de la région lyonnaise au XIVe et XVe siècles* (Lyon, 1974), pp. 217, 240–5 and 317.

There is widespread evidence for recovery towards the end of the fourteenth century. From 1400 output levels in many areas of France plunged again. The chronology of changing output levels contrasts with that in Durham where there is little evidence of recovery before 1400. Just at the time when French grain production shows a renewed downturn in the early years of the fifteenth century there was a modest and short-lived recovery in Durham. Despite these differences, grain production was at a low ebb in both Durham and the parts of France examined by the middle decades of the fifteenth century.

The most prominent causal factor in long-term changes in production levels appears to have been population change. Many French studies suggest that there was a demographic low point about 1450, with fewer than half the number of people populating the countryside than at the beginning of the fourteenth century.[47] The decline was not gradual and even, however, and a body of evidence suggests there was some recovery during the late fourteenth century only to be reversed subsequently. Unfortunately, Neveux's population statistics are not detailed enough for him to be able to place a temporary halt in the decline corresponding to his 'respite' in production levels in the late fourteenth century.[48] Bocquet's evidence from Artois, however, does reveal an increase in population between 1384–1414 which would coincide well with Neveux's period of recovery.[49] Bois' population evidence is more detailed. There was an overall decline between the early fourteenth and mid fifteenth centuries but this was punctuated by a period of recovery in the late fourteenth century. In the viscounty of Arques, for example, he found a growth in population of some 35 per cent between 1374/1380 and 1398/1401.[50] Brief recoveries in population levels in parts of England in the fifty years after the Black Death have not been ruled out but nothing on this scale has been suggested.[51]

Patterns of population change may have been affected by the varied impact and timing of renewed plague outbreaks after 1370. The recovery in production levels in parts of France up to *c.* 1400 may have been permitted by the relative absence of plague from these regions in the final third of the fourteenth century. Bois suggests that plague only reemerged in Normandy as a significant cause of high death rates after the turn of the century.[52] Neveux and Fourquin found evidence for very serious renewed outbreaks of disease in the early fifteenth century.[53] It is possible that output trends in the Lyonnais, which did not match those in other parts of France, were affected by a pattern of demographic change more similar to that proposed for

47 Bois, *Crisis*, pp. 49, 60–2 and 67; Ladurie, *Peasants of Languedoc*, p. 14; Fourquin, *Les Campagnes*, p. 358. Neveux conveniently summarises local and regional studies in Neveux, 'Déclin et reprise', p. 74.

48 Neveux, *Les Grains*, pp. 171–6.

49 A. Bocquet, *Recherches sur la population rurale de l'Artois et du Boulonnais pendant la période bourguignonne (1384–1477)*, Mémoires de la Commission Départementale des Monuments Historiques du Pas-de-Calais 13 (Arras, 1969), pp. 80–2.

50 Bois, *Crisis*, pp. 58–9 and 417.

51 Razi, *Life, marriage and death*, p. 117; D. Postles, 'Demographic change in Kibworth Harcourt, Leicestershire, in the later middle ages', *Local Population Studies* 48 (1992), p. 46.

52 Bois, *Crisis*, pp. 310–11.

53 Neveux, *Les Grains*, pp. 341–2; Fourquin, *Les Campagnes*, p. 333.

Durham than Normandy or Artois. Lorcin used numbers of wills proved in Lyon to chart the timing of surges in mortality, one of which occurred in 1391.[54]

While demographic change may have been the most important long-term determinant of production levels, all historians of France emphasise the importance of military activity on regional economies. Normandy and the Cambrésis were severely affected by the Hundred Years War. Bois stresses that the recovery of 1360–1400 was made possible by a gap in hostilities following the Treaty of Brétigny and subsequent limited military activity. The serious downturn in output during the early fifteenth century was precipitated by increased English pressure from 1410 followed by conquest and occupation.[55] The Bordelais was another region at the mercy of conflict between the English and French and Boutruche's study takes the form of a description of military events for each sub-period followed by details of their economic consequences.[56] The area around Paris was also badly affected in the early fifteenth century by conflict between the Burgundians and Armagnacs. Fourquin emphasised the devastating economic impact of civil wars between 1410–18 and Anglo-Burgundian occupation thereafter.[57] Although there were conflicts and unrest in the Lyonnais, the area was removed from the various theatres of the Hundred Years War. This must explain the relative economic stability of the region during the first half of the fifteenth century.

The precise impact of military activity is difficult to determine and presumably only extended beyond the short term in the most serious circumstances. Recovery around Durham after 1400 was feeble and reversed during the 1430s even though the region was free from conflict on the scale of that experienced in Normandy. Deeper underlying differences between the French and English rural economies are suggested by the scale of the demographic recovery in France before 1400.

Castile

There is no Castilian evidence for sustained low production levels around 1450. The most direct output indicators come from Andalusian grain tithes received by the archbishops of Seville and, despite great annual fluctuations in production levels, the pattern is of gradual increase throughout the first half of the fifteenth century.[58] Casado Alonso's tithe material from Burgos is more continuous, although reliant on deflated sold tithes, and presents a more detailed pattern. Between 1400 and 1450, production levels were certainly stable and even showed slight gradual increase. There is evidence of a subsequent low point in his production data but this did not come until the seventh and eighth decades of the century. Even these difficulties

54 Lorcin, *Les Campagnes*, p. 212.

55 Bois, *Crisis*, p. 317.

56 Boutruche, *La Crise d'une société*.

57 Fourquin, *Les Campagnes*, pp. 291–331.

58 Ladero Quesada and González Jiménez, *Diezmo eclesiástico*, p. 45. Some of these data are also presented in J. Valdeón Baruque, 'Parte primera: los países de la corona de Castilla', in *idem* and J. L. Martín Rodríguez (eds), *Historia de España Menéndez Pidal, Tomo XII: La Baja Edad Media peninsular siglos XIII al XV: la población, la economía, la sociedad* (Madrid, 1996), p. 136.

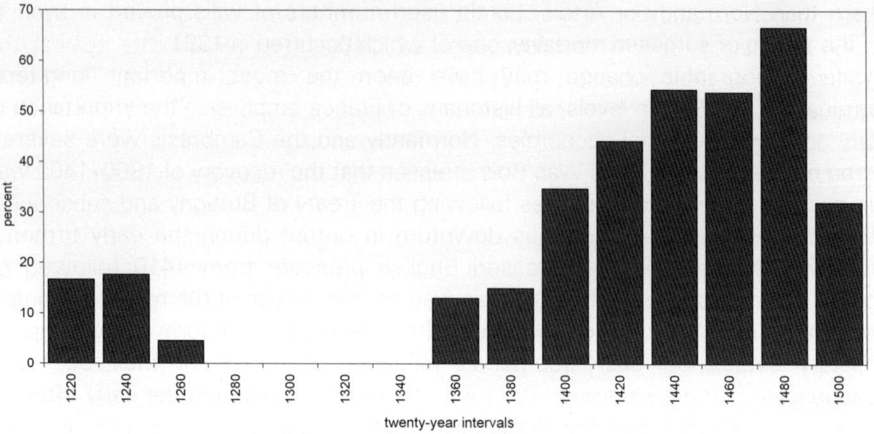

Figure 7.3 Percentage of San Clodio do Ribeiro (Galicia) documents mentioning newly cultivated or populated land
Source: M. Lucas Álvarez and P. Lucas Domínguez, *El monasterio de San Clodio do Ribeiro en la Edad Media: e studio y documentos* (La Coruña, 1996), p. 63.

were preceded and succeeded by rising production.[59] The tithe evidence is supplemented by abundant non-statistical signs of fifteenth-century recovery. For example, the great reforming abbot Fray Alonso de Urueña (1420–84) was able to reverse the fortunes of the Cistercian house of Santa Espina near Valladolid. One means he employed was the return of the abbey's windmills to direct management, made possible by the increase in the amount of grain ground by the peasants.[60]

There are scraps of evidence suggesting parts of Castile, like Durham, suffered from agrarian difficulties during the 1430s. The harvest appears to have been poor around Burgos in 1438–9; disastrous years around Durham also.[61] Andalusian evidence suggests that freak weather conditions caused the total 1435 harvest to be lost in Seville, however, the production index is much higher for Andalusia than for Durham in this year.[62] Whereas there were several years of very poor harvests around Durham in the 1430s and 1440s, the Castilian low points appear to be blips caused by exceptional weather conditions. Indeed, Casado Alonso describes 1427–36 and 1441–2 as years of *bonanza*.[63] Trends in arable output in Spain during the first half of the fifteenth century contrast strongly with the spiralling decline in parts of France and falling production levels around Durham, punctuated only by a short and feeble recovery.

The early-fifteenth-century Castilian recovery is, however, difficult to interpret given

59 Casado Alonso,'Producción agraria', pp. 73–7, 100–1

60 J. M. López García, *La transición del feudalismo al capitalismo en un señorío monástico castellano. El Abadengo de la Santa Espina (1147–1835)* (Valladolid, 1990), pp. 47–8.

61 Casado Alonso,'Producción agraria', p. 73.

62 M. A. Ladero Quesada,'Los cereales en la Andalucía del siglo XV', *Homenaje a Menéndez Pidal I, Revista de la Universidad de Madrid* 18, part 69, (Madrid, 1969), p. 225. Taking 1408 to equal 100, the Seville index is 110 and the Durham index 59: Ladero Quesada and González Jiménez, *Diezmo eclesiástico*, p. 45.

63 Casado Alonso,'Producción agraria', p. 73.

the lack of comparable data from the fourteenth century. One quantitative source, although not based on tithe receipts, does set 1400–50 developments against the difficulties of the previous century. Calculations made by Lucas Álvarez and Lucas Domínguez show the number of documents in the archive of the Orense monastery of San Clodio do Ribeiro de Avia referring to newly ploughed and populated lands for each period of twenty years between 1220 and 1500. These are given as percentages of the total number of documents surviving in Figure 7.3. During the seventy-nine years between 1280 and 1359 none of the surviving documentation refers to the extension of cultivation. This evidence is certainly indirect and subject to the vicissitudes of documentary survival. Nevertheless, it is a strong indication that new lands ceased to be broken in this area of northern Spain from the late thirteenth century until after the Black Death. Recovery appears to have begun around 1360 and, in keeping with the more direct production evidence, the number of references to newly ploughed lands multiplies rapidly for the first half of the fifteenth century.[64] As Figure 7.1 would suggest, evidence for the number of uncultivated townships between the Tyne and Tees shows the opposite trend to the Galician evidence, with a sharp increase in the 1370s and expansion into the early-fifteenth century.[65]

Other evidence leaves little doubt of the seriousness of the mid-fourteenth-century crisis in Castile. Government records make abundant mention of waste lands (*tierras yermas*) in the years around the Black Death and this impression is supported by Cabrillana's statistical evidence for the abandonment of nearly 20 per cent of settlements in the bishopric of Palencia.[66] Valdeón Baruque, admitting the lack of quantitative evidence, used incidental references in chronicles and government records to highlight crisis years throughout the fourteenth century. Aware that crisis years do not indicate depression, however, he turned to food prices and judged that the real difficulties were in the early to mid fourteenth century.[67]

The Galician evidence of improvement towards the end of the fourteenth century can also be supplemented. As in Durham, the years around the turn of the century saw disastrous harvests in parts of Castile. In Seville, for example, cereal production in 1399–1400 was badly affected by rain and a renewed outbreak of the plague. Then, in 1402–3, zones surrounding the Guadalquivir produced little because of flooding.[68] Again, however, the crisis years do not indicate general decline in production levels; evidence of cultivated area presents a picture of recovery at the very end of the

---

64 M. Lucas Álvarez and P. Lucas Domínguez, *El monasterio de San Clodio do Ribeiro en la Edad Media: estudio y documentos* (La Coruña, 1996), p. 63.

65 B. Dodds,'Peasants, Landlords and Production', p. 180.

66 J. Sobrequés Callicó,'La peste negra en la península ibérica', *Anuario de Estudios Medievales* 7 (1970–1), p. 87; N. Cabrillana,'La crisis del siglo XIV en Castilla: la peste negra en el obispado de Palencia', *Hispania* 109 (1968), p. 255. García de Cortázar is cautious about using evidence of abandoned settlements to infer a proportional decline in production: García de Cortázar, *La sociedad rural*, p. 190.

67 J. Valdeón Baruque,'La crisis del siglo XIV en Castilla: revisión del problema', *Estudios de Historia Económica II, Revista de la Universidad de Madrid* 20, part 79 (Madrid, 1971), pp. 169–76; Valdeón Baruque,'Parte primera: los países de la corona de Castilla', pp. 129–33.

68 Ladero Quesada,'Los cereales en la Andalucía del siglo XV', p. 224.

69 García de Cortázar, *La sociedad*, p. 194.

fourteenth century.[69] Díaz de Durana drew on 14 pleas raised in courts between 1393 and 1430 concerning the definition of various communities' control over surrounding lands to argue there was renewed interest in arable cultivation in the Basque province of Álava. He also found the first direct evidence since 1302 of land being brought newly under the plough in 1408.[70]

The Castilian evidence for production levels 1370–1450 is bitty and comes from regions as different as the Basque country, Galicia, the environs of Burgos and Andalusia. Nevertheless, a pattern can be tentatively proposed. Recovery seems to have begun early: in Galicia lands were being newly occupied before 1370. Around the turn of the century, a period of great difficulties around Durham, the evidence for expansion of the cultivated area multiplies. So far, the pattern is comparable to that proposed for certain parts of France. However, the fifteenth century tithe series from Burgos and Andalusia demonstrate that the first half of the fifteenth-century did not see the end of recovery. Production levels were stable, at least allowing for annual harvest fluctuations and occasional bad weather, and even demonstrated a slight upward trend.

Castilian patterns of demographic change may explain this pattern. García de Cortázar distinguished patterns of population growth following the mid-fourteenth-century crisis in Castile from those elsewhere in the Iberian peninsula. In Navarra and Catalonia the process was slow and incomplete, but progress was much faster in Castile.[71] Díaz de Durana's data from the Álava province of the Basque country substantiate this claim. The population of Bernedo increased by nearly 51 per cent between 1366 and 1427. Recovery was not always so early, however, and did not begin in Labraza until around the latter date.[72] Evidence for later-fifteenth-century recovery is much more widespread. The number of hearths in Treviño (Basque country) increased by 30 per cent between 1456 and 1522 and a similar pattern repeated itself elsewhere, with only temporary halts caused by weather and disease.[73] There was demographic increase in fifteenth-century Andalusia also, partly caused by renewed emigration from the north.[74] The demographic data are very thin but it appears that Castilian trends were similar to those in Normandy and Artois in the late-fourteenth century: there was strong recovery. Unlike in these parts of France, however, population recovery did not cease around the turn of the century in Castile. Indeed, numbers appear to have continued rising throughout the fifteenth century.

---

70 J. R. Díaz de Durana, *Álava en la Baja Edad Media. Crisis, recuperación y transformaciones socioeconómicas (c. 1250–1525)* (Vitoria, 1986), pp. 145–8.

71 García de Cortázar, *La sociedad*, p. 193. The Navarra evidence showing recovery during the final third of the fifteenth century is presented in M. Berthe, *Famine et epidémies dans la campagne Navarraise à la fin du Moyen Âge* (Paris, 1984), pp. 443–52. For the recent Catalan evidence, showing a pattern of decline and stagnation throughout the fifteenth century, see E. Mallorquí, *Les Gavarres a l'edat mitjana; poblament i societat d'un massís del nord-est català* (Girona, 2000), pp. 204–6.

72 Díaz de Durana, *Álava*, pp. 109–10 and 116.

73 *Ibid.*, pp. 112 and 151–69.

74 M. González Jiménez, *En torno a los orígines de Andalucía: la repoblación del siglo XIII* (Seville, 1980), p. 91; M. Borrero Fernández, *El mundo rural sevillano en el siglo XV: Aljarafe y Ribera* (Seville, 1983), pp. 149, 152–7 and 186–7.

Production evidence is not yet available from the other Spanish kingdoms. Nevertheless, the Castilian demographic and production data suggest trends from the end of the fourteenth century that are atypical in both Iberian and wider European contexts. The reconquest of Muslim territory, especially the rapid gains made in the thirteenth century, meant the balance between population and resources during the fourteenth and fifteenth centuries was highly unusual in Castile. Migrations southwards, especially after the conquest of Andalusia and subsequent expulsion of the Mudéjars, meant there was little pressure on land in northerly areas of Spain during the late thirteenth and early fourteenth centuries.[75] Indeed, villages were deserted long before the Black Death.[76] The result was that the demographic catastrophes of the second half of the fourteenth century affected a kingdom already under-populated. This may mean later-fourteenth-century recovery represented an improvement on very low levels of production.

Later population movement was complicated, and the long-term economic impact of the repopulation of the south on different parts of Castile is little understood, at least in precise terms. Sparsely populated lands in Extremadura and La Mancha, and later in Andalusia, had been turned over to large-scale livestock farming. Particularly after the establishment of the Mesta system in 1273, it became difficult for arable farmers to defend their interests against the encroaching flocks and herds.[77] It is possible that changing landlord-tenant relations in the late fourteenth century gave the arable farmers increased freedom and enabled them to bring land back into cultivation.

Castilian production levels were not only affected by the relationship between population and resources. As in France, violence of various kinds must have had an impact. Most spectacularly, there was a long conflict in Castile from 1350 to 1389 which began with the struggle between Peter I and his illegitimate half brother Henry of Trastámara. The conflict escalated in scale and embroiled foreign powers.[78] Large numbers of armed men were responsible for pillaging and destruction, causing the desertion of some settlements.[79] Groups of English and French mercenaries were particularly damaging.[80] Nevertheless, the impact of war must have been highly selective geographically. During the period of English involvement in Castile in the early-1380s, Galicia was one of the main theatres of war and yet the evidence in Figure 7.3 suggests new land continued to be broken during these years. Like in France, the impact of war is difficult to quantify. Nevertheless, it seems to have been partly responsible for the very serious difficulties of the mid fourteenth century and a reduction in military destruction following the truces of Leulingham and Monção in 1389 may have facilitated the subsequent recovery.

---

75 T. F. Ruiz, *Crisis and continuity: land and town in late medieval Castile* (Philadelphia, 1994), p. 291; A. MacKay, *Spain in the middle ages; from frontier to empire, 1000–1500* (London, 1977), pp. 70–2; González Jiménez, *Los orígines de Andalucía*, pp. 71 and 86–7.

76 Ruiz, *Crisis and continuity*, p. 309; García de Cortázar, *La sociedad*, p. 189.

77 Ruiz, *Crisis and continuity*, p. 300; MacKay, *Spain*, p. 168; J. Vicens Vives, with J. Nadal Oller, *An economic history of Spain* (Princeton, NJ, 1969), p. 163.

78 MacKay, *Spain*, pp. 121–2; E. Mitre Fernández, 'Algunas cuestiones demográficas en la Castilla de fines del siglo XIV', *Anuario de Estudios Medievales*, 7 (1970–1), p. 615.

79 N. Cabrillana, 'Los despoblados en Castilla la Vieja', *Hispania*, 119 (1971), p. 547.

80 Valdeón Baruque, 'Parte primera: los países de la corona de Castilla', p. 126.

Contrasts

This comparative study of changes in arable production levels in three parts of Europe during the late Middle Ages shows a multitude of different trends, not only between countries but even between individual villages. Nevertheless, three broad patterns emerge. In Durham, 1370–1450 saw ongoing decline in arable production, with only a brief flicker of recovery in the first decades of the fifteenth century. In France, by contrast, the final quarter of the fourteenth century saw some recovery, although this was not sustained in the first half of the fifteenth century. The Castilian pattern is one of sustained recovery from the end of the fourteenth century.

Well-known exogenous factors must have played an important part in these differences. The history of conquest and settlement in Castile may have meant arable production levels were at such a low ebb in the aftermath of the Black Death that an apparent recovery would not require much absolute increase in production. Military factors were clearly important in determining the French patterns, especially since the best French tithe series from Normandy and the Cambrésis are from areas seriously affected by war.

Neither of these explanations fit the English pattern of sustained decline from the final quarter of the fourteenth century, however. It is inconceivable that the limits of expansion in arable production could have been reached around Durham by *c.* 1375: waste remained abundant throughout the period even in the lowland areas of the Tyne Tees region.[81] In other words, the area was relatively sparsely populated, just like Castile. Yet there was no sustained recovery in arable production around Durham. Just like France in the decades after the Treaty of Brétigny, Durham was spared the destruction caused by warfare after the disasters of the early fourteenth century. Yet there was no sustained recovery.

French and Castilian recovery from *c.* 1370 may have had its roots in processes of demographic change different to those in England. Endemic plague, probably mixed with other diseases, did not affect all countries and regions in the same way. Especially after the 1370s, outbreaks tended to be more local but not necessarily less severe. This may have brought about divergent long-term demographic trends. The contrast is striking between widespread French and Castilian evidence for strong recovery even before the beginning of the fifteenth century and a growing body of evidence for further decline and stagnation in England. Given the persuasiveness of the explanations based on age-specific outbreaks of pestilence in England, and their support in detailed Italian evidence, it is by no means clear what the mechanism for demographic recovery could have been in France and Castile.

Detailed comparative work on demographic indicators is needed to test this hypothesis. Such indicators are not abundant, however. On the other hand, indicators of arable production levels in the form of tithe data are relatively plentiful. Further research into these would answer some crucial questions. The compilation of more

---

81 H. M. Dunsford and S. J. Harris, 'Colonisation of the wasteland in County Durham, 1100–1400', *EcHR* 56 (2003), pp. 39–40; R. H. Britnell, 'Fields, farms and sun-division in a moorland region, 1100–1400', *AHR* 52 (2004), pp. 20–37.

English series would clarify whether the Durham decline is representative of the rest of the country. Analysis of fourteenth-century Castilian tithe data would establish whether subsequent recovery is anything other than an illusion created by the low ebb to which production had fallen.[82] Another potential area for study is the Iberian peninsula outside Castile. It is hoped that future work will provide further details in describing and explaining the contrasting trends in output suggested in this paper.

82 The scope for work on fourteenth- and even thirteenth-century tithe receipts in the Burgos Cathedral archive is suggested in Casado Alonso, 'Producción agraria', p. 69.

Chapter 8

Lord, tenant and the market: some tithe evidence from the Wessex region[1]

John Hare

Historians are the victims of their sources and perhaps few more than students of the medieval agrarian economy. The manorial account rolls provide a remarkable level of detail about the agriculture of the lord, but we rightly worry about how typical such material may be. How far does our good knowledge of demesne agriculture distort our view of the much greater non-demesne sector in this period?[2] Was demesne agriculture, with its high capital investment and large scale of production, noticeably more efficient than peasant farming? Or was it noticeably less efficient compared with peasants' higher labour inputs and vested interest in working harder for greater returns? How did the cropping and marketing of lord and of tenant compare? Sources exist for the agricultural activities of this wider population of small producers, whether peasant or small landowner. The records of tithes, incorporated into rectory or parsonage accounts, provide one such source. In this chapter such evidence from an area of Wessex or central southern England, especially in Wiltshire and Hampshire, is examined in the context of the region's agriculture. The tithe evidence needs to be studied in relation to the demesne agriculture of the parish, and where this is not possible, in comparison with that of neighbouring demesnes. Just as the lord's agriculture needs to be seen in the context of the deep regional variations that lay within medieval agriculture, so too must that of the tenantry.

The evidence

Medieval villagers and lords were required to pay tithes to their church. Over the

1 The agrarian background for this article is provided in my forthcoming book on later medieval Wiltshire, *A prospering society: Wiltshire in the later middle ages*. In the meantime something of this context may be found in J. N. Hare,'Change and continuity in Wiltshire agriculture: the later middle ages', in W. E. Minchinton (ed.), *Agricultural improvement: medieval and modern,* Exeter Papers in Economic History, 14 (Exeter, 1981), pp. 1–18; *idem,*'Agriculture and rural settlement in the chalklands of Wiltshire and Hampshire from c.1200 to c.1500', in M. Aston and C. Lewis (eds), *The medieval landscape of Wessex* (Oxford, 1994), pp. 159–69; *idem,*'Regional prosperity in fifteenth-century England: some evidence from Wessex', in M. Hicks, (ed.), *Revolution and consumption in late medieval England* (Woodbridge, 2001), pp. 105–26 and *idem,*'The bishop and the prior: demesne agriculture in medieval Hampshire', *AHR* 54 (2006), pp.187–212. See also R. Scott,'Medieval agriculture', in *The Victoria history of the county of Wiltshire,* IV, and E. Miller's discussions of the southern counties of England in *AHEW,* III. Some of the Overton material was collected for me as part of the Fyfield and Overton project. My thanks are due to P. J. Fowler for arranging this and to E. Roberts for his work.

2 It is impossible to state accurately the proportion of demesne agricultural output to the national total. Campbell suggests a range of a third to a fifth: B. M. S. Campbell, *English seigniorial agriculture, 1250–1450* (Cambridge 2000), p. 60.

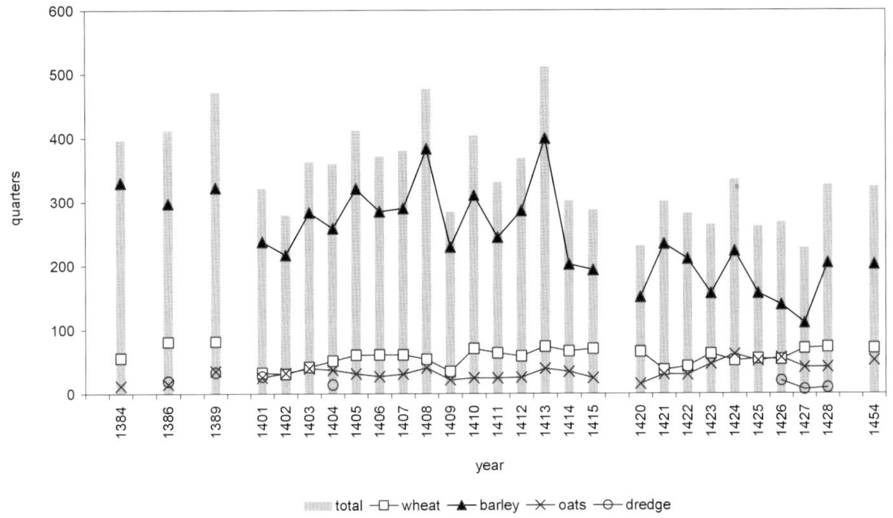

Figure 8.1 Downton grain tithe receipts, 1384–1454
Source: WCM 5362-5453.

course of the Middle Ages, many of these rights fell into the hands of ecclesiastical lords and occasionally they are recorded in a form which permits comparison to be made between lords and their tenants. Such a comparison will help establish the balance between demesne production and that in the parish as a whole. Such sources are rare from this region and time period. They have occasionally been considered in the secondary literature but rarely given any prominence.[3] A particularly extensive study of medieval Wiltshire has located only six manors with surviving documentation that allows the grain to be quantified.

Usually the sources simply do not survive and when they do their form is not always helpful. On small manors, where tithes also belonged to the lord of the manor, they might be incorporated within the main lease. When Winchester College received Andwell (Hampshire), it collected the tithes in the first year but then incorporated them into the lease from 1393. Large manors were also leased, whether separately or as part of the main lease, as at Urchfont (Wiltshire) in 1478, Andover (Hampshire) and Adderbury Rectory (Oxfordshire).[4] Tithes were collected in barns and then sold.[5] But even where there are long sequences of demesne and tithe receipts, as for example at Downton (Wiltshire) and East Meon (Hampshire), there are considerable difficulties.

---

3 Published figures include R. H. Hilton, *The economic development of some Leicestershire estates in the 14th and 15th centuries* (London, 1947), p. 66; R. H. Britnell, 'The occupation of the land: the eastern counties', in *AHEW*, III, p. 164; M. Mate, 'The occupation of the land: Kent and Sussex', in *ibid.*, p. 133; R. H. Britnell, *Growth and decline in Colchester, 1300–1525* (Cambridge 1986), pp. 150 and 155. The first substantial treatment of medieval English tithes is in B. Dodds, 'Estimating arable output using Durham Priory tithe receipts, 1341–1450', *EcHR* 57 (2004), pp. 245–85.

4 WCM 2656, 2695, Wiltshire and Swindon RO (Chippenham), 24/2; T. B. Hobson (ed.), 'Adderbury "rectoria"', Oxford Record Society VIII (1926), pp. 1–23.

5 As at East Meon (Hampshire): C. Harper-Bill (ed.), *The register of John Morton, archbishop of Canterbury, 1486–1500* (3 vols, Leeds and Woodbridge, 1987–2000), I, pp. 88–100.

Table 8.1
Parish tithes and demesne crops of five manors, 1270–1338

Parish tithe (crops as a percentage of the total)							
	Wheat	*Bere*	*Rye*	*Barley*	*Oats*	*Dredge*	*Legumes*
Alton Priors (Wilts.)							
1303	51.1	0.0	2.5	34.0	1.8	4.4	6.2
1304	54.6	0.0	2.5	32.8	0.0	5.7	4.4
1309	50.6	0.0	0.0	40.8		7.7	0.9
1311	40.4	0.0	0.0	41.9	1.7	14.0	3.8
1316	50.8	0.0	0.0	48.5	0.7	0.0	0.0
Enford (Wilts.)							
1309[1]	21.8	0.0	0.0	51.9	12.5	0.0	5.3
1311	19.5	6.8	0.0	56.2	9.3	0.0	8.3
Overton (Wilts.)							
1307	32.3	10.5	0.0	48.3	0.0	8.8	0.0
1311	20.5	6.1	0.0	57.8	2.4	7.6	5.5
1312	32.7	3.3	0.0	48.4	8.4	4.4	3.0
1316	24.7	8.4	0.0	47.1	6.1	13.6	0.0
East Meon (Hants.)[2]							
1305–14	39.6	0.0	0.0	19.5	32.2	0.0	0.0
Hambledon (Hants.)[2]							
1305–14	35.0	0.0	0.0	25.4	31.1	0.0	0.0
Combe (Hants.)							
1307	32.5	14.0	0.0	27.9	26.2	?[3]	0.0
1308	30.7	21.0	0.0	22.7	25.6	0.0	?[3]
Wootton (Hants.)							
1338	31.7	9.8	0.0	29.0	29.5	0.0	0.0
Stratton parish and demesne (Wilts.)[4]							
1286–8[4]							
1294	30.2	0.0	0.0	29.1	24.3	8.3	8.1[5]
1295	37.6	0.0	0.0	22.8	29.7	0.8	9.1[5]
1299	21.8	0.0	0.0	45.0	6.8	20.3	6.1[5]
Inglesham (Wilts.)[6]							
1270	30.2	0.0	0.0	57.4	0.0	0.0	12.4
Coxwell (Berks.)[6]							
1270	34.3	0.0	15.7	50.0	0.0	0.0	0.0
Faringdon (Berks.)							
1270	31.1	0.0	5.2	28.8	9.7	16.5	8.8

Notes:
[1] At Enford in 1309, the parish figures are for the parish and demesne together. The separate demesne figures have been taken from the demesne accounts.
[2] The demesne cropping at East Meon and Hambledon is for the year 1302 only.
[3] The account makes no distinction between demensne output and tithe receipts.
[4] The demesne in question is that of Sevenhampton with Stratton.
[5] Beans.
[6] At Coxwell and Inglesham, tithes from the demesne do not seem to have been included in the issues of the tithes.

Demesne output (crops as a percentage of the total)						
Wheat	*Bere*	*Rye*	*Barley*	*Oats*	*Dredge*	*Legumes*
61.4	0.0	0.0	29.4	9.0	0.0	0.2
68.8	0.0	0.0	30.5	0.0	5.7	0.7
65.8	0.0	0.0	24.3	8.6	0.0	1.3
56.4	0.0	0.0	32.1	11.0	0.0	0.5
56.5	0.0	0.0	33.0	8.9	0.0	0.0
19.6	5.8	0.0	44.9	26.3	0.0	3.3
17.8	15.3	0.0	41.0	17.0	0.0	9.0
34.7	8.2	0.0	21.2	24.6	9.1	2.3
17.7	8.7	0.0	40.2	23.1	6.6	4.5
25.8	6.6	0.0	35.9	20.6	5.1	5.9
30.2	1.3	0.0	30.0	30.3	8.2	0.0
25.5	17.2	0.0	14.3	43.0	0.0	0.0
23.1	0.0	0.0	22.3	51.8	0.0	0.0
33.9	18.9	0.0	30.0	17.6	?[3]	0.0
15.8	32.1	0.0	8.2	44.0	0.0	?[3]
30.9	14.3	0.0	18.9	35.9	0.0	0.0
56.5	0.0	0.0	28.2	15.2	0.0	0.0
?	?	?	?	?	?	?
?	?	?	?	?	?	?
?	?	?	?	?	?	?
46.2	0.0	0.0	40.7	10.0	0.0	3.1
51.4	0.0	27.0	18.6	0.0	0.0	3.0
?	?	?	?	?	?	?

Sources: Alton, Enford and Overton: HRO 111 M94 W N2/1 and 2/2; WCL Composite accounts 1307, 1309, 1311, 1312 and 1316; Stratton: M[erton] C[ollege] M[uniments] 4307, 4308 and 4309; M. W. Farr (ed.), *Accounts and surveys of the Wiltshire lands of Adam de Stratton*, Wiltshire Record Society 14 (1959), pp. 161–85; Inglesham, Great Coxwell and Faringdon, S. F. Hockey (ed.), *The account-book of Beaulieu Abbey*, Camden Society, 4th series 16 (1975), pp. 71 and 92–3; Combe: M. Chibnall (ed.), *Select documents of the English lands of the abbey of Bec*, Camden Society, 3rd series 73 (1951), pp. 146–71; East Meon, Hambledon: HRO 97M97C1 (calculations by J. Z. Titow), and see M. Page (ed.), *The pipe roll of the bishopric of Winchester, 1301–2*, Hampshire Record Series 14 (Winchester, 1996); Wootton: G. W. Kitchen, *The manor of Manydown*, Hampshire Record Society (1895), pp. 150–3.

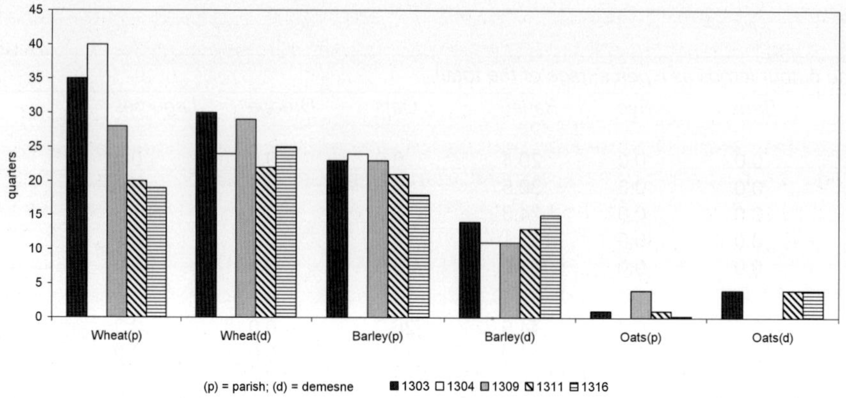

Figure 8.2 Alton Priors grain tithe receipts, 1303–16
Source: Winchester Cathedral Library. Composite accounts 1309, 1311, 1316; Hampshire Record Office 111 M94 W N2/1 and 2/2.

At Downton, the accounts survive almost completely from the time of Winchester College's acquisition of the rights in 1385, but the exceptionally long run of tithe figures includes three periods when the tithes were leased, and this practice became permanent after 1454. At East Meon, there were times when the tithes of particular settlements were leased; there was wholesale leasing in the early fourteenth century, and more and more was leased from the later 1420s. Sometimes, as at Longbridge Deverill (Wiltshire) or Andover, this flexibility incorporated sales from individual fields, preventing us from establishing totals for the lord, tenant or individual crops.[6] Finally, the surviving material is not in a standard format: sometimes we are able to compare the size of demesne and tenant production, sometimes only the cropping patterns of demesne and tenant together.

How far can the few surviving records be treated as reliable? For centuries tithes were a source of confrontation, so might these accounts be little more than a medieval fiction? It is probable that there was an element of struggle between the tithe owner, with an interest in maximising tithe income, and the tithe payer, with contrasting priorities. It is not possible to test the reliability of these sources directly but examination of the material from a few particularly well-documented manors justifies a cautious confidence, and reinforces the evidence of ecclesiastical sources that there was no widespread refusal to pay tithes.[7] This does not mean that the tithe accounts tell the whole story, any more than the manorial accounts give a completely accurate representation of the situation on the demesne. As Drew reminded us long ago, writing of the relationship between the reeve and the lord, 'It is impossible to look through these rolls, so often full of auditors' corrections from end to end, without realising that on many manors a battle of wits was going on all the time'.[8] We should expect nothing less of tithe accounts.

---

6 Longleat Mss 10699–9609; WCM 2660.

7 A. D. Brown, *Popular piety in late medieval England* (Oxford, 1995), p. 81.

8 J. S. Drew, 'Manorial accounts of St Swithun's Priory Winchester', reprinted in E. M. Carus-Wilson (ed.), *Essays in economic history* (3 vols, London, 1954–62), II, p. 29.

However, these sources have a variety that cannot be explained other than as a record of real and meaningful transactions. For example, the figures for Downton show a substantial fall in tithe produce in the fifteenth century, such as might suggest nothing more than the lord's growing inability to collect the produce: a decline in seigneurial power, with little relationship to any agrarian factors (see Figure 8.1). However, the figures show that oats and wheat tithe output were relatively constant while a massive collapse occurred in barley. Are we to believe that the rapacious tithe owner was simply less able to collect barley tithes than those of wheat or oats? This seems unlikely, and we are left to explain a massive fall in this crop's production. Downton has a particularly long series of tithe records, as does East Meon. Alton Priors (Wiltshire), which belonged to St Swithun's Cathedral Priory, Winchester, provides a more usual example with five accounts (see Figure 8.2).[9] Such sequences show that the proportions of various crops produced fluctuated from year to year, both on the demesne and parishioners' holdings. They also show the sharp drop in the 1315 harvest as seen in the 1316 account. As Kershaw concluded, 'the harvest of 1315 was a disaster'.[10] Interestingly, this harvest was noticeably better for the demesne than for the tenantry. Could it be that food shortages in previous years had led many of them to consume their seed corn as food? In conclusion, an initial look at the tithe evidence suggests it provides a worthwhile set of data which should not be discarded even if it needs treating with caution.

The following section of this chapter will use accounts from before the Black Death to compare patterns of production on demesne and tenant land and in different geographical areas. This earlier period does not provide us with any long series of tithe records, but it offers a wider geographical spread than is later available. The remaining sections examine the situation after the Black Death, looking at cropping patterns and trends in production. This last section explores the effect of external factors on demesne and tenant producers. Particular attention is given to Downton because of its very full coverage, spanning seventy years.

Arable farming in Wessex before the Black Death

The area covered by this study was itself divided into different agricultural regions, but was dominated by chalklands. The chalkland parishes generally comprised high chalk downland and more fertile lower soils, and their agriculture was characterised by large demesnes, arable farming and large sheep flocks. Around the chalk lay claylands with their smaller demesnes and sheep flocks. Table 8.1 shows data from 11 manors which can be used to compare cropping patterns on demesne land and in the parish as a whole. Three Wiltshire chalkland manors belonging to the cathedral priory of St Swithun at Winchester (Alton Priors, Enford and Overton) allow direct comparison of demesne and tenant production. Comparative chalkland material is available from

---

9 Three are among the cathedral records, two are among the records of St Cross, Winchester, in the Hampshire Record Office.

10 I. Kershaw, 'The great famine and agrarian crisis in England, 1315–22', reprinted in R. H. Hilton (ed.), *Peasants, knights and heretics* (Cambridge, 1981), p. 89. See also J. Z. Titow, 'Evidence of weather in the account rolls of the bishop of Winchester, 1209–1350', *EcHR* 12 (1959–60), p. 403.

Hampshire: Combe (a manor of the Abbey of Bec), Hambledon and East Meon (the bishopric of Winchester), and Wootton (St Swithun's Priory). Two Wiltshire manors lay outside the chalklands: Inglesham (Beaulieu Abbey) in the Thames valley and Stratton St Margaret (Merton College Oxford) on the corallian limestone and adjacent claylands. These provide more restricted information and have been supplemented with the two Berkshire manors of Coxwell and Faringdon (Beaulieu Abbey). The percentages show the proportion by volume represented by each crop in output from the demesne and the parish tithe. Harrison's tabulation of the some of the same material based on cash valuation has the effect of increasing the importance of expensive wheat and diminishing the importance of barley and oats.[11]

The importance of peasant and tenant production is shown by the three St Swithun's manors in Wiltshire. Even where the demesnes were large, peasant and tenant production was extremely important. In 1311, the demesne at Alton produced 44 per cent of the total tithe of the parish, and the demesnes of Overton and Enford much less, at 29 per cent and 17 per cent respectively. The remaining production and tithes were not just the work of the peasantry but included the output of sub-manors, as at Enford where the tenants included men of gentry status. The figures remind us that even the greatest landowners were responsible for only a small proportion of total production from the soil. Demesne and parish usually show a similar balance of crops, suggesting that the evidence of the demesne can be taken as representative, providing some welcome reassurance to the agrarian historian. There were, however, significant differences, particularly in the tenants' greater preference for barley (see Table 8.1): at Overton barley represented on average 50.4 per cent of tenant and 31.8 per cent of demesne output in 1307–16. This may reflect different emphases on production for consumption and the market in the demesne and tenant sectors. By contrast, oats were much more important on the demesne lands where they represented about a quarter of production. Thirteenth-century lords had massively expanded their cultivation of thin downland soils, suited to large-scale oats production. However, it is important to emphasise that large-scale demesne oats production was of only minor significance as a part of the total output of tenants and demesne together. At Overton in 1307, for example, oats made up only 7 per cent of the total production of the parish. Here the demesne accounts are misleading.

Cropping patterns can be examined both within Wiltshire and beyond. In Wiltshire the chalkland manors showed some variations, between Alton Priors in the fertile vale of Pewsey with its greater prevalence of wheat, to the more typical demesnes of Overton and Enford with their greater emphasis on barley and to a lesser extent oats. But they also differed sharply between the agrarian regimes of the chalklands and the claylands and mixed soils beyond.[12] At Inglesham, in the Thames valley, wheat and barley made up the two main crops with the latter more important on the tenants' land. As on the chalklands, oats were more important on the demesne. At Stratton St Margaret the accounts only provide a breakdown of crops for the parish as a whole. Wheat was again the most important crop, followed fairly closely by barley and then

11 B. Harrison, 'Field systems and demesne farming on the Wiltshire estates of Saint Swithun's Priory, Winchester', *AHR* 43 (1995), pp. 1–18, table 6.

12 Hare, 'Change and continuity'.

oats, with oats being particularly important. On one large demesne within the parish, that of Stratton and Sevenhampton, the rank order of the crops by output was the same but the dominance of wheat was even greater.

We may now extend our coverage to examine the cropping patterns in the whole area including Wiltshire, Hampshire and Berkshire, although most of the documented manors come from the chalklands. Wheat was usually the main cash crop throughout the area, and made up between 30 and 40 per cent of the tithe grain of the parish (tenant and demesne) as at Overton, Stratton, Great Coxwell (Berkshire), Hambledon and East Meon (in east Hampshire), Wootton and Combe (in north Hampshire). It was more important on the demesnes at Alton and Inglesham, where there are signs of demesne specialisation in wheat, but marginally less important in the chalkland at Enford.

Barley was very important in both the Thames valley and in the Wiltshire chalklands, where it could also be supplemented by bere (winter barley). It was the most important crop at Enford and Overton, and was very important outside the chalkland on the tenant land at Inglesham and Great Coxwell in the Thames valley. Barley together with bere constituted a greater proportion of total output than wheat in the north Hampshire chalklands at Combe and at Wootton. In Stratton barley was usually second, as it was in Alton Priors. In east Hampshire, however, barley was much less important. It was only the third crop at Hambledon (25 per cent) and East Meon (20 per cent), reflecting the greater and traditional predominance on the Hampshire demesnes of wheat and oats combinations.[13] Tenants generally seem to have been more involved in barley and bere production than demesne managers. This was the case at Overton, Enford, Alton (slightly), Inglesham, Great Coxwell and Wootton.

Oats was the least important of the main crops on most of the Wiltshire demesnes and was even less important on the tenant land. Nor does it seem to have been important on the vale manors of Wiltshire and Berkshire as at Alton, Inglesham, and Faringdon, with the exception of Stratton. It was much more important in Hampshire amongst the tithes, but this also reflects the pattern of demesne agriculture there. It was clearly the second tithe crop at Hambledon and East Meon. At Combe and Wootton, it produced at least 25 per cent of the tenant tithes, in contrast to the 10 per cent more general in the Wiltshire chalkland. Rye was a very unusual crop in Wiltshire; the demesne at Bromham was the only documented place where it seems to have been important. It was, however, grown on a significant scale over the Berkshire border at Coxwell, and to a lesser extent at Faringdon. Vetch, peas and beans were relatively unusual, but since they were only grown in small quantities their collection may have been less reliable.

The picture that emerges reflects both environmental and commercial factors. Wheat was generally the main crop and some places showed a particular emphasis or specialisation. Barley was more important in the Wiltshire manors than in those in east Hampshire. This may be because of the greater dominance of high downland settlement in Hampshire or perhaps it corresponds to different marketing strategies

---

13 J. Z. Titow, 'Field crops and their cultivation in Hampshire, 1200–1350, in the light of documentary evidence', unpublished paper in Hampshire RO (Winchester) 97/M97/C1; Hare, 'Bishop and the prior', pp. 194–5.

and less concentrated demand for ale there. Barley was generally more important on tenant holdings than on demesne land. It is not clear whether this was a result of its importance for subsistence or of a greater peasant responsiveness to a growing demand for ale. One of the advantages of barley may have been that it could serve both purposes and allow short-term shifts between consumption and the market, depending on the circumstances. The high proportion of barley on tenant and demesne land at Enford may reflect the demand of the Salisbury market. Oats was pre-eminently a demesne crop in the Wiltshire chalklands and even more so in those of Hampshire. At East Meon and Hambledon this was usually the main crop. Oats would probably be more attractive to a lord faced with a large area of poor soil, cultivated outside the open field, and producing for sale, than to a tenant wondering how to get the best possible returns from a limited space within the open fields.

Downton: its regional and agrarian characteristics

The rest of this chapter focuses on an especially long series of accounts for Downton rectory, spanning seventy years and with an almost complete coverage for a quarter of a century. These accounts also allow comparison with the production on the better-known bishopric of Winchester's demesne at Downton which also has exceptionally good documentation. While it may seem rash to examine one manor in isolation, Downton shows several features that reflect the wider changes taking place in Wiltshire and beyond during this period, and so has some claim to represent broader regional experience. Comparison will also be made with the situation on a few other manors where documentation survives, and in particular the even longer series of tithe returns from East Meon in east Hampshire.

Downton lies to the south of Salisbury. It was one of the great blocks of land given to the church before the Norman Conquest and belonged to the bishop of Winchester.[14] The parish consisted of a series of settlements on both sides of the valley of the Avon linked by the bishop's new town of Downton.[15] East of the valley there were areas of different agriculture on the claylands. Here, some of the fields originated in small-scale enclosures but the bishop had also carried out some large-scale intakes which were later converted to pasture. The parish also saw the desertion or shrinkage of settlements between the late fourteenth century and the early sixteenth century.[16] There are now five deserted settlements in the parish. In addition to receiving tithes from all the settlements, the rector also had his own demesne lands and rents in East Downton.

In 1385 Bishop Wykeham gave the rectory to his new foundation of Winchester College, hence the survival of its tithe returns within the college archives. They cover the years 1384–9, 1401–15, 1420–9 and 1454, and largely relate to the settlements in the rich, wide chalkland valley. In the former woodland settlements, the tithes were

---

14 On Downton, see *VCH Wiltshire*, XI, pp. 19–77 (especially pp. 27–9); J. Z. Titow, Land and population on the bishop of Winchester's estates (unpublished Ph.D. thesis, University of Cambridge, 1962); J. Z. Titow, *English rural society, 1200–1350* (London, 1969), pp. 106–36.

15 For a map see *VCH Wilts*, XI, pp. 20–1.

16 Hare, 'Agriculture and rural settlement', p. 166.

Table 8.2
Parish tithes and demesne crops, 1350–1450

	Parish tithe (percentage of total)					Demesne output (percentage of total)			
	Wheat	*Barley*	*Oats*	*Beans etc.*		*Wheat*	*Barley*	*Oats*	*Beans etc.*
Downton[1]									
1407–12 (6)	15.1	77.5	7.1	-	1407–12 (4)	18	65.8	16.2	-
1424–8 (5)	21.7	60.2	18.1	-	1324–8 (5)	23.4	59.4	17.2	-
East Meon									
1404–14	40.6	30.4	25.5	3.4	1409	46.4	22.0	28.1	3.5
Oakshott and Froxfield (in E. Meon)									
1410–14	32.8	7.6	59.5	0.1	1410–14			no data	
Hambledon									
1381–92	32.8	30.4	25.5	3.4	1407	17.9	55.9	21.5	4.6
1410	31.5	46.1	22.4	-	1410	19.7	59.8	16.0	4.4
1465	61.0	24.3	14.7	-	1465			no data	
Harmondsworth (Middlesex)[2]									
1398	59.0	41.0	-	-	1398	58.5	41.5	-	-
1407	30.8	69.2	-	-	1407	39.9	60.1	-	-

Sources: Downton, WCM rectory accounts, and HRO bishopric pipe rolls. East Meon, Oakshott and Froxfield see Table 8.3. Hambledon, Titow's notes in HRO 97M97C1; M. Page (ed.), *The pipe roll of the bishopric of Winchester 1409–10*, Hampshire Record Series 16 (Winchester, 1999), pp. 281–92; HRO 11M59/B2/22/9 and B1/197. Harmondsworth, WCM 11501, 2 and 4.
Notes:
[1]At Downton the tithes do not include beans and other leguminous crops so that they have been excluded from both the tithe and demesne percentages. The bishopric figures for 1407–12 including these extra items would have been 17.2 (not 18.0), 62.8 (not 65.8) and 15.5 (not 16.2) per cent of the total grain produced.
[2]Harmondsworth. The accounts separate the wheat and barley into the demesne and tithe granges. Oats and pulses were not separated in this way and have been excluded from the tabulated figures. As a percentage of the total grain, oats and pulse made up the following: 1398 1.5% and 4.4%; 3.8% and 9.0%; 0.1% and 5.7%.

sold in sheaves, presumably to the tenant cultivators themselves.[17] Pulses were generally sold in the fields.[18] The Downton evidence provides a rare opportunity to compare the parish production of different types of grain with those on the great estate, in this case that of the bishop of Winchester (see Table 8.2). Here the tithes from the bishopric demesne would have contributed to the parish totals, and this would have reduced any apparent variations between the relative cropping of the parish and the demesne.

The most notable feature of both demesne and tithe output is the exceptional prevalence of barley production. It had grown in importance on the bishop's demesne

17 WCM 5365 and 5380.

18 WCM 5382.

by the beginning of the fifteenth century, reflecting both its increasing national importance, and the particular pressures of the great city of Salisbury.[19] This evidence clearly shows how urban demand could affect the agrarian output of the region surrounding it. As people's standard of living improved, they could afford more expensive ale rather than cheaper, and much more dangerous, water. Ale may have been a necessity in towns. This interpretation is supported by examination of the cropping acreages of other Wiltshire demesnes which show that the highest acreages for barley were to be found in southern Wiltshire in Salisbury's immediate hinterland. Over a third of the sown acreage was given over to barley at Downton, Durrington, Winterborne Stoke, Ebbesbourne Wake, Enford and Fonthill Bishop.[20] With the exception of the last two, all of these were within a ten-mile radius of the city. At Downton, five miles from Salisbury, 44 per cent of the sown acreage of the demesne was under barley in 1410, one of highest percentages yet located in the county at any time in the Middle Ages. Thus the evidence from demesnes near Salisbury fits with that of smaller Cambridge where wheat and barley were generally bought from within a radius of between two and ten miles.[21] This is also seen in Andover, immediately around the town, and in the London area at Harmondsworth (Middlesex).[22]

The tithe evidence from areas near towns suggests that tenants attached even greater importance to barley than did the great lord. At Downton, barley constituted 66 per cent of grain produced on the bishop's demesne, but about 77 per cent for the parish tithes (see Table 8.2). This tenant emphasis on barley is clearly seen on the small parsonage demesne. In some years it grew nothing but barley and a few acres of oats. This was the case in 1366, 1379, 1405, 1406 and 1408, and in the last three years the demesne was given over entirely to barley. There was not such a great difference in the importance of barley on demesne and tenant land in Harmondsworth but barley was the largest single crop in both sectors (see Table 8.2).

This overwhelming dominance of one crop may be exceptional in the immediate vicinity of Salisbury and other urban centres. It was not found at the parsonage demesne of Longbridge Deverill, another chalkland manor much further from the city, where the proportion dedicated to barley was similar to that on manorial demesnes on the chalkland, at about 30–40 per cent.[23] Nor was it found at the chalkland rectories of East Meon and Hambledon (in east Hampshire), where the balance of crop production was again much more even. Producers in East Meon showed no significant

---

19 B. M. S. Campbell, K. C. Bartley and J. P. Power, 'The demesne-farming systems of post-Black Death England: a classification', *AHR* 44 (1996), pp. 133–4; J. A. Galloway, 'London's grain supply: changes in production, distribution and consumption during the fourteenth century', *Franco-British Studies* 20 (1995), pp. 31–2.

20 These figures are for barley alone; using dredge as well would have brought in Heytesbury, Teffont and Alton Priors. See further Hare, *Prospering society*.

21 J. S. Lee, 'Feeding the colleges: Cambridge food and fuel supplies, 1450–1560', *EcHR* 56 (2003), pp. 248–51.

22 WCM 2753, where 30 quarters of wheat and 140 quarters of malt are recorded as sent to Winchester College.

23 I. J. E. Keil, 'Impropriator and benefice in the later middle ages', *Wiltshire Archaeological and Natural History Magazine* 58 (1963), p. 359.

preference for barley, and wheat dominated in the early fifteenth century, with about 45 per cent of demesne output, followed by barley and oats with similar percentages of the tithe produce (Table 8.2). At Hambledon, the three main crops were similar in scale, with a slight preference for wheat.[24] Here the shifts since the fourteenth century seem very limited. Two tithings at East Meon whose tithes were collected separately show a different picture. At Oakshott and Froxfield, little barley was grown but almost 60 per cent of the cropping came from oats. This probably reflects the domination of oats on the poor clay with flint soils which were found on much of the higher downlands, in contrast to the more fertile land around Meon itself.

It is worth noting, however, that even beyond the areas of high urban demand, barley cultivation was sometimes more widespread on tenant land than on the demesne. In East Meon in 1410, 29 per cent of the parish tithe output was in barley, compared with 22 per cent of the produce of the bishop's demesne. Here, in selected years during the period 1350–1441, barley made up 25 per cent of the parish production of grain, and 16 per cent of that of the demesne.[25] Barley was more important amongst the tenants, but the situation was less distorted than at Downton. A similar emphasis on tenant barley production has also been seen in the Midlands.[26] But such an emphasis was not universal and at Hambledon barley was more important on the demesne than on tenant land.

In general, however, the tenants showed even greater sensitivity to the market than did the bishop's demesne managers. Ale was less efficient in its use of calories as a foodstuff, so that conversion to malt would have increased the need for its production, as well as requiring extra employment to convert grain to malt. When the lessee at Urchfont had his rents in kind converted into a cash payment, the barley was assessed at £8, the conversion into malt an additional £1. Both developments and their impact on generating employment and prosperity would be underestimated if we looked only at the records of the demesne.

Downton: changing levels of output

In this final section, trends in total production of grain are examined in Downton parish as a whole (excluding the eastern tithings) over a period of over half a century (see Figure 8.1). This can be usefully compared with similar but longer coverage at East Meon. The Downton figures show interesting developments. Here, as elsewhere on demesne estates in the region, the 1380s seem to be a period of high output, at levels that do not appear to have been reached again. The first two decades of the fifteenth century were periods of relative stability in production, followed by one of dramatic decline in the 1420s, with a fall of about 20 per cent. This is a far cry from the stability found in the north of England on the Durham estates in the same decade.[27] Crucially, however, this fall was not uniform and occurred largely in one crop. In the 1420s,

---

24 Hampshire RO 97M97C1, based on the calculations of J. Z. Titow.

25 E. Miller, 'Tenant farming and tenant farmers: the southern counties', in *AHEW*, III, p. 719.

26 Dyer, 'Farming practice and technique: the west midlands', in *AHEW*, III, p. 229. See also the figures for Leicester Abbey in Hilton, *Economic development*, p. 66.

27 Dodds, 'Estimating arable output', pp. 271 and 275.

Table 8.3
Tithe production at Meon Church, 1348–1436

	Wheat	Barley	Oats	Legumes	Total (qtrs.)
1348–55 (3)	33.2	23.5	29.1	5.0	90.8
1357–61 (3)	46.3	26.8	24.5	6.5	104.0
1363–9 (3)	48.7	30.5	34.3	5.8	119.3
1374–83 (3)	55.6	37.5	33.0	7.0	133.1
1386–94 (3)	63.1	44.2	44.1	5.0	156.4
1404–10 (3)	54.3	50.0	37.7	5.1	147.1
1412–13 (2)	63.5	40.2	38.1	5.0	146.8
1414–15 (2)	67.9	39.7	34.4	6.0	147.9
1420–5 (4)	53.5	29.3	35.1	3.6	121.4
1435–6 (2)	38.6	38.3	31.4	3.8	112.1
1438–42 (3)	10.6	13.9	20.2	2.5	70.8

Source: HRO 11M59/B2/18/1–32; supplemented by B1/137, 140, 144, 161, 166, 168, 169, 170, 171, 172 and 173.
Notes: Tigenhall is excluded 1361–1383, Tigenhall and Langrish are included 1404–28, Ramsdean is included 1414–28. Langrish and Ramsdean are excluded 1435–6, and these and Meon and Coombe from 1438. These may have accounted for much of the fall in the last two rows. The figure for 1389 is exceptionally high compared with any other year (201 qtr 6 bs). The figure for 1386–94 should therefore be treated with caution.

barley production fell to 64.8 per cent of what it had been in the period 1400–15 (see Figure 8.1). Wheat and oats, by contrast, retained their new fifteenth-century level, while the production of the latter even increased in the later 1420s.

The East Meon figures reinforce this picture although under different circumstances (see Table 8.3). Here, parish production showed an unexpected high and steady increase until the late 1380s and early 1390s, with a growth of about 50 per cent since the 1340s and 1350s.[28] Production remained high at the start of the fifteenth century, and then fell in the 1420s. Barley seems to have flourished in the first decade of the fifteenth century as at Hambledon and Harmondsworth. The fall in barley production in the 1420s was also significant. Although it fell by about one quarter, the collapse was less dramatic than at Downton since it was cushioned by the smaller dependence on barley. The year 1423 seems to have been particularly disastrous for barley at East Meon, and to a lesser extent for oats, but not for wheat. It was similarly poor at Downton. There were signs of evident difficulty in barley production at Urchfont too where an assessment of the grain produced was included on the court rolls of the period. Normally the demesne produced more barley than wheat but, in four of the twelve years (1421, 1423, 1426 and 1429) this was reversed.[29]

The collapse of barley production requires explanation. It was evidently not an isolated development in Downton since it also occurred at East Meon and Urchfont. Evidence from the bishop's demesne at Downton suggests that low yields were an important factor. The yields given on the bishopric demesnes initially look healthy but a substantial proportion consisted of grain charged to make up for shortcomings in crop production. In reality yields

28 The scale of this growth is surprising, and is unlikely to be a product of the Black Death. The production was already low in 1348, and the individual years reinforce the picture of the table, of steady growth until the late 1380s.

29 Wiltshire and Swindon RO, 192/20.

seem to have been low on the bishopric estates in 1423, 1426 and 1429. As mentioned above, the decline in barley production was not matched by falling production of other grains. Nor can such a fall be explained by any reduction in the sown acreage, for while the area of barley was reduced, from 70 acres (1407–12) to 61 acres (1424–8), this was nothing like the dramatic drop in barley production. One cause of this dramatic fall in barley production probably lay in difficult weather conditions. The evidence of the bishopric of Winchester accounts from other demesnes suggests that the 1420s saw very dry summers, particularly in the growing season. Above all, however, there seems to have been a series of wet autumns when the harvest was due to be collected.[30] On the estates of Battle Abbey in west Sussex the decade was characterised by excessive rain and poor spring crops.[31]

Partly in response to these difficulties, cultivators reduced their dependence on barley. By the later 1420s, the acreage of barley on the bishop's demesne had been reduced to 87 per cent of its early-fifteenth-century figure, although the acreage of wheat and oats remained constant. Production of barley fell more sharply (to 77 per cent) reflecting the specific difficulties of this crop (see Figure 8.1). Meanwhile, the parsonage demesne shifted from its almost exclusive preoccupation with barley in the first decade of the century and turned to more wheat cultivation. Between 1401–6 and 1424–9, the proportion of the sown acreage under barley fell from 88 to 66 per cent, while wheat rose from 6 to 23 per cent. It was still very much the lesser crop, but the shift had been significant. There was little change in oats.

The consequences of the difficulties of the early fifteenth century could be serious for demesne and tenant producers alike. The tithe receipts show the presence of substantial agrarian difficulties in the countryside in the 1420s, as has also been observed in a group of manors south of Salisbury. At nearby Coombe Bisset, the rent of the demesne was cut by £2 in 1421, and there were reductions in virgate rents. At Downton and Coombe Bisset, the income of the manors was cut, at the latter by 12 per cent between the two decades, and the rent by 14 per cent. These difficulties may have reflected problems in the cloth industry in and around Salisbury. However, the evidence presented above suggests the impact of difficult weather conditions is a more likely explanation for the dramatic changes of the 1420s. Earlier boom-time conditions meant farmers developed dependence on one crop, leaving them extremely vulnerable to particularly difficult weather conditions, since a bad harvest in one crop could not be compensated for by relative success in others. The area was never to recover its former rent levels during the century. North of the city, however, any similar decline was subsequently compensated for by the growth of industry in western Wiltshire. This agrarian crisis may have encouraged the shrinkage and desertion of some of Downton's villages, although Winchester College's building in

---

30 For documentation on weather conditions see J. Z. Titow, 'Le Climat à travers les rôles de comptabilité de l'évêché de Winchester (1350–1458)', *Annales ESC* 25 (1970), pp. 337–40 and 342. See also A. Ogilvie and G. Farmer, 'Documenting the medieval climate' in M. Hulme and E. Barrow (eds), *Climates of the British Isles : present, past and future* (London 1997), p. 128, which notes 1421, 1423 and 1428 as years of severely or very severely wet harvests.

31 P. F. Brandon, 'Late-medieval weather in Sussex and its agricultural significance', *Transactions of the Institute of British Geographers* 54 (1971), pp. 4, 7 and 12.

tenements in the town in the 1440s suggests, recovery in the main settlement at least.[32]

Some conclusions

In many ways the tithe records provide some reassurance to students of demesne agriculture. They do not suggest that there was usually any dramatic difference between demesne and tenant sectors in the crops they grew: the evidence of the tithe records reflects the regional pattern of agriculture established from work on the demesnes. But there were differences between the two sectors in the relative balance of crops and in long-term developments. There was already a greater emphasis on barley production on tenant holdings in early-fourteenth-century Wiltshire. Moreover, the Downton evidence shows how the agriculture of both the lord and, more particularly, the tenant was influenced by the changing demands of the market, in this case Salisbury. It was not merely in the London area that urban demand affected the regional distribution of agrarian activity. At Downton, the parsonage lands seem at one point to have practised a virtual barley monoculture, whose dangers were to be seen in the difficult harvests of the 1420s.

The tithe records have enormous and neglected potential importance. Downton and East Meon, as well as far-off Durham, provide long sequences of figures for total production. These, and the others that must surely exist, have considerable significance in shaping our understanding of total, as opposed to demesne, production. The divergences between the two southern sequences and the important Durham material make research on tithe data series even more necessary. A few rectories also record tithes of lambs and wool, and here again their potential to reach beyond the demesne to the tenant sheep flocks is considerable.[33] Frustrating as these tithe records may sometimes be, they can nevertheless provide us with important insights into the agriculture of the later Middle Ages. They provide the opportunity to go beyond the demesne and make contact with 'a fair feeld ful of folk', and they give insight into the regional and commercial influences that were affecting the changing world of the medieval countryside.

32 For economic trends in Wiltshire, see J. N. Hare, 'Growth and recession in the fifteenth-century economy: the Wiltshire textile industry and the countryside', *EcHR* 52 (1999), pp. 1–26. On the cloth industry in Salisbury, see Hare, *Prospering society*, and A. R. Bridbury, *Medieval English clothmaking: an economic survey* (London, 1982), pp. 74–5.

33 As at Downton, the Deverills and East Meon; Hare, *Prospering society*

Part 3

Land, Lordship and Peasant Communities

Chapter 9

Land and lordship: common themes and regional variations

Richard Britnell

Earlier discussions have already commented on the decline in population in Europe during the half century after the Black Death of 1347–50, which continued in many places well into the fifteenth century. At the local level differences of experience were very marked, if only because people tended to migrate out of some sorts of settlement and into others.[1] But Josiah Cox Russell's broad analysis of European populations, comparing large regional units, concluded that 'the [demographic] effects of the plague were much the same everywhere', and that except in drier areas numbers had fallen by 40 per cent by 1400. Despite recovery in some regions during the fifteenth century, he also concluded that Europe's population did not recover to the level of the early fourteenth century until after 1500. Most historians, as Russell's statement implies, ascribe this demographic recession chiefly to the impact of epidemic disease, particularly the Black Death of 1347–50.[2] It is true that epidemic disease was not the only demonstrable cause of population change. In many regions, at different times, warfare was sufficiently destructive to be considered a major supplementary cause of devastation and raised mortality.[3] But epidemics were so universal and so severe that their impact was both more widespread and more sustained than any other cause of declining population between 1350 and 1450. We shall soon have to examine just how the impact of falling population varied amongst European populations, but for the moment it will be enough to comment on some of the changes most directly attributable to it. It will then be necessary to establish how far that takes us in understanding the rural history of the late medieval period.

---

1 E.g. M.Yates,'Change and continuities in rural society from the later middle ages to the sixteenth century: the contribution of west Berkshire', *EcHR* 52 (1999), pp. 620–1.

2 This cannot be a final explanation, of course, since the severity of the Black Death and the frequency of subsequent epidemics also needs accounting for. See, in particular, M. Baillie, *New light on the Black Death: the cosmic connection* (Stroud, 2006).

3 G. Bois, *The crisis of feudalism: economy and society in eastern Normandy c.1300–1550* (Cambridge, 1984), pp. 316–32 and 335–45; R. Boutruche, *La Crise d'une société. Seigneurs et paysans du Bordelais pendant la Guerre de Cent Ans* (Paris, 1963), pp. 196–9, 213–15, 227–9 and 523–9; F. L. Carsten, *The origins of Prussia* (Oxford, 1954), pp. 101–2; C. Meek, *Lucca, 1369–1400: politics and society in an early renaissance city-state* (Oxford, 1978), pp. 81–105; H. Neveux, 'Déclin et reprise: la fluctuation biséculaire, 1340–1560', in *idem* (ed.), *Histoire de la France rurale, 2: De 1340 à 1789* (Paris, 1975), pp. 57–8; J. Tricard, *Les Campagnes limousines du XIVe au XVIe siècle: originalité et limites d'une reconstruction rurale* (Paris, 1996), pp. 15–35 and 93–6.

Depopulation

People in the mid fourteenth century lived mostly in villages and hamlets. Although the urban proportion varied greatly, as we saw in Chapter 1, it is likely that across Europe as a whole rural population was at least 80 per cent of the total. Even many of the places that historians classify as small towns, because of their occupational structure and marketing functions, were so small, and so dependent upon suppliers and customers from their immediate neighbours, that their urban status is questionable. There were hundreds of thousands of rural settlements across Europe; many were isolated farms and many were hamlets accommodating only a few families. The severe loss of population following the Black Death and later epidemics, especially when exacerbated by war, affected both the average size of settlements and their number.

The shrinking of settlements was the most universal sign of depopulation. In most villages the number of inhabitants and dwellings declined, and the occupied area shrank, although the degree of contraction varied because some locations offered a better livelihood than others. Former house plots are sometimes still identifiable from earthworks on the edge of surviving villages.[4] Not surprisingly, meanwhile, some settlements disappeared altogether, and these constitute another widely observed phenomenon of the late Middle Ages, high on the agenda of medieval archaeological and settlement studies since the publication of seminal texts on the subject in the mid twentieth century.[5] The sites of about 3,000 deserted medieval villages are known in England alone, not counting hamlets and isolated farms. Abel concluded that within the boundaries of the Germany of 1933 about 23 per cent of all settlements (40,000 out of 170,000) were abandoned after 1300, and that such desertions were as characteristic of regions of new settlement in eastern Germany as of the older lands to the west.[6] In Sardinia the proportion of deserted settlements was as high as 50 per cent. As these comments imply, the extent of desertion varied greatly across Europe, in accordance with different local circumstances. Settlements were abandoned because they were disadvantageously situated, as well as on account of inhospitable soils, and were probably most frequent in areas remote from commercial outlets. But even in Tuscany it is estimated that 10 per cent of villages were abandoned during the fourteenth and fifteenth centuries.[7]

Beside deserted villages there were many isolated farms, often created from the wastelands of Europe in the twelfth and thirteenth centuries, whose attractions

---

4 E.g. the English villages of Boarstall, Ogle and Chippenham: M. W. Beresford and J. K. S. St Joseph, *Medieval England: an aerial survey*, 2nd edition (Cambridge, 1979), pp. 109–16.

5 W. Abel, *Die Wüstungen des ausgehenden Mittelalters*, 1st edition (Stuttgart, 1943); 3rd edition (Stuttgart, 1976); M. Beresford, *The lost villages of medieval England* (London, 1954).

6 W. Abel, 'Landwirtschaft, 1350–1500', in H. Aubin and W. Zorn (eds), *Handbuch der deutschen Wirtschafts- und Sozialgeschichte* (2 vols, Stuttgart, 1971), I, p. 302; Carsten, *Origins*, pp. 101–3 and 106–7.

7 C. Klapisch-Zuber and J. Day, 'Villages désertés en Italie. Esquisse', in G. Duby *et al.*, *Villages désertés et histoire économique, XI–XVIII siècles*, École Pratique des Hautes Études, Centre de Recherches Historiques (Paris, 1965), p. 456.

waned as better land became easily available. In parts of Europe, such as Scandinavia, the abandonment of farms gives a more meaningful index of the contraction of settlement than that of villages. In Norway the evidence is dramatic; it is estimated that 56 per cent of all farms were abandoned between 1300 and 1520.[8] Simon Harris, in Chapter 10, supplies a case study relating to land that had been drawn into cultivation during the thirteenth century from the moors of north-eastern England; its abandonment was accompanied by the desertion of farm sites that had been established during the period of colonisation.[9]

Villages that were permanently deserted have a particular archaeological importance, as they permit the excavation and analysis of entire settlements. It is usually only by such research that the chronology of desertion can be established with any reliability. The best known such excavation in Britain has been that of Wharram Percy in the Yorkshire Wolds, where there were about 30 households in 1368, and at least 16 still in 1435. By the end of the fifteenth century there were only four, and those were evicted when their landlord put down the village lands to pasture.[10] The decay of Wharram Percy illustrates a very common feature of larger sites; their depopulation was usually gradual rather than sudden. In some cases, indeed, it is a delicate matter defining just at what point the term 'desertion' is appropriate to a village reduced to one or two households.[11]

Labour costs and landlord enterprise

The shrinkage or desertion of settlements was one of the most predictable consequences of declining population. Another was an improvement in the ratio of land to population. This created at least a potential for higher average standards of living, given that before 1349 productivity levels were checked by land hunger in the more crowded parts of Europe. In parts of Europe, including Britain, wage-earners were amongst the principal beneficiaries. The number of hands available to work the available land declined suddenly and dramatically. Labour shortages seem to have been common in Europe during the period 1350–1450, and created upward pressure on wages, although to very different degrees in different places.[12] In the past those who worked on the lands of others, or engaged in some other by-employment, had characteristically come from families without land enough to feed themselves. The

---

8 J. Sandnes, 'Settlement developments in the late middle ages (*c.* 1300–1540)', in S. Gissel *et al.*, *Desertion and land colonization in the nordic countries, c. 1300–1600* (Stockholm, 1981), pp. 91–5.

9 Chapter 10, pp. 176–7.

10 M. Beresford and J. Hurst, *Wharram Percy: deserted medieval village* (London, 1990), pp. 15 and 27.

11 G. Duby, *Hommes et structures du moyen âge* (Paris, 1973), p. 321; E. Kühlhorn, *Die mittelalterlichen Wüstungen in Südniedersachsen* (4 vols, Bielefeld, 1994–6), I, p. 5. Kühlhorn supplies 416 case studies.

12 D. Farmer, 'Prices and wages, 1350–1500', in *AHEW*, III, pp. 467–83; F. Lütge, 'Das 14./15. Jahrhundert in der Sozial- und Wirtschaftsgeschichte', in *idem*, *Studien zur Sozial- und Wirtschaftsgeschichte* (Stuttgart, 1963), pp. 314–16; E. Perroy, 'Revisions in economic history, XVI: wage labour in France in the later middle ages', *EcHR* 8 (1956), pp. 234–9.

shortage of such workers in England after 1349 was the result not simply of high mortality, but also of the capacity of survivors to manoeuvre themselves into freedom from dependence on wage incomes, either by taking up land inherited from deceased relatives or by actively seeking empty holdings. The rapidity with which abandoned land was reoccupied on many estates after the Black Death is striking testimony to this social transformation.

The rising aspirations of workers prompted a variety of public and private strategies on the part of the employing classes to control them more tightly. Some governments attempted to impose a general wage restraint by legislation. The best researched case is that of England, where new regulations came promptly in the wake of the Black Death in the form of the Ordinance of Labourers of 1348 and the Statute of Labourers of 1350.[13] Across Europe, the aims of labour legislation varied, and were often driven by panic.[14] In France, where the upward pressure on wages was less marked than in England, there was nonetheless an edict of 1351 to control labour, and municipal authorities attempted to regulate wages by means of by-laws. In Castile the cortes of Valladolid enacted measures to control wages in 1351. Other labour policies were pursued by German territorial lords, such as that imposed in Upper Bavaria and the Tyrol by Ludwig von Wittelsbach in 1352.[15] Insofar as they aimed to control wages they did not work as well as their instigators hoped, chiefly because many landlords undermined them. Even in Prussia, where increasingly elaborate wage controls were introduced from 1407 onwards, they were unsuccessful in checking wage increases or alleviating the problem of labour shortage.[16] Landlords had no incentive to maintain a landless class simply for the sake of keeping wages low. They could not individually influence the prevailing wage rate, but they could improve their incomes by taking new tenants onto their land; it was in their individual interests to encourage the uptake of land by poorer families who could supply the right credentials for consideration as good tenants. At the same time, manorial lords who could afford to pay higher wages, because their wage bill was small relative to their total outlay, had a strong incentive to circumvent labour laws to get the labour they needed, and so negotiated wages upwards at the expense of those of their neighbours who were more short of cash.[17]

Labour costs represented a large proportion of the costs of managing larger agricultural units, such as manorial demesnes, and especially of those engaged in

13 R. C. Palmer, *English law in the age of the Black Death, 1348–1381: a transformation of governance and law* (Chapel Hill, 1993), pp. 14–23.

14 S. Coen, 'After the Black Death: labour legislation and attitudes towards labour in late-medieval western Europe', *EcHR* 60 (2007), pp. 457–85.

15 J. Aberth (ed.), *The Black Death: the great mortality of 1348–1350. A brief history with documents* (Boston, Mass., 2005), pp. 89–91; F. Lütge, 'Das 14./15. Jahrhundert in der Sozial- und Wirtschaftsgeschichte', in *idem, Studien zur Sozial- und Wirtschaftsgeschichte* (Stuttgart, 1963), p. 316; E. Miller, 'The economic policies of governments: France and England', in M. M. Postan, E. Rich and E. Miller (eds), *The Cambridge economic history of Europe, III: economic organization and policies in the middle ages* (Cambridge, 1963), p. 322; Perroy, 'Revisions', pp. 234–9.

16 Carsten, *Origins*, pp. 103–4.

17 J. Hatcher, 'England in the aftermath of the Black Death', *PP* 144 (1994), pp. 19–25; L. R. Poos, 'The social context of Statute of Labourers enforcement', *Law and History Review* 1 (1983), pp. 35–7.

extensive crop production. Even pastoral farming, although it attracted more investment to meet a better sustained demand for wool, meat and dairy produce, and was less adversely affected by rising wages, was rarely profitable enough, at least before 1450, to justify the expansion of demesne lands. As a result of steeply rising costs, landlords' profits were squeezed. Over the century following the Black Death the direct management of large estates by their owners went into retreat, and in many cases large units were split up between smaller producers who could manage them with family labour. This tendency has been most spectacularly and consistently represented by evidence from southern and midland England, where the direct management of demesnes had been general practice before the Black Death; the evidence is particularly rich here because of exceptionally good manorial records.[18] But direct management was by no means a peculiarly English phenomenon, and many landlords elsewhere faced similar problems. Direct management followed the same chronological pattern of retreat in France; here it was replaced either by share-cropping or leasehold. In northern Italy, where direct demesne farming was already much reduced by 1350, it continued to shrink to the point of almost disappearing by 1400, and by that time even the lords of demesnes in southern Italy were switching over to leasing their land.[19] The argument against direct management was so strong by the end of the fourteenth century that the French poet Eustache Deschamps put it into verse.[20]

The rentier class of the later Middle Ages included many families and institutions whose wealth was newly acquired. Rising costs of labour did nothing to deter the accumulation of miscellaneous properties by those with money to invest. Land conferred a degree of security and social status that was valued even by men whose principal income derived from other sources. But as the role of landlord enterprise declined, the creation of new fortunes became more commonly a matter of accumulating scattered rents rather than building up working farms. The estates of churches, hospitals and guilds similarly increased as a result of random bequests, gifts and purchases.[21] Such accumulations resulted simply in long rent rolls of scattered properties, as acquisitive buyers, or the fortunate beneficiaries of bequests and donations, interposed themselves as a new level of tenure above those occupying the land. Such was the estate of the Basel merchant Ulrich Meltinger, whose rent book of 1491 records scattered properties mostly within a radius of 15 km. from the city, paying rents in grain, fodder, wine and other products.[22] The geographical incidence of

---

18 Chapter 2, pp. 26–9; C. Dyer, *An age of transition? Economy and society in England in the later middle ages* (Oxford, 2005), pp. 194–210.

19 G. Duby, *Rural economy and country life in the medieval West*, trans. C. Postan (London, 1962), pp. 320–7; P. J. Jones, 'Medieval agrarian society in its prime: Italy', in M. M. Postan (ed.), *Cambridge economic history of Europe, I: the agrarian life of the middle ages*, 2nd edition (Cambridge, 1966), pp. 411–12.

20 Neveux, 'Déclin et reprise', pp. 64–5; M. Bompaire, S. Lebecq and J.-L. Sarrazin, *L'Économie médiévale* (Paris, 1993), pp. 3–62.

21 D. Herlihy, 'Santa Maria Impruneta: a rural commune in the late middle ages', in N. Rubinstein (ed.), *Florentine studies: politics and society in renaissance Florence* (Evanston, 1968), p. 274.

22 D. Rippman, *Bauern und Städter: Stadt-Land Beziehungen im 15. Jahrhundert. Das Beispiel Basel* (Basel, 1990), pp. 192–202.

such new accumulations varied, if only because there were marked variations across Europe in the possibility of making new fortunes from commercial, professional or military activities. They were most common in the more fertile and densely populated parts of the Continent. In the more urban regions, wealthy townsmen with no interest in farming their land in person often invested in rural property that had previously belonged to country families, and leased it out to sub-tenants.[23] This might be because they were too heavily committed to a mercantile or professional career to engage in active agricultural management, or in some circles it might simply reflect an aristocratic commitment to non-involvement in productive or mercantile activity.[24]

Yet the prominence of rentier incomes amongst the wealthy did not mean that all agricultural enterprise passed into the peasant sector. Although high costs tended to discourage the direct management of large, scattered estates, they were often more easily absorbed by compact units managed on the spot, especially if the scheme of farming and marketing was one that avoided heavy inputs of hired labour. Landlords often preferred to maintain their demesnes intact, rather than see them split up into smaller leaseholds. Many such units continued to be worked as single leasehold farms. Not only did many demesne farms survive, but the piecemeal creation of new ones became easier after 1350, because there was more land on the market, and it was often commercially viable. Amalgamation of holdings for the convenience of commercial farming, sometimes organised by rentier landlords with untenanted properties on their hands, sometimes by new purchasers, was a common feature of investment in property.

There were also many parts of Europe where circumstances continued to favour the commercial involvement of major landlords in the processing or disposal of peasant produce. This might be the case in wine-making, for example, since the quality of some products benefited from close supervision.[25] Landlords were also more likely to engage in commerce in regions where long-distance, mercantile trade created greater profit opportunities than production for local markets. There were numerous scenarios here, including some that involved landlords in trading contracts without their being responsible for overseeing production. In Norfolk, for example, the profitability of coastal and overseas trade in grain, particularly barley, induced many landlords to take a large part of their fixed rents in kind; in this way they passed onto tenants the costs of production but accepted the transaction costs involved in bulk marketing.[26] In southern Europe these arrangements were especially characteristic of contractual tenures such as share-cropping or fixed-rent leases. Landlords in parts of France controlled a large share of peasant output through various forms of rent in kind; by contracts of *terrage* (Anjou) or *carpot* (the Bourbonnais) they took a share of their

---

23 G. Cherubini, *Signori, contadini, borghesi: ricerche sulla società italiana del basso medioevo* (Florence, 1974), pp. 79–81.

24 G. Pinto, '"Honour" and "profit": landed property and trade in medieval Siena', in T. Dean and C. Wickham (eds), *City and countryside in late medieval and renaissance Italy: essays presented to Philip Jones* (London, 1990), pp. 88–9.

25 J. C. Brown, *In the shadow of Florence: provincial society in renaissance Pescia* (New York, 1982), pp. 98–9.

26 R. H. Britnell, 'The Pastons and their Norfolk', *AHR* 36 (1988), p. 134.

tenants' crops and wine-making, or by share-cropping contracts they took a half of all their grain.[27] Share-cropping was by far the commonest form of leasing vineyards in the central Rhine valley between Koblenz and Bingen throughout the fourteenth and fifteenth centuries.[28] In much of Tuscany the importance of share-cropping continued to increase at the expense of fixed rents during the fourteenth century, although many fixed rents also required the tenants to surrender goods rather than cash.[29] Such arrangements may look non-commercial, but this would be a mistaken judgement for the period 1350–1450 in most of Europe. Only in very outlying parts, remote from centres of consumption, did rents in kind survive for want of an alternative. In general they survived because they served the interests of landlords who could get a better income by marketing farm produce in bulk than by allowing tenants to market it piecemeal. The resulting systems can be criticised for their tendency to weaken tenant initiative, but their social consequences were more benign than those of landlord enterprise that diverted peasant labour into compulsory work on demesne lands.

Even rents in kind and share-cropping represent a rentier style of management that was very different from the direct farming methods of the thirteenth century, and does not greatly qualify the general proposition that landlords were withdrawing from direct involvement. However, retreat from direct landlord enterprise was not always the most appropriate response to the changing relationship between population and resources. This point has been emphasised by a stimulating debate about historical causation, initiated by an article published in 1976 by Robert Brenner.[30] He emphasised that regional variations in the power and interests of landlords and governments should not be left out of account in explaining social change after the Black Death, and that it is a mistake to assume that the effects of depopulation on landlord enterprise were the same everywhere. Falling population, economic context and institutional inheritance must be complementary parts of any explanation of social change in the later Middle Ages.[31]

---

27 R. Germain, *La France centrale médiévale: pouvoirs, peuplement, société, économie, culture* (Saint-Étienne, 1999), p. 269; M. Le Mené, *Les Campagnes angevines à la fin du moyen âge* (Nantes, 1982), pp. 170–92.

28 O. Volk, *Wirtschaft und Gesellschaft am Mittelrhein vom 12. bis zum 16. Jahrhundert* (Wiesbaden, 1998), p. 164.

29 Cherubini, *Signori, contadini, borghesi*, pp. 80–3; D. Herlihy, *Medieval and renaissance Pistoia: the social history of an Italian town, 1200–1430* (New Haven, 1967), pp. 136–7; Herlihy, 'Santa Maria Impruneta', pp. 273–4; G. Pinto, *La Toscana nel tardo medio evo* (Florence, 1982), pp. 225–46; P. Jones, 'From manor to mezzadria: a Tuscan case-study in the medieval origins of modern agrarian society', in, Rubinstein (ed.), *Florentine studies*, pp. 222–7; L. A. Kotel'nikova, *Mondo contadino e città in Italia dall'XI al XIV secolo* (Bologna, 1975), pp. 289–90. See also Tricard, *Campagnes*, pp. 79–86.

30 R. Brenner, 'Agrarian class structure and economic development in pre-industrial Europe', *PP* 70 (1976), pp. 30–75, reprinted in T. H. Aston and C. H. E. Philpin (eds), *The Brenner debate: agrarian class structure and economic development in pre-industrial Europe* (Cambridge, 1985), pp. 10–63.

31 See, in particular, S. H. Rigby, *English society in the later middle ages* (Basingstoke, 1995), pp. 141–3; *idem*, 'Historical causation: is one thing more important than another', *History* 80 (1995), pp. 227–42.

In some contexts the advantages of producing and marketing in bulk were so great that forms of demesne farming survived and expanded, with adverse consequences for the rural population. In Castile the direct involvement of landlords in agrarian activity increased to take advantage of the growing demand for Spanish wool. Since the thirteenth century wool production had become not only big business but a dominant feature of land use in southern Spain and in the central plateau across which vast sheep flocks migrated annually between summer pastures in the north and winter pastures in the south. From about the 1420s the fine Spanish merino wools were establishing a growing market in Flanders. The complex rights of grazing that this transhumance required were supervised by the Mesta, whose operations by 1447 involved 2.5 million sheep, many of which were owned by the Castilian churchmen and nobility. In the lightly populated lands of the Guadalquivier Valley in Andalusia, where demographic recovery waited until the mid fifteenth century, townsmen and noblemen accommodated the expansion of sheep flocks by usurping control of commons and unoccupied lands, a procedure that met little opposition, and was accompanied by the growth of seigniorial territorial rights. Other parts of Spain differed from most of western Europe because population levels both stabilised and started to recover early, so that already by 1400 it is no longer appropriate to consider them for the effects of declining population. A rising output of grain encouraged a more direct involvement in agriculture by landlords than that characteristic of most of fifteenth-century Europe, and helps to account for the growing power of the Castilian nobility over the land and its occupants through this period.[32]

The growth of demesne farming also characterised some coastal parts of the Baltic region, where the emphasis was upon arable husbandry. The Baltic was a 'poor man's Mediterranean'; although the towns there had developed some regular trade with inland centres, they depended on exporting grain, timber and other goods to more urbanised parts of western Europe.[33] Lübeck, the largest Baltic city, had perhaps 28,000 inhabitants before the Black Death, which made it about equivalent in numbers to Perugia, Mantua, Messina or Naples, but it was alone in this class, and in Italy at least a dozen cities were larger.[34] The population of the rural hinterland was also sparse by the standards of western Europe. Even before the Black Death, the population density in the lands of German occupation east of the River Elbe, as in Poland, averaged below ten people to the square kilometre, which compares with only the most rural areas of western and Mediterranean Europe. Because the opportunities offered by trade through Baltic ports were significantly greater than any offered by local markets, it was advantageous for landlords both to produce grain and to bear the

---

32 Chapter 7, pp. 128–30; E. Cabrera, 'The medieval origins of the great landed estates of the Guadalquivir Valley', *EcHR* 42 (1989), pp. 478–9; J. Munro, 'Spanish *merino* wools and the *nouvelles draperies*: an industrial transformation in the late medieval Low Countries', *EcHR* 58 (2005), pp. 457–61; R. S. Smith, 'Medieval agrarian society in its prime: Spain', in Postan (ed.), *Cambridge economic history of Europe*, I, p. 439; C. Dyer, 'Rural Europe', in C. Allmand (ed.), *The new Cambridge medieval history, VII: c. 1415–c. 1500* (Cambridge, 1998), p. 112; J. Vicens Vives, with J. Nadal Oller, *An economic history of Spain* (Princeton, NJ, 1969), pp. 244–7.

33 M. Małowist, 'The problem of inequality of economic development in Europe in the later middle ages', *EcHR*, 2nd series 19 (1966), pp. 23–4.

34 J. C. Russell, *Medieval regions and their cities* (Newton Abbot, 1972), pp. 39–76 and 106–11.

costs of selling in bulk to merchants. The economic power of landlords was enhanced by the fact that small peasant communities had little organisation to fall back on when their status was threatened.[35] These circumstances may be expected to have produced significant differences in social development from those of western Europe.[36] Even before 1400 landlords in eastern Holstein, unlike those of England, were extending their demesnes by adopting waste peasant holdings, and were able to enforce their seigniorial rights to exact rates in labour rather than in cash.[37] In Brandenburg some landlords were apparently successful in extracting heavier labour services.[38]

These implications of the distinctive combination of resources and opportunities in the Baltic nevertheless remained very localised before 1450, chiefly because the opportunities for expanding long-distance trade were adversely affected by depopulation in western Europe. In 1450 exports of grain consisted mostly of Prussian rye exported through Danzig.[39] Growth of landlord enterprise in eastern Europe was not, and could not be, a general response to the demographic crisis of the fourteenth century. Many features of landlordship there between 1350 and 1450 are reminiscent of what was happening in England or France. In some regions of Prussia demesne farming declined just as in England and France. Direct management of demesne land had been a characteristic of Polish estate management before the Black Death, and here, too, it was being abandoned after 1350.[40] The new rural order in north-eastern Europe, with its accompanying 'second serfdom', spread away from coastal areas and became characteristic of a wider region, only from the later fifteenth century when population growth, and a growing demand for cereals and other Baltic commodities, became more general.[41]

---

35 Brenner, 'Agrarian class structure', in Aston and Philpin (eds), *Brenner Debate*, pp. 42–3; H. Wunder, 'Peasant organization and class conflict in eastern and western Germany', in Aston and Philpin (eds), *Brenner Debate*, p. 94; N. J. G. Pounds, *An historical geography of Europe, 450 BC–AD 1330* (Cambridge, 1973), p. 335.

36 This argument is now associated with Brenner, 'Agrarian class structure', in Aston and Philpin (eds), *Brenner debate*, pp. 40–6. For an earlier version of the argument, see M. M. Postan, 'Economic relations between eastern and western Europe', in G. Barraclough (ed.), *Eastern and western Europe in the middle ages* (London, 1970), pp. 168–74.

37 W. Prange, 'Die Entwicklung der adlingen Eigenwirtschaft in Schleswig-Holstein', in H. Patze (ed.), *Die Grundherrschaft im späten Mittelalter* (2 vols, Sigmaringen, 1983), I, pp. 550–1.

38 Carsten, *Origins*, p. 109.

39 P. Dollinger, *The German Hansa*, trans. D. S. Ault and S. H. Steinberg (London, 1970), p. 232.

40 Carsten, *Origins*, p. 108; R. C. Hoffmann, *Land, liberties and lordship in a late medieval countryside: agrarian structures and change in the duchy of Wrocław* (Philadelphia, 1989), pp. 98–104, 115–23 and 306–18; H. Wunder, 'Serfdom in later medieval and early modern Germany', in T. H. Aston, P. R. Coss, C. Dyer and J. Thirsk (eds), *Social relations and ideas: essays in honour of R. H. Hilton* (Cambridge, 1983), pp. 267–8.

41 Hoffmann, *Land, liberties and lordship*, pp. 352–69; M. M. Postan and J. Hatcher, 'Population and class relations in feudal society', *PP* 78 (1978), p. 27.

Tenant holdings

The improved ratio of land to potential tenants, and the abandonment of demesne land by landlords, both created circumstances in which many peasant farmers, if they wished, could increase their stake in the land. Some of the possible welfare gains for tenants were realised quite widely, not least in Britain, whose late medieval social history is generally written in optimistic terms. Tenant enterprise and income here, as elsewhere, tended to expand relative to that of large aristocratic estates.[42] As among rentier entrepreneurs, the increased availability of land accelerated the development of a land market, and the accumulation of formerly independent tenements, by purchase, lease, or a combination of the two, to increase the average size of holdings.[43] In some more commercialised regions such engrossing of property occurred before the Black Death under the stimulus of commercial incentives, although the fragmentation of former tenures, was probably the more dominant trend so long as population was growing. After the Black Death pressure to fragment tenements was greatly reduced, for obvious reasons, and the possibilities for combining them were much greater. Estates that had once discouraged the dismemberment of traditional tenements, like that of the bishopric of Winchester, became inured to it during the following hundred years.[44] In the Angevin countryside the amalgamation of smallholdings by peasants often allowed the reconstitution of tenements that had earlier become fragmented in the course of earlier population growth.[45]

This process of reorganisation was compatible with all sorts of different outcomes, but commonly there was both a reduction in the proportion of smallholders in village populations and the emergence of peasant elites wealthier than their predecessors. The former can be explained by the search for more secure subsistence amongst the poorer peasantry (since smallholding families were the most vulnerable to unemployment and dearth) and the latter by acquisitiveness among the well-to-do, although such a distinction is inevitably artificial, and draws attention away from the general propensity of villagers of all levels of wealth to better their condition where given the opportunity. This change was not confined to western Europe. It can be shown that in villages of the duchy of Wrocław by 1450, fewer peasants each had appreciably more land than in the fourteenth century as a result of such acquisition, and property was more equally distributed.[46] Such improvement was often achieved through migration rather than by sitting still; the evidence of the bishop of Winchester's estate, discussed by John Mullan in Chapter 11, suggests that already

---

42 Chapter 11, pp. 193–7.

43 Duby, *Rural economy*, pp. 338–40; Neveux, 'Déclin et reprise', pp. 69–70.

44 J. Mullan and R. H. Britnell, *Land and family: the land market on the estates of the bishops of Winchester, 1263–1415* (forthcoming). The peasant land market in England is discussed extensively in two collections of local studies: P. D. A. Harvey (ed.), *The Peasant land market in medieval England* (Oxford, 1984), and R. M. Smith (ed.), *Land, kinship and life-cycle* (Cambridge, 1984). There is also further information in the various contributors' sections titled 'Tenant farming and tenant farmers', in *AHEW* III, pp. 587–743.

45 Le Mené, *Campagnes angevines*, pp. 432–3.

46 Hoffmann, *Land, liberties and lordship*, pp. 298–9.

Table 9.1
The distribution of land in the territory of Chieri (Piedmont) in 1327 and 1437

	Size of holding			
	<2 hectares (% in brackets)	*2–10 hectares (% in brackets)*	*10–100 hectares (% in brackets)*	*>100 hectares (% in brackets)*
1327				
proprietors	1416.0 (66.2)	553.0 (25.9)	165.0 (7.7)	5.0 (0.2)
hectares	1042.3 (11.9)	2344.9 (26.7)	4492.7 (51.2)	891.2 (10.2)
1437				
proprietors	366.0 (36.6)	464.0 (46.4)	157.0 (15.7)	12.0 (1.2)
hectares	350.1 (4.0)	2244.5 (25.7)	3918.6 (44.8)	2228.3 (25.5)

Source: C. Rotelli, *Una campagna medievale: storia agraria del Piemonte fra il 1250 e il 1450* (Turin, 1973), pp. 332 and 335.

well-established families were the most likely to improve their lot by staying in one place and accumulating land, while smallholders were the most likely to move around in search of better properties.[47]

Table 9.1, showing changes in the distribution of land in the territory of Chieri in Piedmont, gives an exceptionally clear demonstration of how a reduction in the number of proprietors could permit a general improvement in the size of holdings. Most of the land recorded in 1327 continued to be occupied (the total was reduced only from 8,771.1 hectares to 8,741.5) but the number of proprietors recorded in a tax assessment of 1437 was less than half the number in 1327 (down from 2,139 to 999). The average landholding had more than doubled from 4.1 to 8.8 hectares. The most striking change was the decline in the number of miniscule holdings of less than two hectares and the growth of the proportion of holdings in each of the larger categories. The figures unambiguously imply that older tenements were being amalgamated; the proportion of the land in holdings of over 100 hectares increased from 10.2 per cent of the total to 25.5 per cent.

To some extent the growth of peasant holdings was accompanied by the more convenient disposition of units of property. In parts of the Tuscan countryside townsmen and urban institutions combined older tenements to multiply the number of small compact farms on which a single family lived, a development already under way by 1350.[48] The resulting units were very varied in size. In areas of land scarcity they might be just adequate for subsistence; the *poderi* of the hospital of San Gallo in Florentine territory averaged only 8.6 acres. But in Sienese territory 55 such *poderi* of the Scala Hospital in Siena whose size is known averaged 26.5 acres, and those of the abbey of Rofeno to the south-east of Siena averaged about 64.2 acres, which implied a wish to attract tenants strongly committed to commercial agriculture.[49] In north western Europe, the greater availability of land similarly encouraged the amalgamation

47 Chapter 11, pp. 193–5.

48 Jones,'From manor to mezzadria', pp. 227–36.

49 Cherubini, *Signori, contadini, borghesi*, pp. 82, 169 and 171–2; S. R. Epstein, *Alle origini della fattoria toscana: l'ospedale della Scala di Siena e le sue terre (metà'200–metà '400)* (Florence, 1986), pp. 110–12 and 121–2; P. Jones, *Economia e società nell'Italia medievale* (Turin, 1980), p. 305; Jones, 'From manor to mezzadria', p. 222.

of adjacent units of cultivation in open fields, although the resulting farms were rarely as compact or detached as Italian *poderi* and frequently remained subject to rights of common pasture. Once created, however, more compact units of tenure were often enclosed with hedges, especially when they were converted from arable to pasture.[50] The profits of enclosure often depended on their occupants' specialising in response to current market opportunities, by concentrating on wool production, for example, or on dairy farming.[51]

Although the average size of holding increased, there was no uniformity of outcome; regional circumstances allowed extensive smallholding to survive in many parts of Europe in spite of a diminished population. Sometimes this was because of particular agricultural specialisations that required high inputs of labour and a high value output per acre. The cultivation of vines, in some upland regions of Mediterranean Europe, served to keep family holdings small even in regions where population densities were low.[52] In some areas, usually more heavily populated, numerous smallholdings survived in conjunction with exceptional opportunities for by-employments. Already by 1350 an existing abundance of smallholders seeking employment had often attracted entrepreneurs looking for a dependable labour force, but the exceptional regional availability of by-employments then served to perpetuate the prevalence of minute holdings between 1350 and 1450. Some of the highest densities of German smallholders were in the Rhineland and Neckar region, where commerce and town-country dependency were particularly advanced.[53] These were the circumstances that encouraged the survival of a mass of smallholders in parts of Piedmont, where textile industries, manufacturing woollens, linen and silk were widely diffused in villages and small towns.[54] In parts of Flanders, too, as in the castellany of Courtrai, a high proportion of smallholders were associated with textile manufacture.[55] Mining for coal and metallic ores, which expanded in parts of Europe during the later fourteenth and fifteenth centuries, also gave rise to numerous pockets of wage dependency that affected patterns of landholding as well as relations between lords and tenants.[56] All such developments drew rural areas into dependence upon distant markets, and meant that they were vulnerable to severe recession if for any reason the demand for their products was interrupted. There was

---

50 C. Dyer, *Lords and peasants in a changing society: the estates of the bishopric of Worcester, 680–1540* (Cambridge, 1980), pp. 250–1, 259–60 and 331–9; R. H. Hilton, *The English peasantry in the later middle ages* (Oxford, 1975), pp. 161–73; G. Sivery, *Structures agraires et vie rurale dans le Hainaut à la fin du moyen-âge* (2 vols, Villeneuve-d'Ascq, 1977–80), I, pp. 119 and 133.

51 Dyer, *Age of transition*, pp. 204–6.

52 Cherubini, *Signori, contadini, borghesi*, p. 101.

53 W. Rösener, *Agrarwirtschaft, Agrarverfassung und ländliche Gesellschaft im Mittelalter*, Enzyklopädie deutscher Geschichte 13 (Munich, 1992), p. 44.

54 R. Comba, *Contadini, signori e mercanti nel Piemonte medievale* (Bari, 1988), pp. 126–30, 149–50 and 156–7.

55 D. Nicholas, *Medieval Flanders* (London, 1992), pp. 257 and 279.

56 F. Lütge, *Deutsche Sozial- und Wirtschaftsgeschichte. Ein Überblick*, 3rd edition (Berlin and Heidelberg, 1966), pp. 264–5; J. U. Nef, 'Mining and metallurgy in medieval civilisation', in M. M. Postan and E. Miller (eds), *The Cambridge economic history of Europe, II: trade and industry in the middle ages*, 2nd edition (Cambridge, 1987), p. 474.

even continuing division of former holdings in parts of Flanders and Brabant.[57]

In England, too, high fertility of the soil and the availability of alternative sources of income sometimes combined to maintain a high proportion of smallholders, as in parts of eastern England; there were many more smallholders in East Anglia, for example, than in Cambridgeshire or most of Lincolnshire away from the fenlands.[58] There is no reason to suppose that these examples argue against a tendency for standards of living to rise, since the survival of smallholding was likely to be accompanied by smaller families dependent on each holding, higher earnings, and easier terms of tenure. In some cases families gave up farming altogether to go into manufacturing or service industries at a time when average real wages were high.

Terms of tenure

Where lords sought to divest themselves of land – both vacant tenant holdings and their own demesne lands – they often had to do so on terms attractive to peasant farmers, to the advantage of those who could take them on. Benefiting from the scarcity of potential competitors, tenants were able to escape inherited roles. The search for better conditions of tenure or employment was not only permitted but even encouraged by the active market in land and labour. The period 1350–1450 was one of exceptional mobility, not only amongst wage-earners seeking employment but also of tenants seeking better conditions.[59]

Despite strenuous attempts to defy the implications of market forces by bullying tenants into maintaining terms of tenure as they had been before the Black Death, rents and services were commonly forced downwards. There were exceptional regions where particular commercial success encouraged a rising demand for land against the wider trend. For example, there was a general increase in rents in Flanders through the later fourteenth and fifteenth centuries, as well as in parts of Brabant before 1435, accompanying an exceptionally vigorous recovery of population.[60] In England during the century after the Black Death rents rose on manors of the duchy of Cornwall situated in tin-mining regions of Cornwall.[61] Sometimes upward movements of rent were brought about by purely monetary causes, as in Scotland between 1366 and 1424.[62] In the absence of inflationary pressures brought about by debasement of

---

57 E. Van Cauwenberghe and H. Van der Wee, 'Productivity, evolution of rents and farm size in the southern Netherlands agriculture from the fourteenth to the seventeenth century', in H. Van der Wee and E. Van Cauwenberghe (eds), *Productivity, land and agricultural innovation in the Low Countries (1250–1800)* (Louvain, 1978) pp. 151–7.

58 R. H. Britnell, 'Tenant farming and farmers: eastern England', in *AHEW*, III, pp. 616–17.

59 J. A. Raftis, *Tenure and mobility: studies in the social history of the medieval English village* (Toronto, 1964), pp. 153–82.

60 Van Cauwenberghe and Van der Wee, 'Productivity', pp. 141–3, but see also M.-J. Tits-Dieuaide, 'Peasant dues in Brabant: the example of the Meldet farm near Tirlemont, 1380–1797', in *ibid.*, pp. 114–16.

61 J. Hatcher, *Rural economy and society in the duchy of Cornwall, 1300–1500* (Cambridge, 1970), pp. 148–59.

62 E. Gemmill and N. Mayhew, *Changing values in medieval Scotland: a study of prices, money, and weights and measures* (Cambridge, 1995), p. 377.

the currency, however, the price of grain was normally sluggish in the face of rising costs in the period 1350–1450, with a correspondingly depressive effect on rents, especially those of arable land, unless there were offsetting considerations.[63] Rent movements depended in part on the extent to which rents were contractual. In Tuscany, where various forms of lease had largely replaced traditional tenures, the 1340s were an early turning-point, when a period of generally increasing rents was succeeded by one when rents fell and terms of tenure became more favourable to tenants.[64] Yet although the chronology of change varied greatly for both institutional and environmental reasons, most parts of Europe had experienced significant reductions of rental values by the mid fifteenth century. Sicilian rents in the first half of the fifteenth century were only two-thirds of what they had been before the Black Death.[65] Rents paid in grain on the estate of the count of Leiningen near Worms fell by 20–47 per cent between 1426 and 1488, and proportionately greater reductions in money rents are recorded from elsewhere in Germany.[66] Rent reductions on the estates of the counts of Namur in Wallonia were particularly severe in the crisis years between 1391–1413 and 1432–9.[67] There were large rent reductions on farms in parts of Scandinavia, especially in Norway, where the incidence of desertion was also exceptionally high.[68] Landlords were often obliged to make concessions to avoid the desertion of tenements. Lowered rents were vital to the restabilising of seigniorial authority in the Limousin in the late fourteenth and early fifteenth centuries, for example.[69]

Sometimes new rent levels were accompanied by other improvements in terms of tenure. Freer tenures, in particular leasehold, became more usual than in the past.[70] In the Norman barony of Neubourg the number of leased properties grew even as their rents fell in the early fifteenth century.[71] In some circumstances villagers negotiated with lords to be communally responsible for the payment of rents and other seigniorial dues.[72] In upper Bavaria special terms of tenure, known as *Ödrecht*, were devised to encourage tenants to lease untenanted holdings, and these were accompanied by

---

63 Duby, *Rural economy*, pp. 303–5 and 327–30.

64 Herlihy, *Medieval and renaissance Pistoia*, pp. 271–3.

65 S. R. Epstein, *An island for itself: economic development and social change in late medieval Sicily* (Cambridge, 1992), p. 325

66 W. Abel, *Geschichte der deutschen Landwirtshaft* (Stuttgart, 1962), p. 123; T. Zotz, 'Zur Grundherrschaft der Grafen von Leiningen: Güterbesitz, bäuerliche Dienste und Marktbeziehungen im 15. Jahrhundert', in Patze (ed.), *Grundherrschaft*, II, p. 199.

67 L. Genicot, *La Crise agricole du bas moyen âge dans le Namurois* (Louvain, 1970), p. 101.

68 S. Gissel, 'Rents and other economic indicators', in *idem et al.*, *Desertion and land colonization*, pp. 159–68.

69 Tricard, *Campagnes*, pp. 66–73.

70 R. H. Britnell, *The commercialisation of English society, 1000–1500*, 2nd edition (Manchester, 1996), pp. 221–2; Neveux, 'Déclin et reprise', pp. 64–6.

71 A. Plaisse, *La Baronnie de Neubourg. Essai d'histoire agraire, économique et sociale* (Paris, 1961), pp. 321–32.

72 J. P. Molénat, 'La Seigneurie rurale en Nouvelle Castille au XVe siècle', in G. Anes, B. Vincent *et al.*, *Congreso de historia rural, siglos XV al XIX* (Madrid, 1984), p. 595.

reductions in the burden of both rents and taxes.[73] The decline of demesne farming meant that in this context, too, the amount of rented land was increasing even as land values fell. This is well known from England, but was a more general phenomenon across Europe; it can be observed, for example, in the mark of Brandenburg in the later fourteenth century or duchy of Wrocław during the fifteenth.[74] Many traditions of leasing included an understood right to renewal by the tenant, and indeed some were formally hereditary. Hereditary leases were general in the vineyards of the central Rhine wine-growing region, accounting for over 90 per cent of leases known from the fifteenth century.[75] In these circumstances a section of the peasantry was liable to benefit from both increased disposable income and greater freedom. This possibility depended, of course, upon the landlord being able to rely upon tenants for the successful commercial management of their property, without which they would not have been able to pay their rents. Such tenants had to be able to manage their farming operations without being deterred by high labour costs. They also had to have access to local marketing opportunities to dispose of surplus produce. It was only because such economic and social conditions were widely met by 1350 that landlords were so strongly motivated to reduce their entrepreneurial role in favour of tenants.

The social changes of the period 1350–1450 universally involved changes in the relationships between landlords and tenants in ways that ran against the traditions of the previous two centuries at least, so it is not surprising that they were frequently accompanied by conflict, and sometimes by violent disturbances. Such conflicts were not new after 1350; the great Flemish peasants' revolt of 1323–8 was outstanding for both its tenacity and its achievements.[76] Nor was the determination of tenants to resist their lords a peculiarity of north-western Europe. In Prussia in 1440–2, the peasants of Warmia (Ermland) opposed attempts to impose additional carriage services and new customs.[77] German historians have counted 44 examples of peasant uprisings between 1336 and 1500, all but one after the Black Death.[78] Likewise, the people of Fuenteorejuna, near Córdoba in Castile, rose up against the lordship of Gómez de Guzmán, a commander of the powerful military order of Calatrava.[79] In the best-known examples of rural revolt, resistance to burdensome customs was accompanied by political unrest as a result of misgovernment. The French Jacquerie of 1358 occurred when it did because of the failure of the king and nobility to resist English invasion and protect the security of their tenants. The English Peasants' Revolt of 1381 would not have happened in the way it did had it not been

---

73 W. Rösener, *Peasants in the middle ages*, trans. A. Stützer (Cambridge, 1992), p. 261.

74 H. Helbig, *Gesellschaft und Wirtschaft der Mark Brandenburg im Mittelalter* (Berlin, 1973), pp. 80–1; Hoffmann, *Land, liberties and lordship*, p. 146.

75 Volk, *Wirtschaft und Gesellschaft*, p. 161.

76 W. H. TeBrake, *A Plague of insurrection: popular politics and peasant revolt in Flanders, 1323–1328* (Philadelphia, 1993).

77 Wunder, 'Peasant organization', pp. 94–5 and 98.

78 P. Bierbrauer, 'Bäuerliche Revolten im alten Reich. Ein Forschungsbericht', in P. Blickle, P. Bierbrauer, R. Blickle and C. Ulbrich, *Aufruhr und Empörung. Studien zum bäuerlichen Widerstand im alten Reich* (Munich, 1980), pp. 26 and 62–4.

79 E. Cabrera and A. Moros, *Fuenteorejuna: la violencia antiseñorial en el siglo XV* (Barcelona, 1991).

for the government's imposition of a national poll tax. There is no space here to analyse these revolts, which have been widely studied by historians.[80] The extent to which they were transformative events, and can be thought of as revolutions, rather than expressions of social tensions that were more usually concealed, is difficult to judge. Their principal importance for long-term development was probably in the formation of attitudes and values rather than in any immediate changes.

Serfdom and community: some English issues

In the English Peasants' Revolt there were many concurrent causes of grievance, but one of the most prominent was the survival of unfree status amongst the peasantry. Serfdom disappeared after 1381 more by a process of attrition than by revolutionary activity.[81] That said, its waning was remarkably speedy, given what was at stake, and testifies to the very widespread determination of customary tenants to escape from the stigma of servility. Regional studies have shown that, as in England, personal serfdom was of diminishing importance during the later Middle Ages in some other parts of Europe, as in the Nivernais, in Berry and in Hainault.[82] The disappearance of serfdom, however, is not easily generalised as a phenomenon of European significance. Particularly in the days when English economic history was regarded as providing a general model of economic development, many writers adopted this as a defining feature of the transition from medieval to modern times as if it had been a universal feature of European social history in this period. It was not. England was outstandingly conservative in the extent to which landlords had clung to customary relationships with tenants; labour services and other servile dues had long been in decline in other parts of Europe.[83]

This is another case where the effects of depopulation have to be understood within the context of given power relationships and given social institutions. Serfdom in England had a distinct institutional form because the common law had imposed a much sharper legal division between free and unfree tenurial and personal status than was characteristic of most of Europe. The English model does not even fit Scotland, where an independent institutional and legal structure had developed by 1300, and where the construction of unfreedom was accordingly quite different. Personal serfdom in Scotland, already greatly diluted by 1300, died out during the fourteenth century.[84] English legal distinctions had encouraged landlords to preserve the labour

80 P. Freedman, 'Rural Society', in M. Jones (ed.), *The new Cambridge medieval history, VI: c.1300–c.1415* (Cambridge, 2000), pp. 95–101, and bibliography pp. 913–20; R. H. Hilton, *Bond men made free: medieval peasant movements and the English rising of 1381* (London, 1973); R. H. Hilton and T. H. Aston (eds), *The English rising of 1381* (Cambridge, 1984); M. Mollat and P. Wolff, *The popular revolutions of the late middle ages* (London, 1973).

81 Britnell, *Commercialisation*, pp. 217–23; R. H. Hilton, *The decline of serfdom in medieval England* (London, 1969).

82 Germain, *La France centrale*, pp. 225–35.

83 Jones, *Economia e società*, pp. 246–7; *idem*, 'From manor to mezzadria', pp. 211–14; Kotel'nikova, *Mondo contadino*, pp. 143–229; Rösener, *Peasants*, pp. 27–8.

84 A. A. M. Duncan, *Scotland: the making of the kingdom* (Edinburgh, 1975), pp. 328–48.

services and other servile personal dues by which villeinage was defined under the law. But as lords found it harder to keep tenants on the old terms after 1349, they were obliged to abandon servile obligations, and the way was open to the gradual renegotiation of customary tenures as leasehold or copyhold. The relative clarity of the distinction between freedom and unfreedom in England meant that as that line started to shift the concept of unfreedom lost practical significance.

The decline of villeinage was of undoubted importance for the development of English society, but even in England it was of indirect significance for the formation of capitalist relationships. A large number of English peasants before the Black Death were free tenants; villeins accounted for perhaps only 59 per cent of peasant households in the east and central Midlands in 1279, and less in the country as a whole since there were significantly fewer villeins in the northern and eastern counties. The proportion had, in any case, already tended to decline all through the thirteenth century.[85]

Similar caution is needed with respect to the contribution of the period 1350–1450 to the weakening of communal and family bonds and the growth of economic individualism among the English peasantry. It is true that, as a result of the fragmentation of many demesnes, and the leasing of others to peasants, the share of peasant farmers in total market supply increased relative to that of manorial lords and their agents. It is true, too, that in some respects the development of the market in villein tenements after the Black Death undermined former family attachments to land and weakened the hold of former village customs. Yet, quite apart from the large and growing number before 1349 of free men who could buy and sell their property at will, some historians attribute a distinctive English individualism even among villeins to much deeper roots.[86] The changes in this respect after 1350 were not without preceding developments in the direction of peasant freedom. Yet when families survived the onslaughts of plague, their attachment to inherited lands was often strong, where they were of good quality.[87]

It is seriously to be doubted, too, whether village communities were in fact greatly weakened in the long term as a result of the freeing of the land market after 1349. The peasant elite that emerged during the course of the period 1350–1450 was likely to exercise a powerful control over village affairs if its members could work together. The experience of Durham Priory estates suggests that a period of exceptional disorder in the later fourteenth century gave way to greater stability under the aegis of such families in the fifteenth century.[88] Responsibility for managing village fields and commons, maintaining the parish church, administering the property of village fraternities, collecting taxes, negotiating with landlords and their servants, handling the business of manorial courts, all implied the need for co-operation among villagers and

---

85 E. Kosminsky, *Studies in the agrarian history of England*, R. H. Hilton (ed.), trans. R. Kisch (Oxford, 1956), p. 206.

86 Notably A. Macfarlane, *The origins of English individualism* (Oxfords, 1978).

87 Z. Razi,'Family, land and the village community in later medieval England', *PP* 93, pp. 16–36.

88 Chapter 12, pp. 205–12.

the disciplining of recalcitrant members.[89] There were restrictions on the possibility of extreme economic individualism among even the larger farmers in such village society.

Leaseholders and yeoman farmers did not make English agriculture precociously individualistic or capitalist in its mode of operations; fifteenth-century agriculture was in many respects less capitalist in its organisation than the structure it superseded.[90] Yet for all that, the changes that occurred were of permanent significance for economic development. The decline of villein tenure and personal status between 1350 and 1450 was never reversed, so that ancient institutional barriers to personal mobility and the transferability of property were permanently weakened. Large leasehold farmers became more prominent in English rural society. The population growth of the sixteenth century started from a distribution of properties and a structure of economic power and property rights very different from those prevailing when population surged in the twelfth and thirteenth centuries, and this is important for explaining why later population growth had effects different from what had gone before.

Chapters 10–12

Of the three chapters in this section, the one by Simon Harris is most directly concerned with the impact of depopulation upon agriculture in a closely specified regional context. He provides a case study of a single area of moorland, in a county where moors were exceptionally extensive in the Middle Ages.[91] Agriculture on Spennymoor had been developed in the later thirteenth century by the villagers of Kirk Merrington, Middlestone, Westerton, Hett, Tudhoe, Whitworth and Sunderland Bridge, to the advantage of the bursar of Durham Priory who received additional money rents as a result. After the Black Death tenants gave up the cultivation of these lands in favour of the core township lands of these villages, and two new farms that had been created from the moor were deserted. This study supplies an unambiguous example of the implications of declining population for cereals output and land use. It also supplies direct evidence that, to some extent at least, land abandoned for cereals cultivation might be converted to use as pasture. Spennymoor also supplies an instance of land whose 'marginal' quality as arable – implied by its late development and early abandonment – had more to do with accessibility and access to markets than with the qualities of the soil.

John Mullan's chapter uses the rich documentation of the estates of the bishopric of Winchester to compare the implications of depopulation for the operation of the

89 W. O. Ault, *Open-field farming in medieval England* (London, 1972); V. Bainbridge, *Gilds in the medieval countryside* (Woodbridge, 1996); Dyer, *Age of transition*, pp. 75–8, 138 and 244–5; C. Dyer,'Taxation and communities in late medieval England', in R. H. Britnell and J. Hatcher(eds), *Progress and problems in medieval England: essays in honour of Edward Miller* (Cambridge, 1996), pp. 168–90; M. K. McIntosh, *Controlling misbehaviour in England, 1370–1600* (Cambridge, 1998).

90 R. H. Britnell,'Commerce and capitalism in late medieval England: problems of description and theory', *Journal of Historical Sociology* 6 (1993), pp. 359–76.

91 H. M. Dunsford and S. J. Harris,'Colonization of the wasteland in County Durham, 1100–1400', *EcHR* 56 (2003), pp. 34–56.

land market in two regions of southern England. His findings underline the importance of past developments as well as of current opportunities for trade and employment. He considers both the lower and upper reaches of the resulting peasant society in the later fourteenth century. Although these new opportunities to accumulate property imply the polarisation of landholding between a peasant elite and the surviving cottagers and smallholders, he points out that the welfare implications of this widening gap are far from obvious. Even though smallholders had little opportunity to accumulate, some regions more than others offered them opportunities for wage-earning. Some migrants may have improved their lot as sub-tenants, or as tenants on other manors. The welfare gains of peasants who accumulated larger holdings are more apparent partly because they were less mobile and more easily followed through our records. Tenants who already had substantial holdings, and who were often leaders of village society, were likely to accumulate properties around what they already possessed, especially if they were lucky enough to survive recurrent epidemics and enjoy a long life.

Peter Larson's paper discusses the period of adaptation to changed structures of property ownership and authority within village communities that followed the Black Death. This period is more commonly analysed as one of greater conflict between landlords and tenants, as lords tried to protect their incomes and restrict the mobility of their tenants.[92] Such conflict was undoubtedly a feature of the period, even on the Durham Priory estates, but comparable adjustments had also to be made within village societies. Larson shows that on the estates of Durham Priory that transition was a painful one, characterised by the breakdown of former social norms and increased violence between villagers. It was resolved only by new structures of authority, chiefly associated with the small groups of wealthy peasants whose emergence was one of the more pervasive features of social change in the English countryside after 1349. Even within the same region, differences of institutional context – differences of estate management in this case – could affect the way in which rural communities adapted to changing circumstances. Village communities remained more robust on the estates of the bishops of Durham than on those of Durham Priory with which they were intermingled.

---

92 E. B. Fryde and N. Fryde, 'Peasant rebellions and peasant discontents', in *AHEW*, III, pp. 744–819; R. H. Hilton, *The English peasantry in the later middle ages* (Oxford, 1975), pp. 54–76; see also P. L. Larson, *Conflict and compromise in the late medieval countryside: lords and peasants in Durham, 1349–1400* (New York, 2006), pp. 77–110.

Chapter 10

Changing land use in a moorland region: Spennymoor in the fourteenth and fifteenth centuries

Simon J. Harris

Driving from Bishop Auckland along the A688 towards Durham the route skirts the south-eastern edge of the limestone escarpment that divides northern and western County Durham from the south-eastern lowlands. The land rises dramatically and is capped by a row of settlements, Westerton, dominated by the eighteenth-century gothic tower built as an astronomical observatory for the mathematician and astronomer Thomas Wright, is clearly visible. So is the larger settlement of Kirk Merrington, formerly known also as Great or East Merrington, dominated as the name suggests by its church, although the medieval one has been rebuilt.[1] While these elements dominate the local landscape, what is less apparent, as the route swings around the northern edge of the escarpment, is that the road follows the approximate boundary of the old enclosed fields of the string of settlements on the escarpment, and that north of this lay what once was the great moor of Spennymoor (see Figure 10.1).[2] Spennymoor as an open tract of wasteland has long gone, its vestiges being enclosed in the eighteenth century, and it is now lost under the decayed industrial settlement to which it has given its name. However, records of its former condition allow us to examine in some detail one of the problems discussed by agrarian historians of the late Middle Ages, namely the extent to which the newly colonised lands of the twelfth and thirteenth centuries were abandoned, or underwent changes of use, during the fourteenth and fifteenth centuries.

Throughout the thirteenth and early-fourteenth centuries the interaction between a growing population and the need for resources to maintain and sustain them had led to a substantial expansion of land under the plough. In the heavily populated Midlands this meant that little land remained to be brought into cultivation by the mid thirteenth century. In northern counties, including Durham, settlement was less dense and substantial new acreages were still being put under crops in the early fourteenth century.[3] Even here, however, this expansion was effectively brought to a close after about 1314. A combination of changing weather conditions, harvest failure and warfare combined to halt the expansion, and to cause some contraction.[4] The arrival

1 N. Pevsner, *The buildings of England: County Durham*, 2nd edition, revised E. Williamson (London, 2000), pp. 345 and 499.

2 The name means 'moor with (or by) a fence or enclosure': A. D. Mills, *A dictionary of English place-names*, corrected edition (Oxford, 1995), p. 304; V. Watts, *A dictionary of County Durham place-names* (Nottingham, 2002), p. 116.

3 H. M. Dunsford and S. J. Harris, 'Colonization of the wasteland in County Durham, 1100–1400', *EcHR* 56 (2003), pp. 34–56.

4 I. Kershaw, 'The great famine and agrarian crisis in England 1315–1322', *PP* 59 (1973), pp. 3–50; B. M. S. Campbell (ed.), *Before the Black Death: studies in the 'crisis' of the early fourteenth century*

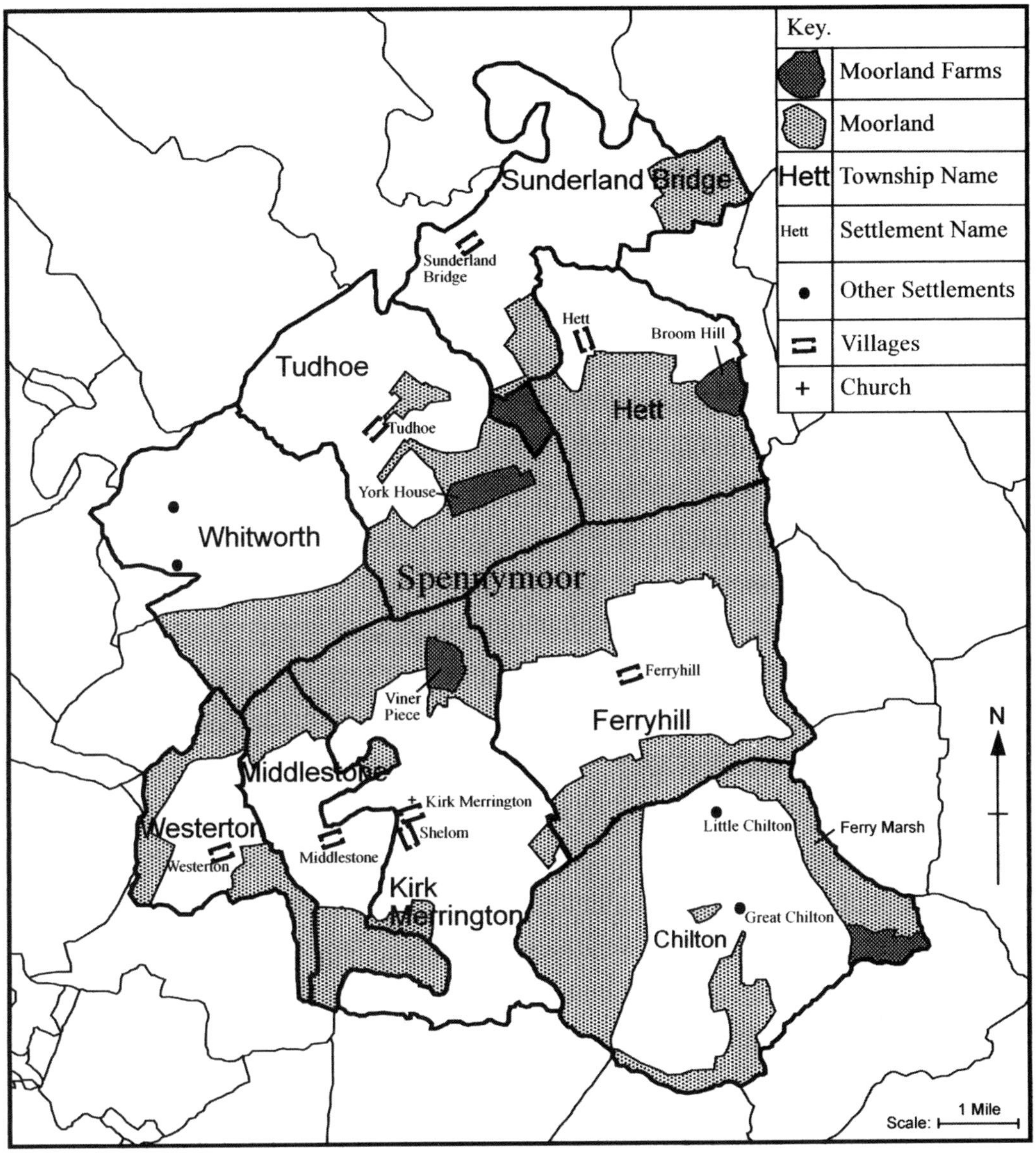

Figure 10.1 Settlements, town lands and moorland farms of the townships around Spennymoor, showing the extent of the moor in the later Middle Ages

Source: The map is based upon the field pattern analysis and moorland maps produced by Dr Helen M. Dunsford, and upon maps of the extent of the town fields of Kirk Merrington produced by Dr E. J. Morrin in *idem*, Merrington: land, landlord and tenants, 1541–1840. A study of the estate of the dean and chapter of Durham (unpublished Ph.D. thesis, University of Durham, 1997).

of the plague in 1349 and the substantial decline of the population that ensued had a great impact throughout England. The initial dislocation is very noticeable in surviving records, and although in many parts of the country there was some temporary demographic and economic recovery in the third quarter of the fourteenth century, recurrences of plague meant that the population effectively stagnated or declined for at least the following hundred years.[5] How much land, and what kind of land, was taken out of cultivation in these circumstances have proved difficult questions to answer. The association of contraction with marginality has been questioned; land abandoned was not always the last to be colonised. In any case, marginality is not to be defined solely by reference to the appropriateness of particular soil types for arable farming.[6] Moreover lords might find that properties could no longer be let for customary rents, and yet be able to find tenants who would take them on negotiated terms.[7] 'Marginal' quality is a topic of particular interest in a region of extensive moorlands such as the medieval palatinate of Durham.

This chapter grows out of a project specifically devised to investigate changing land use in the palatinate of Durham.[8] Some core findings of the project reveal that the extent of the wasteland in the county in the twelfth and thirteenth centuries was far larger than hitherto expected, and stretched from the High Pennines, where substantial moors still survive, right across the county to the eastern seaboard where they have now almost totally vanished. The findings also emphasise the importance of the episcopal estates, in part because of the power of the bishops and their administration, and the size of their estate, but also because of the strong surviving evidence.[9] In a county where so much of the sown acreage in 1300 was recently colonised, the kinds of land that were abandoned, the extent of the abandonment, and the alternative uses to which former arable was put, are questions of particular importance. On the episcopal estate overall, it has been argued elsewhere that the

---

4 *cont.*

(Manchester, 1991); L. R. Poos, *A rural society after the Black Death: Essex 1350–1525* (Cambridge, 1991).

5 J. Hatcher, *Plague, population and the English economy, 1348–1530* (London, 1977), pp. 21–30; R. M. Smith, 'Human resources', in G. Astill and A. Grant (eds), *The countryside of medieval England* (Oxford, 1988), pp. 208–11.

6 M. Bailey, 'The concept of the margin in the medieval English economy', *EcHR*, 2nd series 42 (1989), pp. 1–17.

7 J. Z. Titow, 'Lost rents, vacant holdings and the contraction of peasant cultivation after the Black Death', *AHR* 42 (1994), pp. 97–114.

8 The project was funded by the ESRC and supervised by Richard Britnell and Brian Roberts.

9 Dunsford and Harris, 'Colonization', pp. 34–56. The evidence is principally drawn from the surviving charters of the bishops of Durham, the majority of the pre-1300 charter now being available in editions: H. S. Offler (ed.), *Durham episcopal charters 1071–1152*, Surtees Society 179 (1964); M. G. Snape (ed.), *English episcopal acta 24: Durham 1153–1195* (Oxford, 2002); *idem* (ed.), *English episcopal acta 25: Durham 1196–1237* (Oxford, 2002); and C. M. Fraser (ed.), *Records of Antony Bek, bishop and patriarch 1283–1311*, Surtees Society 162 (1947). In addition two surveys provide invaluable material: W. Greenwell (ed.), *Boldon Buke: a survey of the possessions of the see of Durham*, Surtees Society 25 (Durham, 1852); *idem* (ed.), *Bishop Hatfield's survey: a record of the possessions of the see of Durham*, Surtees Society 32 (1857).

amount of land totally abandoned by tenants was relatively small, and later colonised land was only slightly more likely to be abandoned. Indeed, the estate in the later fourteenth and fifteenth centuries faced a very different problem. Getting tenants to pay their rents was more difficult than keeping tenants on the land.[10]

The early development of Spennymoor can be briefly summarised. At the division of the pre-Conquest patrimony of St Cuthbert with the bishops of Durham in *c.* 1082, the priory received estates at Ferryhill and Merrington (Kirk or East Merrington). Not only did these two estate centres develop, but additional villages were established at Middlestone and Westerton (Middle Merrington and West Merrington respectively), and at Hett; a subsidiary settlement, Shelom, was appended to Kirk Merrington. This meant a substantial increase in the population, probably both by increased fertility and by migration. But it also meant that the new peasant communities in collaboration with the priory brought new lands into cultivation. New fields were drawn from Spennymoor, lying to the north of the Merrington villages and Ferryhill on the lower lands north of the limestone escarpment towards the River Wear, and from other wastes that lay to the south towards Coundon and Old Eldon. This was a characteristically late northern development. Writing in the 1330s, the Durham monk historian Robert de Graystanes, recalling the days of Prior Richard de Hoton (elected in 1290), recorded that 'this prior converted Spennymoor to cultivated land, but at great expense; although the men of Tudhoe and Hett resisted him, claiming common pasture there, the prior contented them all by paying compensation for their grievances'.[11] These events probably date to the 1290s, before Prior Hoton became embroiled in a great dispute with Bishop Antony Bek in 1300.[12] They marked the high point of the priory of Durham's colonisation of the moor, which lay to the north of a concentration of its estates centred on Ferryhill and Kirk Merrington.

The priory had brought only parts of the moor into cultivation; it used other parts to pasture stock. However, later evidence shows that the priory estates, while possessing a pastoral side, were predominantly arable, producing some wheat and barley, but with a marked preference for oats.[13] The priory did not stop at this development; in the later thirteenth century it continued to enclose, buying out the rights of the commoners in Ferry Marsh, which lay along the eastern edge of the township of Ferryhill.[14] But its main efforts were focused on Spennymoor. Prior Hoton, as we have seen, enclosed moorland and bought out the common rights of the tenants of Hett and Tudhoe.[15] Although the priory kept stock at both Kirk Merrington

---

10 S. J. Harris, 'Wastes, the margins and the abandonment of land: the bishop of Durham's estate, 1350–1480', in C. D. Liddy and R. H. Britnell (eds), *North-east England in the later middle ages* (Woodbridge, 2005), pp. 196–219.

11 'Iste Prior Spendingmor redegit in culturam, none sine magnis sumptibus; resistebant enim homines de Tudow, et de Hett, ibi clamantes pasturam communem, sed Prior vexationes redimiens, omnibus satisfecit': J. Raine (ed.), *Historiae Dunelmensis scriptores tres, Gaufridus de Coldingham, Robertus de Graystanes, et Willelmus de Chambre*, Surtees Society 9 (1839), p. 74.

12 C. M. Fraser, *A history of Antony Bek, bishop of Durham, 1283–1311* (Oxford, 1957), pp. 123–75.

13 DCM Loc. IV, fol.146d.

14 DCM 2.12.Spec.17; DCM 4.12.Spec.11, 16 and 18; DCM 1.13.Spec.18.

and Ferryhill, these new enclosures cannot have been entirely for its own several pasture. Some at least were granted to tenants and cultivated as arable. Some of these enclosures, too, remained subject to rights of common. They were thrown open for pasture only once the crop had been harvested, subject to careful measures of control. References to the 'open time' (*tempus apertum*), when fields were made available for livestock, occur in many of the charters relating to Spennymoor.[16]

The era of arable expansion in Spennymoor, as in the rest of Durham, probably ended early in the fourteenth century. Although not ravaged to the same extent as Northumberland or Cumberland, the palatinate was subjected to frequent visits by the Scots during the later years of Edward II's reign. The substantial payments made by the county to buy off raiders could only partly have mitigated the impact of their ravaging.[17] Combined with the bad harvest years of 1315–17, the second and third decades were particularly hard for northern estates and their tenants. The arable enclosures on Spennymoor nevertheless remained well occupied in 1340–1; a rental of that year shows that the priory had tenants there, mostly holding small parcels, owing a total of £24 13s 9½d. In the surviving bursars' accounts from the 1330s the rents of assize from Spennymoor are recorded, and were only slightly higher than this, at about £25 to £26. An initial rental entry of the rental of 1340–1 under the heading 'Spennymore' records two larger properties enclosed from the waste which are described as manors, one later called Yorkhouse (because it had belonged some time before 1341 to Roger of York), and the other an enclosure later known as Moorhouse (probably because it belonged in 1341 to Adam de Mora). Following this, the tenures of peasants from neighbouring vills, not all of which were priory estates, are recorded under seven separate headings: East Merrington [Kirk Merrington] in Spennymoor, Middle Merrington [Middlestone] in Spennymoor, West Merrington [Westerton] in Spennymoor, Hett in Spennymoor, Tudhoe in Spennymoor, Whitworth in Spennymoor, and Sunderland [Sunderland Bridge] in Spennymoor. Under each of these headings is a list of tenants holding small parcels of the moor, the largest being of 30 acres. Tenures more commonly ranged from four to ten acres. No part of the colonised moor is attributed to the nearby townships of Chilton and Ferryhill.[18]

It is at this time that we have the first real opportunity to gauge the extent of the scale of the rented enclosures. The acreage of rents in Spennymoor is summarised in Table 10.1. The two 'manors' on Spennymoor had between them 110 acres of arable. The land attributed to the seven separate adjacent townships 'in Spennymoor' amounted to a further 606.63 acres, presumably Durham acres. This implies a total intake of at least 717.63 acres. It is unfortunately impossible from the rental to estimate the extent of township lands in tenants' hands – those cultivated before the last intakes – in all the adjacent townships, but an attempt is feasible for three of them

---

15 DCM 4.12.Spec.13, 14, 17 and 20; DCM Cart. II, fols 228r–229r.

16 For a good example, see DCM 4.12.Spec.18. This relates to Ferry Moor, probably an extremity of Spennymoor.

17 C. McNamee, *The wars of the Bruces: Scotland, England and Ireland 1306–1328* (East Linton, 1997).

18 R. A. Lomas and A. J. Piper (eds), *Durham Cathedral Priory Rentals, I: Bursars Rentals,* Surtees Society 198 (1986), pp. 62–4. Yorkhouse was the sixty-acre manor of John of Morpeth, formerly occupied by Roger of York. Roger was perhaps its first tenant: *ibid.*, p. 62.

Table 10.1

Arable acres attached to two manors and nine townships around Spennymoor, 1340–1

	Arable in township fields ac.	*Arable 'in Spennymoor' ac.*	*Total ac.*
Two manors	0.00	110.00	110.00
Chilton	159.00	0.00	159.00
Westerton	343.75	139.13	482.88
Middlestone	54.25	67.50	121.75
East Merrington	629.00	54.50	683.50
Ferryhill	728.00	0.00	728.00
Hett	?	106.50	106.50+
Tudhoe	?	54.00	54.00+
Whitworth	?	68.00	68.00+
Sunderland Bridge	?	118.00	118.00+
Total	1914.00	717.63	2631.63+

Source: R. A. Lomas and A. J. Piper (eds), *Durham Cathedral Priory Rentals*, I: *Bursars Rentals*, Surtees Society 198 (1986), pp. 56–60 and 62–4.

Table 10.2

Arable acres attached to two manors and nine townships around Spennymoor, 1396–7

	Arable in township fields ac.	*Arable 'in Spennymoor' ac.*	*Total ac.*
Two manors	0.00	?	?
'in Spennymoor'	-	97.00	97.00
Chilton	160.00	0.00	160.00
Westerton	332.78	66.00	398.78
Middlestone	429.50[1]	(0.00)	429.50
East Merrington	1101.00[2]	(0.00)	1101.00
Ferryhill	977.00[3]	0.00	977.00
Hett	?	(0.00)	?
Tudhoe	?	(0.00)	?
Whitworth	?	(0.00)	?
Sunderland Bridge	?	(0.00)	?
Total	3000.28+	163.00	3163.28+

Source: R. A. Lomas and A. J. Piper (eds), *Durham Cathedral Priory Rentals*, I: *Bursars Rentals*, Surtees Society 198 (1986), pp. 112–19 and 125.

Note:

[1] including 13 acres now recorded under East Merrington

[2] subtracting 37 acres formerly in Ferryhill and Middlestone

[3] including 24 acres now recorded under East Merrington

together with Chilton and Ferryhill. If one takes the recorded acreages for tenanted priory lands at Chilton, the three Merringtons and Ferryhill, this amounts to 1,914 acres. This figure needs to be increased to take account of 36 bondage tenures in Ferryhill, Shelom in East Merrington, and Middlestone that are recorded in later bursars' rentals but not noted in 1340–1 as owing a money rent, probably because at that time they rendered labour services.[19] Since a bondage holding in this region was

19 Ibid., pp. 114, 116 and 118.

enclosures made on the moor that were variously described as manors or granges, although they are best thought of as moorland farms with several arable enclosures. Their tenants had pastured livestock on the moor. The instrument of 1447 records details of tithe rents for Yorkhouse for 1358 and 1361 which imply that grain was still grown there in those years. It also cites a letter addressed to Richard of Chesterfield, rector of Brancepeth, some time between 1363 and 1384, to the effect that thirty years previously Yorkhouse and Moorhouse had been heavily cultivated (*in plenissima cultura*), and that their occupants had then had many ewes and other animals. It then observes that for the last twenty years both properties had been uninhabited and their lands used only as pasture.[28] If a true report, this would push the abandonment of residence and arable farming on both farms to before 1364. The record goes on to say that since Lord Neville, earl of Westmorland, had acquired Tudhoe (in Brancepeth parish), 30 new houses had been added there, that now the arable lands of the village were less than a third of what was required, and that the pastures were also inadequate. As a result the people of Tudhoe needed to lease Yorkhouse and Moorhouse to compensate for the deficiencies of their own townlands. The Neville's reported expansion of an estate village was some achievement in a period when village populations were more likely to be declining, but some caution is needed in interpreting the pleadings of the people of Tudhoe. As we have seen, they had been strongly opposed to the priory's colonisation of Spennymoor in the first place, and considered themselves to have been deprived of common rights there. It seems likely, to judge from what else we know, that their requirements of additional land were overstated. The most impressive part of this testimony is that Moorhouse and Yorkhouse had been abandoned by at least 1363 and that arable husbandry there had collapsed within the space of ten years. That sounds like the immediate aftermath of the Black Death.

The information supplied by the priory rentals is limited but nevertheless helpful in identifying some changes of the later fourteenth century. They imply that the land-hunger of the inhabitants of Tudhoe was a transient one, and that finding tenants for land on Spennymoor in fact became more difficult between 1340–1 and 1396–7. By the latter date the two manors of Moorhouse and Yorkhouse are represented only by a blank entry for 'Morhous in Spenningmor', which implies that no rent was expected. The only separate heading for 'Spenyngmor' in the rental records 97 acres of arable in ten peasant holdings of varying sizes between 2 and 16 acres.[29] These are difficult to relate to tenures recorded in 1340–1. Another 66 acres 'in Spennyngmor' or 'in Spen', in three holdings each of 22 acres, were assigned to three tenants of Westerton among the township lands.[30] This total of 163 acres is seemingly all that remains in the rental of the 717.64 acres recorded in 1340–1. Of course, it may be that lands in

28 Richard of Chesterfield was presented to Brancepeth Rectory in 1363 and had been replaced by 1384: D. S. Boutflower (ed.), *Fasti Dunelmenses*, Surtees Society, 139 (1926); R. Donaldson, Patronage and the Church: a study in the social structure of the secular clergy in the diocese of Durham (1311–1540) (2 vols, unpublished Ph.D. dissertation, University of Edinburgh, 1955), II, p. 52.

29 Lomas and Piper (eds), *Durham Cathedral Priory rentals*, I, p. 125.

30 *Ibid.*, pp. 118–19.

Spennymoor were no longer recorded separately to the extent that they were in the 1340s, so that their importance in the 1390s is understated.

On the other hand, the evidence from 1396–7, little though it can concede to optimism, may itself conceal the true extent of abandonment of land on Spennymoor. The priory maintained a subsidiary set of accounts of waste and decayed rents. Only a few examples of these survive, the earliest being from 1396–7, but the figures show that at this time £17 6s 6d of the rents for Spennymoor were waste out of a sum of £18 18s 10d in the corresponding bursar's account.[31] These perhaps exclude the 8s 6d due from the 66 acres assigned to Westerton in the rental of that year. In the accounts for 1397–8 and 1399–1400, the total of waste rents had fallen back to £14,[32] but by the account for 1404–5 this had reached parity with the sum charged to the bursar's rental of the same date, implying total abandonment, and this was the situation in the remaining waste accounts up until 1436–7, after which the accounting practice changed.[33] From the mid 1390s until at least the late 1430s the Spennymoor enclosures appear to have been effectively abandoned, with only smaller parcels being spasmodically cultivated. The bursars' accounts from 1419–20 to 1425–6 merely hint that the sum charged to the account for rents in Spennymoor 'as appears by the rental' was unlikely to be realised,[34] but more specifically in 1426–7 and 1427–8, the clerk records 'nothing received here from rents of assize from le Spenyngmor because it is waste, but we ought to receive £18 18s 10d'.[35] When rent was received for land in Spennymoor, it seems to have been for isolated years, or runs of years when the priory was able to rent parts of the moor for pasture. Even in 1495–6 rents from Spennymoor totalled only £2 18s. There were four parcels of rented land, one held by a member of the gentry and three by groups of tenants from Hett, Sunderland Bridge and Tudhoe, the latter two vills not being priory estates. The abandonment of Yorkhouse and Moorhouse as compact farms some time in the mid fourteenth century seems to have been permanent, and the subsequent use of their land intermittent. An inventory of 1446 records that various tenants held in Yorkhouse, and in the rent book of 1495–6, and the final bursar's rental of 1539, just before the priory's dissolution, the tenants of Tudhoe leased Yorkhouse. It would seem that the actual farmstead had never been reoccupied.[36]

The abandonment of tenures on Spennymoor implied a reduction there of land under the plough, and this is confirmed by a further strand of evidence from the priory

31 DCM Bursar's Account, Waste 1396–7.

32 DCM Bursars'Accounts, Waste 1397–8 and 1399–1400.

33 DCM Bursars' Accounts, Waste 1404–5, 1406–7, 1418–19, 1426–7, 1427–8, 1428–9, 1429–30, 1431–2, 1432–3, 1433–4, 1434–5, 1435–6 and 1436–7.

34 DCM Bursar's Accounts 1419–20, 1420–1, 1421–2, 1422–3, 1423–4, 1424–5 and 1425–6.

35 DCM Bursar's Account 1426–7.

36 Raine (ed.), *Historiae Dunelmensis scriptores tres*, appendix, p. ccci; W. Greenwell (ed.), *Feodarium Prioratus Dunelmensis: a survey of the estates of the prior and convent of Durham compiled in the fifteenth century, illustrated by the original grants and other evidences*, Surtees Society 58 (1871), pp. 178 and 323; Lomas and Piper (eds), *Durham Cathedral Priory rentals*, I, pp. 182–3. Although the farm does not seem to have been reoccupied in the medieval period, it must have remained identifiable. It was subsequently reoccupied, and still survives today.

archives. The surviving accounts of tithes sold in parishes where the priory had appropriated the church show that the production of grain on Spennymoor fell dramatically immediately after the Black Death. Recovery of cereals output seems to have been swift, so that by the 1360s, the sale of grain tithes was again nearing the estimated level for the 1340s. The letter to Richard of Chesterfield may belong to just this time. But from the late 1370s onwards conditions became less favourable for cereals cultivation. Between 1375 and 1378, and again between 1388 and 1390, Spennymoor was recorded as waste. The arable there had not been wholly abandoned before 1400, for grain tithes were received from Spennymoor in the surviving accounts for 1373, 1383, 1386, 1396, 1397 and 1399. From then on, however, no grain tithes are recorded as collected from Spennymoor.[37]

The evidence of Spennymoor and its surrounding townships implies that, as elsewhere in England, the period 1350–1450 was one of declining arable acreages. The details relating to Spennymoor itself, implying that land there was under crops for so short a period of its recorded history, suggest that it was unattractive in more ways than one. Its abandonment as arable makes much sense. With a much smaller population in the later fourteenth century, retrenchment towards the core lands around the settlements on the escarpment would be attractive. This probably had as much to do with inconvenience of access to the Spennymoor enclosures, and to the limited commercial possibilities for regional specialisation, as to the intrinsic qualities of the moor as arable. In addition, if weather conditions had deteriorated during the course of the fourteenth century, the attractions of the settlements and lands on the escarpment with their freer draining soils are obvious. Spennymoor, lying on the lower lands north of the escarpment, consequently became less attractive for the regular cultivation of arable crops. This seems, then, to be a case of 'last in, first out', the arable that had been inned from the waste only in the late thirteenth century having been very largely abandoned as ploughland within the following hundred years. The Merrington estates in the seventeenth century were largely pastoral, as they are now.[38]

---

37 B. Dodds, Tithe and agrarian output between the Tyne and the Tees, 1350–1450 (unpublished Ph.D. thesis, University of Durham, 2002), appendix 2.

38 E.J. Morrin, Merrington: land,, landlord and tenants, 1541–1840. A study in the estate of the dean and chapter of Durham (unpublished Ph.D. thesis, University of Durham, 1997), pp. 109–10.

Chapter 11

Accumulation and polarisation in two bailiwicks of the Winchester bishopric estates, 1350–1410: regional similarities and contrasts

John Mullan

Amongst the entry and marriage fines in the Winchester pipe roll for 1399–1400 the following record occurs for a land transaction on the manor of East Meon:

> And 106s 8d from Nicola, widow of Thomas Knoller, to retain one messuage and one virgate of villein land in Comb', one toft one garden, 4 acres of villein land called Spyghtes in Meon', 3½ acres of wood in Hyden', 8 acres of old purpresture in Comb', a piece of meadow in M..., one cottage 10 acres of villein land called Budellond in Meon', lately of John Parker', one toft, 2 crofts of villein land containing 8 acres, lately of Richard Couk' and 40 acres from the lord's demesne, in Selescomb' from Thomas Knoller her husband.

This transfer of property on the manor of East Meon in south-east Hampshire, in comparison to the vast majority of transfers of customary land over the course of the latter part of the fourteenth century, is striking. This collection of properties adds up to an impressive whole, certainly on a scale that we might not commonly associate with the lands of the customary tenants of medieval England. We are seeing at least ten apparently separate holdings totalling somewhere in the region of over 100 acres. We know relatively little about the process of how such estates were formed, and an entry such as this raises a number of important questions, the answers to which may facilitate not only a greater appreciation of the peasant land market in this period but also a better understanding of the local structures upon which peasant agriculture rested. It is well known that the accumulation of tenements, and a simultaneously growing polarisation of land occupancy between richer and poorer customary tenants, became more frequent from the late fourteenth century, but we have few explanations for variations in its timing and extent. They are, of course, phenomena to be set against the background of the Black Death and subsequent plagues, of a fall in population, of dereliction, abandonment and the vacancy of properties and of peasants better able to make decisions and strike bargains over tenancies with their lords.[1]

Historians of the medieval peasantry have sought to answer these questions from the evidence of a variety of individual manors, but the pipe rolls of the bishopric of Winchester allow us an unparalleled opportunity to study the nature and process of accumulation with comparative data. They are our chief evidence for the dynamics of the estate's land market.[2] These estates were vast, covering some 60 manors, liberties and boroughs spread across south and south-western England. The section

---

1 Chapter 9, pp. 149–67.

2 The Winchester pipe rolls are housed at Hampshire Record Office, Winchester. For a handlist of reference numbers corresponding to the dates given in the text see R. H. Britnell (ed.), *The Winchester pipe rolls and medieval English society* (Woodbridge, 2003); M. Page, *The medieval bishops of Winchester: estate, archive and administration* (Winchester, 2002), pp.183–7.

within each manorial account that is of particular interest to us is that part known as 'Fines and Marriages', for these record the transfer of lands between peasants and sometimes from lord to peasant in the forms of waste and demesne. The rolls offer a remarkable amount of detail; between 1350 and 1410 there are some 22,000 such transfers distributed over the bishop's manors. The larger manors secure the bigger share of these; in any one typical year a manor such as Bishops Waltham in Hampshire or Farnham in Surrey may record 30 or 40 transactions, while smaller manors such as Culham in Buckinghamshire or Upton in Wiltshire may record one or two, or sometimes none at all.

The different forms of customary holdings available within any one manor necessarily influenced the character of any composite holdings. There was a vast array of types of tenement being transferred and, although not always necessarily easy to determine, between 40 per cent and 50 per cent of these were standard holdings or standard holdings with additional properties. The remainder were smaller plots, messuages, irregular acreages of arable, meadow, pasture, assarts and other small, undifferentiated pieces of land, as well as woods, mills and fish-weirs; many of these were the result of the fragmentation of holdings in the period of land pressure in the years before the Black Death. The larger composite holdings of the late fourteenth and early fifteenth centuries commonly included both standard holdings and accumulations of smaller properties (see Tables 11.1 and 11.2). A typical example is from the manor of Staplegrove, where in 1397 Juliana inherited from her husband, John Gaburdel, a messuage and a virgate with a cottage with curtilage containing one and a half acres, a second cottage with curtilage and two dayworks of overland, and a further two dayworks of overland. It lay in the three tithings of Illebere, Bourland and Nailsbourne.

One advantage of this voluminous data is that we are not restricted by the narrow horizons of a single manor. Rather, the near unbroken series of rolls allows us the opportunity to see the broader picture, to look at regional as well as inter-manorial contrasts, and so to see what was happening to holdings and families over a wide area and a relatively long period of time. This chapter uses this diversity to examine and compare two regions: the manors clustered around Taunton in Somerset and a geographically distant group focused on the manor of East Meon in south-eastern Hampshire. The Taunton set consisted of the manors of Bishops Hull, Holway, Nailsbourne, Staplegrove, Poundisford, Otterford and Rimpton. The East Meon manors were East Meon itself and its associated manor East Meon Church, Fareham, Hambledon and Brockhampton.[3] These are not artificial groupings; in the course of the period under review it became episcopal policy to cluster manors for administrative purposes into regional bailiwicks.[4] Our two groups, therefore, could each be said to have some administrative as well as geographical homogeneity. Our first task is to examine the general characteristics of the customary holdings within these bailiwicks and to look at trends in the accumulation of properties over the course of the later

---

3 The cluster also included Gosport, Alverstoke and Berleigh. They have been excluded as Gosport and Berleigh record no fines over the period, and Alverstoke includes only reliefs for free tenants.

4 J. Z. Titow, Land and population on the bishop of Winchester's estates, 1209–1350 (unpublished PhD thesis, University of Cambridge, 1962), p. 6.

Table 11.1
The largest accumulated holdings in the Taunton bailiwick, 1350–1410

Name (and manor)	*Probable period of activity*	*Description of holding*
William Shaldew (Bishops Hull)	1350–1378	messuage, ½ virgate of overland, cottage, cottage with curtilage containing 1 daywork, 2 acres, 3 cottages with curtilages
Nicholas Chelwardeswood ([a] Holway and [b]) Bishops Hull)	1350–1389	[a] messuage, ½ virgate containing 20 acres, 2 messuages, 2 ferlings containing 20 acres, cottage; [b] 3 ½ acres of overland meadow, 1 acre of overland meadow
Adam Moor (Holway)	? –1391*	messuage, 3 ferlings, 18 ½ acres overland meadow, ploughland containing 4 acres overland, acre, 7 ½ dayworks, 9 feet overland, plot of overland, cottage with plot containing 3 roods, 9 dayworks overland, 6 cottages, plot containing 5 acres, cottage with curtilage containing 2 ½ dayworks overland, 9 acres meadow, 2 ½ acres overland, 9 acres 3 roods overland meadow
William Knight (Staplegrove)	1351–1376	messuage, virgate containing 40 acres, 2 acres overland, messuage, ferling containing 10 acres, cottage with curtilage containing 2 dayworks overland
Robert Stokes (Holway)	1356–1372	messuage, virgate containing 40 acres, messuage, ½ virgate in villeinage containing 20 acres, 3 acres overland, 4 dayworks overland meadow, cottage with curtilage, 1 acre overland
Richard Spiring (Bishops Hull)	1350	messuage, ½ virgate, cottage with curtilage containing daywork overland, cottage with curtilage containing 2 dayworks, 1 acre meadow, 1 acre meadow
John Gaburdel (Staplegrove)	1360–1410	messuage, virgate, cottage with curtilage containing 1½ acres, cottage with curtilage, 2 dayworks overland, 2 acres overland
Walter Hatherich (Poundisford)	1391–1409	messuage, ½ virgate, 10 acres overland, cottage with curtilage containing 1 acre overland, cottage with curtilage containing 7 dayworks overland, 3 roods meadow
Richard Mode (Holway)	1351–1362	messuage, 3 ferlings, pasture for 8 beasts, 8 acres overland, 8 acres overland meadow, 2 acres overland meadow, ½ acre
Adam Marsh (Nailsbourne)	1352–1403	messuage, ½ virgate, 1½ acre meadow, messuage, ½ virgate
Adam Culling (Nailsbourne)	–1403*	messuage, ½ virgate, ferling, 7 acres overland, 2 acres overland, 2 acres overland
John Monk (Holway)	1351–1403	messuage, ½ virgate, messuage, virgate, 3 acres, 2 acres overland meadow, 1 acre overland
John Pound (Holway)	1361*	cottage with curtilage containing 2 dayworks overland, cottage containing 1½ dayworks overland, cottage with curtilage containing 1 rood 2 dayworks overland, 3 acres overland, 3 acres overland, 1 acre overland
John Sweet (Holway)	1350–1362	10 acres overland, cottage with curtilage containing 3 ½ acres overland, 1 acre overland, 3 roods meadow overland, 1 acre overland, cottage with curtilage containing 1 daywork overland

Note: An asterisk denotes that there is some difficulty tracing the formation of the holding, usually because of the existence of more than one family with the same surname.

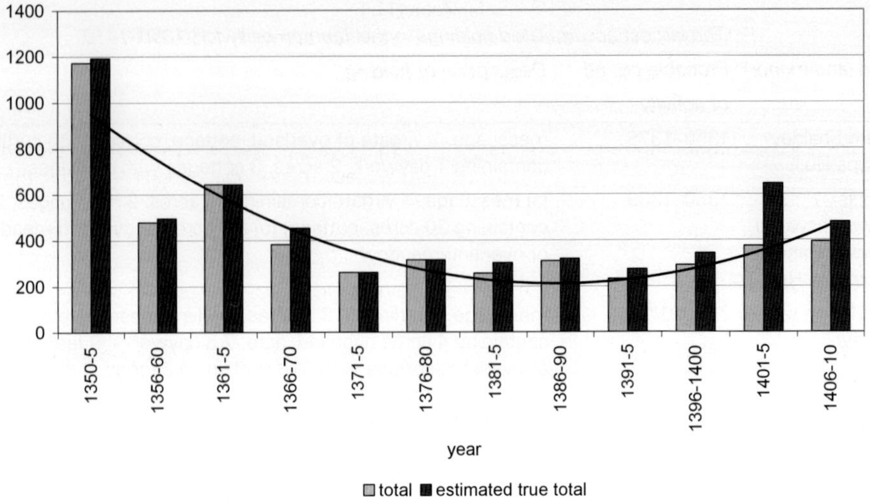

Figure 11.1 Number of land transactions on the Taunton manors, 1350–1410

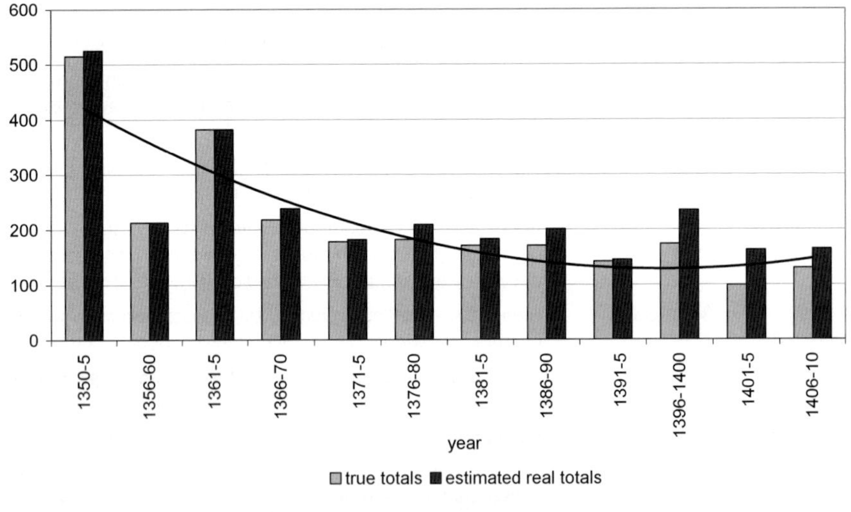

Figure 11.2 Number of land transactions in the East Meon bailiwick, 1350–1410

fourteenth century. We shall then examine some of the patterns and methods in which some of the larger composite holdings were brought together. A comparison between the two bailiwicks reveals that they have much in common, although there were some differences arising from past patterns of development or new developments after the Black Death.

The transactions to be analysed were not evenly spread over time, for both bailiwicks witnessed a massive surge in transfers immediately after the Black Death with a comparable rise following the great pestilence of 1361–2. A decline in the volume of transfers in the later fourteenth century was brought about by a fall in population, the abandonment of land, and also possibly by the accumulation of holdings. A perceptible rise in the number of transfers is again apparent at the turn of the century, more vigorously on the Taunton manors than in East Meon bailiwick.

Table 11.2
The largest accumulated holdings in East Meon bailiwick, 1350–1410

Name (and manor)	*Probable period of activity*	*Description of holding*
Thomas Knoller [a]East Meon and [b]East Meon Church)	1350–1400	[a] messuage, virgate, toft, garden, 4 acres, 3 ½ acres wood, 8 acres purpresture, piece of meadow, cottage, 10 acres, toft, 2 crofts containing 8 acres, 40 acres demesne; [b] cottage with curtilage, purpresture, 4 acres, 3 acres, cottage with curtilage, cottage, 10 acres
Thomas Molin (Brockhamton)	1363–1391	messuage, virgate, 10 acres, cottage, piece containing 1 acre
John Sole (East Meon)	1352[?]–1401	messuage, virgate, toft, virgate, water-mill with 2 acres purpresture
John Neng (East Meon)	1354–1393	2 messuages, 2 virgates, grange containing 8 acres purpresture…[ms damaged}
John Roger (East Meon)	1366–1377[?]	messuage, virgate in villeinage, toft containing 8 acres, 9 acres wood purpresture, cottage and 2 acres purpresture
Alice, mother of Richard Pewel (Hambledon)	–1410*	messuage, virgate, cottage, 4 acres, cottage with curtilage, messuage, 10 acres, 2 acres purpresture
John Forcombe (East Meon)	1349–1384	messuage, 2 virgates, water-mill, 9 acres
William Hook (East Meon)	1350–1364	messuage, virgate, toft, virgate, croft containing 1 acre, 1 acre, cottage, croft containing ½ acre
Henry Napier (Brockhampton)	1351–1395	messuage, ½ virgate, messuage, ½ virgate, cottage with curtilage containing ½ acre
John and Emma Burton (Brockhampton)	1362–1390	messuage, 2 ½ virgates in villeinage, messuage, 2 virgates in villeinage, messuage, 3 half acres, cottage with curtilage, toft with curtilage, 1 acre, shop, purpresture
Thomas Gust (Brockhampton)	–1384	messuage, virgate, 3 crofts, 2 crofts containing 4 acres, 3 crofts containing 24ac.
Walter Mayle	1357–1410 (Fareham)	messuage, ½ virgate, messuage, 8 acres, toft, ½ virgate, toft, ½ virgate
William Oxshutte (Fareham)	1410	messuage, ½ virgate, croft containing 8 ½ acres purpresture, toft with curtilage containing ½ acre, cottage with curtilage, 2 tofts containing 4 acres
John Langrissh (East Meon)	1383–1399	cottage with curtilage, 4 acres, toft, 10 acres, grove, 2 crofts containing 24 acres
John Cous (East Meon)	1352–96[?]	cottage with curtilage containing 1 acre, 5 acres purpresture, toft with curtilage, 10 acres in villeinage, toft with curtilage, 10 acres in villeinage

Note: An asterisk denotes that there is some difficulty tracing the formation of the holding, usually because of the existence of more than one family with the same surname.

Figures 11.1 and 11.2 show these developments; they estimate totals for years when rolls are missing (1381, 1391, 1398, 1404, 1405 and 1408) by adopting the preceding year's total. The same procedure has been adopted in the case of destroyed or illegible accounts of individual manors.[5] It is against this picture that we must view tenurial accumulations.

The most obvious difference between the two bailiwicks was one of scale. The Taunton group was the larger of the two and it witnessed far more transactions of all types of customary land over the period. Between 1350 and 1410 there were 5,109 transfers of property, the largest number of these were on Holway manor, although Poundisford and Staplegrove were not far behind. There were about half the number (2,575) in the East Meon bailiwick, with East Meon itself easily taking the larger share.

On the conservative estates of the bishop of Winchester standardised customary holdings, either whole or fragmented, remained strongly in evidence. The central position of the messuage and virgate in the lands of Thomas Knoller, our prime example of tenant accumulation, suggests that the standard holding was the core around which other, smaller, pieces were gathered. The virgate and its sub-divisions were standard units in both the bailiwicks under review, but there were differences in the nature of the virgate whose origins were ancient. The virgate on the Taunton manors was generally a standard 40 acres, so the half virgate and quarter virgate were regularly 20 and 10 acres respectively. By contrast, there was considerable variation in the acreage of virgates in the East Meon bailiwick; although Fareham and Brockhampton were consistent with virgates of 32 and 20 acres respectively, on other manors in the bailiwick we find a range of sizes of virgate, ranging between 16 and 60 acres. The acre in the Hampshire manors may have been considerably smaller than in Somerset.[6]

A more significant difference between the two bailiwicks resulted from the higher degree of land hunger in the more westerly group during the past hundred years or more. On the Taunton manors the fragmentation of standard holdings had proceeded farther by the mid fourteenth century; the half virgate and the ferling, or quarter virgate, were common, whilst the whole virgate was relatively unusual. The small manor of Rimpton, with a correspondingly small number of transfers, stands apart within this group, for here transfers of virgates, half virgates and quarter virgates constituted 46.5 per cent of all transactions, suggesting a more conservative market. In the East Meon group, by contrast, the complete virgate was predominant, with few half virgates and very few quarter virgates. There were also some two-virgate holdings. The prevalence of the virgate was particularly characteristic of East Meon itself and its associated manor of East Meon Church, in both of which the quarter virgate was entirely absent, in name at least. At Fareham, Hambledon and Brockhampton, virgate and half-virgate holdings took up a smaller share of the market, and a correspondingly higher share of transactions was in cottages, tofts and crofts. As a result of these differences, the full virgate was more frequently the core unit of accumulated property in East Meon than in the Taunton group, whereas accumulating half or quarter virgates

---

5 East Meon: 1355 and 1387; East Meon Church: 1394; Brockhampton, 1367; Fareham: 1375, 1401 and 1406; Hambledon: 1384; Nailsbourne: 1352, 1360, 1369 and 1388; Holway: 1369; Poundisford; 1369; Staplegrove: 1359.

6 A. E. Levett, *The Black Death on the estates of the see of Winchester* (Oxford, 1916), p. 69.

Table 11.3
Standard holdings with engrossments in the Taunton bailiwick, 1350–1410

	Virgate			*Half virgate*			*Quarter virgate*		
year	*T*	*A*	*A%*	*T*	*A*	*A%*	*T*	*A*	*A%*
1350–55	17	6	35.3	121	45	37.2	151	45	29.8
1356–60	4	2	50.0	29	14	48.3	56	26	46.4
1361–65	11	4	36.4	69	38	55.1	87	28	32.2
1366–70	4	1	25.0	19	10	52.6	31	7	22.6
1371–75	7	4	57.0	32	18	56.3	32	11	34.4
1376–80	3	2	66.7	28	8	28.6	41	15	36.6
1381–85	4	1	25.0	19	7	36.9	26	12	46.2
1386–90	1	1	100.0	15	9	60.0	14	7	50.0
1391–95	10	3	30.0	23	9	39.1	12	3	25.0
1396–1400	6	3	50.0	28	11	39.3	28	11	39.3
1401–05	5	2	40.0	29	14	48.3	30	16	53.3
1406–10	5	3	60.0	32	12	37.5	22	8	36.4

Note: T = total numbers of virgates, half virgates and quarter virgates repsectively; A = number in each category that was augmented; A% = A as a percentage of T.

were more numerous in the latter than in the former. In fact, in the East Meon bailiwick accumulating quarter virgates were very few (see Tables 11.3 and 11.4).

In both bailiwicks the enormous number of cottages transferred (nearly 26 per cent of all transfers in East Meon and 19 per cent in Taunton) meant that they formed the most active part of the market. We shall return to their significance in the growth of composite holdings later in this chapter. Their large numbers suggests that they too should be regarded as a standard unit of tenure.

The character of the accumulation of customary holdings

Even a casual glance at the lists of transferred properties in our two bailiwicks from 1350 onwards show many similarities between the two. We have so far presupposed that once an individual had accumulated different properties the resulting agglomeration formed a new farming unit. But on examination the appearance of many of these new holdings is decidedly lacking in any perceptible single identity. The parcels of which they were made up were often scattered. In 1390 Emma Burton inherited from her husband John an estate consisting of three messuages, 4½ virgates, three half acres, a cottage with curtilage, a toft with a curtilage and acre of land, and a shop, lying in at least four separate locations. Moreover, the evidence also suggests that the separate parts often retained the names of former tenants. The Burton's half virgate was called 'Mourhous' and one of the virgates was called 'Rayes', both of which lay in the township of Hailing. The first of these was acquired in 1363 from the lord, to whom it had escheated when Joan widow of Adam Moor died without kin. The Rayes virgate was acquired under the same conditions and in the same year from one John Ray. Yet, thirty years later the association of the former family names persisted. The virgates never became known as 'Burtons'. Other examples of this phenomenon can be readily found. John Cous' unusual composite estate of 1396 in East Meon made up solely of cottages and tofts had within it a toft and ten acres of villein land called 'Chepman' in the township of Oxenbourne. This can

Table 11.4.
Standard holdings with engrossments in the East Meon bailiwick, 1350–1410

	Virgate			Half virgate			Quarter virgate		
year	*T*	*A*	*A%*	*T*	*A*	*A%*	*T*	*A*	*A%*
1350–55	80	15	18.8	71	3	4.2	26	5	19.2
1356–60	16	3	18.8	30	8	26.7	2	0	0
1361–65	65	22	33.8	41	8	19.5	5	0	0
1366–70	30	15	50.0	22	3	13.6	4	0	0
1371–75	17	5	29.4	22	2	9.1	7	5	71.4
1376–80	18	8	44.4	20	6	30.0	3	1	33.3
1381–85	19	13	68.4	14	6	42.8	3	1	33.3
1386–90	22	4	18.8	18	6	33.4	4	2	50.0
1391–95	24	11	45.8	12	6	50.0	0	0	0
1396–1400	34	12	35.3	14	4	28.5	4	0	0
1401–05	21	10	47.6	10	3	30.0	2	0	0
1406–10	30	8	26.6	14	4	28.5	0	0	0

Note: T = total numbers of virgates, half virgates and quarter virgates repsectively; A = number in each category that was augmented; A% = A as a percentage of T.

be traced back to Richard Chapman's surrender of the land more than thirty years before in 1365. The other toft in the estate was called 'Hugheslond', again suggesting a persistent identification with a former tenant. Complex composite holdings, even in the early fifteenth century, continued to be viewed as a combination of parts with separate origins and associations rather than as a unified whole. The large composite holdings surrendered by William Oxshutte to his son William in Fareham in 1410 contained within it a croft known as 'Kaytescroft'.[7]

The absence of any necessary consolidation of property is demonstrated in both bailiwicks by the fact that some of these wealthy peasants also had tenurial horizons beyond the manor. Thomas Molin of Brockhampton, who died in about 1390, left property stretching over three tithings. Although it has been difficult to trace all individuals' enterprises within the Taunton bailiwick, it is very likely that at least three from a list of 14 had interests in properties in other manors of the bailiwick. John Gaburdel of Staplegrove, for example, also held a further set of four properties in Nailsbourne manor, mostly of one or two acres but one of a messuage and 25 acres in villeinage and 10 acres of overland. Similarly, an examination of a list of 15 selected

7 M. Page (ed.), *The pipe roll of the bishopric of Winchester, 1409–10* (Winchester, 1999), p. 296.

names across the East Meon bailiwick shows that in two instances there is evidence of these successful tenants holding in more than one manor. John Hardescombe of East Meon may be the same as held a cottage in Hambledon some years before, and John Rogers may be the man who held some additional small property in Fareham. The evidence from the East Meon bailiwick is less conclusive than that from the Taunton bailiwick, but this may be explained by the fact that East Meon manor, where many of the largest accumulations were taking place, was some distance from the rest of the bailiwick manors; it does not necessarily signify any real difference in the operations of accumulating tenants. Although composite holdings were usually not unified and consolidated farms, accumulators were often concerned to improve their portfolio of properties. Ambitious tenants made large numbers of acquisitions by surrendering an existing tenure, which suggests that they were keen to secure the best lands.

The accumulation of customary holdings had been a relatively uncommon feature of the Winchester estate before the Black Death, and the records prior to 1348 reveal that manor courts had made some attempt to prevent it.[8] Nevertheless, the availability of other types of holding allowed peasant accumulation to proceed farther in the Taunton bailiwick than in the East Meon bailiwick before 1349, despite higher land values in the former. After the Black Death, however, the East Meon bailiwick rapidly caught up. By dividing the whole period 1350–1410 into five year sub-divisions it has been possible to separate solitary full, half and quarter virgates from those augmented by other properties (see Tables 11.3 and 11.4, and Figures 11.3–11.7). In both bailiwicks, augmented virgates and half virgates increased their share of the total market. In the Taunton group, despite an overall fall in the number of land transactions over the period, the percentage of full virgates with added lands, albeit with a number of peaks and troughs, reveals a slight upward trend (Figure 11.3). This is also true of the quarter virgate. A trend for the half virgate is not immediately apparent by simple counting of accumulated holdings, although there was a peak in the later 1380s (see Figures 11.4 and 11.5). In the East Meon group the full virgate, a much larger part of the market than at Taunton, shows a more marked trend towards an increasing proportion of accumulations between 1350 and 1385 (Figures 11.6 and 11.7). Messuages with half virgates in the East Meon group were also increasingly augmented. In both bailiwicks depopulation had released properties for acquisition by accumulating peasants, but this happened more rapidly in the East Meon bailiwick than in Taunton. It seems that more rapid accumulation in the Taunton bailiwick before 1348–9 was a feature of high demand for land in the context of secure commercial opportunity, whereas in East Meon after that date it was more the result of an excess supply of land and the consequently greater ease with which property could be obtained.

Polarisation: the fortunes of cottagers

The emergence of the tenurially enriched peasantry in the last few decades of the fourteenth century is clearly detectable in both the Taunton and the East Meon

---

8 See the report on ESRC Award no R000236499 (The Peasant Land Market in Southern England, 1260–1350), which is available searching on the ESRC website.

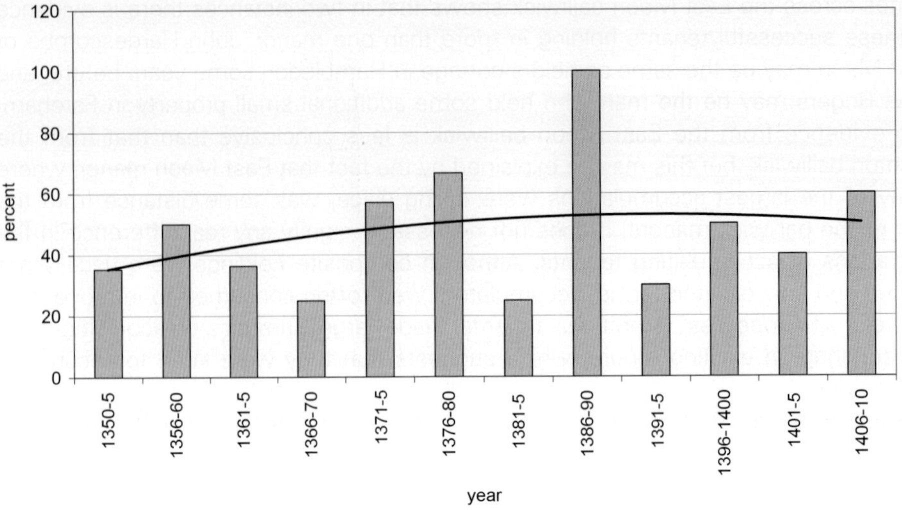

Figure 11.3 Percentage of augmented virgates on the Taunton manors, 1350–1410

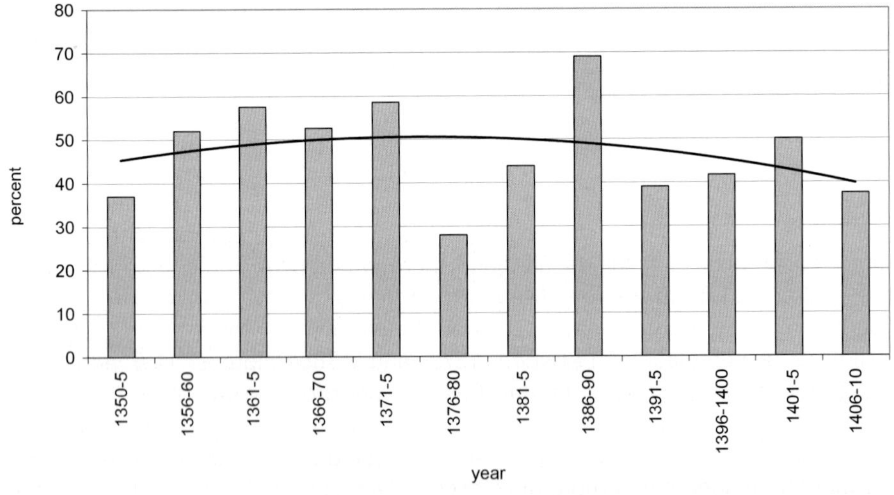

Figure 11.4 Percentage of augmented half virgates on the Taunton manors, 1350–1410

bailiwicks. Do we see a corresponding tenurial impoverishment of the poorer or less able peasant that has been detected by Hilton and several others elsewhere? Certainly both quarter virgates and cottages showed a weaker propensity to accumulate than the larger standard holdings. A huge number of cottages were transferred in both bailiwicks over the period, often simply described as 'one cottage', but often, too, 'one cottage with a curtilage containing one acre of purpresture' or 'one cottage with curtilage containing in all half an acre'. Entries such as these would seem to indicate that a small holding was standard and unadorned with later accumulations, at least in the more recent past. Many others are ambiguous and may or may not indicate the addition of other lands to the cottager's basic holding. 'One cottage with a curtilage and five acres of villein land', for example, is common, but whether the five acres

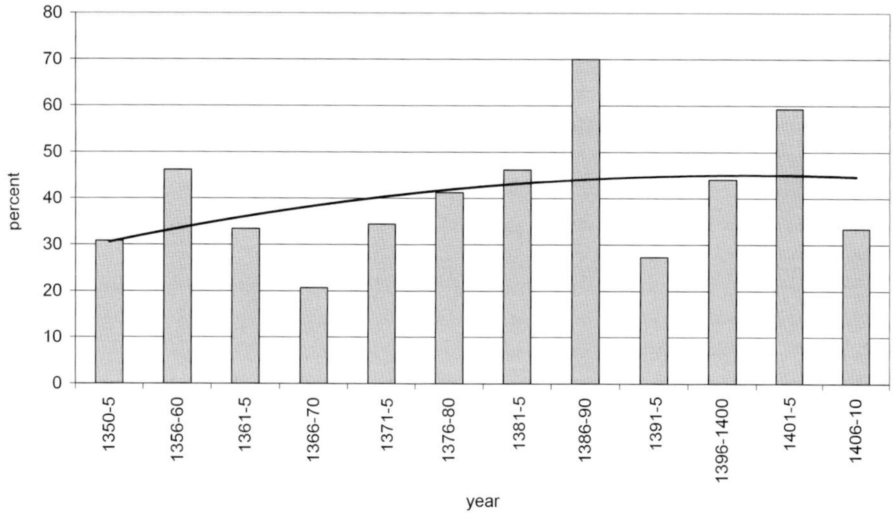

Figure 11.5 Percentage of augmented quarter virgates on the Taunton manors, 1350–1410

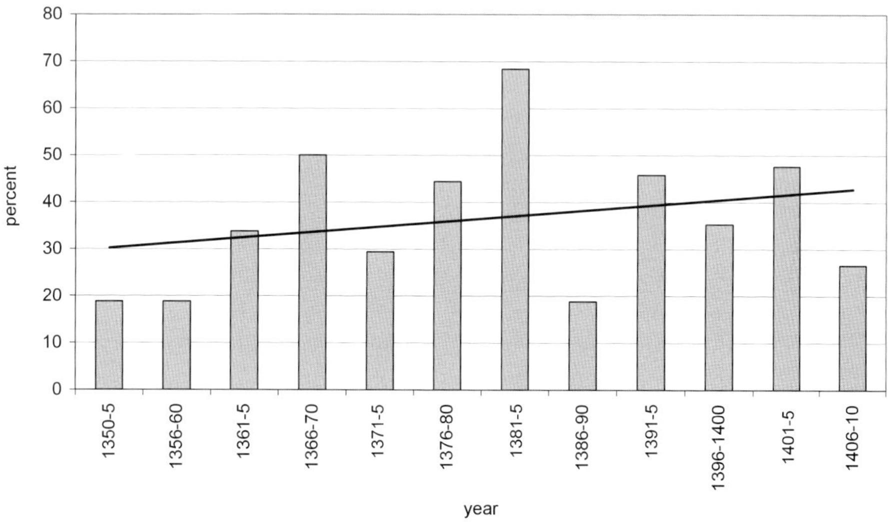

Figure 11.6 Percentage of augmented virgates in the East Meon bailiwick, 1350–1410

were an engrossment beyond the standard holding is not clear. We are also faced with the difficulty of how to interpret the comparatively small number of two-cottage holdings and whether they are, in some way, standard. Thirty-nine of these occur in the Taunton group. The abbreviated Latin does not allow us to know whether they had more than one curtilage. Two-cottage holdings are usually described as 'containing' some additional property, such as 'two cottages containing three dayworks of overland'. This would incline one to interpret these holdings as standard single units of tenure, as both cottages are seen to be intimately involved in the same piece of land. The difficulty of distinguishing between standard units and those augmented with additional lands is further complicated, particularly in the Taunton bailiwick, by the presence of tenurial units ('dayworks' and 'overland') unique to the bishopric estate.

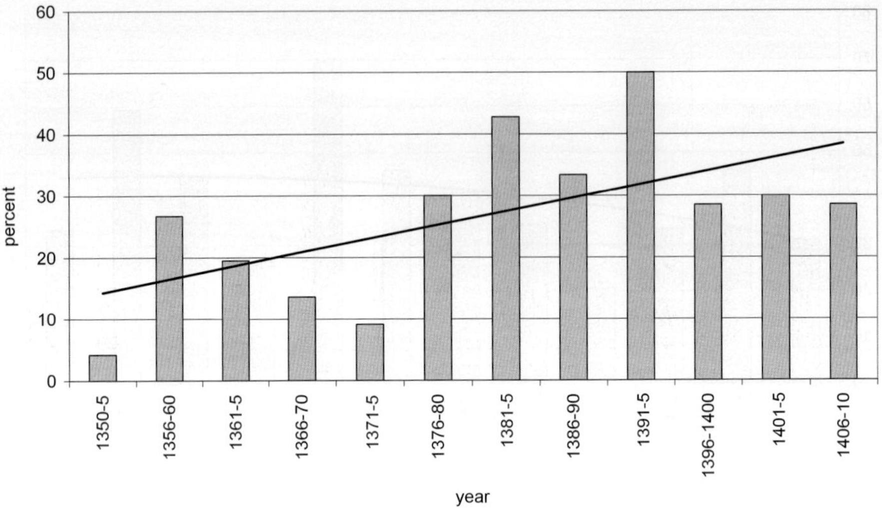

Figure 11.7 Percentage of augmented half virgates in the East Meon bailiwick, 1350–1410

We read, for example, of a cottage with curtilage containing three roods of villein land and three dayworks of overland. It could well be that the overland was a 'traditional' appendage to the cottage, but equally could represent an encroachment into the lord's waste.

In other instances, though, the description of a property suggests more distinctly the accumulation of more than one holding. On the manor of East Meon Church, for example, we read of a transaction in 1396 of 'one cottage with a curtilage and one toft and ten acres of villein land'. Such transactions at least allow us an estimate of cottages with accumulations. It is abundantly clear that in both bailiwicks lands additional to a cottage were, in almost every instance, very small in scale, acres, half acres, roods, dayworks and plots. In the Taunton group between 1350 and 1379 there were some 832 transfers of single cottages, of which only 50 could be said to have fairly distinct additions. Between 1380 and 1410 only 356 cottages were transferred, and of these only 31 had engrossed other lands. It was in turn a tiny fraction of these either before or after 1380 whose total accumulation comprised three or more constituent parts, and none lay in more than one tithing. The only example of a cottage transferred with three or more components was at Holway in 1391; it was conveyed with 'a plot containing three roods, nine dayworks overland of villein land, six cottages, a plot of villein land containing five acres'. The evidence thus indicates quite clearly that it was extremely rare for the cottagers to engross other properties. In the few instances where they did so the additional lands were usually very small.

In both bailiwicks, too, family attachments to cottages and other smallholdings were significantly weaker than those to larger units of tenure. On the manor of Nailsbourne, by way of example, we find that 95 cottages were transferred between 1350 and 1410. From the record of these transfers we are able to extract the names of 85 outgoing tenants; in the other 10 cases either the new tenant was taking up a vacant holding or the name is illegible. Only 19 of these 85 tenants reappear in later records as fining for any sort of holding, and the length of time between some of these repeated names reduces the likelihood that they were the same person. For

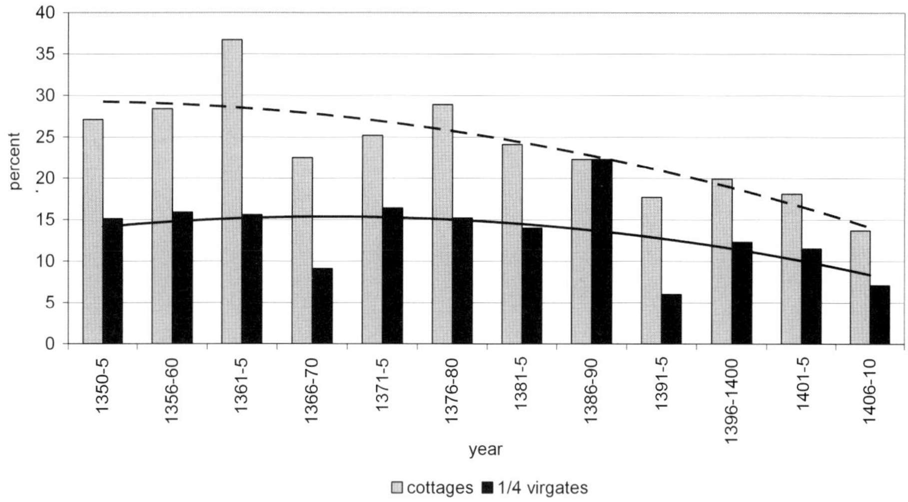

Figure 11.8 Transfer of cottages and quarter virgates (ferlings) as a percentage of total transfers: Taunton bailiwick

example, William Brite left his cottage in Nailsbourne in 1361; we next hear of a William Brite as an incoming tenant in 1409. It is hardly likely to be the same man; more probably the first of these Williams died in the plague of 1361–2. Nearly three-quarters of cottage transfers were by surrender to people outside the family; only about a quarter were *post mortem* transfers. In two examples we are specifically told that a tenant had abandoned the cottage and refused to hold it any longer. In one of these instances, at Nailsbourne in 1371, the incoming tenant was compelled to take on the tenement (*ad hoc compulsus*). Of the 28 cottages that changed hands by *post mortem* transfers, 10 had escheated to the lord because, as the text puts it, 'no one of the kin cared to fine although a proclamation was made according to the custom of the manor'; most of these examples were from before 1380. This stands in contrast to the half virgates, where of the 43 relinquished on the manor, only 14 went outside the family except by marriage. Only one of these was as a result of a refusal by the previous tenant, and only three (all between 1350 and 1362) escheated to the lord because no one of the kin cared to fine. Augmented half virgates were even more likely than unaugmented ones which remained in family hands.

Meanwhile on the manor of Hambledon in Hampshire 91 individuals whose names can be recovered left a cottage holding in the period. Of those transferred outside the family following a tenant's death, about 12 escheated to the lord because no one of the kin cared to fine and 38 were surrendered to be taken up by another family. Of the 91 names of cottagers whose cottages were transferred, only 8 appear in the rolls again within a time period likely to imply a reference to the same person. In contrast, of the names abstracted for fining for virgate holdings in Hambledon, 12 out of 37 reappear at a later date fining for other holdings, and some of the others were women who perhaps cannot be traced later because they married. These were the more active players in the market whilst at the same time the tenure of their virgate holdings was more stable; half of all transfers were intrafamilial. Only 13 per cent were transferred *inter vivos* outside the family, as against 42 per cent of transferred cottages.

There are nevertheless contrasts between the two bailiwicks that merit consideration. Between 1350 and 1410 in the Taunton bailiwick there was a proportional reduction in the number of cottages and quarter virgates transferred, whether with additional holding or not (see Figure 11.8). Perhaps cottages and ferlings were being absorbed into the engrossments of the virgaters and half virgaters, especially after 1380. Cottage holdings in the East Meon bailiwick present us with a contrast, for cottagers here displayed greater capacity to survive through the period with none of the proportional fall off in the number of transfers seen in the Taunton manors. The percentage of transfers of cottages year by year remains remarkably stable. The near complete incapacity of the cottager to accumulate would nevertheless even here seem to suggest polarisation between richer and poorer households.

This evidence strongly suggests some general polarisation of property ownership, with a growing gap between the tenures of mere cottagers and those of the higher echelons of peasantry. This would strongly support Hilton's model of a growing polarisation of property ownership between richer and poorer peasants.[9] However, the different experience of cottagers between the two bailiwicks has implications for the relative welfare of different groups within village society that are difficult to assess. Some of the abandonment of cottages, especially between 1380 and 1410, belongs to periods of high mortality when the number of independent households was probably falling, and in these circumstances it can have had little direct relevance to the material welfare of their former owners. It seems unlikely, though, that differences in mortality among cottagers between the two bailiwicks was great enough to explain the evident difference between them in the demand for cottages. This is more likely to be explicable in terms of new employment opportunities for wage-earners. To the extent that poor families were able to migrate to secure good employment in towns, or in other villages – a common feature of the later fourteenth and early fifteenth centuries – the abandonment of their cottages was an indication of rising, rather than falling prosperity.[10] There may have been a greater abandonment of cottages on the Taunton manors because this was a region where the urban industry was creating an exceptional amount of new employment. Taunton was one of the towns whose ranking rose through the fourteenth and fifteenth centuries, and whose population showed a positive increase between 1377 and 1525.[11]

Some of the cottages accumulated by wealthier tenants engaged in arable farming on extended acreages were perhaps used as tied cottages for attracting workers, by a process of increasing dependence whose implications for welfare are ambiguous.[12]

---

9 Hilton, *Economic development*, pp. 94–105.

10 J. A. Raftis, *Tenure and mobility: studies in the social history of the medieval English village* (Toronto, 1964), p. 153.

11 A. Dyer, 'Ranking lists of medieval English towns', in D. M. Palliser (ed.), *The Cambridge urban history of Britain, I: 600–1540* (Cambridge, 2000), pp. 755–7, 759 and 762; A. Dyer, '"Urban decline"', in England. 1377–1525', in T. R. Slater (ed.), *Towns in decline, AD 100–1600* (Aldershot, 2000), p. 278. See also E. M. Carus-Wilson, *The expansion of Exeter at the close of the middle ages* (Exeter, 1963), pp. 19–22.

12 H. S. A. Fox, 'Servants, cottagers and tied cottages during the later middle ages: towards a regional dimension', *Rural History* 6 (1995), pp. 125–54.

But again, it needs to be remembered that this was a period when labour was scarce and wages were generally rising. A farm worker in 1410 was likely to be earning significantly more regularly, and at a better wage rate, than his predecessor before 1349, and was likely to be able to maximise his earnings by occasional moves from cottage to cottage, depending on where there was good employment to be had. It is difficult to be sure that in years of labour scarcity a wage-earning family's acceptance of a tied cottage would represent a decrease in its welfare.

The greater disappearance of cottagers from the record in the Taunton bailiwick is therefore probably less an indicator of insecurity amongst poorer villagers than evidence of improved terms of employment. Given the divergence between (generally lower) grain prices and (generally higher) wage rates between 1375 and 1410 it is likely that the welfare gap between wage-earning cottagers and arable-dependent virgaters and half-virgaters was in fact narrowing rather than widening.

The process of accumulation

We now need to turn our attention to the actual process of accumulation to attempt to understand a little further the manner in which properties were collected and by whom. To find common threads it is appropriate that we focus on a selection of the largest from each bailiwick. For this purpose the 14 properties in the Taunton bailiwick and 15 of comparable extent from the East Meon bailiwick listed in Tables 11.1 and 11.2 have been selected as a study sample. Despite the contrasts we have commented on so far, the similarities between accumulators in the two bailiwicks prove to be much greater than any differences.

In the first instance it is worth repeating that not all of these larger holdings were first formed in the later fourteenth century. A few of those in existence in the post-Black Death period were of more ancient origin. Page has noted earlier examples as a characteristic feature of the manor of Bishop's Waltham.[13] The Forcombe holding in East Meon, for example, consisting of a messuage and two virgates, a water-mill and nine acres, which was inherited by Agnes, widow of John Forcombe, in 1384, and then by her son in 1386, can be traced back to a similar holding in 1308. Similarly, the messuage and virgate, toft and virgate, mill-site and a moor of two acres inherited by Edith the widow of William Sole can be traced back to a like holding in 1328. But instances such as these are relatively unusual; the mills included in these two instances might suggest that the holdings were anciently organised around the running of the mill and were not built up by a process of accumulation. In the main, like that of the Knoller holdings, the formation of larger accumulated estates, in general, can be seen to be happening from the mid fourteenth century onwards. The Black Death and the second great pestilence of 1361–2 are central to accounting for this phenomenon. Some of the most significant steps towards the creation of these large composite holdings took place within a short time of the plagues of 1348–9 and 1361–2. These were moments when inheritance as a form of land transfer became temporarily dominant. Although *post mortem* transfers do not feature as largely as

13 Page, 'The peasant land market on the estate of the bishopric of Winchester before the Black Death', in Britnell (ed.), *Winchester pipe rolls*, p. 72.

Table 11.5
Transfer of augmented virgates inside and outside the family in the Taunton bailiwick

	Total	*By inheritance*	*By intrafamilial transfer*	*%*	*By marriage transfer post mortem*	*%*	*By extrafamilial transfer inter vivos*	*By extrafamilial*	*%*
Before 1380	17	9	1	5	3	18	1	3	24
After 1380	16	8	3	69	2	13	1	2	19
			Family: 64%					Non-family: 21%	

Table 11.6
Transfer of augmented half virgates inside and outside the family in the Taunton bailiwick

	Total	*By inheritance*	*By intrafamilial transfer*	*%*	*By marriage*	*%*	*By extrafamilial transfer post mortem*	*By the extrafamilial transfer inter vivos*	*%*
Before 1380	149	77	6	56	36	24	5	31	24
After 1380	88	35	10	51	13	15	2	26	32
			Family: 54%					Non-family: 28%	

inter vivos transfers in the overall development of larger holdings, they were, perhaps, often critical in their early formation. Nonetheless, it is no accident that Thomas Knoller was able to secure a significant multiple holding by transfer *inter vivos* in 1362.

Larger holdings were often made possible by inheritance from deceased relatives, and this inevitably allowed well-established families a better chance to accumulate than others. In the East Meon bailiwick the surnames of the tenants of about half of the selected group of 15 accumulated holdings can be traced back to the later thirteenth century, and it is probable that at least some of these can be seen a lot earlier.[14] Only four family names are not attested before the Black Death. The accumulators, then, were mostly from long-settled local families. We are able to trace the name of Knoller on the manor of East Meon back to the late thirteenth century and the family, or at least branches of it, also had interests in the neighbouring manor of East Meon Church.[15] Such established families were more likely to have larger holdings, more likely than cottagers and smallholders to feel committed to family property, and more likely to retain what they had and add to it.

If we look at the Taunton evidence from the fourteenth century the majority of virgates with additional holdings both before and after 1380 were transferred by inheritance; marriage and non-family transfers formed a comparatively small proportion (see Table 11.5). With the much larger number of augmented half virgates a similar pattern emerges (see Table 11.6). The transfer of these properties within families was compatible with frequent transfers of the same parcels of land by marriage and inheritance. For example, Juliana, widow of John Rogers, inherited her

14 E.g. Langrish, Knoller, Sole, Napier, Oxshutte, Rogers, Hook and Mayle.

15 The name Knoller has a locational derivative 'by the hill', but whether the name came from outside as migrants or whether it is associated with a particular hill in East Meon is unknown.

multiple tenancies in East Meon in 1362 from her husband, who perhaps died in the second great pestilence. By 1366 she too had died and the property passed to her son John, who added to it further. In the later 1370s it passed in turn to Agnes, John's widow. By the end of that decade Agnes married John Reynold who acquired the property intact. It had passed through six hands in fifteen years. A further instance is that of Christine, daughter of William Hook who, again, inherited her father's extensive holding at East Meon in 1364, in the same year she married Adam Radesole with the complete holding. Joan Sole became an attractive heiress in 1350, when she inherited from her mother, Matilda, two messuages and 1½ virgates, a water-mill and two acres on the manor of East Meon. Two years later, with the complete estate still intact, she married John Wood, who in turn continued to add to the holding.

Better established tenants also, of course, had the added advantage that they were more likely than others to be able to pay large entry fines, which gave them a better chance both of securing inherited lands and of acquiring land by transfer *inter vivos*. In this latter case, of course, the fine was additional to the purchase price paid to the vendor. Thomas Knoller paid a total of £15 10s 4d in fines in East Meon over the course of his career. Some of these fines were levied at between £1 and £2 in addition to the more usual fines of a few shillings and pence. The average fine in the East Meon bailiwick for the whole period was 16s 6d, but we may regard sums such as 13s 4d or 3s 4d as the more typical amounts. Nor was Thomas alone. John and Emma Burton, for example, paid fines of £3 6s, £1 6s and £1 as well as smaller ones. Thomas Molin of Brockhampton paid one of £12 in 1363 for the composite holding of Clement Bachesmere, a figure almost matched by the £10 fine levied on his nephew when he succeeded to the estate in 1391. John Langrish paid £16, the highest fine in the bailiwick within the period, to succeed to his father's accumulated holdings in 1356. In turn his son was fined £10 to secure his inheritance, as well as the large sum of £2 13s 4d for a marriage that brought him the large Forcombe holding in 1382. The size of these fines bears a relationship with the large size of the holdings. Henry Napier built up his estate almost exclusively from small properties, and entirely by the surrender of fellow villagers, did not pay fines of this order. His highest fine was £2 for a virgate, the only holding of any size that he acquired. Nonetheless, despite the small size of Henry's individual acquisitions, there were 19 of them, and the fines totalled £7 14s 4d. Although we find that the average fine in the Taunton bailiwick over the period was similar, some of the totals paid by the wealthier peasants here outstrip even our East Meon examples. The average for the bailiwick over the period was 15s 10d. Yet, Simon Mode, who built up a large holding in Holway, on one occasion paid £15 for a messuage and virgate with pasture in Hanlade tithing at Holway in 1357. Simon's entry fines total £19 11s 6d. William Shaldew of Bishops Hull, to give a further example, was levied a total of £4 4s 9d between 1359 and 1383. Such sums become even larger if we look at those who held lands in more than one manor. Nicholas Chelwardeswood, for instance, who held various portions of land in both Bishops Hull and Holway, paid fines totalling £24 17s. On top of this one needs also to be aware of the unrecorded cash payments made to the out going tenants by those securing properties *inter vivos,* and one may guess that these may have been considerable even in relation to the fines. One can only speculate where the money might have come from. It was unlikely to have been derived from wage labour. Not only were these wealthier peasants able to make relatively large profits from the scale of their agricultural output but it is likely that they also drew rents from sub-tenants occupying surplus dwellings or outlying properties.

In neither bailiwick did demesne lands contribute greatly to the formation of large peasant accumulations. Thomas Knoller's holding was unusual in this respect. Of the 36 payments for parts of the lord's waste or demesne in the East Meon bailiwick, most of which occur at East Meon itself, only five took significant advantage of released demesne, and three of these five involve Thomas Knoller. Acquisitions of waste were more common in the Taunton group of manors, amounting to more than 244 fines over the whole bailiwick, but they were not prominent components of large multiple holdings. The one exception was the estate of Thomas Bacot, who died, probably some time after 1410, holding an accumulation of properties made up largely of parcels of waste and demesne land, mostly in Staplegrove but also in Holway and Nailsbourne. He had paid 16 separate fines between 1390 and 1407, of which 8, and possibly as many as 13, were for waste or demesne land.

Besides family background and personal wealth, longevity was an especially striking feature of the principal accumulators of peasant land. Thomas Knoller is an example of this. It seems that he had been active in the land market for forty-seven years, from as early as 1350 until as late as 1397. Over that period he was involved in 13 land transactions in East Meon and five in the neighbouring manor of East Meon Church, nearly all of which were for lands secured *inter vivos* from other families. In only two transactions did he surrender properties. His first fine in East Meon itself was for four acres of villein land by surrender in 1352. In 1358 he fined for a messuage and ten acres at East Meon from John Parker and in 1362 for a toft and ten acres of villein land from Richard Cook, both by surrender. The most significant acquisition also took place in 1362 when he received, by surrender of John, son of Nicholas Bere, and for the huge fine of £6, an extensive composite holding in Combe, Meon and Hyden. These properties were to be found in Thomas' inheritance in 1400. For a fine of 13s 4d, he acquired 40 acres of land with pasture from the bishop's demesne at East Meon in 1370. This was one of three fines during the 1370s in which he took up demesne land, one parcel of which we are specifically told 'lay between his cottage and the barn'. Other pieces of land, demesne as well as customary, were also acquired over the period – a cottage at East Meon with curtilage containing a rood of villein land in 1363, a cottage with curtilage and five acres of purpresture in 1385. Some of them can be ascribed to those additional marginal holdings which Thomas' son inherited independently of his mother Nicola in 1400.[16] The length of Thomas Knoller's career as an accumulator of property was far from unrepresentative amongst the tenants of large composite holdings. Of the 29 sample holdings at least 16 individuals – 10 in the East Meon bailiwick and 6 in the Taunton bailiwick – had been active in the land market for more than twenty-five years, some considerably longer than that (see Tables 11.1 and 11.2).

The position of accumulating tenants was also enhanced by their ability to influence the practices of the manorial court. They established the right to fine to have an earlier quitclaim upon a property enrolled in the court records, as extra surety that neither the previous tenant nor his heirs would make any further claim. Use of the device appears

16 Thomas, son of Thomas' inheritance can be reconstructed from acquisitions made in East Meon and East Meon Church in 1352, 1370 and 1379, and in East Meon Church in 1399.

15 times in the East Meon bailiwick, but not before 1360, perhaps testifying to the increased need for tenurial security occasioned by the increase of extra-familial acquisitions in the period after plagues. Thomas Knoller employed the device in 1397, when he fined for the clerk to enrol a quitclaim to 1½ acres in Combe acquired from Thomas Neng some time previously. Thomas was not alone in this, and other occurrences involve our selected wealthier peasants. In 1365 John Burton, for example, paid 6d to have recorded the quitclaim all right in a curtilage in Brockhampton by Matthew Cook and Richard Gamlin and Mary his wife. Another useful device for those who leased out part of their acquisitions for periods of years, or for the life of a lessee, was the practice of registering rights of reversion. John Langrish, who built up a considerable estate of cottages, at some point surrendered a grove and two crofts to William and Nicola Morton 'with reversion after their deaths'. William Hook, in building up his large estate in East Meon in 1351, surrendered a newly acquired cottage and croft to Joan Hatch with the stipulation that the tenement would revert to William on Joan's death. Likewise, in 1351 John Sole and his wife conceded their water mill and two acres in the Forcomb tithing of East Meon to Robert and Isabel Baker for their lives, with subsequent reversion. In a sense these devices were attempts to combat the fragility and disparate character of some of these complex holdings.

Conclusions

This research has opened up some interesting avenues and there are, of course, several areas which would merit further research. One would, for example, like to know something of the subsequent histories of these holdings and how long they survived beyond our period. Perhaps some of these successful tenants had also had careers as manorial officials putting them in some position of advantage. One would also like to know whether the bishop's administration had a policy to control or even to encourage large accumulations at this time. Nonetheless, we have attempted to focus on some of the primary features of the accumulation and polarisation of customary land in the two bailiwicks. In general the larger composite holdings were gathered around a virgate or half virgate. They were frequently made up of a combination of other, smaller standard holdings and a multitude of other pieces of land. Not only were accumulated holdings growing in number over the period, particularly after about 1380, but also in scale, made up of many pieces, often in several tithings and occasionally in more than one manor. We have noted that both the past history of the land market before 1349 and the commercial environment affected the rapidity and extent of accumulation. Although the Taunton bailiwick was the larger of the two, the fragmentation of virgates had proceeded further there by 1349 because of a high demand for land. The very largest accumulations in the later fourteenth century tended to be found in the East Meon group, where good properties were relatively cheaper.

We are also able to detect a corresponding polarisation of property ownership. Partly, this can be seen through the fact that very few cottages became the core of larger holdings. But we have questioned whether this implies relative impoverishment of cottagers. We note, particularly in the Taunton bailiwick, a decline in the number of independent cottages in the land market and the disappearance of many of their tenants, presumably because many of them could improve their lot by migrating to work elsewhere.

As far as the actual process of accumulation is concerned several common features stand out. Many accumulating peasants in both bailiwicks were from well established families with relatively high incomes, and they were active on their manors for a long time. Although plagues gave survivors short-term opportunities for accumulating inheritances, their longer-term ambitions were especially orientated towards acquisitions *inter vivos*, rather than *post mortem*, perhaps indicating an interest in the better and more valuable properties. This is further emphasised by the ability of these successful peasants to use the manorial courts to secure their title to these holdings against potential claims either from the previous holders and their families or from the lessees to whom surplus properties were entrusted.

Chapter 12

Rural transformation in northern England: village communities of Durham, 1340–1400[1]

Peter L. Larson

When the Black Death reached Durham in 1349, it was only the latest disaster to befall the county. Famine and the wars with Scotland had already weakened the population, but the scale of the disaster of the Black Death was greater than anything the peasants had faced.[2] The mortality during the first outbreak alone averaged approximately 60 per cent; the plague killed slightly over half of the tenants of Durham Priory, ranging from 21 to 78 per cent in different vills.[3] Lords and peasants attempted to carry on as before, but the subsequent social, political, and economic upheaval ushered in transformations in both agriculture and village society throughout Durham, particularly on the Durham Priory main estate.[4] Changes in agriculture, economy, and demography do not determine the nature of changes in social or political relations. Even the continuance of 'traditional' practices required an active choice on the part of the peasants; but some saw an opportunity to choose a new path. In the priory's villages, these changes did not come easily. The concept of community itself became contested as the priory peasantry clashed over agriculture, politics, and perhaps even the order of society in the villages itself. While the Black Death and subsequent economic conditions initiated this period of change, in the end peasants themselves decided how to order their communities.[5]

---

1 This chapter has benefited from the comments of numerous readers. In particular, James Masschaele and Maryanne Kowaleski commented on an early form of this paper, and Sarah Blick and Ben Dodds have read and commented on the current version. I also would like to thank Ben Dodds for his comments and suggestions on the overall project of which this is a part. All errors remain my own.

2 The war with Scotland and the Great Famine took their toll on the economy. R. A. Lomas, Durham Cathedral Priory as a landowner and landlord, 1290–1540 (unpublished Ph.D. thesis, University of Durham, 1973), p. 30, and *North-east England in the middle ages* (Edinburgh, 1992), pp. 54–74. There was a decrease in the arable land under cultivation in Durham before 1340: B. Dodds, *Peasants and production in the medieval North-East: the evidence from tithes, 1270–1536* (Woodbridge, 2007), pp. 28 and 55–70.

3 R. A. Lomas, 'The Black Death in County Durham', *Journal of Medieval History* 15 (1989), p. 129. I have estimated the overall mortality for tenants at 50–60 per cent, which is only slightly higher than the mortality of the monks themselves, at about 58 per cent: P. L. Larson, *Conflict and compromise in the late medieval countryside: lords and peasants in Durham, 1349–1400* (New York, 2006), p. 73.

4 These changes are the subject of Larson, *Conflict.*

5 For the late medieval history of the priory main estate (consisting of the majority of the villages belonging to the priory, administered primarily by the bursar) see Lomas, 'Durham Cathedral Priory'.

As the Durham peasantry tried to rebuild their society in a new and changing environment, they struggled not only with their lords, but with their neighbours as well.[6] Villagers had different conceptions of what a normal village society should be, and these views could be incompatible. Thus, an understanding of these conflicting opinions, or at the very least the acceptance of their divergence, is necessary to explain the transformations that took place. A new social order could be hammered out only with the consent of others, whether willingly given or grudgingly exacted. In many of the villages of the Durham Priory main estate, some peasants chose change, and the resultant conflict tore those communities apart. Social dynamics, attitudes, and mentalities drove this complex situation, and rather than simple reasons such as the Black Death or an economic slump, the answer lies in a crisis of order and control in conjunction with increasing individualism in agricultural practices. The Black Death initiated a period of instability that permitted these changes to occur. While the transformations would not be complete until the fifteenth century, the new orders and organisation were solidly in place by 1400.

The question of community

The use of 'village community' and 'village communities' is deliberate, as the villages in Durham each constituted a separate community, even when the nature of those communities altered. The ways in which communities functioned changed during the late-fourteenth century, in some villages quite substantially, but communities continued to exist in a demonstrable sense. This is clear from the briefest examination of the surviving halmote court rolls for both estates. Nevertheless, the village was not the only form of collective identity available to the Durham peasants, or for manorial jurisdiction. Villagers could be divided between different status groups of free men or neifs, for example. At the same time, in some instances individual settlements were linked together in larger complexes comprising more than one village.[7]

The most telling criticism of the historical concept of 'community' is that it obscures the many fissures and factions within a given group, simplifying and reducing motivation and coherence into a caricature.[8] Sometimes this failing is ascribed to the 'Toronto School' of Raftis, whose works often describe rather organic and harmonious village communities that functioned quite independently of the local lord. However, as Schofield has pointed out, many Marxist approaches share this failing, as they emphasise 'class consciousness' and solidarity in resistance to lordly oppression, glossing over fractures in the community as minor or as less important

---

6 The use of loosely applied closure theory is helpful in this instance; a strict use of the theory is difficult given the absence of many crucial details: S. H. Rigby, *English society in the later middle ages: class, status, and gender* (New York, 1995), pp. 9–14.

7 One example would be the three Merrington villages; another would be Over and Nether Heworth, referred to here simply as the Heworths, as priory officials normally treated them as a single unit.

8 On the debate over 'community', see C. Carpenter, 'Gentry and community in medieval England', *Journal of British Studies* 33 (1994), pp. 340–80. For a recent summary of the debate, see P. R. Schofield, *Peasant and community in medieval England 1200–1500* (New York, 2003), pp. 1–8.

than resistance to seigniorial oppression.[9] Rather than abandon the term 'community' altogether, however, some historians have argued for the importance of the village community in medieval society, and its continuing existence within the manorial system, as the bearer of distinctive rights and duties that can be demonstrated from documentary evidence. In this sense its existence does not depend upon our reading medieval society through the distorting lens of imposed theoretical and ideological constructs. Despite the criticisms of their methods, Raftis and his students have presented a strong, if sometimes problematic, argument for a cohesive village community.[10] The emerging consensus is that the term remains useful, especially as medieval records constantly employ the term or its synonyms.

Although this debate has brought to light the diversity of identity and allegiance among medieval English men and women, the community itself has not received the attention it deserves despite a plethora of works on the English village.[11] The Toronto School historians' division of families into strata based on appearances in manorial court rolls has illuminated the structure of medieval villages, and the studies of changes in landholding and migration in and out of the villages have strengthened the history of the late medieval countryside.[12] However, village institutions and the idea of community in these works generally appear static.[13] According to Dyer, 'the village

---

9 Schofield, *Peasant and community*, p. 5; Rigby, *English society*, pp. 2–5, 49–59 and 104–44.

10 In particular, C. Dyer, 'The English medieval village community and its decline', *Journal of British Studies* 33 (1994), pp. 407–29; H. M. Cam, 'The community of the vill', in V. Ruffer and A. J. Taylor (eds), *Medieval studies presented to Rose Graham* (Oxford, 1950), pp. 1–14. J. A. Raftis points out how a strong village community could co-exist within the manorial system in 'Social change versus revolution: new interpretations of the Peasants' Revolt of 1381', in F. X. Newman (ed.), *Social unrest in the late middle ages: papers of the fifteenth annual conference of the Center for Medieval and Early Renaissance Studies* (Binghamton, New York, 1989), especially pp. 6–8. See also B. Kümin, *The shaping of a community: the rise and reformation of an English parish, c. 1400–1560* (Brookfield, Vermont, 1996), p. 2.

11 Early modern historians have devoted far more time to this aspect of village society, in particular to the conflict over 'right order' as a response to Protestantism or 'puritanism': K. Wrightson and D. Levine, *Poverty and piety in an English village: Terling, 1525–1700*, new edition (Oxford, 1995); M. Spufford, 'Puritanism and social control?', in A. Fletcher and J. Stevenson (eds), *Order and disorder in early modern England* (Cambridge, 1985), pp. 41–57; M. K. McIntosh, 'Local change and community control in England, 1465–1500', *Huntingdon Library Quarterly* 49 (1986), pp. 219–42; eadem, *A community transformed: the manor and liberty of Havering, 1500–1620* (Cambridge, 1991), pp. 250–7.

12 The most important works of the Toronto School are J. A. Raftis, *Tenure and mobility: studies in the social history of the mediaeval English village* (Toronto, 1964); *idem*, 'Social structures in five east midland villages: a study in the possibilities of court roll data', *EcHR*, 2nd series 18 (1965), pp. 83–100; *idem*, 'The concentration of responsibility in five villages', *Mediaeval Studies* 28 (1966), pp. 92–118; E. B. DeWindt, *Land and people in Holywell-cum-Needingworth: structures of tenure and patterns of social organization in an east midlands village, 1252–1457* (Toronto, 1971); A. DeWindt, 'Peasant power structures in fourteenth-century King's Ripton', *Mediaeval Studies* 38 (1976), pp. 236–67; E. Britton, *The community of the vill: a study in the history of the family and village life in fourteenth-century England* (Toronto, 1977).

13 For critiques of the Toronto School's approach, see Z. Razi, 'The Toronto School's reconstruction of medieval peasant society: a critical view', *PP* 85 (1980), pp. 141–57, and Rigby, *English society*, pp. 6–9 and 45–9.

community has a shadowy existence in historical writing about the English Middle Ages . . . scholars have been reluctant to assign to the village any central place in their account of medieval society'.[14] Although his list of 'notable exceptions' covers most recent historiography on the village, his point is accurate. Too often, the village community is represented as the context within which change occurred, rather than as an active part of the rural dynamic. The history of the manorial system, peasant demography, and even questions of law and order in village society are fairly well served; yet the effect of the many changes from the Black Death onward on the idea of community is largely unknown.

The large series of surviving halmote court rolls and other relevant estate records make the villages of Durham Priory an excellent starting point to study the village community, and the records also provide a convincing spatial basis for the existence of the 'village community' throughout the main estate of Durham Priory.[15] In contrast, the lack of records for the bishopric estate from certain periods complicates any comparison with the bishopric village communities, which is frustrating, as the bishopric village communities apparently did not undergo the same upheaval as on the priory estate.[16] In order to establish a model of how the priory villages changed, the present argument will focus on one vill, Billingham, to allow some basic quantitative and prosopographical analysis, and thus provide depth within the broader approach. Although this vill and its families receive special attention, the ways in which the villagers there reordered their society (as well as some of the problems in interpreting the village community) apply to the majority of the villages of the estate.

Village communities in Durham before the Black Death

Sparsity of evidence for the period before the Black Death hampers any attempt to construct a definite baseline for any study of the Durham villages. The few court rolls older than 1364, combined with other priory estate records, nevertheless provide enough information to sketch out a probable picture of the village communities just before and after the Black Death.[17] During this time, most settlements on both estates were located in the southern and eastern areas of the county, in areas of lower elevation and along rivers. While these lowland villages appear similar to the 'typical' English nucleated village, there were significant differences. The greatest differences lay in the agricultural emphasis of the village and its concomitant social dynamics. There was a strong pastoral element even in Durham villages with

14 Dyer, 'English medieval village community', p. 407.

15 On the leasing of customary land by Durham Priory, see Larson, *Conflict*, pp. 162–7 and 201; for the leasing of customary land elsewhere in England, see B. Harvey, *Westminster Abbey and its estates in the middle ages* (Oxford, 1977), pp. 244–55, and P. R. Schofield, 'Tenurial developments and the availability of customary land in a later medieval community', *EcHR*, 2nd series 49 (1996), pp. 250–67.

16 Larson, *Conflict*, pp. 195–8.

17 DCM Halmote Rolls 1295; 1296, Summer, Autumn; 1297, Spring; 1340 Autumn; 1345 Autumn; and 1358, Summer and Autumn. R. A. Lomas and A. J. Piper (eds), *Durham Cathedral Priory rentals, I: bursars rentals*, Surtees Society CXCVIII (Durham, 1986).

'Midland' features. Regarding the practice of arable agriculture, there is much we do not know, including how village fields were divided, but it is evident that common fields occupied a smaller portion of the land than in the Midlands.[18] In part, all these differences were due to the smaller size of the Durham villages, which Britnell characterised as islands in a sea of waste, because substantial tracts of moorland existed between the settlements. As a result, he speculated that '[t]heir few inhabitants could have managed their agrarian resources with a degree of informality that would hardly have been tolerated in a large Midland village'.[19]

Such informality is visible in the earliest court records after the Black Death, as well as in the handful of rolls from the late-thirteenth century.[20] Before the later 1360s, the repetition of byelaws in the court was as rare as were amercements for breaking them, to the extent that it is difficult to define the rules and regulations that operated in the villages. It is possible that the clerks copying the court rolls omitted such repetition as unnecessary because everyone knew the rules, as was sometimes the case with the terms of landholding. However, later practice would imply that the restatement of byelaws was the norm whenever they needed to be enforced in court. The fact that byelaws rarely appear in the bishopric halmote books distinguishes these northern villages from those in the Midlands, and points to their looser organisation.[21]

While the village reeve, jury, and pinder existed in nearly all medieval English manors and villages, in Durham their powers were broader and less well defined.[22] The reeve and jurors held the roles of headman and elders in the village, dominating the major offices for years, often for life. In some villages, these men represented the wealthiest and best established of the customary tenants; elsewhere, they held little land in the village, but rented demesne land. In terms of regulation and enforcement, the seigniorial hand fell upon the villages relatively lightly; priory officials were well aware of the events of their villages, but saw little reason to intervene in village affairs other than as an outside arbitrator and judge. All of this is of course difficult to quantify in any degree; nonetheless, the records portray loosely regimented village communities. Disputes were settled by negotiation and compromise more than by litigation or violence. Only a strong sense of communal identity, and perhaps a good store of social capital, notably effective peace-keeping institutions and a tradition of communal action, would allow the villages to function in this way, or so it seems.[23]

---

18 For the most recent treatment on the division of Durham fields and the use of field systems, see R. H. Britnell, 'Fields, farms and sun-division in a moorland region, 1100–1400', *AHR* 52 (2004), pp. 20–36.

19 Britnell, 'Fields', p. 37; see also W. O. Ault, *Open-field husbandry and the village community: a study of agrarian by-laws in medieval England,* Transactions of the American Philosophical Society, new series 55 no. 7 (Philadelphia, 1965), p. 12.

20 DCM Halmote Rolls, 1295 to 1401 (with gaps). Extracts of the priory rolls up to 1384 have been printed in H. Longstaffe and J. Booth (eds), *Halmota Prioratus Dunelmensis,* Surtees Society 82 (Durham, 1889).

21 For the standard history of village byelaws, see Ault, *Open-field husbandry*.

22 On the village officers in Durham, see Larson, *Conflict,* pp. 58–61. Officers in the Durham villages held their positions for long periods, possibly for life, and as such have a strong presence in the court record.

Other than apparent co-operation and a general appearance of harmony based on the court rolls, is there evidence of the villages as communities? 'Community' is rarely attested in normal situations, and its existence can be argued only from negative evidence (when rules were broken) or from the reaction of villagers to external threats, (ranging from lawsuits to the acts of oppressive lords). The bishopric villages eventually came together as communities in resistance to the 'feudal reaction' of Bishop Thomas Hatfield (1345–81), but there is far less evidence for the priory villages.[24] Villagers could sue and be sued together in the halmote courts. They were capable of executing communal activities, particularly those of a seigniorial nature such as the repair of the local mill, and did so with few absences. Priory officials recognised the villages as communities, often addressing orders to 'all tenants of the vill' or to 'the entire vill', and they expected the communities to act as such. All told, the argument for the existence of village communities rests on the priory's viewpoint, the lack of any consistent evidence for serious feuds or divisions, and the ability of the tenants in the village to hold to common byelaws.[25] Construing the Durham villages as communities does not preclude dissent or conflict but, as used here, implies a loose cohesion of people with common rules and responsibilities.

The village of Billingham, located in south-eastern Durham, was roughly representative of the priory main estate and serves as a useful case study. The village contained demesne lands, and the tenants owed works there as well as at the nearby manor of Bellasis and at the prime sheep-rearing centre at Saltholme.[26] Most tenants were free men, yet they held customary lands of the prior and lacked certain rights that the freeholders in the village possessed.[27] The bursars' rental of 1340–1 recorded 63 tenants in the village, so a rough estimate of a total population of between 300 and 400 souls is not unreasonable.[28] Agriculture there was primarily arable but had a strong pastoral element, not surprising given the links to the priory's main sheep-

---

23 On the idea of social capital in late medieval and early modern English villages, see M. K. McIntosh, 'The diversity of social capital in English communities, 1300–1640 (with a glance at modern Nigeria)', in R. I. Rotberg (ed.), *Patterns of social capital: stability and change in historical perspective* (Cambridge, 2001), pp. 121–52; see also R. I. Rotberg, 'Social capital and political culture in Africa, America, Australasia, and Europe', *ibid*., pp. 1–18.

24 On Bishop Hatfield's feudal reaction, see R. H. Britnell, 'Feudal reaction after the Black Death in the palatinate of Durham', *PP* 128 (1990), pp. 28–47, and Larson, *Conflict*, pp. 77–141.

25 Raftis makes a strong case for community, in which byelaws play a significant part, in *Tenure and mobility*, pp. 104–27. See also Ault, *Open-field husbandry*.

26 The demesne at Billingham was worked by the monks until 1359, that at Bellasis until 1373, while Saltholme was brought back into direct management in 1350: Lomas and Piper (eds), *Bursars rentals*, I, p. 208.

27 P. L. Larson Conflict and compromise in the late medieval countryside: lords and peasants in Durham, 1349–1430 (unpublished Ph.D. dissertation, Rutgers, the State University of New Jersey, 2004), pp. 80–90.

28 Lomas and Piper (eds), *Bursars rentals*, I, pp. 46–9. The population figure given is not meant to be precise; it assumes approximately 4.7 to 4.9 people per tenant family: see Schofield, *Peasant and community*, pp. 83–4 for acceptable multipliers for average peasant household size. It also takes into account that there may have been a small group of landless or sub-tenant villagers, as well as the possibility that some individuals with multiple holdings really were different people.

rearing centre. The village offices were filled by men who usually held standard customary tenements (known as bondlands) and the village 'government' such as it was conformed to the basic pattern described above. The primary evidence for the period comes from the rolls of the priory's halmote court. While not completely equivalent to manorial courts, the halmotes heard much of the same business and provide a window onto the lives of the peasantry.[29]

The Black Death and the transformation of the community

Although the Black Death was a disaster on a grand scale in Durham, it was not unprecedented. The early fourteenth century had seen the Great Famine and associated cattle and sheep murrains (1315–22), as well as continued depredations by the Scots.[30] This helps explain why the Durham peasantry stoically went on with life even as the *prima pestilencia* slew more than half of the population; they had developed strategies to cope with adversity. On the bishopric estate, which provides most of our information for the years immediately following the Black Death, there is little evidence of panic in the face of the plague. Some peasants fled, not from fear, but from the rent collectors. Likewise, while many peasants balked at taking up new lands, this too was pragmatism in the face of yet another disaster rather than a specific reaction to the Black Death. By and large, society and agriculture continued to function, and the halmote courts met according to their regular schedule.[31] In 1350, immediately following the plague, many bishopric peasants formed new marriages and began taking up lands.[32] Life went on, yet, the situation was increasingly difficult. Tenements lay empty from the very outbreak of the plague, particularly on the bishopric estate, and the records of the bishopric halmote courts tell of considerable upheaval.[33]

There was a good deal of disruption on the priory main estate, as tenants must have operated under the same conditions as their neighbours, and the priory's policies later in the century certainly were not lenient. Still, later records contain no hints of any feudal reaction or resistance; if either occurred, it must have ended as quickly as on the bishopric estate. However, underlying economic and demographic problems did exist, and the drop in population coupled with an economic downturn destabilised the situation further. Although the peasants had learned to cope with hardship, the effects of the Black Death on the population and economy of the county eventually proved too hard to ride out.

---

29 DCM Halmote Rolls, 1340–1401 (with gaps). On the halmote courts, see P. L. Larson, 'Local law courts in late medieval Durham', in C. D. Liddy and R. H. Britnell (eds), *North-east England in the later middle ages* (Woodbridge, Suffolk, 2005), pp. 97–109.

30 See n. 2 above.

31 There were some isolated difficulties on the bishopric estate, including a reluctance to take new lands or sow old ones, but these issues disappeared by 1350: PRO DURH 3/12, fols. 1–60. The priory managed to collect its tithes in 1349 and in some cases sell them: Dodds, 'Durham Priory tithes and the Black Death between Tyne and Tees', *Northern History* 39 (2002), p. 18.

32 Britnell, 'Feudal reaction', pp. 30–2.

33 Larson, *Conflict*, pp. 77–169.

true that court records are biased against recording co-operation.[44] A shift towards increased conflict in Durham at this time is nevertheless demonstrable.[45] In just about every sphere of activity, tenants committed unneighbourly acts, often deliberately. Judging by the court rolls, common sense and the golden rule had disappeared suddenly from the priory main estate; this may be seen when the bursar fined William del Rawe of Billingham £1 'because he maliciously ejected the goods of William Sparrow from his house contrary to the order of the lord [prior]'.[46] These and similar incidents required the bursar to order his tenants not to trespass against each other in words and deeds, and to enjoin the men of the estate to keep their wives and servants in line because of the problems of insult and slander.[47]

Throughout the priory main estate, violence and feuding followed and compounded the disrespect and lack of communal co-operation. While the number of affrays did not increase substantially, the recorded circumstances of those acts indicate an escalation of the violence as the halmote heard more complaints of daggers drawn and of ambushes.[48] Peasants from every strata of village society, even the village officers and jurors, were embroiled in these conflicts.[49] The Miryman family found itself at the centre of several quarrels.[50] Thomas Miryman became embroiled in a feud with Richard Walker, another prominent villager, with the result that Thomas was suspended from his office.[51] Thomas' kinsman John and William Jackson of Wolviston were ordered to stay away from each other, and if they or their servants, or anyone acting in their names, trespassed against the other they were to forfeit £5. Three years later, the same John Miryman and Robert Hardgill found pledges for the sum of £20 each to keep the peace between themselves and their servants.[52] Incidentally, the involvement of the Miryman family in the village of Wolviston indicates the dangers of focusing solely on the village community, as many families had social and economic links with other villages.

---

44 McIntosh, *Autonomy and community*: the royal manor of Havering, 1500–1620 (Cambridge, 1991) pp. 183–4.

45 Larson, *Conflict*, pp. 178–82.

46 DCM Halmote Rolls, 1375, Summer, Billingham.

47 For examples of this behaviour and the priory's response, see DCM Halmote Rolls, 1365, Autumn, Newton Bewley; 1368, Autumn, Southwick and Monkwearmouth; 1371, Autumn, Monkwearmouth; 1372, Summer, Heworths; 1373, Spring, South Shields; 1374, Spring, Hesilden; 1376, Summer, South Shields. The bursar fined one scold twenty shillings for stirring up trouble despite warnings to desist: 1376, Spring, Hesilden. It is unclear if these women and men were punished by anything other than fines, as some villages, such as South Shields, did not have cucking stools in defiance of the bursar: Halmote Rolls, 1365, Summer and 1366, Summer, South Shields.

48 There are no homicides prosecuted in the halmotes, as is true of much other violent crime; as the records for these courts do not survive, an approach similar to that of B. Hanawalt, *Crime and conflict in English communities 1300–1348* (Harvard, 1979) is not possible. Further research into violence in Durham is in progress.

49 DCM Halmote Rolls, 1369, Spring, Wolviston.

50 Larson, *Conflict*, pp. 186–9.

51 DCM Halmote Rolls, 1371, Summer (Billingham) and 1382, Autumn.

The involvement of prominent villagers or village officers (the pinder excepted) in acts of violence and feuds was a new development, as before 1370 such activity was extremely rare. Even the rescue of animals and goods from the pinder's care rarely had been violent before then. But as wealthier and more prominent villagers became embroiled in conflicts, they affected the tenor of those conflicts. This was more than personal feuding, however; factions were developing. Most pledges to keep the peace extended not only to the main men involved, but to their families, servants, and even friends. Given the nature of the violence, the men who were involved, and the creation of factions, the bursar and prior proclaimed numerous injunctions against drawing weapons or disturbing the peace, the penalties for which continued to climb.[53] By 1381, when lords elsewhere in England were dealing with peasant unrest and anti-seigniorial sentiment, the prior and bursar of Durham were scrambling to keep their village communities together.

Even after the violence lessened in the early 1380s, the lack of co-operation and the disrespect persisted. It was not, however, only in village activities that the absence of common effort was displayed; villagers no longer worked together for seigniorial projects as they had before, and their lack of respect for each other extended to the priory. The power and impartiality of the priory was undercut by the frequent pardoning of amercements and fines by the prior, terrar, and bursar, especially to the benefit of village officers and tenants who worked for the priory.[54] Tenants refused to provide food and lodging for priory officers, and wilfully neglected their carrying duties. To judge by the bursar's injunctions, the estate was a complete mess, with ruinous buildings, overflowing ditches, and rough or obstructed roads throughout. Communal activities of all sorts had disappeared. The bursars issued the usual injunctions regarding the price of ale, providing pinders and folds, and so forth with disturbing frequency, even commanding the tenants of Wolviston not to reap early in 1387.[55] The communal agricultural practices of Durham had broken down. Something was truly wrong with peasant society in Durham society in order to require such paternalism on the part of priory officials.[56]

A new village order

The violent disputes peaked in 1378 and 1379 and had largely disappeared by 1384, although the upheaval and conflict continued to simmer. But what did all of this violence and conflict produce? In some villages, such as South Shields where mercantile and commercial factors were important, but also in a few of the more 'traditional' villages, the result was continuous quarrelling. Elections to replace jurors, almost unheard of before, became a more frequent occurrence. No new consensus or single community identity emerged; instead, the struggle over who controlled the

---

53 See Larson, *Conflict*, pp. 183–91.

54 Larson, *Conflict*, p. 176.

55 DCM Halmote Rolls, 1387, Spring, Wolviston.

56 Others, including Ault and Dyer, see this as common throughout England, however; see W. O. Ault, 'Village by-laws by common consent', *Speculum* 29 (1954), pp. 378–94, and Dyer, 'Medieval village community', pp. 422–3.

community continued and precluded cooperation of any sort. However, this was not a common outcome, as what happened in Billingham was more representative. There, a small group of tenants had come to dominate the village to a greater extent than before.[57] The newly dominant families had always loomed large in village affairs, but only as part of a larger community; now, they were in control. In many villages, including Billingham, these men had been at the centre of the violence during the preceding decades, but their side had won. In Billingham, Hardgills and Monctons had served on the village jury alongside the men of the Miryman and del Tonne families. By 1377, the Hardgills were firmly in charge of Billingham, along with families such as Gris, Grisby, Raynald and May, to the exclusion of the other families. These men concentrated control of the demesne lands into their own hands and used it to bolster their positions in the village. The leasing of demesne lands was all the more important for the distribution of land in that there was little engrossment of holdings in Billingham and little alternative opportunity for tenurial redistribution.[58]

In Billingham, domination by an elite, sometimes contested, had replaced consensus and solidarity. However, initial examinations of the fifteenth-century halmote records reveal little long-term dominance by specific families, instead showing turnover in the members of the village oligarchy. Conflict diminished considerably, indicating just how firmly the leaders were in control, and the change is clearly reflected in the halmote records. During the 1360s, an average of 14 cases were heard per halmote tourn (excluding demises, general injunctions, and the assize of ale), on average involving 23 individuals, including members of the upper stratum but also a variety of other personages. From 1385 to 1400, there was an average of four to five such cases, involving 17 individuals on average. With the exception of some mass amercements, including one for the playing of football in 1386, most of the parties involved (excepting women presented for merchet or fornication) were from the families of office holders or other wealthy peasants.[59] Much of the interpersonal business disappeared; debts and trespasses must have been solved out of court through the personal power of the elite peasants, and many poorer or less well connected tenants perhaps avoided the court because of its suspected partiality. The halmote court ceased to be a place for the (more-or-less) just settlement of disputes, the decisions of which most peasants had respected. There is no clearer evidence of a change in the community than the change in the business of the halmote court and the people who were active in that forum. It is unlikely that the missing business was

---

57 This would be an excellent starting point for a case study of closure theory in a medieval English village.

58 In the bursar's rental for 1395/6, there are 52 tenants, as opposed to the 63 a half-century earlier: Lomas and Piper (eds), *Bursars rentals*, pp. 96–104.

59 This data is from DCM Halmote Rolls, with samples taken for the village of Billingham from 1364–7, 1385–17, and 1397–1400 (a total of 24 court tourns). To avoid prejudicing the numbers in favour of the jurors, the juror list and assize of ale have been omitted (nearly all of the women amerced for the assize were wives of the jurors); in addition, demises and general injunctions are omitted. Inclusion of demises was statistically insignificant. The method used may understate the number of individuals, as persons described as son/daughter of another were counted as only one person, as it is possible that the parent was deceased.

simply transferred to another court, as the priory forbade its tenants access to other courts .[60]

From 1340 to 1364, the village communities on the priory main estate had been stable and functional, although not idyllic, and the halmote court had provided acceptable dispute resolution.[61] Communal activities, from agriculture to the maintenance of communal structures to the performance of communal seigniorial activities, operated normally, and the bursar had concerned himself more with individual tenants neglecting their duties rather than with the need to issue broad instructions of what to do and what not to do. Interpersonal litigation appeared healthy, and most tenants had faith in the bursar and their own officers to be relatively impartial. By the 1390s, all this had changed. Some villages developed a need for frequent replacement of reeves and sometimes even of jurors; along with the decline of business in the courts, this indicates that the village officers no longer operated with general consent (or even the fiction of it).[62] The engrossment of land was increasing. In Billingham, 54 tenants held the land in the village in 1395/6, which was down from 64 a half century earlier. The leasing of demesne land enabled men to strengthen their power in the village, so that in addition to their customary tenements these men all but monopolised the demesne lands.[63] Access to those lands, in part from power in the villages due to office holding, allowed families to increase their power further, if not necessarily permitting the creation of a dynasty. The transformation was complete if not finished. A new set of community organisations had emerged, although they may hardly be labelled stable at this point. The old consensus that had governed the village communities, however rough and fragmented it may have been, was gone; in its place was either constant conflict, or, as in Billingham, control by a small group of families who abandoned the façade of ruling in the broader interests of the village.

Although the new shape of the village communities had solidified by 1400, the withering of the old ways and the blossoming of the new continued in the fifteenth century, steadily building on the foundations laid in the late fourteenth century. Many villages continued to hold annual elections for reeves, and some frequently held elections for juries as well. The sense of stability in those villages provided by long-serving officers before the crisis was gone, and this further exacerbated the disintegration of the community of the vill. Even in those villages that were more stable, such as Billingham, important families still sometimes struggled for control. The use of short leases for customary land would evolve into syndicates of wealthier

---

60 Larson,'Local law courts', p. 106.

61 On the concept of 'manorial' courts and dispute resolution, see L. Bonfield, 'The nature of customary law in the manor courts of medieval England', *Comparative Studies of Society and History* 31 (1989), pp. 514–34; J. S. Beckerman,'Procedural innovation and institutional change in medieval English manor courts', *Law and History Review* 10 (1992), pp. 157–252, and *idem*, 'Toward a theory of medieval manorial adjudication: the nature of communal judgments in a system of customary law', *Law and History Review* 13 (1995), pp. 1–22. For the applicability of these ideas in the Durham halmotes, see Larson,'Local law courts'.

62 Larson, *Conflict*, pp. 217–21.

63 Lomas and Piper (eds), *Bursars rentals*, pp. 96–104.

tenants leasing their entire vill, resulting in the reconstitution of the village communities as small groups of wealthy peasants and large numbers of poorer cottagers and sub-tenants.[64] These syndicates were the logical conclusion of the steady engrossment of lands by the village elites. Although unfavourable to so many members of the village community, all of this did lead to tenurial stability, at least for those who held tenures of the priory.[65] In 1385, the court records had already begun to reflect only the actions of the greater tenants and their adherents. The poorest tenants were all but disappearing from the court records, seldom appearing in court even for fornication or the marriage of a daughter, both of which concerned the priory; these men and women now mattered very little in village society. The situation was worsening for the majority of the priory peasantry. The many petty, greedy, and divisive actions had transformed rural society permanently. It would take some time to complete the transformation, but the changes could not be undone, and these alterations in the social and political dynamics of the village possibly paved the way for later contests over 'right order' in the village community.

The causes of change

It is easy to demonstrate that change took place on the priory main estate; the conflict and violence are clear, and the difference in activity in the halmotes is readily apparent. Explaining how and why this happened is far more difficult, as the records seldom present the motivations of the actors and the chronology of likely factors is inexact. Based on the conditions in this period, the business recorded in the halmotes, and the nature of conflict, the major cause likely was a shift in agricultural emphasis or orientation, perhaps to a more individual approach.[66] One element in this was an increased emphasis on stock raised by the tenants. Either tenants were increasing the numbers of animals they owned, or they were choosing to look after the animals as they saw fit rather than continue to join in common pasturing. The most common and most divisive acts attested to in the court concerned animals, either overburdening the commons or trespassing in the crops of others. The most frequent commands issued by the bursar, the most common byelaws repeated in the courts, all demanded adherence to the traditional system of herding and pasturing animals belonging to the tenants of the village, generally under the supervision of the pinder, and often common herdsmen as well. These byelaws also concerned the maintenance of the pinfold and the employment of a village pinder to regulate the animals, particularly when they were not under the eye of the herdsmen. As the violence escalated, as village cohesion lessened, the tone of these orders became more insistent, and by the

---

64 Lomas and Piper (eds), *Bursars rentals*, pp. 9 and 199–227. Some syndicates formed early in the fifteenth century, but most were created later.

65 See Lomas, 'Durham Cathedral Priory', p. 39.

66 McIntosh also noted a transformation of agricultural practices after the Black Death in Havering, along with repetition of certain byelaws and injunctions and increased conflict within the manor: M. K. McIntosh, *Autonomy and community*, pp. 137–41 and 176–8, and especially pp. 201–15. This conflict began around 1385, the time that the conflict in Durham was ending. On the progressive nature of peasant agriculture after the Black Death, see J. A. Raftis, *Peasant economic development within the English manorial system* (Montreal, 1996).

end of the fourteenth century injunctions to have pinders and pinfolds had become seasonal occurrences for many vills. This appearance of agricultural upheaval could be an illusion created by the clerks of the court, who began recording byelaws more assiduously. Yet, a change in scribal practice does not eliminate the possibility of agricultural change. A cause still would be necessary for the clerks to begin recording byelaws in such a consistent manner, and conflict over the practice of agriculture would be the most likely culprit of such a change. The evidence of scribal practice is unlikely to be meaningless, given the consistency of the rolls over two centuries, and the coincidence of the repetition of byelaws with the conflict within the communities makes it likely that the latter was a direct cause of the former.[67]

The transformation of land tenure on the priory main estate was another facet of the overall agricultural changes. In the past, the normal process was for tenants to take customary lands for life and pay a money fine on entry (*gressuma*). However, beginning in the 1360s, the priory began leasing the customary land to the tenants for a term of years. The initial terms were fairly long, twenty-one and thirty years being common, but by 1400 the terms had dropped to less than ten years and very few life tenancies remained.[68] Similar changes in the terms of landholding occurred throughout England after the Black Death, but the monks of Durham Priory adopted the practice more quickly and more comprehensively, even if its timing varied from village to village.[69] Although partly a seigniorial initiative, the tenants had much to gain by this change, as the new leases provided more flexibility in land management and the eventual elimination of entry fines threw open the market for land. This is not to say that leasing revived a sluggish land market, but it could permit a tenant to group his holdings together and then enclose them with hedges; there certainly were numerous instances of animals breaking hedges and getting to crops.[70] Chronologically there is no direct correlation between the adoption of leasing and the conflict within the villages. In some villages, the practice of leasing customary lands predates the rise in violence and decline in co-operation, while in other villages, such as Billingham, the tenants truly did not embrace leasing until nearly 1400. While the shift to leasing did not cause or end the transformation, it did contribute and was likely indicative of the instability of the time.

Finally, there was the competition between certain families for control. Earlier, they appear to have shared the offices and perks in the village with each other, ruling as a group through the jury and assuming the consent of the rest of the villagers. Village agriculture and society were loosely organised, and this method of village government worked well. At some point this consensus broke down, and these families began contending with each other. It is hard to say whether this strife was a result of the

---

67 Ault refers to such changes in recording while discussing the enforcement of village byelaws: *Open-field Husbandry*, pp. 40–54.

68 Lomas, 'Durham Cathedral Priory', pp. 38–9.

69 Cf. B. Harvey, *Westminster Abbey*, pp. 244–5, and Schofield, 'Tenurial developments'.

70 On leasing and the Durham land market, see T. Lomas, 'South-east Durham: late fourteenth and fifteenth centuries', in P. D. A. Harvey (ed.), *The peasant land market in medieval England* (Oxford, 1984), pp. 252–317; Lomas, 'Durham Cathedral Priory', pp. 29–39 and 121; and Larson, *Conflict*, pp. 160–7.

changes in the villages or whether the families themselves created much of the upheaval. The latter case makes some sense. These villagers would have had both the means and the motivation to embrace newer, more individualistic agricultural practices, but if only some families did so, that would jeopardise the position of their neighbours. It is also possible that some families with political power but limited lands saw this as an opportunity to increase their wealth, and thus increase their grip on the village even further; in some respects this appears similar to the conflict between the 'A' and 'B' families described in works by the Toronto School.[71] Both these scenarios explain the splitting of the communities down the middle. In the end, however, all the remaining powerful families came to adopt the system of short-term leases and contribute to a newer system of agriculture that, if not individualistic, was certainly narrower in participation. It would perhaps be premature to argue that these changes were related to any shift toward a 'agrarian capitalism'. However, these changes and the social and tenurial structures in Durham (in which serfdom played a very small role) complicate Whittle's argument that the decline of serfdom was integral to the development of 'agrarian capitalism' in England.[72]

All this returns us to the question of community at the beginning of this period of transformation. If cohesive village communities did exist on the priory main estate, how did they disintegrate so rapidly? It is at this point that we can best perceive the limited sense in which village communities were necessarily cohesive groups. When faced with external pressure in the form of lordly oppression from Bishop Hatfield, the bishopric village communities pulled together. In part, the priory communities failed to maintain their shape because of the divided leadership alluded to above. However, on closer inspection, the halmote rolls reveal some clues that, despite the demonstrable existence of communal institutions, the normal village community on the priory estate was not strong to begin with and lacked true solidarity. The priory tenants never truly displayed an ability to work together on their own initiative; they responded to the demands of their officers and of the priory officials, but any form of resistance was sporadic and individual. As long as there was no real pressure on the community, the loose regulation sufficed and obviated the need for investment of social capital in the community. Once pressure increased, in the form of tenurial change and economic and agricultural depression, the weak ties within the communities could not stand the strain and, combined with a divided leadership, the communities began to come apart at the seams. Only when the elite families put aside their differences and accepted the new tenurial and agricultural system did the community resurface, although firmly in the control of the upper stratum of peasant society.

71 A prosopographical study might help illuminate this question, however, certain difficulties with the records may mask the actual wealth and landholdings of the families in question.

72 J. Whittle, *The development of agrarian capitalism: land and labour in Norfolk, 1440–1580* (Oxford, 2000).

Part 4

Conclusion

Chapter 13

Common themes and regional variations

Ben Dodds and Richard Britnell

In principle the task of relating general trends to regional variations during the medieval centuries poses no analytical difficulty that does not recur in later periods. In recent times, while cohorts of economists, sociologists and economic historians have focused on issues relating to industrialisation and economic growth, some of the most difficult problems of analysis and practice have arisen in attempting to explain why performance has differed regionally within single states, as well as between different parts of the world, and to formulate policies to redress inequalities that have arisen. Awareness of regional variation is not merely compatible with a common problematic; it is the inspiration for much of the research that draws scholars and politicians together in seeking to understand. In the same way, our knowledge of the remarkable expansion of European settlement and trade in the period 1000–1300, or of the economic consequences of epidemic disease and warfare in the fourteenth century, has not been built upon the assumption that all parts of Europe were sharing a common experience. We are perhaps more aware now than ever of great differences in detail between the extent to which different regions were affected by crises, and the relative speed with which they were able to recover. This is well attested by the comparison of tithe data from England, France and Castile in Chapter 7. In these concluding comments we shall focus on the implications of the various contributions to this volume for British economic and social history, although the various points to be made are mostly capable of being extended to the other European economies and beyond.

Differences of location, climate, resources and institutions

Our existing literature shows clearly that differences of location, climate, and resources implied very different possibilities even within the bounds of national economic historical awareness. The mountains of Scotland and Wales, the upland regions of the Pennines, the gentler slopes of the Cotswolds or the Chilterns, the low-lying regions of the Lincolnshire and Cambridgeshire fens, the extensive loams of the Midlands, the clay soils of Essex, and the Thames valley, to mention but a few distinctive topographical features of the British landscape, each had their distinctive local economies that affected the structure and availability of employment, the possibilities for commerce, and the rate at which settlement could expand. Across Europe as a whole, contrasts of terrain and climatic differences were even more extreme, affecting decisively the crops that could be grown and the animals that could be kept. Italian farmers could grow not only a wide variety of cereals and industrial crops but olives and vines as well, whereas the farmers of much of upland Britain were constricted to a precarious regime of oats and barley. The tithes of Dunbarrow (Angus) were paid wholly in oatmeal and barley in the late-fifteenth century.[1] No one is tempted to assimilate daily life in medieval Iceland to the experiences of peasants in Andalusia.

Regional contrasts are apparent not only between different geographical environments but also between economic and social institutions, which owed much to a remote past beyond the reach of written records. In England the institutions of central government and the Church have the greatest claim to have national coverage, and although even they show many local divergences of detail it is questionable how far they were 'regional'. The institution of tithing was subject to the canon law of the Church, modified in detail by local custom (see Chapter 6). Nevertheless, structures of lordship, tenures, field systems and pasturing arrangements were less centrally regulated, and were subject to variations that were partly congruent with variations in the natural environment, but had distinctive political and cultural origins. They were sufficiently strong to distinguish midland England from East Anglia, and were much more complex if the whole of Britain is taken into account.[2] Across Europe the differences were much greater, with corresponding variations in their impact on structures of rural authority and decision-making (see Chapter 9). Beyond simply describing these differences and attempting to explain them, economic historians have analysed them principally as evidence for the varying autonomy with which producers could act in responding to commercial incentives. Arbitrary financial levies and excessively restrictive or insecure tenures weakened tenants' inclination and capacity to invest in their lands. Rigid local customs restricting land use similarly reduced the freedom of tenants to adjust the composition of their output in accordance with changes in prices. Such 'feudal' structures of control over peasant farmers, whether seigniorial or collective, have therefore a bad reputation for the way in which they inhibited economic as well as political liberty. If institutional variations had the importance that is often attributed to them we should expect to find more conservative traditions in the English Midlands, where there were both relatively more customary tenants and more common fields, than in East Anglia, where there were more free tenants and more flexible pasturing arrangements. There is some evidence that this was in fact the case.[3]

Inherited differences between institutions did not limit the possible range of variation between regions, however, since those institutions were constantly reshaped in accordance with shifts in the locus of economic and political power. This was a particularly important feature of the period after the Black Death. The old

---

1 R. H. Britnell, *Britain and Ireland, 1050–1530: economy and society* (Oxford, 2004), pp. 395 and 510; P. Jones, 'Medieval agrarian society in its prime: Italy', in M. M. Postan (ed.), *The Cambridge economic history of Europe, I: the agrarian life of the middle ages*, 2nd edition (Cambridge, 1966), pp. 370–3.

2 R. A. Dodgshon, *The origin of British field systems: an interpretation* (London, 1980); H. L. Gray, *English field systems* (Harvard, Mass., 1915); A. R. H. Baker and R. A. Butlin (eds), *Studies in the field systems of the British Isles* (Cambridge, 1973).

3 R. L. Hopcroft, 'The social origins of agrarian change in late medieval England', *American Journal of Sociology* 99 (1994).

structure of tenures was heavily modified by the problems faced by landlords in finding tenants. But these developments, too, were regionally variable, as demonstrated by different patterns of accumulation across the Winchester bishopric estates (see Chapter 11). The halmote courts on the estates of Durham Priory were managed according to local traditions of the Durham palatinate, and although they changed during the later Middle Ages they were far from assimilating to the better known forms of manorial jurisdiction further south (see Chapter 12).

Where, then, lies the justification for contemplating a history of rural economy and society with any common themes?

Common experiences and differing responses

The possibility of an integrated approach to national and international histories of the economy derives above all from repeated observation of common phenomena in different contexts. Just as during the period 1000–1300 historians in all parts of Europe observe the taking in of land from forest and marsh, the multiplication of tenures, rising rents, the foundation of new villages and towns, and the growth of towns and trade, so in the period after 1300, and particularly during the hundred years after the Black Death, they commonly observe the shrinking of settlements, falling rents, and the restructuring of rural employment into pasture farming and other specialisations. The output of arable farming is often observed to decline, although with great differences of severity and chronology (see Chapter 5). These features of declining population were not universal, although they were far more widespread than the foundation of new settlements, the growth of old ones, increases in rent, or the expansion of arable cultivation during this period. They accordingly present themselves as a common research agenda requiring description, quantification if possible, and explanation, to determine when and where agrarian recession occurred, what caused it or prolonged it, how quickly agrarian growth was resumed in different contexts, and what was the foundation of recovery. In other words, the possibility of an integrated economic history embracing different regions has originated from cumulative observation, and has impressed itself on historical study in spite of striking regional variations. Students approaching new data for the first time will expect to find one set of phenomena and be surprised – and surely pleased – if they find something different. As we have seen the depopulation brought about by epidemic disease, climatic change, and the impact of warfare, have all some claim to be general features of the late medieval economy of sufficient force to cause some parallel changes across Europe at different times, even if the chronology of change differed and if other changes they brought about varied because of differences of economic and political environment (see Chapter 7). Study of regional variation is unlikely ever to overturn the weight of evidence that has served to identify common themes in agrarian history, even though it will necessarily continue to modify perception and understanding of them in detail.

Some of the variation arose simply because disease, war and climatic change did not affect all regions to the same extent. In some instances, extreme regional variations exaggerated the impact of widespread changes. Many of the regions and periods where signs of agrarian crisis were most severe, for example, were those where local warfare was most destructive. The English inflicted more of this sort of damage on their neighbours than they suffered in return, but the problems of northern

England during the ten years after the battle of Bannockburn in 1314 can hardly be understood without reference to invasions by the Scots.[4] However, most regional economic development will defy simple explanation at this level of generalisation. It is often inappropriate to dwell on variations in the temporary impact of disease or war as a prime determinant of change in the longer term. The regions most subject to population loss and the contraction of arable husbandry during the fourteenth and fifteenth centuries were not necessarily those where epidemic disease had ravaged most severely, or where warfare was most destructive. In the long term, regional variations were also affected by the environmental differences in location, resources and institutions that we have already observed.

A whole range of circumstances influenced the way in which different regions could or did respond to changing circumstances. It has long been expected that soils that were unattractive to cultivate because they took more labour to plough, or needed more inputs of manure, or were more remote from a village centre, would be more likely to be abandoned than easily worked fertile soils in the vicinity of towns. The change in land use on Spennymoor during the later fourteenth century cannot be ascribed to the effects of climatic change, disease or war, and requires particular local observation for its explanation (see Chapter 10). A region of extensive upland moors, like much of northern England, Wales and Scotland, might be expected to respond differently to declining population from the richer lands of East Anglia or Kent. A development of this line of argument that takes into account local ecology and differential costs of production is capable of leading to many interesting observations that can be integrated into broader themes. There were other contexts, for example, where, both before and after the Black Death, land use was adversely affected by a rising sea level and storm surges that swept away coastal and estuary defences against the sea.[5]

Because of differences in climate and terrain, we should expect regional variation across Europe even in the absence of trade. If we could examine the agriculture of Europe before the urban expansion of the ninth and tenth centuries we should doubtless be able to form some stronger impression of such variation, but in fact it survived to a large extent through the Middle Ages. Sicilian villagers did not eat the same food, drink the same drink or wear the same clothing as self-sufficient Norwegian villagers. The requirement of the Church that wine should be available for the liturgy of the Mass would not induce Scots farmers to invest in vineyards. A papal bull of Nicholas V, issued in 1450, allowed the people of St Andrews diocese in Scotland to use butter and other dairy produce in Lent because olive oil was not readily available.[6] Local diets differed even between parts of Britain in accordance

---

4 B. Dodds, *Peasants and production in the medieval North-East: the evidence from tithes, 1270–1536* (Woodbridge, 2007), pp. 56–61; I. Kershaw, *Bolton Priory: the economy of a northern monastery, 1286–1325* (London, 1973), pp. 14–18.

5 M. Bailey, '*Per impetum maris*: natural disaster and economic decline in eastern England, 1275–1350', in Campbell (ed.), *Before the Black Death: studies in the 'crisis' of the early fourteenth century* (Manchester, 1991), pp. 184–208; R. H. Britnell, 'The occupation of the land: eastern England', in *AHEW*, III, p. 54.

with local resources. Oats constituted a much more important part of the diet of the Scots than of the southern English.[7] In upland areas where arable farming was risky and population relatively sparse, pastoral products like milk and cheese constituted a larger part of the diet than in more densely settled arable regions.[8] These differences inevitably affected the ways in which local farmers responded in detail to common changes in the relationship between land and population. If peasant diets improved across Europe, as they commonly did during the century after 1350, they did not all improve to the same extent or in the same way. There is every reason why an integrated history of Europe should positively welcome studies of regional variation, since they alone can expose the more complicated patterns of cause and effect that explain the long-term impact of more general causes of change.

Trade and specialisation

An integrated approach to the economic history of the late medieval period is further justified by the extent to which the growth of trade created complex links between different regions. Without such trade we should be limited to comparing the responses of self-sufficient communities to the common problems of high mortality and war. However, given the extent of commerce in agricultural produce by the fourteenth century the agenda for research is more complex. The way different settlements, districts and regions developed was at least in part contingent upon the possibilities for local specialisation either in agriculture or in manufacturing and trade. It is not enough to observe the local development of wool production in the English Cotswolds, for example, without recognising it as a response to the growth of cloth-manufacturing centres in other regions of England and Europe, which was in turn governed by changes in disposable income and consumer preference; the economic history of the Cotswold region cannot be self-contained. The extent to which different places were dependent on trade is one of the most important things to observe about them. In the century after the Black Death some of the most interesting economic developments in agriculture, as in manufacturing, were responses to market opportunities. Chapter 1 explored some of the possibilities for discussing levels of trade, specialisation, regional inter-dependence and market integration in Europe as a whole. This approach, too, implies the importance of relating detailed regional histories to wider themes in economic development.

Adam Smith famously observed that the possibility for occupational specialisation was limited by the extent of the market. Such specialisation was an important defining characteristic of regional differences by the fourteenth century, but the spatial scale on which specialisation occurred could vary considerably. Market towns were often the

---

6 T. Thomson (ed.), *Liber cartarum prioratus Sancti Andree in Scotia*, Bannatyne Club 69 (Edinburgh, 1841), pp. 24–5.

7 C. Dyer, *Standards of living in the later middle ages: social change in England c. 1200–1520* (Cambridge, 1989), pp. 152–4; E. Gemmill and N. J. Mayhew, *Changing values in medieval Scotland: a study of prices, money, and weights and measures* (Cambridge, 1995), p. 202.

8 Britnell, *Britain and Ireland*, pp. 10–11

principal source of demand for rural products, and took great pains to encourage and regulate their supply, as we have seen in the case of Aberdeen (see Chapter 4). The importance of Salisbury as a market for nearby villages in the early fifteenth century is demonstrated by their concentration on barley (see Chapter 8). Urban fortunes could either stimulate or discourage the employment of resources within the region that served them. The shift in local urban demand after 1349 away from bread grain towards wool, meat and dairy produce, in conjunction with the general rise in labour costs, was responsible for much of the restructuring of land use, since most grain was sold over relatively short distances. Spennymoor was not only more remote from village centres than the townlands, which fared better, but also more remote from any market centre, so that as transport costs rose relative to the price of grain it was increasingly disadvantaged relative to other more accessible locations. The larger a town became, the greater the likelihood that producers in its trading area could find some specialised product or service with which to supply it. Since the smallest identifiable regional unit is usually a market town and its hinterland, we can classify a good deal of such specialisation as intra-regional.

On a larger territorial scale we can identify much larger trading areas in which smaller regions complemented each other in complex ways. By 1300 there were well-established regional specialisations, shaped by mercantile activity that also served the demands of metropolitan and overseas trade. The concept of regional agrarian specialisation needs careful handling, since every shire had a mixture of farming types. The level of agrarian specialisation was always limited by the great weight of subsistence agriculture and local supply, even in regions of exceptionally intensive agriculture like Flanders.[9] In some respects, too, the degree of local specialisation retreated after 1349, as farmers increased their dependence on livestock, and forms of mixed farming became increasingly the norm. Increased household expenditure on superior consumables such as meat, dairy produce and barley ale did not serve to widen the differences between regions because each urban supply region could to some extent adapt its farming to accommodate a changed structure of demand. Nevertheless, the level of trade remained high enough to maintain many regional distinctions in the balance of commodities produced, particularly within shires supplying London and overseas markets.[10] Norfolk farmers specialised in barley, the superior grain for malting and brewing.[11] In contrast, producers in Feering in Essex specialised in wheat, the superior and most expensive bread grain. In regions of very specialised grain production, such as north-east Kent, it is likely that, having sold their surplus, peasant farmers bought in such fodder crops as they needed, and in that way

---

9 E. Thoen, 'Agricultural progress in England and the north and southern Netherlands during the middle ages: was the demand really so important?', *NEHA-Jaarboek voor economische, berijfs- en techniekgeschiedenis* 61.1 (1998), p. 42.

10 B. M. S. Campbell, K. C. Bartley and J. P. Power, 'The demesne-farming systems of post Black-Death England: a classification', *AHR* 44 (1996), pp. 176–8; J. A. Galloway, 'Town and country in England, 1300–1700', in S. R. Epstein (ed.), *Town and country in Europe, 1300–1800* (Cambridge, 2001), pp. 118–20.

11 Britnell, 'Occupation of the land', pp. 62–7; B. M. S. Campbell and M. Overton, 'A new perspective on medieval and early modern agriculture: six centuries of Norfolk farming, *c.* 1250–*c.* 1850', *PP* 141 (1993), pp. 54–7.

were better off than had they tried to produce everything themselves.[12] The Breckland region of East Anglia was one where arable farming suffered a prolonged contraction in the later Middle Ages, but where the local economy responded to a wide range of alternative opportunities stretching far beyond those offered by a single urban market, such as supplying rabbits to London.[13] The saffron trade of southern Cambridgeshire and northern Essex begins to be documented from the mid fifteenth century.[14]

The range of activities open to rural communities was not restricted to the various branches of agriculture. Many crafts were practised in the rural societies of pre-industrial Europe, and not exclusively for supplying local needs. The growth of the English cloth industry during the course of the late Middle Ages was predominantly an urban phenomenon, but the rapid increase in the number of fulling mills benefited rural areas where merchants found conveniently placed resources of labour or water power.[15] Fishing, coal- and tin-mining, iron-working, pottery, cutlery, brewing and salt-making were all activities that could supplement the incomes of landlords and tenants alike.[16] Agriculture remained everywhere the principal source of rural incomes. Manufacturing and extractive industries were characteristic of some parts of the countryside, often dependent upon particular mercantile networks. The economic diversity between different parts of Britain tended to widen as industrial specialisation followed the stimulus of mercantile trade.[17] Many industrial and mining activities can profitably be studied regionally as long as their dependence upon inter-regional exchange is duly explored.[18]

One of the features of improving resources *per capita* during the fourteenth century and into the fifteenth was that at least during some parts of the period the real disposable incomes of surviving populations increased. Pressure on incomes during the thirteenth century had discouraged the development of a market for consumer goods; surpluses were liable to be used for more food, for necessary repairs and for the replacing or supplementing of household utensils and capital goods. During the course of the fourteenth century, though, the share of income that went to satisfying

---

12 B. Dodds, 'Peasant production and productivity', paper delivered at the Ninth Anglo-American Seminar on the Medieval Economy and Society, Lincoln, 2007.

13 M. Bailey, *A marginal economy? East Anglian Breckland in the later middle ages* (Cambridge, 1989), pp. 149–50.

14 Lee, *Cambridge*, p. 108.

15 J. Langdon, *Mills in the medieval economy: England, 1300–1540* (Oxford, 2004), pp. 40–7.

16 Dodds, *Peasants and production*, pp. 85–93; J. Hatcher, *Rural economy and society in the duchy of Cornwall, 1300-1500* (Cambridge, 1970), pp. 29–36.

17 A. R. H. Baker, 'Changes in the later middle ages', in H. C. Darby, *A new historical geography of England before 1600'* (Cambridge, 1976), pp. 218–36; Galloway, 'Town and country', pp. 122–8.

18 E.g. I. Blanchard, 'Industrial employment and the rural land market, 1380–1520', in R. M. Smith (ed.), *Land, kinship and life-cycle* (Cambridge, 1984), pp. 227–75; R. H. Britnell, 'The woollen textile industry of Suffolk in the later middle ages', *The Ricardian* 13 (2003), pp. 86–99; J. N. Hare, 'Growth and recession in the fifteenth century economy: the Wiltshire textile industry and the countryside', *EcHR* 52 (1999), pp. 1–26; J. Hatcher, *English tin production and trade before 1550* (Oxford, 1973).

basic problems of food, clothing and fuel declined, and families were able to spend rising sums of money on manufactured commodities whose sale had previously been much more restricted.[19] Social critics of the late fourteenth century report in strident terms the way in which ordinary people were beginning to ape their betters, and while some allowances have to be made for literary conventions of snobbery and grumpiness there is good reason to believe that their observations had some basis in fact.[20] This ability of a widening range of townsmen and wealthier peasants to broaden the range and quality of what they purchased gave precisely the conditions required to encourage specialisation in particular manufactures in different places. This phenomenon provides a good example, in fact, of the way in which an understanding of general trends (in this case rising real incomes) is needed to explain regionally varying outcomes.

As the history of England's wool and cloth trades implies, regional specialisation in the late Middle Ages was already shaped to some extent by international trade. Chapter 1 commented on the fact that market incentives varied across Europe, being strongest in areas of greater urbanisation like northern Italy and north-western Europe. In much of western and northern England this was a very secondary influence, and even in the eastern, southern and midland shires it affected only a limited range of commodities. But the production of wool and the manufacture of cloth, both of which had uneven regional distributions, were both strongly geared to export trade, and so was the output of coal and tin. If Phillipp Schofield's interesting analysis of the north-eastern economy is right, it implies that specialisations that brought greater prosperity to a region in normal years could nevertheless imply exceptional risks in years of food shortage, when they depended on increasing their trade with other regions (see Chapter 3). One of the most remarkable instances of late medieval regional specialisation was the wine-growing region of Gascony, whose agriculture had been shaped by the stimulus of demand for wine in England and elsewhere in north-western Europe.[21]

It is unlikely that total English exports normally accounted for more than 5–10 per cent of national income at any stage in the fourteenth and fifteenth centuries, which is about as much as we can say given that our estimates are so few and so rough that no intertemporal comparisons are justifiable. An estimate of £352,000 for the value of export trade in the years 1304–11 may be compared with estimates of £4–5 million for national income around 1300 to suggest a proportion of 7–9 per cent, and it is unlikely to have risen above this even in the 1540s.[22] If we assume there was no increase in

---

19 R. H. Britnell, 'Movable goods before the consumer revolution: England c. 1300', in M. Boone and M. Howell (eds), *In but not of the market: movable goods in the late medieval and early modern economy* (Brussels, 2007), pp. 71–80; B. M. S. Campbell, 'England: land and people', in S. H. Rigby (ed.), *A companion to Britain in the later middle ages* (Oxford, 2003), pp. 11–12; M. Kowaleski, 'A consumer economy', in R. Horrox and W. M. Ormrod (eds), *A social history of England, 1200–1500* (Cambridge, 2006), pp. 238–59.

20 J. Hatcher, 'England in the aftermath of the Black Death', *PP* 144 (1994), pp. 13–19.

21 E. M. Carus-Wilson, *Medieval merchant venturers*, 2nd edition (London, 1967), pp. 269–70; R. Dion, *Histoire de la vigne et du vin en France des origines au XIXe siècle* (Paris, 1959), pp. 365–83.

national income between 1452–61 and 1470 – and there is unlikely to have been very much – we can compare an estimated annual value of overseas trade of about £115,000 in the former years with an estimated national income of £3.5 million in the latter year to imply a proportion of only 3–4 per cent.[23] But since the impact of the export trade was very unequally distributed, there must have been parts of the kingdom where appreciably more than these percentages of income depended upon foreign trade because of the extent to which their employment had become dependent upon merchant intermediaries. These surely included the cloth-making villages of west Wiltshire and south and central Suffolk.

Regional history in historical research

In a period when many modern states did not exist, distinction between 'national' and 'regional' history can be problematic. In some respects, the difference between local, that is referring to one particular place, and regional, relating to an area defined by one or more criterion, is more useful. Nevertheless, historians often want to provide a general picture of development, taking account of both the local and regional, and for this purpose it is necessary to consider how regions are defined. The preceding discussion enables us to classify the types of region in practical use amongst historians of agrarian economy and society in the late Middle Ages.

Two types of region appropriate to certain purposes are independent of the existence of towns and trade, since even in a purely subsistence rural economy historians would recognise regional differences of both agricultural and institutional typology. In the former category are regions identified by similarities of landscape and soil types. Although these sometimes correspond to regions with a particular specialisation (to be noted as type 4), they often have a more complex collection of special features, resulting from distinctive characteristics of the landscape. The Breckland and Fenland of eastern England are both in this category, and in both cases their description and interpretation has had important implications for economic history.[24] In the second category are regions of similar rural institutions, defined by such long-established institutions as the Midland open fields, the East Anglian foldcourse system, or by the structure of tenures. Such differences are often very ancient, and can supply valuable clues to the course of economic and social developments in periods before the availability of regional documentary evidence. They can also contribute to debates about the extent to which institutional structures

---

22 R. H. Britnell, 'The English economy and the government, 1450–1550', in J. L. Watts (ed.), *The end of the middle ages?* (Stroud, 1998), p. 94; T. H. Lloyd, 'Overseas trade and the money supply in the fourteenth century', in N. J. Mayhew (ed.), *Edwardian monetary affairs (1279–1344)* (Oxford, 1977), pp. 100–3; N. Mayhew, 'Modelling medieval monetisation', in R. H. Britnell and B. M. S. Campbell (eds), *A Commercialising economy: England 1086–c. 1300* (Manchester, 1995), pp. 58 and 72; G. D. Snooks, 'The dynamic role of the market in the Anglo-Norman economy and beyond, 1086–1300', in Britnell and Campbell (eds), *Commercialising economy*, p. 50.

23 J. L. Bolton, *The medieval English economy, 1150–1500* (London, 1980), p. 307; N. J. Mayhew, 'Population, money supply and the velocity of circulation in England, 1300–1700', *EcHR* 48 (1995), p. 244.

24 E.g. Bailey, *Marginal Economy?*; H. C. Darby, *The medieval fenland* (Cambridge, 1940).

favoured or impeded economic development as commercial pressures became more pervasive.[25]

The growth of commerce superimposes on those patterns further forms of region. A third type of region is defined by the territory that supplied a particular town with agricultural produce – which is likely to have been divided into sub-regions that concentrated on different commodities, perhaps in accordance with the principles of Von Thünen. Although bulky items were unlikely to travel more than 20 miles overland in normal circumstances, access to water transport could greatly extend the area of a town's supply even of grain and fuel, and livestock were likely to travel over larger distances because they could be made to walk.[26] Many smaller towns lay within the supply region of larger ones, and small-town merchants often acted as suppliers to larger neighbours.[27]

A fourth type of region is defined by reference to particular specialisations of agriculture, fishing or industrial production serving distant markets and dependent on mercantile enterprise for its market. The wool-producing Cotswolds, the fisheries of the South-West, and the textile villages of western Wiltshire had regional characteristics in this sense.[28] There can be no very sharp division between 'regional' and 'local' developments, since some specialisations were particular to particular towns or villages, like Thaxted's cutlery industry, or to a few settlements widely distributed amongst others of a different character.[29] Some activities were dependent upon very specific localised mineral resources, for example, and would only occur where certain deposits were easily accessible. Care is needed, too, in discussing developments in textiles as regional phenomena, since specialisations of this kind

25 E.g. D.C. Douglas, *The social structure of medieval East Anglia* (Oxford. 1927); J. E. A. Jolliffe, *Pre-feudal England: the Jutes* (London, 1933); *idem*, 'Northumbrian institutions', *English Historical Review* 41 (1926), pp. 1–42; E. B. Fryde, 'South-western and south-central shires: a region of conservative and oppressive lordship', in *idem, Peasants and landlords in later medieval England, c. 1380–c. 1525* (Stroud, 1996), pp. 209–19.

26 E.g. Campbell *et al., Medieval capital*; C. Dyer, 'Market towns and the countryside in late medieval England', *Canadian Journal of History* 31 (1996), pp. 18–35; J. A. Galloway, D. Keene and M. Murphy, 'Fuelling the city: production and distribution of firewood and fuel in London's region, 1290–1400', *EcHR* 49 (1996), pp. 447–72; M. Kowaleski, *Local markets and regional trade in medieval Exeter* (Cambridge, 1995); Lee, *Cambridge*; *idem*, 'The trade of fifteenth century Cambridge and its region', in M. Hicks (ed.), *Revolution and consumption in medieval England* (Woodbridge, 2001), pp. 127–39.

27 J. A. Galloway, 'One market or many? London and the grain trade of England', in *idem* (ed.), *Trade, urban hinterland and market integration c. 1300–1600* (London, 2000), pp. 23–42; J. Masschaele, *Peasants, merchants and markets: inland trade in medieval England, 1150–1350* (New York, 1997).

28 E.g. E. B. Fryde, 'Sheep and wool of the Cotswolds', and 'Sheep and wool of central and western counties of southern England', in *idem, Peasants and landlords*, pp. 87–112; J. Hare, 'Growth and recession in the fifteenth century economy: the Wiltshire textile industry and the countryside', *EcHR* 52 (1999), pp. 1–26; M. Kowaleski, 'The expansion of the south-western fisheries in late medieval England', *EcHR* 53 (2000), pp. 429–54.

29 C. Dyer, *Making a living in the middle ages. The people of Britain, 850–1520* (New Haven, 2002), p. 205.

were often distributed unevenly across a predominantly agrarian landscape, to be found in some villages but not others.[30]

The relative density of towns supplies a fifth criterion for identifying regions on a yet larger scale of historical geography. Drawing boundaries in this instance is bound to be exceptionally arbitrary, but the existence of such regions is implied by the comments on differing urban densities across Europe in Chapter 1, which observed the exceptional number and size of urban populations in northern Italy and north-western Europe. One well-known attempt to collect data and define such urban regions was that of J. C. Russell.[31] Although defined by reference to urban phenomena, regional differences of this kind had direct implications for many aspects of rural life, such as the volume of local trade in agricultural products, the quantity of money in circulation, the demand for land, the composition of agricultural production and the structure of rural employment.

Apart from these types of region, historians also frequently study regions that have little *a priori* justification except ease of research, as when they study a single county or group of counties, making no strong assumptions about the distinctive regionality of their study area.[32] Studies of taxable wealth or the distribution of the tax-paying population usually compare county or hundred units, because of their unambiguity in the records, rather than attempting to employ regional boundaries defined according to social or environmental criteria.[33] The geographical basis of studies has also often been defined for institutional reasons, especially the survival of a particularly good body of documentation from one source.[34] A good deal of our most coherent evidence about land management and lord-tenant relations comes from the archives of particular episcopal or monastic estates.

Numerous other types of region could be proposed that are not currently much employed for comparative purposes, but which may have more application in future, such as regions of equivalent population density, or of some similar agrarian technology. Because these different types of region are so different in the research purposes for which they are constructed, overlap in complex ways, and are often difficult to define with any exactitude, they rule out the possibility of any absolute definition of regionality. Medieval agrarian regions can only be defined in relation to each problem in hand, and cannot be assumed to have any single and absolute structuring. They became more complex in the course of economic development, and that is necessarily one of the phenomena that it behoves historians to explore.

---

30 R. H. Britnell, *Growth and decline in Colchester, 1300–1525* (Cambridge, 1986), p. 85.

31 J. C. Russell, '*Medieval regions and their cities* (Newton Abbot, 1972).

32 E.g. *AHEW, III*, chapters 2, 3 and 7; G. Platts, *Land and people in medieval Lincolnshire* (Lincoln, 1985); L. R. Poos, *A rural society after the Black Death: Essex, 1350–1525* (Cambridge, 1991); J. Whittle, *The development of agrarian capitalism: land and labour in Norfolk, 1440–1580* (Oxford, 2000).

33 E.g. Baker, 'Changes', pp. 190–6; R. S. Schofield, 'The geographical distribution of wealth in England, 1334–1649', *EcHR*, 2nd series 18 (1965), pp. 483–510.

34 C. C. Dyer and P. R. Schofield, 'Recent work on the agrarian history of medieval Britain', in I. Alfonso (ed.), *The rural history of medieval European societies: trends and perspectives* (Turnhout, 2007), pp. 46–7.

Regional studies and economic trends

To speak of common national or international economic trends, as opposed to local and regional ones, implies that it would be appropriate to employ the concept of a national economy, or group of national economies, in interpreting late medieval data, so that the analogy between modern and medieval economies with which we began this chapter is not so far-fetched as it might seem. England and Wales had a national currency, a common legal system, a fairly well unified system of taxation on property and external trade, and extensive internal trade. The crown of Scotland was less intrusive, but the kingdom had similar features of economic unification to a lesser degree. These institutional features would not of themselves guarantee the viability of writing about economic trends in England, Scotland or Britain. Yet it is possible to show that because markets were fairly well integrated, output, prices, rents, and wages moved with some consistency across different regions, implying the existence of trends in national income that could in principle be measured if we had appropriate data. Defining these common trends as carefully as possible, and attempting to assess degrees of regional variation, has repeatedly proved a meaningful task.

British aggregate data are in some respects exceptionally good. There are price series for numerous commodities and wage series for a few different categories of labour.[35] English and Scottish customs accounts give continuous evidence for fluctuations in exports, although we have no continuous aggregate measure of output for any commodity whether agricultural or industrial.[36] We have rough estimates of English population in 1377 and 1524, and rather more estimates of the coinage in circulation.[37] The high quality of English archives, and particularly that of the central government, has also permitted some remarkable nationwide surveys of particular aspects of rural economy.[38] For historians of continental Europe, it is not always as feasible to compare regional and aggregate data. In Italy, for example, this is partly explained by the absence of a central medieval archive, although rich documentary sources survive in individual places, often kept by individual families.[39] In Spain, the problem appears to be that insufficient research has been undertaken on particular regions, and particular themes, to permit the comparison of varying patterns.[40]

---

35 Chapters 2–4, above; D. L. Farmer, 'Prices and wages, 1350–1500', in *AHEW*, III, pp. 431–525; E. Gemmill and N. J. Mayhew, *Changing values in medieval Scotland: a study of prices, money, and weights and measures* (Cambridge, 1995).

36 E. M. Carus-Wilson and O. Coleman, *England's export trade, 1275–1547* (Oxford, 1963); M. Rorke, 'English and Scottish overseas trade, 1300–1600', *EcHR* 59 (2006), pp. 265–88.

37 M. Allen, 'The volume of the English currency, 1158–1470, *EcHR* 54 (2001), pp. 607–8; B. M. S. Campbell (ed.), *English seigniorial agriculture, 1250–1450* (Cambridge, 2000), p. 403.

38 B. M. S. Campbell, *English seigniorial agriculture, 1250–1450* (Cambridge, 2000); *idem* and K. Bartley, *England on the eve of the Black Death: an atlas of lay lordship, technological innovation: the use of draught animals in English farming from 1066 to 1500* (Cambridge, 1986); *idem*, *Mills in the medieval economy: England, 1300–1540* (Oxford, 2004).

39 L. Provero, 'Forty years of rural history for the Italian middle ages', in Alfonso (ed.), *Rural history*, pp. 153–4.

40 J. A. García de Cortázar and P. Martínez Sopena, 'The historiography of rural society in medieval Spain', in Alfonso (ed.), *Rural history*, p. 120.

Yet even in Britain, where both regional and national data are available, evidence relating to common trends has to be laboriously constructed from sources not intended for the purpose. The resulting observations are insufficient to model economic change after the Black Death without the addition of a large amount of guesswork. There remains much uncertainty about how to describe the course of development, and a great need for ongoing research. In this work regional studies and the aggregate analysis of the medieval economy will complement each other in ways unlike those of modern economies with more securely based statistical information. The distinction between aggregate trends and regional diversity has continually to be redefined in the light of new findings. The most precise data concerning trends in population, wages and prices, output and productivity during the fourteenth and fifteenth centuries come from documentary material relating to particular locations or regions, and common trends can be established only by studying the concordance of such data.

The general outline currently remains fuzzy on many points (see Chapter 2), yet this is likely to be improved by carrying observation, analysis and comparative methodology as far as they will go. Regional studies will continue to make a vitally necessary contribution to knowledge of change in the economy as a whole. At the same time they can only benefit from awareness of more general developments. Given the multiplicity of regions we have discussed, and the evident interaction between them that arose through commercial exchange, agricultural history cannot have any coherent structure unless historians bear in mind the existence of such common problems, and spend part of their time at least in attempting to improve our understanding of them. Only under such circumstances will they be able to place regional diversity in context, and to improve our understanding of the course by which some regions became richer or poorer than others. That this is far from being a forlorn hope is demonstrable from the readiness with which agrarian historians not only of England, but across Europe, meet, discuss, and recognise each other's work as relevant to their own.

Bibliography

Abel, W., *Agricultural fluctuations in Europe from the thirteenth to the twentieth centuries*, trans. O. Ordish (London, 1980).

—, *Geschichte der deutschen Landwirtshaft* (Stuttgart, 1962).

—, 'Landwirtschaft, 1350–1500', in H. Aubin and W. Zorn (eds), *Handbuch der deutschen Wirtschafts- und Sozialgeschichte* 2 vols, Stuttgart (1971), I, pp. 300–33.

—, *Die Wüstungen des ausgehenden Mittelalters*, 2nd edition, (Stuttgart, 1955).

Aberth, J. (ed.), *The Black Death: the great mortality of 1348–1350. a brief history with documents* (Boston, Mass., 2005).

Abulafia, D., 'Southern Italy and the Florentine economy, 1265–1370', *EcHR*, 2nd series 33 (1981), pp. 377–88.

—, *The two Italies: economic relations between the Norman kingdom of Sicily and the northern communes* (Cambridge, 1977).

Alfonso, I. (ed.),*The rural history of medieval European societies: trends and perspectives* (Turnhout, 2007).

Allen, M., 'The volume of the English currency, 1158–1470', *EcHR* 54 (2001), pp. 595–611.

Anderson, P. J. (ed.), *Charters and other writs illustrating the history of the royal burgh of Aberdeen, MCLXXI–MDCCCIV* (Aberdeen, 1890).

Appleby, A. B., 'Grain prices and subsistence crises in England and France, 1590–1740', *JEH* 39 (1979), pp. 865–87.

Astle, T., Ayscough, S. and Caley, J. (eds), *Taxatio ecclesiastica Angliæ et Walliæ, auctoritate P. Nicholai IV, circa A.D. 1291*, RC (London, 1802).

Aston, T. H. (ed.), *Landlords, peasants and politics in medieval England* (Cambridge, 1987).

—, and Philpin, C. H. E. (eds), *The Brenner debate: agrarian class structure and economic development in pre-industrial Europe* (Cambridge, 1985).

Ault, W. O., *Open-field farming in medieval England* (London, 1972).

— *Open-field husbandry and the village community: a study of agrarian by-laws in medieval England*, Transactions of the American Philosophical Society, new series 55 no. 7 (Philadelphia, 1965).

—, 'Village by-laws by common consent', *Speculum* 29 (1954), pp. 378–94 .

Aymard, M., 'Monnaie et économie paysanne', in V. B. Bagnoli (ed.), *La moneta nell' economia europea, secoli XIII-XVIII* (Florence, 1981), pp. 553–65.

Babington, C. and Lumby, J. R. (eds), *Polychronicon Ranulphi Higden monachi Cestrensis*, Rolls Series 41 (9 vols, London, 1865—86).

Baehrel, R., *Une Croissance: La Basse-Provence rurale (fin du XVIe siècle -1789): essai d'économie historique statistique* (Paris, 1961).

Baigent, F. J. (ed.), *The registers of Johan de Sandale and Rigaud de Asserio, bishops of Winchester (A.D. 1316–1323)*, Hampshire Record Society (1897, for 1893).

Bailey, M., 'Peasant welfare in England, 1290–1348', *EcHR* 51 (1998), pp. 223–51.

— 'The concept of the margin in the medieval English economy', *EcHR*, 2nd series 42 (1989), pp. 1–17.

—, *The English manor, c. 1200–c. 1500* (Manchester, 2002).

—, *A marginal economy? East Anglian Breckland in the later Middle Ages* (Cambridge, 1989).

—, 'Peasant welfare in England, 1290–1348', *EcHR* 51 (1998), pp. 223–51.
—, '*Per impetum maris*: natural disaster and economic decline in eastern England, 1275–1350', in Campbell (ed.), *Before the Black Death* (below), pp. 184–208.
—, 'The rabbit and the medieval East Anglian economy', *AHR* 36 (1988), pp. 1–20.
—, 'Rural society', in R. Horrox (ed.), *Fifteenth-century attitudes: perceptions of society in late medieval England* (Cambridge, 1994), pp. 150–68.
Baillie, M., *New light on the Black Death: the cosmic connection* (Stroud, 2006).
Bailly-Maître, M. C., and Benoit, P., 'Les Mines d'argent de la France médiévale', in Société des Historiens Médiévistes de l'Enseignement Supérieur Public, *L'Argent* (below), pp. 17–59.
Bainbridge, V., *Gilds in the medieval countryside* (Woodbridge, 1996).
Baker, A. R. H., 'Changes in the later middle ages', in H. C. Darby, *A new historical geography of England before 1600* (Cambridge, 1976), pp. 186–247.
—, 'Evidence in the "Nonarum inquisitiones" of contracting arable lands in England in the early fourteenth century', *EcHR*, 2nd series 19 (1966), pp. 518–32.
— and Butlin, R. A. (eds), *Studies in the field systems of the British Isles* (Cambridge, 1973).
Baldwin, J. W., *The medieval theories of the just price: romanists, canonists and theologians of the twelfth and thirteenth centuries* (Philadelphia, 1959).
Barron, C. M., *London in the later middle ages: government and people, 1200–1500* (Oxford, 2004).
Bean, J. M. W., 'Landlords', in *AHEW*, III, pp. 526–86.
Béaur, G., 'From the North Sea to Berry and Lorraine: land productivity in northern France, 13th–19th centuries', in Van Bavel and Thoen (eds), *Land productivity* (below), pp. 136–67.
Becker, M. J., *Rochester Bridge, 1387–1856: a history of its early years* (London, 1930).
Beckerman, J. S., 'Procedural innovation and institutional change in medieval English manor courts', *Law and History Review* 10 (1992), pp. 157–252.
—, 'Toward a theory of medieval manorial adjudication: the nature of communal judgments in a system of customary law', *Law and History Review* 13 (1995), pp. 1–22.
Benedictow, O., *The Black Death, 1346–1353: the complete history* (Woodbridge, 2004).
Bennett, J. M., *Ale, beer and brewsters in England* (Oxford, 1996).
Bennett, M. J., 'The Lancashire and Cheshire clergy, 1379', *Transactions of the Historic Society of Lancashire and Cheshire* 124 (1972), pp. 1–30.
Bennett, N. H. (ed.), 'Blunham rectory accounts, 1520–1539', in J. S. Thompson (ed.), *Hundreds, manors, parishes and churches: a selection of early documents for Bedfordshire*, Bedfordshire Historical Record Society 69 (1990), pp. 124–69.
Beresford, M., *The lost villages of medieval England* (London, 1954).
—, and Hurst, J., *Wharram Percy: deserted medieval village* (London, 1990).
—, and St Joseph, J. K. S., *Medieval England: an aerial survey*, 2nd edition (Cambridge, 1979).
Berthe, M., *Famine et epidémies dans la campagne Navarraise à la fin du Moyen Age* (Paris, 1984).
Beveridge, W., *Prices and wages in England from the twelfth to the nineteenth century*, I (London, 1939).
—, 'A statistical crime of the seventeenth century', *Journal of Economic and Business History* 1 (1929), pp. 503–33.
Bickley, W. B., and Carter, W. F. (eds), *Abstract of the bailiffs' accounts of monastic and other estates in the county of Warwick under the supervision of the Court of Augmentations for the year ending at Michaelmas, 1547*, Dugdale Society Publications 2 (London, 1923).
Bierbrauer, P., 'Bäuerliche Revolten im alten Reich. Ein Forschungsbericht', in P. Blickle, P.

Bierbrauer, R. Blickle and C. Ulbrich, *Aufruhr und Empörung. Studien zum bäuerlichen Widerstand im alten Reich* (Munich, 1980), pp. 1–68.
Blanchard, I., 'The continental European cattle trades, 1400–1600', *EcHR*, 2nd series 39 (1986), pp. 427–60.
—, 'Industrial employment and the rural land market, 1380–1520', in Smith (ed.), *Land, kinship and life-cycle* (below), pp. 227–75.
—, *Mining, metallurgy and minting in the middle ages* (3 vols, Stuttgart, 2001—5).
—, Gemmill, E., Mayhew, N., and Whyte, I. D., 'The economy: town and country', in Dennison, Ditchburn and Lynch (eds), *Aberdeen before 1800* (below), pp. 129–158.
Blaschke, K., *Geschichte Sachsens im Mittelalter* (Munich, 1990).
Blockmans, F. and Blockmans, W. P., 'Devaluation, coinage and seignorage under Louis de Nevers and Louis de Male, counts of Flanders, 1330-84', in N. J. Mayhew (ed.), *Coinage in the Low Countries (880–1500)* (Oxford, 1979), pp. 69–94.
Blomquist, T. W., 'The dawn of banking in an Italian commune: thirteenth century Lucca', in Centre for Medieval and Renaissance Studies, University of California, Los Angeles, *The dawn of modern banking* (New Haven, 1979), pp. 53–75.
Bocquet, A., *Recherches sur la population rurale de l'Artois et du Boulonnais pendant la période bourguignonne (1384–1477)*, Mémoires de la Commission Départementale des Monuments Historiques du Pas-de-Calais 13 (Arras, 1969).
Bois, G., *Crise du féodalisme. Economie rurale et démographie en Normandie orientale au début du XVIe siècle* (Paris, 1976), published in English as *The crisis of feudalism: economy and society in eastern Normandy c.1300–1550* (Cambridge, 1984).
Bolton, J. L., *The medieval English economy, 1150–1500* (London, 1980).
Bompaire, M., Lebecq, S., and Sarrazin, J.-L., *L'Économie médiévale* (Paris, 1993).
Bonfield, L., 'The nature of customary law in the manor courts of medieval England', *Comparative Studies of Society and History* 31 (1989), pp. 514–34.
Borrero Fernández, M., *El mundo rural sevillano en el siglo XV: Aljarafe y Ribera* (Seville, 1983).
Borsch, S. J., *The Black Death in Egypt and England: a comparative study* (Austin, 2005).
Boutflower, D. S. (ed.), *Fasti Dunelmenses*, Surtees Society, 139 (1926).
Boutruche, R., *La Crise d'une société. Seigneurs et paysans du Bordelais pendant la Guerre de Cent Ans* (Paris, 1963).
Bowden, P., 'Statistical appendix', in *AHEW*, IV, pp. 814–70.
Brandon, P. F., 'Late-medieval weather in Sussex and its agricultural significance', *Transactions of the Institute of British Geographers* 54 (1971), pp. 1–17.
Bray, G., *Tudor Church reform: the Henrician canons of 1535 and the* Reformatio legum ecclesiasticarum, Church of England Record Society 8 (2000).
Brenner, R., 'Agrarian class structure and economic development in pre-industrial Europe', *PP* 70 (1976), pp. 30–75, reprinted in Aston and Philpin (eds), *Brenner debate* (above), pp. 10–63.
Bridbury, A. R., 'The Black Death', *EcHR* 26 (1973), pp. 577–92, reprinted in *idem*, *The English economy from Bede to the Reformation* (Woodbridge, 1992), pp. 200–17.
—, *Economic growth: England in the later middle ages* (London, 1962).
—, *Medieval English clothmaking: an economic survey* (London, 1982).
Brie, F. W. D. (ed.), *The Brut. or the Chronicles of England*, Early English Text Society, original series 131 and 146 (2 parts, London, 1906–8).
Britnell, R. H., *Britain and Ireland, 1050–1530: economy and society* (Oxford, 2004).
—, 'Commerce and capitalism in late medieval England: problems of description and theory', *Journal of Historical Sociology* 6 (1993), pp. 359–76.
—, *The commercialisation of English society, 1000–1500,* 2nd edition (Manchester, 1996).
—, 'The economic context', in A. J. Pollard (ed.), *The Wars of the Roses* (Basingstoke, 1995), pp. 41–64.

—, 'The English economy and the government, 1450–1550', in J. L. Watts (ed.), *The end of the middle ages?* (Stroud, 1998), pp. 89–116.
—, 'La commercializzazione dei cereali in Inghilterra (1250–1350)', *Quaderni Storici* 32 (1997), pp. 631–61.
—, 'Feudal reaction after the Black Death in the palatinate of Durham', *PP* 128 (1990), pp. 28–47.
—, 'Fields, farms and sun-division in a moorland region, 1100–1400', *AHR* 52 (2004), pp. 20–36.
—, 'Forstall, forestalling and the Statute of Forestallers', *English Historical Review*, 102 (1987), pp. 89–102.
—, *Growth and decline in Colchester, 1300–1525* (Cambridge, 1986).
—, 'Local trade, remote trade: institutions, information and market integration, 1270–1330', in S. Cavaciocchi (ed.), *Fieri e mercati nella integrazione delle economie europee, secc. XIII–XVIII* (Florence, 2001), pp. 185–203.
—, 'Markets, shops, inns, taverns and private houses in medieval English trade', in B. Blondé, P. Stabel, J. Stobart and I. Van Damme (eds), *Buyers and sellers: retail circuits and practices in medieval and early modern Europe* (Turnhout, 2006), pp. 109–23.
—, 'Minor landlords in England and medieval agrarian capitalism', *PP* 89 (1980), pp. 3–22, reprinted in Aston, (ed.), *Landlords* (above), pp. 227–46.
—, 'Movable goods before the consumer revolution: England c. 1300', in M. Boone and M. Howell (eds), *In but not of the market: movable goods in the late medieval and early modern economy* (Brussels, 2007), pp. 71–80.
—, 'The occupation of the land: eastern England', in *AHEW*, III, pp. 53–67.
—, 'The Pastons and their Norfolk', *AHR* 36 (1988), pp. 132–44.
—, 'Price-setting in English borough markets, 1349–1500', *Canadian Journal of History* 31 (1996), pp. 2–15.
—, 'Rochester Bridge, 1381–1530', in N. Yates and J. M. Gibson (eds), *Traffic and politics: the construction and management of Rochester Bridge, AD 43–1993* (Woodbridge, 1994), pp. 41–106.
—, 'Tenant farming and farmers: eastern England', in *AHEW*, III, pp. 611–24.
—, 'Urban demand in the English economy, 1300-1600', in Galloway, ed., *Trade,* (below), pp. 1–21.
—, 'Uses of money in medieval Britain', in D. Wood (ed.), *Medieval money matters* (Oxford, 2004), pp. 16–30.
—, (ed.), *The Winchester pipe rolls and medieval English society* (Woodbridge, 2003).
—, 'The woollen textile industry of Suffolk in the later middle ages', *The Ricardian* 13 (2003), pp. 86–99.
—, and Campbell, B. M. S. (eds), *A commercialising economy: England 1086 to c. 1300* (Manchester, 1995).
— and Hatcher, J. (eds), *Progress and problems in Medieval England: essays in honour of Edward Miller* (Cambridge, 1996).
Britton, E., *The community of the vill: a study in the history of the family and village life in fourteenth-century England* (Toronto, 1977).
Brown, A. D., *Popular piety in late medieval England* (Oxford 1995).
Brown, J. C., *In the shadow of Florence: provincial society in renaissance Pescia* (New York, 1982).
Cabrera, E., 'The medieval origin of the great landed estates of the Guadalquivir Valley', *EcHR* 42 (1989), pp. 465–83.
— and Moros, A., *Fuenteorejuna: la violencia antiseñorial en el siglo XV* (Barcelona, 1991).
Cabrillana, N., 'La crisis del siglo XIV en Castilla: la Peste Negra en el obispado de Palencia', *Hispania* 109 (1968), pp. 245–58.
—, 'Los despoblados en Castilla la Vieja', *Hispania* 119 (1971), pp. 485–550.

Caley, J., and Hunter, J. (eds), *Valor ecclesiasticus*, RC (6 vols, London, 1810–34).
Cam, H. M., 'The community of the vill', in V. Ruffer and A. J. Taylor (eds), *Medieval studies presented to Rose Graham* (Oxford, 1950), pp. 1–14.
Campbell, B. M. S., 'Agricultural progress in medieval England: some evidence from eastern Norfolk', *EcHR* 36 (1983), pp. 26–46.
—, 'Arable productivity in medieval England: some evidence from Norfolk', *JEH* 43 (1983), pp. 379–404.
—, (ed.), *Before the Black Death: studies in the 'crisis' of the early fourteenth century* (Manchester, 1991).
—, *English seigniorial agriculture, 1250–1450* (Cambridge, 2000).
—, 'Commercial dairy production on medieval English demesnes: the case of Norfolk', *Anthropozoologica* 16 (1992), pp. 107–18.
—, 'England: land and people', in Rigby (ed.), *Companion to Britain in the later middle ages* (below), pp. 3–25.
—, 'A fair field once full of folk: agrarian change in an era of population decline', *AHR* 41 (1993), pp. 60–70.
—, 'The land', in Horrox and Ormrod (eds), *Social history of England* (below), pp. 179–237.
—, 'Land, labour, livestock and productivity trends in English seignorial agriculture, 1208–1450', in B. M. S. Campbell and M. Overton (eds), *Land, labour and livestock: historical studies in European agricultural productivity* (Manchester, 1991), pp. 144–82.
—, 'Matching supply to demand: crop production and disposal by English demesnes in the century of the Black Death', *JEH* 57 (1997), pp. 827–58.
—, 'Measuring the commercialisation of seigneurial agriculture c. 1300', in R. H. Britnell and B. M. S. Campbell (eds), *A commercialising economy: England 1086 to c. 1300* (Manchester, 1995), pp. 132–93.
—, and Bartley, K., *England on the eve of the Black Death: an atlas of lay lordship, land, and wealth, 1300–49* (Manchester, 2006).
—, Bartley, K. C. and Power, J. P., 'The demesne-farming systems of post -Black Death England: a classification', *AHR* 44 (1996), pp. 131–79.
—, Galloway, J. A., Keene, D. and Murphy, M., *A medieval capital and its grain supply: agrarian production and distribution in the London region c. 1300* (London, 1993).
— and Overton, M., 'A new perspective on medieval and early modern agriculture: six centuries of Norfolk farming, *c.* 1250–*c.* 1850', *PP* 141 (1993), pp. 38–105.
Carpenter, C., 'Gentry and community in medieval England', *Journal of British Studies* 33 (1994), pp. 340–80.
Carsten, F. L., *The origins of Prussia* (Oxford, 1954).
Carus-Wilson, E. M., *The expansion of Exeter at the close of the middle ages* (Exeter, 1963).
—, *Medieval merchant venturers*, 2nd edition (London, 1967).
— and Coleman, O., *England's export trade, 1275–1547* (Oxford, 1963).
Casado Alonso, H., 'Producción agraria, precios y coyuntura económica en la diocesis de Burgos y Palencia a fines de la Edad Media', *Studia Historica Historia Medieval* 9 (1991), pp. 67–101.
Cazelles, R., *Nouvelle Histoire de Paris: De la fin du règne de Philippe Auguste à la mort de Charles V, 1223–1380* (Paris, 1972).
Cervantes Bello, F. J., 'Crisis agrícola y guerra de independencia en el entorno de Puebla. El caso de San Martín y sus cercanías, 1800–1820', *Estudios de Historia Novohispania*, 20 (1999), pp. 107–33.
Chadwick, S. J., 'The Dewsbury moot hall', *Yorkshire Archaeological Journal* 21 (1911), pp. 345–478.
Chayanov, A. V., *The theory of peasant economy* (ed.) D. Thorner, B. Kerblay and R. E. F. Smith (Manchester, 1986).

Cherubini, G., 'Foires et marchés dans les campagnes italiennes au moyen âge', in Desplat (ed.), *Foires et marchés* (below), pp. 71–84.
—, *L'Italia rurale del basso medioevo* (Rome, 1984).
—, *Signori, contadini, borghesi: ricerche sulla società italiana del basso medioevo* (Florence, 1974).
Chibnall, M. (ed.), *Select documents of the English lands of the abbey of Bec*, Camden Society, 3rd series 73 (1951).
Childs, W. (ed.), *Vita Edwardi Secundi* (Oxford, 2005).
Clark, E., 'Debt litigation in a late medieval English vill', in J. A. Raftis (ed.), *Pathways to medieval peasants* (Toronto, 1981), pp. 247–79.
Clemente Ramos, J., *La economía campesina en la Corona de Castilla (1000–1300)* (Barcelona, 2003).
Cobban, A. B., *The King's Hall within the university of Cambridge in the later middle ages* (Cambridge, 1969).
Coen, S., 'After the Black Death: labour legislation and attitudes towards labour in late-medieval western Europe', *EcHR* 60 (2007), pp. 457–85.
Comba, R., *Contadini, signori e mercanti nel Piemonte medievale* (Bari, 1988).
Cornia, G. A., 'Farm size, land yields and the agricultural production function: an analysis for fifteen developing countries', *World Development* 13 (1985), pp. 513–34.
Creighton, C., *A history of epidemics in Britain from A.D. 664 to the extinction of the plague* (2 vols., Cambridge, 1891–4).
Darby, H. C., *The medieval fenland* (Cambridge, 1940).
Davis, J., 'Baking for the common good: a reassessment of the assize of bread in medieval England', *EcHR* 57 (2004), pp. 465–502.
Day, J., *The medieval market economy* (Oxford, 1987).
Dejongh, G. and Thoen, E., 'Arable productivity in Flanders and the former territory of Belgium in a long-term perspective (from the middle ages to the end of the ancien régime)', in Van Bavel and Thoen (eds), *Land productivity* (below), pp. 30–65.
Dennison, E. P., Ditchburn, D. and Lynch, M. (eds), *Aberdeen before 1800: a new history* (East Linton, 2002).
Denton, J. H., 'The valuation of the ecclesiastical benefices of England and Wales, 1291–2', *Historical Research* 66 (1993), pp. 231–50.
Derville, A., *L'Agriculture du Nord au moyen âge (Artois, Cambrésis, Flandre wallonne),* (Villeneuve-d'Ascq, 1999).
—, 'Dîmes, rendements du blé et "révolution agricole" dans le nord de la France au moyen âge', *Annales ESC* 42 (1987), pp. 1411–32.
Desplat, C. (ed.), *Foires et marchés dans les campagnes de l'Europe médiévale et moderne* (Toulouse, 1996).
Desportes, F., *Le Pain au moyen âge* (Paris, 1987).
DeWindt, A., 'Peasant power structures in fourteenth-century King's Ripton', *Mediaeval Studies* 38 (1976), pp. 236–67.
DeWindt, E. B., *Land and people in Holywell-cum-Needingworth* (Toronto, 1971).
Díaz de Durana, J. R., *Alava en la baja Edad Media. Crisis, recuperación y transformaciones socioeconómicas (c. 1250–1525)* (Vitoria, 1986).
Dickinson, W. C. (ed.), *Extracts from the early records of Aberdeen, 1317, 1398–1407,* Scottish History Society, 3rd series 49 (1957).
Dion, R., *Histoire de la vigne et du vin en France des origines au XIXe siècle* (Paris, 1959).
Dobson, R. B., *Durham Priory, 1400–1450* (Oxford, 1973).
Dodds, B., 'Durham Priory tithes and the Black Death between Tyne and Tees', *Northern History* 39 (2002), pp. 5–24.
—, 'Estimating arable output using Durham Priory tithe receipts, 1341–1450', *EcHR* 57 (2004), pp. 245–85.

—, 'Managing tithes in the late middle ages', *AHR* 53 (2005), pp. 125–40.
—, 'Peasants, landlords and production between the Tyne and Tees, 1349–1450', in Liddy and Britnell (eds), *North-east England* (below), pp. 173–96.
—, *Peasants and production in the medieval North-East: the evidence from tithes, 1270–1536* (Woodbridge, 2007).
—, 'Peasant production and productivity', paper delivered at the Ninth Anglo-American Seminar on the Medieval Economy and Society, Lincoln, 2007.
—, Tithe and agrarian output between the Tyne and Tees, 1350–1450 (unpublished Ph.D. thesis, University of Durham, 2002).
—, 'Workers on the Pittington demesne in the late middle ages', *Archaeologia Aeliana* 28 (2000), pp. 147–61.
Dodgshon, R. A., *The origin of British field systems: an interpretation* (London, 1980).
Dollinger, P., *The German Hansa*, trans. D. S. Ault and S. H. Steinberg (London, 1970).
Donaldson, R., Patronage and the Church: a study in the social structure of the secular clergy in the diocese of Durham (1311–1540) (2 vols, unpublished Ph.D. dissertation, University of Edinburgh, 1955).
Douglas, D. C., *The social structure of medieval East Anglia* (Oxford. 1927).
Drew, J. S., 'Manorial accounts of St Swithun's Priory Winchester', reprinted in E. M. Carus-Wilson (ed.), *Essays in economic history* (3 vols, London, 1954–62), II, pp. 12–30.
DuBoulay, F. R. H., *The lordship of Canterbury* (London, 1966).
Duby, G., *Hommes et structures du moyen âge* (Paris, 1973).
—, 'Medieval agriculture, 900-1500', in C. M. Cipolla (ed.), *The Fontana economic history of Europe: the middle ages* (London, 1972), pp. 175–220.
—, *Rural economy and country life in the medieval West,* trans. C. Postan (London, 1962).
—, *et al., Villages désertés et histoire économique, XI-XVIII siècles,* École Pratique des Hautes Études, Centre de Recherches Historiques (Paris, 1965).
Duncan, A. A. M., *Scotland: the making of the kingdom* (Edinburgh, 1975).
Dunsford, H. M. and Harris, S. J., 'Colonization of the wasteland in County Durham, 1100–1400', *EcHR* 56 (2003), pp. 34–56.
Dyer, A., 'Ranking lists of medieval English towns', in D. M. Palliser (ed.), *The Cambridge urban history of Britain, I: 600–1540* (Cambridge, 2000), pp. 747–70.
—, '"Urban decline"' in England. 1377–1525', in T. R. Slater (ed.), *Towns in decline, AD 100–1600* (Aldershot, 2000), pp. 266–88.
Dyer, C., *An age of transition? economy and society in England in the later middle ages* (Oxford, 2005).
—, 'Changes in diet in the late middle ages: the case of harvest workers', *AHR* 36 (1988), pp. 21–37, reprinted in *idem, Everyday life* (below), pp. 77–99.
—, 'The English medieval village community and its decline', *Journal of British Studies* 33 (1994), pp. 407–29.
—, *Everyday life in medieval England* (London and Rio Grande, 1994).
—, 'Farming practice and technique: the west midlands', in *AHEW*, III, pp. 222–38.
—, 'Gardens and orchards in medieval England', in *idem, Everyday life* (above), pp. 113–31.
—, 'The hidden trade of the middle ages: evidence from the west midlands of England', *Journal of Historical Geography* 18 (1992), pp. 283–303, reprinted in *idem, Everyday life* (above), pp. 283–303.
—, *Lords and peasants in a changing society: the estates of the bishopric of Worcester 680–1540* (Cambridge, 1980).
—, *Making a living in the middle ages. The people of Britain, 850–1520* (New Haven, 2002).
—, 'Market towns and the countryside in late medieval England', *Canadian Journal of History* 31 (1996), pp. 18–35.
—, 'The occupation of the land: the west midlands', in *AHEW*, III, pp. 77–92.

—, 'Peasants and coins: the uses of money in the middle ages', *British Numismatic Journal* 67 (1997), pp. 30–47.
—, 'Rural Europe', in C. Allmand (ed.), *The new Cambridge medieval history, VII: c. 1415–c. 1500* (Cambridge, 1998), pp. 106–20.
—, 'A small landowner in the fifteenth century', *Midland History* 1 (1972), pp. 1–14.
—, *Standards of living in the later middle ages: social change in England c. 1200-1520* (Cambridge, 1989).
—, 'Taxation and communities in late medieval England', in Britnell and Hatcher (eds), *Progress and problems* (above), pp. 168–90.
—, 'Were there any capitalists in fifteenth-century England?', in J. Kermode (ed.), *Enterprise and individuals in fifteenth-century England* (Stroud, 1991), pp. 1–24, reprinted in *idem, Everyday Life* (below), pp. 305–27.
—, and Schofield, P. R., 'Recent work on the agrarian history of medieval Britain', in Alfonso (ed.), *Rural history* (above), pp. 21–55.
Dyer, G., 'Output per acre and size of holding: the logic of peasant agriculture under semi-feudalism', *Journal of Peasant Studies* 24 (1996), pp. 103–131.
Elrington, C. R., 'Assessments of Gloucestershire: fiscal records in local history', *Transactions of the Bristol and Gloucestershire Archaeological Society* 103 (1985), pp. 5–16.
Epstein, S. R., *An island for itself: economic development and social change in late medieval Sicily* (Cambridge, 1992).
—, *Alle origini della fattoria toscana: l'ospedale della Scala di Siena et le sue terre (metà '200 – metà '400)* (Florence, 1986).
Evans, T. A. R. and Faith, R. J., 'College estates and university finances, 1350–1500', in J. I. Catto and R. Evans (eds), *The history of the university of Oxford, II: late medieval Oxford* (Oxford, 1992), pp. 635–707.
Faith, R., 'Berkshire: fourteenth and fifteenth centuries', in Harvey (ed.), *Peasant land market* (below), pp. 107–58.
Farmer, D. L., 'Grain yields on Westminster Abbey manors, 1271–1410', *Canadian Journal of History* 18 (1983), pp. 331–47.
—, 'Grain yields on Winchester manors in the later middle ages', *EcHR* 2nd series 30 (1977), pp. 555–66.
—, 'Marketing the produce of the countryside, 1200–1500', in *AHEW*, III, pp. 324–430.
—, 'Prices and wages, 1350–1500', in *AHEW*, III, pp. 431–525.
Farr, M. W. (ed.), *Accounts and surveys of the Wiltshire lands of Adam de Stratton*, Wiltshire Record Society 14 (1959).
Favier, J., *Nouvelle historie de Paris: Paris au XVe siècle, 1380–1500* (Paris, 1974).
Flett, I. and Cripps, J., 'Documentary sources', in M. Lynch, M. Spearman and G. Stell, (eds), *The Scottish medieval town* (Edinburgh, 1988), pp. 18–41.
Fogel, R. W., 'Second thoughts on the European escape from hunger: famines, chronic malnutrition and mortality rates', in S. R. Osmani (ed.), *Nutrition and poverty* (Oxford, 1992), pp. 243–86.
Fournial, É., *Histoire monétaire de l'Occident médiéval* (Paris, 1970).
Fourquin G., *Les Campagnes de la région parisienne à la fin du moyen âge du milieu du XIIIe siècle au début du XVIe siècle* (Paris, 1964).
Fowler, J. T. (ed.), *Extracts from the account rolls of the priory of Durham, 1303–1541*, Surtees Society 99, 100, 102 (3 vols, London, 1898–1901).
Fox, H. S. A., 'Exploitation of the landless by lords and tenants in early medieval England', in Z. Razi and R. M. Smith (eds), *Medieval society and the manor court* (Oxford, 1996), pp. 518–68.
—, 'The people of Woodbury in the fifteenth century', *The Devon Historian* 56 (1998), pp. 3–8.

—, 'Servants, cottagers and tied cottages during the later middle ages: towards a regional dimension', *Rural History* 6 (1995), pp. 125–54.
Fraser, C. M., *A history of Antony Bek, bishop of Durham, 1283–1311* (Oxford, 1957).
—, 'The pattern of trade in the north-east of England, 1265–1350', *Northern History* 4 (1969), pp. 44–66.
—, (ed.), *Records of Antony Bek, bishop and patriarch 1283–1311*, Surtees Society 162 (1947).
Fray, J.-L., *Villes et bourgs de Lorraine: réseaux urbains et centralité au moyen âge* (Clermont-Ferrand, 2006).
Freedman, P., 'Rural society', in M. Jones (ed.), *The new Cambridge medieval history, VI: c.1300–c.1415* (Cambridge, 2000), pp. 82–101.
Fryde, E. B., *Peasants and landlords in later medieval England* (Stroud, 1996).
— and Fryde, N., 'Peasant rebellions and peasant discontents', in *AHEW* III, pp. 744–819.
Galloway, J. A., 'London's grain supply: changes in production, distribution and consumption during the fourteenth century', *Franco-British Studies* 20 (1995), pp. 23–34.
—, 'One market or many? London and the grain trade of England', in *idem* (ed.), *Trade* (below), pp. 23–42.
—, 'Town and country in England, 1300–1700', in S. R. Epstein (ed.), *Town and country in Europe, 1300–1800* (Cambridge, 2001), pp. 106–31.
— (ed.), *Trade, urban hinterland and market integration c. 1300–1600* (London, 2000).
—, Keene, D. and Murphy, M., 'Fuelling the city: production and distribution of firewood and fuel in London's region, 1290–1400', *EcHR* 49 (1996), pp. 447–72.
García de Cortazar, J. A., *La sociedad rural en la España medieval* (Madrid, 1988).
—, and Martínez Sopena, P., 'The historiography of rural society in medieval Spain', in Alfonso (ed.), *Rural history* (above), pp. 93–139.
Geertz, C., *Agricultural involution: The process of ecological change in Indonesia* (Berkeley and Los Angeles, 1963).
Gemmill, E., 'Signs and symbols in medieval Scottish trade', *Review of Scottish Culture* 13 (2000–1), pp. 7–17.
— (ed.), *Aberdeen guild records, 1437–1468*, Scottish History Society, 5th series 17 (2005).
—, and Mayhew, N., *Changing values in medieval Scotland: a study of prices, money, and weights and measures* (Cambridge, 1995).
Genicot, L., *La Crise agricole du bas moyen âge dans le Namurois* (Louvain, 1970).
—, 'Crisis: from the middle ages to modern times', in Postan (ed.), *Cambridge economic history of Europe*, I (below), pp. 660–741.
Germain, R., *La France centrale médiévale: pouvoirs, peuplement, société, économie, culture* (Saint-Étienne, 1999).
Gissel, S., 'Rents and other economic indicators', in *idem et al.*, *Desertion and land colonization* (below), pp. 143–71.
—, *et al.*, *Desertion and land colonization in the nordic countries, c. 1300–1600* (Stockholm, 1981).
Glennie, P., 'In search of agrarian capitalism: manorial land markets and the acquisition of land in the Lea Valley, c.1450–c.1560', *Continuity and Change* 3 (1988), pp. 11–40.
Goldberg, P. J. P., 'Mortality and economic change in the diocese of York, 1390–1514', *Northern History* 24 (1988), pp. 38–55.
González Jiménez, M., *En torno a los orígines de Andalucia: la repoblación del siglo XIII* (Seville, 1980).
Gordon, J., *Aberdoniae vtrivsque descriptio: a description of both touns of Aberdeen*, ed. C. Innes, Spalding Club 5 (1842).
Gottfried, R. S., *Epidemic disease in fifteenth-century England; the medical response and*

the demographic consequences (New Brunswick, 1978).
Goy, J., and Le Roy Ladurie, E. (eds), *Les Fluctuations du produit de la dîme. Conjoncture décimale et domaniale de la fin du moyen âge au XVIIIe siècle* (Paris, 1972).
—, and — (eds.), *Prestations paysannes dîmes, rente foncière et mouvement de la production agricole à l'époque préindustrielle* (Paris, 1982).
Graham, R., *English ecclesiastical studies; being some essays in research in medieval history* (London, 1929).
Gras, N. S. B. and Gras, E. C., *The economic and social history of an English village (Crawley, Hampshire) A.D. 909–1928* (Cambridge, Mass., 1930).
Gray, H. L., *English field systems* (Harvard, Mass., 1915).
Greenwell, W. (ed.), *Bishop Hatfield's survey, a record of the possessions of the see of Durham*, Surtees Society 32 (1857).
— (ed.), *Boldon Buke: a survey of the possessions of the see of Durham*, Surtees Society 25 (Durham, 1852).
— (ed.), *Feodarium Prioratus Dunelmensis: a survey of the estates of the prior and convent of Durham compiled in the fifteenth century, illustrated by the original grants and other evidences*, Surtees Society 58 (1871).
Halcrow, E. M., 'The decline of demesne farming on the estates of Durham Cathedral Priory', *EcHR*, 2nd series 7 (1954–5), pp. 345–56.
Hanawalt, B., *Crime and conflict in English communities 1300–1348* (Harvard, 1979).
—, *The ties that bound: peasant families in medieval England* (Oxford, 1986).
Hanham, A., *The Celys and their world: an English merchant family of the fifteenth century* (Cambridge, 1985).
Hare, J. N., 'Agriculture and rural settlement in the chalklands of Wiltshire and Hampshire from c.1200–c.1500', in M. Aston, and C. Lewis (eds.), *The medieval landscape of Wessex* (Oxford, 1994), pp. 159–69
—, 'The bishop and the prior: demesne agriculture in medieval Hampshire', *AHR* 54 (2006), pp. 187–212.
—, 'Change and continuity in Wiltshire agriculture: the later middle ages', in W. E. Minchinton (ed.), *Agricultural improvement: medieval and modern,* Exeter Papers in Economic History 14 (Exeter, 1981), pp. 1–18.
—, 'Growth and recession in the fifteenth-century economy: the Wiltshire textile industry and the countryside', *EcHR* 52 (1999), pp. 1–26.
—, *A prospering society: Wiltshire in the later middle ages* (forthcoming).
—, 'Regional prosperity in fifteenth-century England: some evidence from Wessex', in M. Hicks (ed.), *Revolution and consumption in late medieval England* (Woodbridge, 2001), pp. 105–26.
Haren, M., *Sin and society in fourteenth-century England: a study of the* Memoriale presbiterorum (Oxford, 2000).
Harper-Bill, C. (ed.), *The register of John Morton, archbishop of Canterbury, 1486–1500* (3 vols, Leeds and Woodbridge, 1987–2000).
— (ed.), *Religious belief and ecclesiastical careers in late medieval England* (Woodbridge, 1991).
Harris, S. J., 'Wastes, the margins and the abandonment of land: the bishop of Durham's estate, 1350–1480', in Liddy and Britnell (eds), *North-east England* (below), pp. 197–219.
Harrison, B., 'Field systems and demesne farming on the Wiltshire estates of Saint Swithun's Priory, Winchester', *AHR* 43 (1995), pp. 1–18.
Harrison, C. J., 'Grain price analysis and harvest qualities, 1465–1634', *AHR* 19 (1971), pp. 135–55.
Hartridge, R. A. R., *A history of vicarages in the middle ages* (Cambridge, 1930).
Harvey, B. F., *Living and dying in England, 1100–1540: the monastic experience* (Oxford, 1993).

—, *Westminster Abbey and its estates in the middle ages* (Oxford, 1977).
Harvey, P. D. A., *Manorial records* (London, 1984).
—, *A medieval Oxfordshire village: Cuxham, 1240 to 1400* (London, 1965).
—(ed.), *The peasant land market in medieval England* (Oxford, 1984).
Harwood Long, W., 'The low yields of corn in medieval England', *EcHR* 32 (1979), pp. 459–69.
Hatcher, J., 'England in the aftermath of the Black Death', *PP* 144 (1994), pp. 3–35.
—, *English tin production and trade before 1550* (Oxford, 1973).
—, 'English serfdom and villeinage: towards a reassessment', *PP* 90 (1981), pp. 3–39, reprinted in Aston (ed.), *Landlords* (above), pp. 247–83.
—, 'The great slump of the mid-fifteenth century', in Britnell and Hatcher (eds), *Problems and progress* (above), pp. 237–72.
—, 'Mortality in the fifteenth century: some new evidence', *EcHR*, 2nd series 39 (1986), pp. 19–38.
—, *Plague, population and the English economy, 1348–1530* (London, 1977).
—, *Rural economy and society in the duchy of Cornwall, 1300–1500* (Cambridge, 1970).
—, and Bailey, M., *Modelling the middle ages: the history and theory of England's economic development* (Oxford, 2001).
—, Piper, A. J. and Stone, D., 'Monastic mortality: Durham Priory, 1395–1529', *EcHR* 59 (2006), pp. 667–87.
Heath, P., *Medieval clerical accounts*, St Anthony's Hall Publications 26 (York, 1964).
—, 'North Sea fishing in the fifteenth century: the Scarborough fleet', *Northern History* 3 (1968), pp. 53–68.
Hector, L. C. and Harvey, B. F. (eds), *The Westminster Chronicle, 1381–1394* (Oxford, 1982).
Henry, A., 'Silver and salvation: a late fifteenth-century confessor's itinerary throughout the parish of Bere Ferrers, Devon', *Report and Transactions of the Devonshire Association for the Advancement of Science* 133 (2001), pp. 17–96.
Heers, J., *Gênes au XVe siècle* (Paris, 1971).
Helbig, H., *Gesellschaft und Wirtschaft der Mark Brandenburg im Mittelalter* (Berlin, 1973).
Herlihy, D, *Medieval and renaissance Pistoia: the social history of an Italian town, 1207–1430* (New Haven and London, 1967).
—, 'Santa Maria Impruneta: a rural commune in the late middle ages', in Rubinstein (ed.), *Florentine studies* (below), pp. 242–76.
— and Klapisch-Zuber, C., *Les Toscans et leurs familles* (Paris, 1978), later published in an English version as *Tuscans and their families: a study of the Florentine catasto of 1427* (New Haven, Conn., 1985).
Hilton, R. H., *Bond men made free: medieval peasant movements and the English rising of 1381* (London, 1973).
—, *Class conflict and the crisis of feudalism* (London, 1985).
—, *The decline of serfdom in medieval England* (London, 1969).
—, *The economic development of some Leicestershire estates in the 14th and 15th centuries* (Oxford, 1947).
—, *The English peasantry in the later middle ages* (Oxford, 1975).
—, *A medieval society: the west midlands at the end of the thirteenth century*, 2nd edition (Cambridge, 1983).
— and Aston, T. H. (eds), *The English rising of 1381* (Cambridge, 1984).
Hobson, T. B. (ed.), *Adderbury "rectoria"*, Oxford Record Society 8 (1926).
Hockey, S. F. (ed.), *The account-book of Beaulieu Abbey*, Camden Society, 4th series 16 (1975).
Hoffmann, R. C., *Land, liberties and lordship in a late medieval countryside: agrarian structures and change in the duchy of Wrocław* (Philadelphia, 1989).

Holmes, G. A., *The estates of the higher nobility in fourteenth-century England* (Cambridge, 1957).
Holt, R., *The mills of medieval England* (Oxford, 1988).
Hopcroft, R. L., 'The social origins of agrarian change in late medieval England', *American Journal of Sociology* 99 (1994), pp. 1559–95.
Horrox, R. (ed.), *The Black Death* (Manchester, 1994).
— and Ormrod, W. M. (eds), *A social history of England, 1200–1500* (Cambridge, 2006).
Hoskins, W. G., 'Harvest fluctuations and English economic history, 1480–1619', *AHR* 12 (1964), pp. 28–46.
—_, 'Harvest fluctuations and English economic history, 1620–1759', *AHR* 16 (1968), pp. 15–31.
Howell, C., *Land, family and inheritance in transition: Kibworth Harcourt, 1280–1700* (Cambridge, 1983).
Hunt, E. S., *The medieval super-companies: a study of the Peruzzi company of Florence* (Cambridge, 1994).
Hybel, N., 'The grain trade of northern Europe before 1350', *EcHR* 55 (2002), pp. 229–45.
Hyde, J. K., *Society and politics in medieval Italy: the evolution of civil life, 1000–1350* (London, 1973).
Innes, C. (ed.), *Ancient laws and customs of the burghs of Scotland, I: A.D. 1154–1424*, Scottish Burgh Record Society 1 (Edinburgh, 1868).
Jenks, S., 'Von den archaischen Grundlagen bis zur Schwelle der moderne (ca. 1000-1450)', in M. North (ed.), *Deutsche Wirtschaftsgschichte; ein Jahrtausend im Überblick* (Munich, 2000), pp. 15–106.
Jolliffe, J. E. A., 'Northumbrian institutions', *English Historical Review* 41 (1926), pp. 1–42.
—, *Pre-feudal England: the Jutes* (London, 1933).
Jones, P., *Economia e società nell'Italia medievale* (Turin, 1980).
—, 'From manor to mezzadria: a Tuscan case-study in the medieval origins of modern agrarian society', in Rubinstein (ed.), *Florentine studies* (below), pp. 193–241.
—, 'Medieval agrarian society in its prime: Italy', in Postan (ed.), *Cambridge economic history of Europe,* I (below), pp. 340–431.
—, *The Italian city state: from commune to signoria* (Oxford, 1997).
Jordan, W. G., *The great famine: northern Europe in the early fourteenth century* (Princeton, N.J., 1996).
Karakacili, E., 'English agrarian labour productivity rates before the Black Death: a case study', *JEH* 64 (2004), pp. 24–60.
Keen, M., *English society in the later middle ages, 1348–1500* (London, 1990).
Keene, D., 'Medieval London and its region', *The London Journal* 14 (1989), pp. 99–111.
Keil, I. J. E., 'Impropriator and benefice in the later middle ages', *Wiltshire Archaeological and Natural History Magazine* 58 (1963), pp. 351–61.
Kershaw, I., *Bolton Priory: the economy of a northern monastery, 1286–1325* (London, 1973).
—, 'The great famine and agrarian crisis in England 1315–1322', *PP* 59 (1973), pp. 3–50.
King, E., 'The occupation of the land: the east midlands', in *AHEW*, III, pp. 67–76.
Kitchen, G. W., *The manor of Manydown*, Hampshire Record Society (1895).
Kitsikopolous, H., 'Standards of living and capital formation in pre-plague England: a peasant budget model', *EcHR* 53 (2000), pp. 237–61.
Klapisch-Zuber, C. and Day, J., 'Villages désertés en Italie. Esquisse', in G. Duby *et al.*, *Villages désertés et histoire économique, XI–XVIII siècles*, École Practique des Hautes Études, Centre de Recherches Historiques (Paris, 1965), pp. 419–59.
Kosminsky, E., *Studies in the agrarian history of England* (ed.) R. H. Hilton, trans. R. Kisch (Oxford, 1956).
Kotel'nikova, L. A., *Mondo contadino e città in Italia dall' XI al XIV secolo* (Bologna, 1975).

Kowaleski, M., 'A consumer economy', in Horrox and Ormrod, eds., *Social history of England* (above), pp. 238–59.
—, 'The expansion of the south-western fisheries in late medieval England', *EcHR* 53 (2000), pp. 429–454.
—, 'The grain trade in fourteenth-century Exeter', in E. B. DeWindt (ed.), *The salt of common life: individuality and choice in the medieval town, countryside and Church* (Kalamazoo, 1995), pp. 1–52.
—, *Local markets and regional trade* (Cambridge, 1995).
Kühlhorn, E., *Die mittelalterlichen Wüstungen in Südniedersachsen* (4 vols, Bielefeld, 1994–6).
Kula, W., *Measures and men*, trans. R. Szreter (Princeton, 1986).
Kümin, B., *The shaping of a community: the rise and reformation of an English parish, c. 1400–1560* (Brookfield, Vermont, 1996).
Ladero Quesada, M. A., 'Los cereales en la Andalucía del siglo XV', *Homenaje a Menéndez Pidal I, Revista de la Universidad de Madrid* 18, part 69 (Madrid, 1969), pp. 223–40.
— and González Jiménez, M., *Diezmo eclesiástico y producción de cereales en el reino de Sevilla, (1408–1503)* (Seville, 1979).
Lane, F. C., *Venice: a maritime republic* (Baltimore, 1973).
Langdon, J., *Horses, oxen and technological innovation: the use of draught animals in English farming from 1066 to 1500* (Cambridge, 1986).
—, *Mills in the medieval economy: England, 1300–1540* (Oxford, 2004).
—, 'Water-mills and windmills in the west midlands, 1086–1500', *EcHR* 44 (1991), pp. 424–44.
Lardin, P., 'La Crise monétaire de 1420–1422 en Normandie', in Société des Historiens Médiévistes de l'Enseignement Supérieur Public, *L'Argent* (below), pp. 101–43.
La Roncière, C. M. de, *Florence: Centre économique régional au XIVe siècle* (5 vols, Aix-en-Provence, 1976).
—, 'L'Approvisionnement des villes italiennes au moyen âge (XIVe–XVe siècles)', in Centre Culturel de l'Abbaye de Flaran, *L'Approvisionnement des villes de l'Europe occidentale au moyen âge et aux temps modernes* (Auch, 1985), pp. 33–51.
—, *Prix et salaires à Florence au XIVe siècle (1280–1380)* (Rome, 1982).
Larson, P. L., Conflict and compromise in the late medieval countryside: lords and peasants in Durham, 1349–1430 (unpublished Ph.D. dissertation, Rutgers, the State University of New Jersey, 2004).
—, *Conflict and compromise in the late medieval countryside: lords and peasants in Durham, 1349–1400* (New York, 2006).
—, 'Local law courts in late medieval Durham', in Liddy and Britnell eds., *North-east England* (below), pp. 97–109.
Lee, J. S., *Cambridge and its economic region, 1450–1560* (Hatfield, 2005).
—, 'Feeding the colleges: Cambridge food and fuel supplies, 1450–1560', *EcHR* 56 (2003), pp. 243–64.
—, 'The trade of fifteenth-century Cambridge and its region', in M. Hicks (ed.), *Revolution and consumption in medieval England* (Woodbridge, 2001), pp. 127–39.
Leijonhufvud, L., *Grain tithes and manorial yields in early modern Sweden: trends and patterns of production and productivity c. 1540–1680*, Acta Universitatis Agriculturae Sueciae Agraria 309 (Uppsala, 2001).
Lennard, R. V., 'The alleged exhaustion of the soil in medieval England', *Economic Journal* 32 (1922), pp. 12–27.
Le Roy Ladurie, E., *The peasants of Languedoc*, trans. J. Day (Urbana, 1974).
—, *Montaillou: cathars and catholics in a French village, 1294–1324*, trans. B. Bray (Harmondsworth, 1980).
—, *The territory of the historian* (Hassocks, 1979).

—, and Goy, J., *Tithe and agrarian history from the fourteenth to the nineteenth centuries: an essay in comparative history* (Cambridge, 1982).
Levett, A. E., *The Black Death on the estates of the see of Winchester* (Oxford, 1916).
—, *Studies in manorial history* (Oxford, 1938).
Liddy, C. D., and Britnell, R. H. (eds), *North-east England in the later middle ages* (Woodbridge, 2005).
Lloyd, T. H., 'Overseas trade and the money supply in the fourteenth century', in N. J. Mayhew (ed.), *Edwardian monetary affairs (1279–1344)* (Oxford, 1977), pp. 96–124.
—, *The movement of wool prices in medieval England*, Economic History Review Supplement 6 (London, 1973).
Lomas, R. A., 'The Black Death in County Durham', *Journal of Medieval History* 15 (1989), pp. 127–40.
—, Durham Cathedral Priory as a landowner and landlord, 1290–1540 (unpublished Ph.D. thesis, University of Durham, 1973).
—, *North-east England in the middle ages* (Edinburgh, 1992).
—, 'The priory of Durham and its demesnes in the fourteenth and fifteenth centuries', *EcHR*, 2nd series 31 (1978), pp. 339–53.
— and Piper, A. J. (eds.), *Durham Cathedral Priory rentals, I: bursars rentals*, Surtees Society 198 (Durham, 1986).
Lomas, T., 'South-east Durham: late fourteenth and fifteenth centuries', in Harvey (ed.), *Peasant land market* (above), pp. 252–317.
Longstaffe, W. H. and Booth, J. (eds), *Halmota Prioratus Dunelmensis*, Surtees Society 82 (Durham, 1889).
López García, J. M., *La transición del feudalismo al capitalismo en un señorío monástico castellano. 'El Abadengo de la Santa Espina' (1147–1835)* (Valladolid, 1990).
Lorcin, M.-Th., *Les Campagnes de la région lyonnaise au XIVe et XVe siècles* (Lyon, 1974).
Lucas Álvarez, M., and Lucas Domínguez, P., *El monasterio de San Clodio do Ribeiro en la Edad Media: estudio y documentos* (La Coruña, 1996).
Luders, A., *et al.* (eds), *Statutes of the realm* (11 vols, London, 1808–28).
Lunt, W. E., 'The collectors of clerical subsidies', in W. A. Morris and J. R. Strayer (eds), *The English government at work, 1327–1336, II: fiscal administration* (Cambridge, Mass., 1947), pp. 227–80.
—, *Financial relations of the Papacy with England, 1327–1534* (Cambridge, Mass., 1939).
Lütge, F., 'Das 14./15. Jahrhundert in der Sozial- und Wirtschaftsgeschichte', in *idem*, *Studien* (below), pp. 281–335.
—, *Deutsche Sozial- und Wirtschaftsgeschichte. Ein Überblick*, 3rd edition (Berlin and Heidelberg, 1966).
—, 'Die Preispolitik in München im hohen Mittelalter. Ein Beitrag zum Streit über das Problem "Nahrungsprinzip" oder "Erwerbsstreben"', in *idem*, *Studien* (below), pp. 229–30.
—, *Studien zur Sozial- und Wirtschaftsgeshichte* (Stuttgart, 1963).
McCann, J., trans., *The rule of St Benedict* (London, 1976).
McDonnell, J., 'Upland Pennine hamlets', *Northern History* 26 (1990), pp. 20–39.
Macfarlane, A., *The origins of English individualism* (Oxfords, 1978).
McIntosh, M. K., *Autonomy and community: the royal manor of Havering 1200–1500* (Cambridge, 1986).
—, *A community transformed: the manor and liberty of Havering, 1500–1620* (Cambridge, 1991).
—, *Controlling misbehaviour in England, 1370–1600* (Cambridge, 1998).
—, 'The diversity of social capital in English communities, 1300–1640 (with a glance at modern Nigeria)', in R. I. Rotberg (ed.), *Patterns of social capital: stability and change in historical perspective* (Cambridge, 2001), pp. 121–52.

—, 'Local change and community control in England, 1465–1500', *Huntingdon Library Quarterly* 49 (1986), pp. 219–42.
MacKay, A., *Spain in the middle ages; from frontier to empire, 1000–1500* (London, 1977).
McNamee, C., *The wars of the Bruces: Scotland, England and Ireland 1306–1328* (East Linton, 1997).
Mallorquí, E., *Les Gavarres a l'edat mitjana; poblament i societat d'un massís del nord-est català* (Girona, 2000).
Małowist, M., 'The problem of inequality of economic development in Europe in the later middle ages', *EcHR,* 2nd series 19 (1966), pp. 15–28.
Martin, G. H. (ed.), *Knighton's Chronicle, 1337–1396* (Oxford, 1995).
Masschaele, J., *Peasants, merchants, and markets: inland trade in medieval England, 1150–1350* (New York, 1997).
—, 'The public space of the marketplace in medieval England', *Speculum* 77 (2002), pp. 383–421.
Mate, M., 'Agrarian economy after the Black Death: the manors of Canterbury Cathedral Priory, 1348–91', *EcHR*, 2nd series 37 (1984), pp. 341–54.
—, 'The occupation of the land: Kent and Sussex', in *AHEW,* III, pp. 119–36.
—, , 'Pastoral farming in south-east England in the fifteenth century', *EcHR*, 2nd series 40 (1987), pp. 523–36.
—, 'The rise and fall of markets in southeast England', *Canadian Journal of History* 31 (1996), pp. 59–86.
Mayhew, N. J., 'Modelling medieval monetisation', in Britnell and Campbell (eds), *A commercialising economy* (above), pp. 55–77.
—, 'Population, money supply and the velocity of circulation in England, 1300–1700', *EcHR* 48 (1995), pp. 238–57.
Meek, M., *Lucca, 1369–1400: politics and society in an early renaissance city-state* (Oxford, 1978).
Mené, M. le, *Les Campagnes angevines à la fin du moyen âge* (Nantes, 1982).
Miller, E. (ed.), *The agrarian history of England and Wales, III: 1348–1500* (Cambridge, 1991).
—, 'The economic policies of governments: France and England', in M. M. Postan, E. Rich and E. Miller (eds), *The Cambridge economic history of Europe, III: economic organization and policies in the middle ages* (Cambridge, 1963), pp. 290–340.
—, 'Tenant farming and tenant farmers: the southern counties', in *AHEW,* III, pp. 703–22.
—, 'Tenant farming and tenant farmers: Yorkshire and Lancashire', in *AHEW,* III, pp. 596–611.
— and Hatcher, J., *Medieval England: rural society and economic change, 1086–1348* (London, 1978).
Mills, A. D., *A dictionary of English place-names*, corrected edition (Oxford, 1995).
Mitchell, B. R., *British historical statistics* (Cambridge, 1988).
Mitre Fernández, E., 'Algunas cuestiones demográficas en la Castilla de fines del siglo XIV', *Anuario de Estudios Medievales* 7 (1970–1), pp. 615–62.
Molénat, J. P., 'La Seigneurie rurale en Nouvelle Castille au XVe siècle', in G. Anes, B. Vincent *et al., Congreso de historia rural, siglos XV al XIX* (Madrid, 1984), pp. 589–97.
Mollat, M. and Wolff, P., *The popular revolutions of the late middle ages* (London, 1973).
Montanari, M., *Campagne medievali: strutture produttive, raporto di lavoro, sistemi alimentari* (Turin, 1984).
Morrin, E. J., Merrington: land, landlord and tenants, 1541–1840. a study in the estate of the dean and chapter of Durham (unpublished Ph.D. thesis, University of Durham, 1997).
Mullan, J., 'The transfer of customary land on the estates of the bishop of Winchester between the Black Death and the plague of 1361', in Britnell (ed.), *Winchester pipe rolls* (above), pp. 81–107.

— and Britnell, R. H., *Land and family: the land market on the estates of the bishops of Winchester, 1263–1415* (forthcoming).
Munro, J. H., 'Deflation and the petty coinage problem in the late-medieval economy: the case of Flanders, 1334–1484', *Explorations in Economic History* 25 (1988), pp. 387–423.
—, 'Spanish *merino* wools and the *nouvelles draperies*: an industrial transformation in the late medieval Low Countries', *EcHR* 58 (2005), pp. 431–84.
—, *Wool, cloth and gold: the struggle for bullion in Anglo-Burgundian trade, 1340–1478* (Toronto, 1972).
Nef, J. U., 'Mining and metallurgy in medieval civilisation', in M. M. Postan and E. Miller (eds), *The Cambridge economic history of Europe, II: trade and industry in the middle ages*, 2nd edition (Cambridge, 1987), pp. 696–734.
Neveux, H., 'Déclin et reprise: la fluctuation biséculaire, 1340–1560', in G. Duby and A. Wallon (eds), *Historie de la France rurale, 2. De 1340 à 1789* (Paris, 1975).
—, *Les Grains du Cambrésis (fin du XIVe – début du XVIIe siècles). Vie et déclin d'une structure économique* (Paris, 1980).
Newman, C. M., 'Darlington and Northallerton in the later middle ages', in Liddy and Britnell (eds), *North-east England* (above), pp. 127–40.
Nicholas, D., *The growth of the medieval city: from late antiquity to the early fourteenth century* (London, 1997).
—, *The later medieval city, 1300–1500* (London, 1997).
—, *Medieval Flanders* (London, 1992).
Nicholson, R., *Scotland: the later middle ages* (Edinburgh, 1974).
Nightingale, P., 'England and the European depression of the mid-fifteenth century', *JEH* 26 (1997), pp. 631–56.
—, 'Monetary contraction and mercantile credit in later medieval England', *EcHR*, 2nd series 43 (1990), pp. 560–75.
Oestmann, C., *Lordship and community: the Lestrange family and the village of Hunstanton, Norfolk, in the first half of the sixteenth century* (Woodbridge, 1994).
Offler, H. S. (ed.), *Durham episcopal charters 1071–1152*, Surtees Society 179 (1964).
Ogilvie, A. and Farmer, G., 'Documenting the medieval climate', in M. Hulme and E. Barrow (eds), *Climates of the British Isles: present, past and future* (London 1997), pp. 112–33.
Oliva Herrer, H. R., *Ordenanzas de la villa de Becerril de Campos (c. 1492): transcripción y estudio* (Palencia, 2003).
—, *La Tierra de Campos a fines de la Edad Media: economía, sociedad y acción politica campesina* (Valladolid, 2002).
Orme, N., 'A country parish in the 1450s', *Friends of Exeter Cathedral: seventy-second annual report* (Exeter, 2002), pp. 16–24.
Osheim, O., *An Italian lordship: the bishopric of Lucca in the late middle ages* (Berkeley, 1977).
Oschinsky, D. (ed.), *Walter of Henley and other treatises on estate management and accounting* (Oxford, 1971).
Page, F., *The estates of Crowland Abbey: a study in manorial organisation* (Cambridge, 1934).
Page, M., *The medieval bishops of Winchester: estate, archive and administration* (Winchester, 2002).
—, 'The peasant land market on the estate of the bishopric of Winchester before the Black Death', in Britnell (ed.), *Winchester pipe rolls* (above), pp. 61–80.
— (ed.), *The pipe roll of the bishopric of Winchester, 1301–2*, Hampshire Record Series 14 (Winchester, 1996).
— (ed.), *The pipe roll of the bishopric of Winchester 1409–10*, Hampshire Record Series 16 (Winchester, 1999).

Page, W. (ed.), *The chartulary of Brinkburn*, Surtees Society 90 (Durham, 1892).

Palliser, D. M., 'Introduction', in *idem* (ed.), *The Cambridge urban history of Britain: I, 600–1540* (Cambridge, 2000), pp. 1–15.

Palmer, R. C., *English law in the age of the Black Death, 1348–1381: a transformation of governance and law* (Chapel Hill, 1993).

Patze, H. (ed.), *Die Grundherrschaft im späten Mittelalter* (2 vols, Sigmaringen, 1983).

Perroy, E., 'Revisions in economic history, XVI: wage labour in France in the later middle ages', *EcHR* 8 (1955), pp. 232–9.

Pevsner, N., *The buildings of England: County Durham*, 2nd edition, revised E. Williamson (London, 2000).

Pinto, G., '"Honour" and "profit": landed property and trade in medieval Siena', in T. Dean and C. Wickham (eds), *City and countryside in late medieval and renaissance Italy* (London, 1990), pp. 81–91.

— (ed.), *Il Libro del biadaiolo: carestie e annona a Firenze dalla metà del' 200 al 1348* (Florence, 1978).

—, *La Toscana nel tardo medio evo* (Florence, 1982).

Piper, A. J., Muniments of the Dean and Chapter of Durham: medieval accounting material (Durham University Library Archives and Special Collections Searchroom Handlist, 1995).

—, 'The size and shape of Durham's monastic community, 1274–1539', in Liddy and Britnell (eds), *North-east England* (above), pp. 153–71.

Plaisse, A., *La Baronnie de Neubourg. Essai d'histoire agraire, économique et sociale* (Paris, 1961).

Platts, G., *Land and people in medieval Lincolnshire* (Lincoln, 1985).

Pollard, A.J., 'The north-eastern economy and the agrarian crisis of 1438–1440', *Northern History* 25 (1989), pp. 88–105.

—, *North-eastern England during the Wars of the Roses: lay society, war and politics, 1450–1500* (Oxford, 1990).

Poos, L. R., 'The rural population of Essex in the later middle ages', *EcHR*, 2nd series 38 (1985), pp. 515–30.

—, *A rural society after the Black Death: Essex 1350–1525* (Cambridge, 1991).

—, 'The social context of Statute of Labourers enforcement', *Law and History Review* 1 (1983), pp. 27–52.

Poppe, D., *Économie et société d'un bourg provençal au XIVe siècle: Reillanne en Haute Provence* (Wrocław, 1980).

Postan, M. M., ed., *The Cambridge economic history of Europe, I: the agrarian life of the middle ages,* 2nd edition (Cambridge, 1966).

—, 'The economic foundations of medieval economy', reprinted in *idem* (ed.), *Essays* (below), pp. 3–27.

—, 'Economic relations between eastern and western Europe', in G. Barraclough (ed.), *Eastern and western Europe in the middle ages* (London, 1970), pp. 125–74.

—, 'The fifteenth century', *EcHR* 9 (1938–9), pp. 160–7, reprinted in *idem*, *Essays* (below), pp. 41–8.

—, 'Medieval agrarian society in its prime: England', in *idem* (ed.), *Cambridge economic history of Europe,* I (above), pp. 549–632.

—, *The medieval economy and society: an economic history of Britain in the middle ages* (Harmondsworth, 1972).

—, *Essays on medieval agriculture and general problems of the medieval economy* (Cambridge, 1973).

—, 'Some agrarian evidence of declining population in the later middle ages', reprinted in *idem*, *Essays* (above), pp. 186–213.

—, and Hatcher, J., 'Population and class relations in feudal society', *PP* 78 (1978), pp. 24–37.

Postles, D., 'The acquisition and administration of spiritualities by Oseney Abbey', *Oxoniensia* 51 (1986), pp. 69–77.
—, 'Demographic change in Kibworth Harcourt, Leicestershire, in the later middle ages', *Local Population Studies* 48 (1992), pp. 41–8.
Pounds, N. J. G., *An economic history of medieval Europe* (London, 1974).
—, *An historical geography of Europe, 450 BC–AD 1330* (Cambridge, 1973).
Powicke, F. M., and Cheney, C. R. (eds), *Councils and synods, with other documents relating to the English Church, II: A.D. 1205–1313* (2 vols, Oxford, 1964).
Prange, W., 'Die Entwicklung der adlingen Eigenwirtschaft in Schleswig-Holstein', in Patze (ed.), *Grundherrschaft im späten Mittelalter* (above), I, pp. 519–53.
Proudfoot, L. J., 'Parochial benefices in late medieval Warwickshire: patterns of stability and change, 1291 to 1535', in T. R. Slater and P. J. Jarvis (eds), *Field and forest: an historical geography of Warwickshire and Worcestershire* (Norwich, 1982), pp. 203–31.
Provero, L., 'Forty years of rural history for the Italian middle ages', in Alfonso (ed.), *Rural history* (above), pp. 141–72.
Purvis, J. S. (ed.), *Select XVI century causes in tithe from the York Diocesan Registry*, Yorkshire Archaeological Society Record Series 114 (1949, for 1947).
Raftis, J. A., 'The concentration of responsibility in five villages', *Mediaeval Studies* 28 (1966), pp. 92–118.
—, *The estates of Ramsey Abbey: a study in economic growth and organization* (Toronto, 1957).
—, *Peasant economic development within the English manorial system* (Montreal, 1996).
—, 'Peasants and the collapse of the manorial economy on some Ramsey Abbey estates', in Britnell and Hatcher (eds), *Progress and problems* (above), pp. 191–206.
—, 'Social change versus revolution: new interpretations of the Peasants' Revolt of 1381', in F. X. Newman (ed.), *Social unrest in the late middle ages: papers of the fifteenth annual conference of the Center for Medieval and Early Renaissance Studies* (Binghamton, New York, 1989), pp. 3–22.
—, 'Social structures in five east midland villages: a study in the possibilities of court roll data', *EcHR*, 2nd series 18 (1965), pp. 83–100.
—, *Tenure and mobility: studies in the social history of the medieval English village* (Toronto, 1964).
Raine, J. (ed.), *The charters of endowment, inventories and account rolls of the priory of Finchale*, Surtees Society 6 (London, 1837).
— (ed.), *Historiae Dunelmensis scriptores tres, Gaufridus de Coldingham, Robertus de Graystanes, et Willelmus de Chambre*, Surtees Society 9 (London, 1839).
— (ed.), *The inventories and account rolls of the Benedictine houses or cells of Jarrow and Monk-Wearmouth*, Surtees Society 29 (London, 1854).
Razi, Z., 'Family, land and the village community in later medieval England', *PP* 93 (1981), pp. 3–36, reprinted in Aston (ed.), *Landlords* (above), pp. 360–93.
—, *Life, marriage and death in a medieval parish: economy, society and demography in Halesowen 1270–1400* (Cambridge, 1980).
—, 'The Toronto school's reconstruction of medieval peasant society: a critical view', *PP* 85 (1980), pp. 141–57.
— and Smith, R. M., 'The historiography of manorial court rolls', in *idem* and R. M. Smith (eds), *Medieval society and the manor court* (Oxford, 1996), pp. 1–35.
Rees, U. (ed.), *The cartulary of Haughmond Abbey* (Cardiff, 1985).
Reyerson, K. L., *Business, banking and finance in medieval Montpellier* (Toronto, 1985).
Rigby, S. H. (ed.), *A companion to Britain in the later middle ages* (Oxford, 2003).
—, *English society in the later middle ages: class, status and gender* (Basingstoke and New York, 1995).
—, 'Historical causation: is one thing more important than another', *History* 80 (1995), pp.

227–42.
—, *Medieval Grimsby: growth and decline* (Hull, 1993).
Rippman, D., *Bauern und Städter: Stadt-Land Beziehungen im 15. Jahrhundert. Das Beispiel Basel* (Basel, 1990).
Riva, Bonvesin de la, *De magnalibus Mediolani*, (ed.) M. Corti (Milan, 1974).
Roberts, B. K., 'Village plans in County Durham: a preliminary statement', *Medieval Archaeology* 16 (1972), pp. 33–56.
Robinson, W. C., 'Money, population and economic change in late medieval Europe', *EcHR*, 2nd series 12 (1959), pp. 63–76.
Robinson, W. R. B., 'The *Valor ecclesiasticus* of 1535 as evidence of agrarian output: tithe data for the deanery of Abergavenny', *Bulletin of the Institute of Historical Research* 56 (1983), pp. 16–33.
Rogers, J. E. T., *A History of agriculture and prices in England* (7 vols, Oxford, 1866–1902).
Roover, R. de, *L'Évolution de la lettre de change* (Paris, 1953).
Rorke, M., 'English and Scottish overseas trade, 1300–1600', *EcHR* 59 (2006), pp. 265–88.
Rösener, W., *Agrarwirtschaft, Agrarverfassung und ländliche Gesellschaft im Mittelalter*, Enzyklopädie deutscher Geschichte 13 (Munich, 1992).
—, *Peasants in the middle ages*, trans. A. Stützer (Oxford, 1994).
Rosser, G., *Medieval Westminster, 1200–1540* (Oxford, 1989).
Rotberg, R. I., 'Social capital and political culture in Africa, America, Australasia, and Europe', in *idem* (ed.), *Patterns of social capital: stability and change in historical perspective* (Cambridge, 2001), pp. 339–56.
Rotelli, C., *Una campagna medievale: storia agraria del Piemonte fra il 1250 e il 1450* (Turin, 1973).
Rubinstein, N. (ed.), *Florentine studies: politics and society in renaissance Florence* (Evanston, 1968).
Ruiz, T. F., *Crisis and continuity: land and town in late medieval Castile* (Philadelphia, 1994).
Russell, J. C., *British medieval population* (Albuquerque, 1948).
—, *Medieval regions and their cities* (Newton Abbot, 1972).
Ruwet, J., 'La Mesure de la production agricole sous l'Ancien Régime: le blé en pays mosan', *Annales E.S.C.* 4 (1964), pp. 625–42.
Salter, H. E. (ed.), *A subsidy collected in the diocese of Lincoln in 1526*, Oxford Historical Society 63 (Oxford, 1909).
Sánchez Trujillano, M. T., *et al.* (eds), *A la sombra del castillo: la Edad Media en el museo de La Rioja* (Logroño, 2002).
Sandnes, J., 'Settlement developments in the late middle ages (approx. 1300–1540)', in S. Gissel *et al.*, *Desertion* (above), pp. 78–114.
Schofield, P. R., 'England: the family and the village community', in Rigby (ed.), *Companion to Britain in the later middle ages* (above), pp. 26–46.
—, *Peasant and community in medieval England 1200–1500* (New York, 2003).
—, 'Tenurial developments and the availability of customary land in a later medieval community', *EcHR*, 2nd series 49 (1996), pp. 250–67.
Scott, R., 'Medieval agriculture', in *The Victoria history of the county of Wiltshire*, IV, (Oxford 1959).
Seabourne, G., *Royal regulation of loans and sales in medieval England* (Woodbridge, 2003).
Sivery, G., *Structures agraires et vie rurale dans le Hainaut à la fin du Moyen-Âge* (2 vols, Villeneuve-d'Ascq, 1977–80).
Slicher van Bath, B. H., *The agrarian history of western Europe, A.D. 500–1850* (London, 1963).
Smith, R. A. L., *Canterbury Cathedral Priory: a study in manorial administration* (Cambridge, 1943).

Smith, R. M., 'Human resources', in G. Astill and A. Grant (eds), *The countryside of medieval England* (Oxford, 1988), pp. 188–212.
— (ed.), *Land, kinship and life-cycle* (Cambridge, 1984).
Smith, R. S., 'Medieval agrarian society in its prime: Spain', in Postan (ed.), *Cambridge economic history of Europe*, I (above), pp. 432–48.
Snape, M. G. (ed.), *English episcopal acta 24: Durham 1153–1195* (Oxford, 2002).
— (ed.), *English episcopal acta 25: Durham 1196–1237* (Oxford, 2002).
Snooks, G. D., 'The dynamic role of the market in the Anglo-Norman economy and beyond, 1086–1300', in Britnell and Campbell (eds), *Commercialising economy* (above), pp. 27–54.
Sobrequés Callicó, J., 'La peste negra en la península ibérica', *Anuario de Estudios Medievales* 7 (1970–1), pp. 67–101.
Société des Historiens Médiévistes de l'Enseignement Supérieur Public, *L'Argent au moyen âge* (Paris, 1998).
Sopena, P. M., 'Foires et marchés ruraux dans les pays de la couronne de Castille et Léon du Xe au XIIIe siècle', in Desplat (ed.), *Foires et marchés* (above), pp. 47–69.
Spufford, M., 'Puritanism and social control?', in A. Fletcher and J. Stevenson (eds), *Order and disorder in early modern England* (Cambridge, 1985), pp. 41–57.
Spufford, P., *Money and its uses in medieval Europe* (Cambridge, 1988).
—, *Power and profit: the merchant in medieval Europe* (London, 2002).
Stern, D. V., *A Hertfordshire demesne of Westminster Abbey: profits, productivity and weather* (ed.) C. Thornton (Hatfield, 2000).
Stevenson, A., 'Trade with the South, 1070–1513', in Dennison, Ditchburn and Lynch (eds), *Aberdeen before 1800* (above), pp. 180–206.
Stone, D., *Decision-making in medieval agriculture* (Oxford, 2005).
—, The management of resources on the demesne farm of Wisbech Barton, 1314–1430 (unpublished Ph.D. thesis, University of Cambridge, 1998).
—, 'Medieval farm management and technological mentalities: Hinderclay before the Black Death', *EcHR* 54 (2001), pp. 612–38.
—, 'The productivity of hired and customary labour: evidence from Wisbech Barton in the fourteenth century', *EcHR* 50 (1997), pp. 640–56.
—, 'The productivity and management of sheep in late medieval England', *AHR* 51 (2003), pp. 1–22.
Stone, E. D., and Cozens-Hardy, B. (eds), *Norwich consistory court depositions, 1499–1512 and 1518–1530*, Norfolk Record Society 10 (1938).
Stuart, J. (ed.), *Extracts from the council register of the burgh of Aberdeen, I: 1398–1570*, Spalding Club 12 (Aberdeen, 1844).
Swanson, H., *Medieval artisans* (Oxford, 1989).
Swanson, R. N., 'An appropriate anomaly: Topcliffe parish and the fabric fund of York Minster in the later middle ages', in D. Wood (ed.), *Life and thought in the northern Church, c.1100–c.1700: essays in honour of Claire Cross*, Studies in Church History: Subsidia 12 (Woodbridge, 1999), pp. 105–21.
—, *Church and society in late medieval England*, revised edition (Oxford, 1993).
—, 'Clergy in manorial society in late medieval Staffordshire', *Staffordshire Studies* 5 (1993), pp. 13–34.
—, 'Economic change and spiritual profits: receipts from the peculiar jurisdiction of the Peak District in the fourteenth century', in N. Rogers (ed.), *Harlaxton medieval studies, iii: England in the fourteenth century, proceedings of the 1991 colloquium* (Stamford, 1993), pp. 171–95.
—, 'Standards of livings: parochial revenues in pre-reformation England', in C. Harper-Bill (ed.), *Religious belief and ecclesiastical careers in late medieval England* (Woodbridge, 1991), pp. 151–96.

Tawney, R. H., *The Agrarian problem in the sixteenth century* (London, 1912).
TeBrake, W. H., *A plague of insurrection: popular politics and peasant revolt in Flanders, 1323–1328* (Philadelphia, 1993).
Thoen, E., 'Agricultural progress in England and the north and southern Netherlands during the middle ages: was the demand really so important?', *NEHA-Jaarboek voor economische, berijfs- en techniekgeschiedenis* 61.1 (1998), pp. 36–45.
Thomson, T. (ed.), *Liber cartarum prioratus Sancti Andree in Scotia*, Bannatyne Club 69 (Edinburgh, 1841).
Threlfall-Holmes, M., 'The import merchants of Newcastle upon Tyne, 1464–1520: some evidence from Durham Cathedral Priory', *Northern History* 40 (2003).
—, *Monks and markets: Durham Cathedral Priory, 1460–1520* (Oxford, 2005).
—, 'Newcastle trade and Durham Priory, 1460–1520', in Liddy and Britnell (eds), *North-east England* (above), pp. 141–52.
Tillotson, J. H. (ed.), *Monastery and society in the late middle ages: selected account rolls from Selby Abbey, Yorkshire, 1398–1537* (Woodbridge and Wolfeboro, 1988).
Tirado Marínez, J. A., 'Los medios de vida: agricultura, ganadería y artesanía', in M. T. Sánchez Trujillano, P. Alvarez Clavijo, J. A. Tirado Martínez and J. Martínez Flórez (eds), *A la sombra del castillo: la Edad Media en el museo de La Rioja* (Logroño, 2002), pp. 65–91.
Titow, J. Z., *English rural society, 1200–1350* (London, 1969).
—, 'Evidence of weather in the account rolls of the bishopric of Winchester, 1209–1350', *EcHR*, 2nd series 12 (1960), pp. 360–407.
—, 'Field crops and their cultivation in Hampshire, 1200–1350, in the light of documentary evidence', (unpublished paper, Hampshire Records Office, Winchester, 97/M97/C1).
—, Land and population on the bishop of Winchester's estates, 1209–1350 (unpublished Ph.D. thesis, University of Cambridge, 1962).
—, 'Le Climat à travers les rôles de comptabilité de l'évêché de Winchester (1350–1458)', *Annales ESC* 25 (1970), pp. 312–50.
—, 'Lost rents, vacant holdings and the contraction of peasant cultivation after the Black Death', *AHR* 42 (1994), pp. 97–114.
—, *Winchester yields: a study in medieval agricultural productivity* (Cambridge, 1972).
Tits-Dieuaide, M.-J., 'Peasant dues in Brabant: the example of the Meldet farm near Tirlemont, 1380–1797', in Van der Wee and Van Cauwenberghe (eds), *Productivity* (below), pp. 107–23.
Tricard, J., *Les Campagnes limousines du XIV*e *au XVI*e *siècle: originalité et limites d'une reconstruction rurale* (Paris, 1996).
Tuck, J. A., 'Farming practice and techniques: the northern borders', in *AHEW*, III, pp. 175–82.
—, 'The occupation of the land: the northern borders', in *AHEW*, III, pp. 34–42.
Valdeón Baruque, J., 'La crisis del siglo XIV en Castilla: revisión del problema', *Estudios de Historia Económica II, Revista de la Universidad de Madrid*, 20, part 79 (Madrid, 1971), pp. 161–184.
—, 'Parte primera: los países de la corona de Castilla', in *idem* and J. L. Martín Rodríguez (eds), *Historia de España Menéndez Pidal, Tomo XII: La Baja Edad Media peninsular siglos XIII al XV: la población, la economía, la sociedad* (Madrid, 1996), pp. 25–300.
Van Bavel, B. J. P. and Thoen, E. (eds), *Land productivity and agro-systems in the North Sea area (middle ages–20th century) elements for comparison*, Corn Publication Series 2 (Turnhout, 1999).
Van Cauwenberghe, E. and Van der Wee, H., 'Productivity, evolution of rents and farm size in the Southern Netherlands agriculture from the fourteenth to the seventeenth century', in Van der Wee and Van Cauwenberghe (eds), *Productivity* (below), pp. 125–61.

Van der Wee, H. and Van Cauwenberghe, E. (eds), *Productivity, land and agricultural innovation in the Low Countries (1250–1800)* (Louvain, 1978).
Van Werveke, H., 'Currency manipulation in the middle ages: the case of Louis de Male, count of Flanders', *Transactions of the Royal Historical Society*, 4th series 31 (1949), pp. 115–27.
Vanderzee, G. (ed.), *Nonarum inquisitiones in curia scaccarii temp. regis Edwardi III*, RC (London, 1807).
Vicens Vives, J. with Nadal Oller, J., *An economic history of Spain* (Princeton, NJ, 1969).
Vogüé, A. de and Neufville, J. (eds), *La Règle de Saint Benôit, II (ch. VIII-LXXIII)*, Sources Chrétiennes 182 (Paris, 1972).
Volk, O., *Wirtschaft und Gesellschaft im Mittelrhein vom 12. bis zum 16. Jahrhundert* (Wiesbaden, 1998).
Wackerfuss, W., *Kultur- Witschafts- und Sozialgeschichte des Odenwaldes im 15. Jahrhundert* (Breuberg-Neustadt, 1991).
Walter, J. and Schofield, R., 'Famine, disease and crisis mortality in early modern society', in *idem* (eds), *Famine, disease and the social order in early modern society* (Cambridge, 1989), pp. 1–73.
Watkins, A., 'Cattle grazing in the Forest of Arden in the later middle ages', *AHR* 37 (1989), pp. 12–25.
—, 'Peasants in Arden', in R.H. Britnell (ed.), *Daily life in the late middle ages* (Stroud, 1998), pp. 83–101.
Watts, V., *A dictionary of County Durham place-names* (Nottingham, 2002).
Whittle, J., *The development of agrarian capitalism: land and labour in Norfolk, 1440–1580* (Oxford, 2000).
Wood, A. C. (ed.), *Registrum Simonis Langham, Cantuariensis archiepiscopi*, Canterbury and York Society 53 (1956).
Wood, D., *Medieval economic thought* (Cambridge, 2002).
— (ed.), *Medieval money matters* (Oxford, 2004).
Wright, G. T. (ed.), *Longstone records, Derbyshire* (Bakewell, 1906).
Wright, S. M., *The Derbyshire gentry in the fifteenth century*, Derbyshire Record Society 8 (Chesterfield, 1983).
Wrightson, K. and Levine, D., *Poverty and piety in an English village: Terling, 1525–1700*, new edition (Oxford, 1995).
Wrigley, E. A., 'Energy availability and agricultural productivity', in B. M. S. Campbell and M. Overton (eds), *Land, labour and livestock: historical studies in European agricultural productivity* (Manchester, 1991), pp. 323–39.
—, 'Some reflections on corn yields and prices in pre-industrial economies', in J. Walter and R. Schofield (eds), *Famine, disease and the social order in early modern society* (Cambridge, 1989), pp. 235–78.
—, 'The transition to an advanced organic economy: half a millennium of English agriculture', *EcHR* 59 (2006), pp. 435–80.
Wunder, H., 'Peasant organization and class conflict in eastern and western Germany', in Aston and Philpin (eds), *Brenner Debate* (above), pp. 91–100.
—, 'Serfdom in later medieval and early modern Germany', in T. H. Aston, P. R. Coss, C. Dyer and J. Thirsk (eds), *Social relations and ideas: essays in honour of R. H. Hilton* (Cambridge, 1983), pp. 249–72.
Yates, M., 'Change and continuities in rural society from the later middle ages to the sixteenth century: the contribution of west Berkshire', *EcHR* 52 (1999), pp. 617–37.
Zotz, T., 'Zur Grundherrschaft der Grafen von Leiningen: Güterbesitz, bäuerliche Dienste und Marktbeziehungen im 15. Jahrhundert', in Patze (ed.), *Grundherrschaft im späten Mittelalter* (above), II, pp. 177–228.
Zylbergeld, L., 'Les Régulations du marché du pain au XIIIe siècle en Occident et l'"assize

of bread" de 1266–1267 pour l'Angleterre', in J.-M. Duvosquel and A. Dierkens (eds), *Villes et campagnes au moyen âge. Mélanges Georges Despy* (Liège, 1991), pp. 791–814.

and tenant numbers 22–3, 152
and transfers of property 182
and wages 78, 116
Black Sea 12
Blakealler, Elinor 103
Blount, John 99
Blunham (Bedfordshire) 100n, 102, 107
Boarstall (Buckinghamshire) 150n
Boccaccio, Giovanni 74
Boleford, Margery 103, 108
Bonar, Henry 68
Boniface, archbishop of Canterbury 97n
Bordelais (France) 11, 122, 125
borghi see towns
Bourbonnais (France) 154–5
Bourland (Somerset) 180
bovates 174
Bowes Moor 32
Brabant 11, 161
Bradeley, Master Richard 108
Brancepeth (Co. Durham) 176
Brandenburg (Germany) 157, 163
Branscombe (Devon) 103, 108
bread 3
assize of 7–8, 60–2, 68
price of 7–8
Breckland 23, 26, 33, 34, 35, 222, 225
Brétigny, Treaty of 125
Brite, William 190–1
Brockhampton (Hampshire) 180, *183*, 184
Broisour, Andrew 68
Broissour, Thomas 68
Brome, John, of Baddesley Clinton 36
Bromesdon, William 109
Bromham (Wiltshire) 139
Brouhgton (Huntingdonshire) 29
Bruges 19
Buckingham, duke of 36
Burgos (Spain) 125, 126, 128
Burmington (Warwickshire) 110n
Burton, Emma *183*, 184, 195
Burton, John *183*, 184, 195, 197

calves 96–9, 109
Cambrai (France) 75, *121*, 121, 122, 123, 125, 130
Cambridge 142
Cambridgeshire 9, 76, 161, 217, 223
Canada 113
Canterbury
archbishopric 26
Cathedral Priory 23, 27
Carlisle 105
bishopric 105
Castile (Spain)
agricultural techniques 85–6
grain prices 78
grain production 125–9
labour legislation 152
populaton 85–6, 130
survival of data 115, 131
wool production 156
Catalonia (Spain) 128
Cattle-raising 32–3, 35, 66, 99
Cely family 9
Chapel-en-le-Frith (Derbyshire) 108
Chapitre de Saint–Just 123
Chapitre Primatial de Saint-Jean (France) 123
Chapman, Richard 185
Chayanov, Alexander V. 84
cheese 30, 68, 95, 100
price of 22, 26, 32, 35
Chelwardeswood, Nicholas *181*, 195
Chester 92
Chesterfield, Richard of 176, 178
Chieri (Italy) 159
Chillenden, Thomas 27
Chilterns 217
Chilton (Co. Durham) 172, 173, 174, 175
cities *see* towns
cloth *see* textiles
coinage *see* currency
Colchester (Essex) 24
Cologne 5
Combe (Dorset) 108
Combe (Hampshire) *133–4*, 138–9
communities *see* peasants
contracts of sale, 9
Cook, Matthew 197
Cook, Richard 196
Coombe Bisset (Wiltshire) 145
Cornwall 34, 161
Cornwall, duchy of 22, 77, 161
Cotswolds 217, 221, 226
Couk', Richard 179
Counden (Co. Durham) 171
Couper, Matthew 65
Courtrai (Belgium) 160
Cous, John *183*, 185
Coventry (Warwickshire) 24
cows and dairy farming 17–18, 26, 30, 32, 34, 153, 167
price of cows 22, 26, 32, 35
size of herds 28, 32–4, 36–9
tithe of milk 95, 97
see also cattle-raising
Coxwell (Berkshire) *133–4*, 138–9
Crawley (Hampshire) *37*, 38–9
credit 9, 12–14, 66–7
Cromwell, Ralph Lord 36
crops
composition of 137–40, 144–5, 217–18
demesne and tenant compared 137–43, 146
seedcorn ratio 3

yields of 40–3, 47, 51, 81–2
see also arable husbandry, barley and bear, grain, legumes, maslin, oats and oatmeal, rice, rye, saffron, wheat
Crowland Abbey 30
Crukin, Matheus 68
Culane, Andrew 63
Culham (Buckinghamshire) 180
Culling, Adam *181*
Cumberland 172
Cumbria 55
currency 6–7, 14, 228
and bullion famines 14
debasement of 161–2
Curson family 106
customs 8, 17, 218, 225–6
of Scottish burghs 57
Cuxham (Oxfordshire) 22

dairy farming *see* cheese, cows
Danzig (Poland) 157
dearth *see* famine, prices
Deddington (Oxfordshire) 94, 99
Delft (Netherlands) 68
del Tonne family 210
demesne lands 3, 88
cropping of 137–43
expanding 157
leasing of 26–9, 75, 77, 116, 152–4, 157–8, 174–5, 195–6, 203, 211
management of 3, 24, 27–8
and peasant accumulation 163,195–6, 211
Derbyshire 28, 95n
see also Peak District
Deschamps, Eustace 153
Devon 55
Dewsbury (West Riding, Yorkshire) 97n, 98, 101, 103n
Dey, John 36
Diest 11
diet 18, 30–1, 41, 61, 220–2
Ditcheat (Somerset) 82
Dordrecht (Netherlands) 68
Downton (Wiltshire) 33, 135, 136, 137, 140–6
Drakenage (Warwickshire) 36
Dunbarrow (Angus) 217
Dundee (Angus) 57
Durham
geography and land use 23, 166, 168–78
grain prices 16, 19, 40–55
lordship and community 165, 167, 199–214, 218–9
manorial demesnes 26
stock farming 32
tithes and output
Black Death 24, 25, 86
data 100
late fourteenth century 30, 32, 113–31
fifteenth century 34, 35, 113–31, 143, 146
Durrington (Wiltshire) 142
Dutchman, Hans the 68
Dutchman, Henry the 68
dyestuffs 18, 67, 84

Easington (Co. Durham) 53
East Anglia 31, 161, 218, 220, 225
East Meon (Hampshire)
demesne *141*, 142–4
tithes
grain 95, 100, *133–4*, 136, 138–40, *141*, 142–4
livestock 95, 98, 100
landholding 179–98
East Merrington *see* Kirk Merrington
East Rainton (Co. Durham) 206n
Eastry (Kent) 33
Ebbesbourne Wake (Wiltshire) 142
economic fluctuation 14–15, 20–39, 116–31, 144–5
international contrasts 130–1
Edinburgh (Midlothian) 57
Edward II, king of England 172
Edward III, king of England 78
eggs 100
sale of 7, 90–1
Egypt 76
Elbe, River 156
Elkington (Northamptonshire) 75
Elmland *see* Warmia
Elton (Huntingdonshire) 29
Elyott, Michael 103
enclosure 140, 160, 168, 171–8, 213
Enford (Wiltshire) *133–4*, 137, 138–9, 142
English Channel 6, 10
entry fines *see* tenants
epidemics 23–4, 27, 120–1, 124, 130, 149, 170, 179
see also Black Death
Essex
demesne output 29
geography 217
population 25, 27, 34, 39, 120n
saffron 223
tithe output 30
Evers, Master Hugh 108n
Exeter (Devon) 49, 51, 54–5
Exeter Cathedral 100, 102–3
Extremadura (Spain) 129

famine and dearth 12, 27, 51–2, 55, 62, 73–4, 137
Fareham (Hampshire) 180, *183*, 184, 186, 187
Faringdon (Berkshire) *133–4*, 138–9
farms, deserted 150–1, 162, 166, 175–7

Farnham (Surrey) 180
Feering (Essex) 24, 29, 30, 222
Ferryhill (Co. Durham) 171–2, 173, *174*, 175, 206n
Fillingham (Lincolnshire) 109
fish and fisheries 31, 67, 69, 223, 226
Flanders 11, 67, 156, 160, 161, 163, 222
flax 84, 95, 97
Florence (Italy) 5, 6, 159
Foljambe family 106
Fonthill Bishop (Wiltshire) 142
football 210
Forcombe, Agnes, widow of John 193
Forcombe, John *183*
Forman, Thomas 67
France
- currency 6
- famine 49–50
- grain prices 78
- grain production 77, 121–5, 126
- landholding 153, 154
- livestock production 32
- population 77, 124, 130
- survival of data 113–5
- war 32, 77, 125, 130
- wine production 18
- yields 79, 82

fruit 3, 18, 68, 76, 95, 100
fuel 4, 9, 224
Fuenteorejuna (Spain) 163

Gaburdel, John 180, *181*, 186
Gaburdel, Juliana 180
Galicia (Spain) 127, 128, 129
Gamlin, Mary, wife of Richard 197
Gamlin, Richard 197
gardens 3, 97
Gascony (France) 224
Genoa 5
German, John 98
Germany 12, 18, 150, 152, 156, 160
- *see also* Prussia

Ghent 5
Glastonbury Abbey 82
glebe 91–3, 100–1, 104, 107, 110–11
Gómez de Guzmán, lordship of 163
Gosmer, Richard 99, 102
Gosport (Hampshire) 180n
grain
- long-distance trade in 9–12, 54–5, 67–8, 156–7
- price of 22, 26–7, 31–2, 35, 40–55, 58–60, 78
- production of 16–17, 24
- quality of 61–2
- rents paid in 154–5
- sale and distribution of 3–6, 9–12, 19, 102–3, 109
- sale of, by sample 63
- sale in sheaves 140–1
- seedcorn 3
- tithe of 23–5, 30, 95–7, 100–3, 107–9, 217–18
- wages paid in 3
- *see also* barley and beer, maslin, oats and oatmeal, rye, wheat

Graystanes, Robert de 171
Great Waltham (Essex) *38*
Great Wolford (Warwickshire) 95
Grey, Sir Henry, of Wrest 107
Gris family 210
Grisby family 210
Guadalquivir, River 127, 156
Gust, Thomas *183*

Hailing (Hampshire) 185
Hainault (Belgium) 164
Halesowen (Worcestershire) 23–4, 25, 27
Hambledon (Hampshire)
- demesne output 138–40, *141*, 142–4
- grain prices 16
- landholding 180, *183*, 184, 186, 191
- tithe output *133–4*, 138–40, *141*, 142–4

Hampshire 139–40, 184
Hardescombe, John 186–7
Hardgill, Robert 208
Hardgill family 210
Harley (Shropshire) 93
Harlow (Essex) 96
Harmondsworth (Middlesex) *141*, 142, 144
Hatch, Joan 197
Hatfield Survey 1381, 174
Hatfield, Thomas, bishop of Durham 204, 214
Hatherich, Walter *181*
Havering (Essex) 212n
hay 95–6, 108
hemp 95, 97
Henry of Trastámara, king of Castile 129
Henry V, king of England 33
Hereford Cathedral 104
Hesilden (Co. Durham) 208n
Hett (Co. Durham) 166, 171–2, *173*, 174n
Heworths, Over and Nether (Co. Durham) 200n, 206, 208n
Hexham Abbey 107n
Heytesbury (Wiltshire) 142n
hides 5, 64
High Easter (Essex) *38*
Hilborough (Norfolk) 33
Hinderclay (Suffolk) 15–16
Hoggeman, Henry 103
Holme-next-the-Sea (Norfolk) 96
Holstein (Germany) 157
Holway (Somerset) 180, *181*, 184, 195, 196
Holy Island (Northumberland) 96
Holywell (Huntingdonshire) 22

honey 95, 100
Hook, Christine, daughter of William 195
Hooke, John 103
Hook, William *183*, 197
Hornsea (East Riding, Yorkshire) 98, 100n
Hoton, Richard de, prior of Durham 171
Hungary 113

Île-de-France (France) 122
Illebere (Somerset) 180
incentives
    commercial 3, 15–16, 18–19, 27–9, 86, 110–11, 221
    lordship and 218
    for subsistence 83
    see also prices
India 83
'Indian summer' (c.1350–77) 20–6, 77, 116
Indonesia 83
industry *see* manufacturing
Inglesham (Wiltshire) *133–4*, 138–9
Inverory, William 63
Ireland 4, 9
iron 67–8
Isle of Ely 9
Italy
    cereal production 75–6, 217
    estate management 4, 153
    grain prices 78
    pastoral farming 77
    towns 121n, 224, 227
    trade 10, 11
    wine 18, 217

Jackson, William 208
Jameson, John 63
jurisdiction
    over trade, 7–9, 13
    urban, 57

Kelvedon (Essex) 29, 30
Kent 34, 220, 222
Kibworth Harcourt (Leicestershire) 25, 29
King, Gregory 40
King's College, Cambridge 9
King's Law 40–1
Kinsbourne (Hertfordshire) 28
Kirby Malham (West Riding, Yorkshire) 101, 109
Kirk Merrington (Co. Durham) 166, 168, 171–2, 173, *174*, 175, 178, 200n
Knight, William *181*
Knighton, Henry 27, 39, 51, 51n, 74
Kniveton (Derbyshire) 107n
Knoller, Nicola, widow of Thomas 179
Knoller, Thomas 179, *183*, 184, 193–4, 195, 196–7
Koblenz (Germany) 155

Kynros, Gilbert de 63

labour services 17–18, 157
    see also rents, serfdom
Labraza (Spain) 128
La Mancha (Spain) 129
lambs 95–101, 107–9, 146
Lancaster, duchy of 27, 28, 33, 36
land
    demand for 22–3, 29–30, 34–5, 153, 182, 184, 187
    distribution of 82–3, 158–61, 179–98
    market in 158, 178–98
    polarisation of holding size 167, 187–93, 212
    waste 119, 127, 130, 168, 177
landlords
    accumulation by 153–4
    enterprise of 77, 154–7
    exploitation of tenants by 81, 85, 156–7, 218
    see also demesne lands, manors, rents, tenants
Langrish, John 195, 197
Langrissh, John *183*
Languedoc (France) 79, 81
La Rioja (Spain) 76
Lea, River 10
leases *see* demesnes, tenures
Legh, William 106
legumes 24, 139, 141
Leicester 51
Leiningen (Germany) 162
Leith (Midlothian) 67
Lenzi, Domenico, of Florence 10
Lewes Priory 107
Lichfield Cathedral 107n
Limousin (France) 4
Lincoln 91, 92, 105, 161, 217
    Cathedral 107
Little Finborough (Suffolk) 106n
livestock 18–19
    sold for meat, 11
Lombardy (Italy) 77
London
    grain supply 10, 51, 108, 142, 146
    population 5, 6
    trade 19, 54, 222, 223
Longbridge Deverill (Wiltshire) 136, 142
Lorymer, John 68
Lübeck (Germany) 156
Lyon (France) 123, 124, 125
Lytham priory 96–7, 99, 101

Malgham, Thomas 101
malt 60–4, 68, 102, 143, 222
Manfredonia (Italy) 10
manors
    administrative groupings of 180

jurisdiction of 196–7, 203–5, 210–12, 218–19
moorland farms defined as 175–6
officials of 203, 207–9, 211–12
vacant tenancies 22
see also demesnes, rents, tenants, tenures, villages
Mantua (Italy) 156
manufacturing
employment in 4, 54, 77, 160, 221, 223, 226
impact on land values 77
urban 24
manure 82
market integration 10–13, 40–55, 221
market places 7–8, 12, 60–2, 102
abandonment of 13
clerks of 64, 69
forestalling the 63–4
foundation of 13
illegitimate 63
layout of 8
and price-setting 11, 105
price formation in 62
regulation of 7–8, 19, 60–5, 222
sellers in 65–6
tolls and tollbooth in 63–4
in towns 56–69
in villages 6, 11
see also ale, bread, prices, trade
Marsh, Adam *181*
Martham (Norfolk) 84
maslin 68
Masoun, Henry, wife of 66
May family 210
Mayle, Walter *183*
measures 47, 49, 68
boll and firlot 61, 63–5
regulation of 7, 65
meat 11, 17–18, 30, 66, 153, 222
Mediterranean 6, 9, 11, 156
Melksham, vicar of 110n
Meltinger, Ulrich 153
merchants
and the food trades 8–11, 67–9, 156–7
networks of 223
and property 154
institutions of 9–10
see also trade
Merrington *see* Kirk Merrington, Middlestone, Westerton
Merton College, Oxford 138
Messina (Italy) 156
Mesta 129, 156
Middlestone (Co. Durham) 166, 171, 173, *174*, 175
mid-fifteenth-century slump 20, 35–6, 123–4
Midwinter, William, of Northleach 9
migration 22, 29–30, 128–9, 158, 161, 167, 192–3
mills 76, 122, 126, 193, 206
falling numbers 25, 34
profits of 65
rents of 24–5, 65
tithe of 95
Milan 5
mining
of coal 31, 54, 160, 223
of metallic ores 14, 34, 160–1, 223
of tin 34
Miryman family 210
Miryman, John 208
Miryman, Thomas 208
Mode, Richard *181*
Mode, Simon 195
Molin, Thomas *183*, 186, 195
Moncton family 210
money
of account 7
supply of 13–15, 24, 39
see also coinage, credit
Monford 93
Monk, John *181*
Monkwearmouth (Co. Durham) 208n
Montaillou (France) 81
Monza (Italy) 5
Moor, Adam *181*, 185
Moorhouse (Co. Durham) 172, 176, 177
Moor, Joan, widow of Adam 185
moorland 166, 168–78, 220
Mora, Adam de 172
mortality 51, 53–4, 120–1
see also Black Death, epidemics, famine and dearth
Mortehoe (Devon) 102
Morton, Nicola 197
Morton, William 197
multure 65

Nailsbourne (Somerset) 180, *181*, 186, 190, 191, 196
Namur, counts of (Belgium) 162
Napier, Henry *183*, 195
Naples (Italy) 10, 156
national income 224–5, 228
Navarra (Spain) 128
Necker (Germany) 160
Neng, John *183*, 197
Netherlands 11
Neubourg, barony 162
Neville family 176
Newcastle (Northumberland) 54
Newton (Co. Durham) 119
Newton Bewley (Co. Durham) 208n
Nicholas V, pope 220
Nivernais (France) 164

Nonarum inquisitiones 92–3
Norfolk 82, 154, 222
Normandy (France) 122, 123, 124, 125, 128
North Sea 6, 54
North Shields (Northumberland) 54
Northumberland 52n, 172
Norway 151, 162, 220
Norwich (Norfolk) 24, 99
  Cathedral Priory 25, 28

oatcakes 61
oats and oatmeal 24, 61, 63–4, 67, 100, 105, 109, 137–9, 143–4, 171
Ogle (Northumberland) 150n
Oise, River, 10
Old Durham (Co. Durham) *118*, 119
Old Eldon (Co. Durham) 171
olives and oil 18, 221
Ordinance of Labourers, 1348 152
Orense (Spain) 127
Ormsby St Margaret (Norfolk) 35
Otterford (Somerset) 180
Ouse, River 11
Overton (Wiltshire) *133–4*, 137, 138, 139
Oxenbourne (Hampshire) 185
Oxshutte, William *183*, 186

Pakistan 83
Palencia, bishopric 127
'Palframan', Simon 64
Paris (France) 5, 10, 19, 122, 125
parishes
  appropriated 94–5, 132–3, 140
  number of, in England, 94
  unappropriated 95, 106, 135
  see also tithes
Parker, John 196
Paston family 35
pastoral husbandry 21, 30–9, 52–3, 76–7, 112, 129, 202–5, 212, 222
  see also cows, sheep
Peak District 98, 106, 108
peasants
  accumulation of land by 158–9, 167, 179–97
  characteristics of those accumulating 195–7
  common rights of 171–2, 176
  conflicts between 167, 206–9, 213–14
  dominant families among 209–14
  and the labour supply 84, 192–3
  and community organisation 157, 165–7, 200–14, 218
  and household size 204
  revolts and uprisings by 163–4
  and price incentives 16, 18, 80–7
  standards of living of 158, 163, 223–4
  supplying the market 13, 86–7
  syndicates of 211–12
  yeomen 166
  see also tenants, tenures, wage earners
Pennines 32, 170, 217
Perth 57
Perugia (Italy) 156
Peter I, king of Castile 78, 129
Pewell, Alice, mother of Richard *183*
Pewsey, vale of 138
Piedmont (Italy) 76, 160
pigs 66, 95, 100
Pittington (Co. Durham) 206n
plough beasts 85
Plummar, Hugh 63
poderi 159–60
Poland 156, 157
population 219–20
  age profile of 121
  of the eastern Baltic region 156
  of England 13, 25, 27, 34, 38–9, 81, 119–20, 169–70, 228
  of northern England 53, 119–20, 124, 151
  of Europe 149, 219
  of Flanders and Brabant 161
  of France 122, 124, 128, 130
  of Spain 128–30, 156
  and resources, models of 73
poultry 96
Pound, John *181*
Poundisford (Somerset) 180, *181*, 184
prices
  data concerning 43–5, 58–60, 60–1, 228
  density of 156
  fluctuation of 12, 15–16, 21–39, 40–55, 61–2, 78
  and harvests 40–2, 46–7, 51
  inter-regional variation 12, 19, 40–55
  regulation of 7–8, 60–2
  seasonal fluctuations 62
  see also incentives, market integration
productivity
  agricultural 3, 78–87
  restraints on 81–2, 218
Prussia 67, 152, 157, 163

Radesole, Adam 195
Ramsey Abbey 22, 23, 27, 28, 29, 85
Rattray (Aberdeenshire) 67
Rawe, William del 208
Ray, John 185
Raynald family 210
records 74–5, 228
  of Aberdeen 56–7, 60–2
  of the bishopric of Winchester 178–9
  of Durham bishopric and priory 44–5, 202
  relating to demesne production 74
  relating to tithe receipts 74–5, 91–100, 115, 132–3, 146

region
varying definitions of 225–6
regional variation
in access to markets 4–6, 9, 12, 156–7, 166, 178
in the activity of the land market 182, 184
in agricultural productivity 79, 82
in agricultural specialisation 10–11, 18, 142–3, 156, 160, 221–3, 226
in the availability of non-agricultural employment 34, 54, 84–5, 160, 192–3, 197–8, 223
in the balance between arable and pasture 18, 32–3, 52–3. 55
in the character of rents 154–5
in the chronology of change 17, 24–7, 32–5, 76–7, 113–31, 156, 161–2, 229
in commercialisation 4–6, 9, 22, 35, 153–4, 160, 224
in cropping ratios 137–43, 217–18
in currency 7
in diet 220–1
in demesne management 153
in dependence on long-distance trade 18, 67, 221, 224–5
in the desertion of settlements 150–1
in the duration and nature of serfdom 164–5
in the impact of disease 219–20
in the impact of war 219–20, 219
in the incidence of famine and dearth 51–2
in landlord enterprise 154–7
in mercantile activity 8–11
in population density 154, 156
in levels of urbanisation 5, 10, 12–13, 150, 156, 227
in the impact of warfare 32–3, 85, 125, 149, 219–20
in price levels 40–55
in soils, terrain and climate 137–8, 178, 217, 220–1, 225
in trading customs 8
in rural customs and institutions 184, 202–3, 218–19, 225
in the volume of local trade, 4–6
rents 4, 153
declining 107, 145, 161–3
increasing 77, 161, 219
paid in kind 4, 153–5
paid in labour 173, 175
paid in money 4, 173–5, 177
paid by share-cropping 153–5
for pasture 32
recovery after 1349 22
for tithes 104–5
unpaid, 30–1, 67, 171
Repingdon, Philip, bishop of Lincoln 102
Reynold, John 195
Rhine, River 10, 155
Rhineland (Germany) 7, 11, 160, 163
Ribchester (Lancashire) 104
Riccall (East Riding, Yorkshire) 109
rice 68
Rimpton (Somerset) 180, 184
Ripon (West Riding, Yorkshire) 98
Robynson, Henry 109
Rochester 9
Roger, John *183*
Rogers, Juliana, widow of John 194
Rolland, Alexander 64
rye 19, 24, 50–1, 68, 139

Sacriston (Co. Durham) 32
saffron 76
St Alban's Abbey 22
St Andrews (Fife) 68, 220
St George's Chapel, Windsor 94, 99
St James, Tiverton 105
St Mary (Shropshire) 93
St Nicholas Church, Aberdeen 66
St Oswald's parish (Co. Durham) 119
Salerno (Italy) 10
Salisbury (Wiltshire) 24, 140, 142, 145, 146, 222
Cathedral 109, 110n
salt 31, 67–8, 223
Saltholme (Co. Durham) 204
San Clodio do Ribeiro de Avia, monastery *126*, 127
San Gallo, hospital 159
Santa Espina, monastery (Spain) 126
Sardinia (Italy) 77, 150
Saxony 4–5
Sayvile, John 107
Scala Hospital 159
Scandinavia 4, 151, 162
Scarborough (North Riding, Yorkshire) 51, 54
Scotland
currency 15, 161
diet 221
geography 217
government 228
prices 56–69
raids and warfare 105, 172, 205, 220
serfdom 164
towns 6, 19, 56–69
trade 4, 56–69
wool 9
Sedyll, Thomas 104
Seine, River 10
Selby Abbey 90
serfdom
decline of 164–5, 214
'second' 157
Severn, River 11
Seville (Spain) 126, 127

archbishopric 125
Shaldew, William *181*, 195
sheep 18, 95, 98–9, 204
investment in 31
migration of 156
milk from 30
murrain of 24
size of flocks 23–4, 28–34, 36–9
see also wool
Shelom (Co. Durham) 171, 173, 175
Shincliffe (Co. Durham) *118*, 119
ships 67–9
wreck of 69
shops 8
Shrewsbury (Shropshire) 93
Shropshire 93
Sicily 10, 162, 220
Sidbury (Devon) 108
Siena (Italy) 159
Smith, Adam 221
Smot, John, of Edinburgh 67
soap 68
soils
exhaustion 79, 82
and landholding 150, 161
regional variation 16, 137–8, 217
fertility 83, 86
poor soils 140, 143, 166, 170, 178, 220
Sole, Edith, widow of John 193
Sole, Joan 195
Sole, John *183*, 197
Sole, Matilda, mother of Joan 195
Somerset 184
South Shields (Co. Durham) 206, 208n, 209
Southwick (Co. Durham) 206n
Spain 6, 75–7, 156, 228
see also Castile
Sparrow, William 208
specialisation
farming 33, 139, 160
regional 10–11, 18, 36, 51, 54–5, 76–7, 139–42, 156, 219, 221–2, 224–7
restricted opportunities for 178
Spennymoor (Co. Durham) 166, 168–78, 220, 222
Spring, Richard *181*
Staplegrove (Somerset) 180, *181*, 184, 196
Statute of Labourers, 1351 152
Staverton (Devon) 103
Stokes, Robert *181*
Stoke St Milburgh (Shropshire) 93
Stralsund (Prussia) 67, 68
Stratton (Wiltshire) *133–4*, 138–9
subsistence faming 3–4, 222
Suffolk 225
Sunderland Bridge (Co. Durham) 166, *173*, 177
Sussex 34, 145
Swanscombe (Kent) 106n
Sweden 115
Sweet, John *181*
Swynburne, George, of Nafferton 107n
Syon Abbey 36

Taunton (Somerset) 29, 179–98
taverns, trade in, 8–9
Taxatio ecclesiastica of 1291 92–3
Teesdale 32
Teesside 35
Teffont (Wiltshire) 142n
tenants
in conflict with landlords 162–4, 167, 171, 174, 176, 206–7, 209–10, 214
attachment to particular holdings 190–1
bondage 173–4
cottagers and smallholders 3, 53, 82–3, 85, 158–61, 167, 187–94
customary and unfree 85, 164–5, 179–97
entry fines paid by 180, 195, 213
free 165, 204
holding from more than one manor 186–7, 195
numbers of 22–3, 29–30, 35, 120, 123, 175–7, 204–5
smallholding 82–3, 85, 158–61, 167
see also land, peasants, rents, serfdom, tenures
tenures
amalgamation of 154, 158–9, 179–98
bondlands 173–4, 205
carpot 154
cottages 179–81, 183–93, 196–7
fragmentation of 184
increasing freedom of 162–3
inheritance of 194–5
interfamilial transfers 185–6, 191, 193, 195–7
leases 4, 153, 162–3, 166, 211–12, 213–14
named 185–6
Ödrecht 162–3
poderi 159–60
terrage 154
subdivision of 161
tofts and crofts 184–5
unoccupied 22–3, 29–30, 35, 123, 152, 161–2
virgates 183–5, 187–95, 197–8
see also tenants
textiles
production of 54, 145, 160, 223–6
trade in 68, 221
Thames, River 10, 11, 138–9, 217
Thaxted (Essex) 226
Tierra de Campos (Spain) 75
timber, trade in, 5, 9, 68
tin-mining 34
tithes 218

barns for 110
in Castile 115, 125–9
and commercialisation 89–91, 108–12
collection of 99, 101–3, 135
commutation of 97–8
contribution to ecclesiastical incomes 92–3
data relating to 91–100, 102, 115, 122, 125–6, 135, 136–7
declining value of 174
disposal of 100–5
disputes concerning 99–101, 136
evasion of 100
as evidence of economic fluctuations 23–5, 30, 74–6, 87, 91, 93–4, 99–101, 116–31, 137, 143–6, 178
fictional sales of 96–7
in France 115, 121–5
historiography relating to 113–16
leases and farmers of 103–12, 135, 136
rectorial ('great') 94–5, 103–4, 107
sale of 101–3, 108–12, 125, 135, 140–1
valuations of 96–7
vicarial ('small') 94, 98, 100
see also grain, parishes, records
tithing penny 25, 27, 34, 38, 54
Tiverton (Devon) 106
Topcliffe (North Riding, Yorkshire) 98, 102, 110
Topsham (Devon) 101
towns and cities
common land in 66
distribution of 4–5, 224, 227
employment in 5, 192
food supply of 4–5, 9–11, 19, 51, 56, 63, 66–8, 109, 140–2, 221–2, 226, 228
grain production in 66–7
guilds and guildsmen of 57, 60
illegal trade in 63–4
impact on local cropping regimes 141–2
impact on the land market 153–4
lessees of tithes from 109
pigs in 66–7
population of 5–6, 156
scot and lot in 64
size of 4–6, 156
trade
extent of 4–6, 13
'hidden' 9, 63–4
Long-distance 8–13, 64, 67–8, 110, 154–7, 160–1
see also market, integration of, market places, merchants, transport
transport
cost of 102
by river 10–11
by sea 9–12, 51, 66–9, 110, 156–7
Trent, River 11
Treviño (Spain) 128
Trouns, John 103
Tudhoe (Co. Durham) 166, 171–2, *173*, 176, 177
Tunnok, Richard 109
Tuscany (Italy) 74, 150, 155, 159, 162
Tynemouth Priory 53n
Tyrol (Austria) 152

Upper Bavaria (Germany) 152, 162
Upton (Wiltshire) 180
Upwood (Huntingdonshire) 29
Urchfont (Wiltshire) 135, 143–4

Valladolid (Spain) 78, 126, 152
Valor ecclesiasticus (1535) 92–3
Veere (Netherlands) 68
vegetables 3, 18, 68
Venice 5, 6
Vernon family 106
Vigone (Italy) 76
villages
deserted 75, 77, 150–1, 129, 140, 145–6, 150–1
shrinking 175, 219
see also parishes, peasants
villeinage *see* serfdom
virgates *see* tenures
von Thünen, Johann Heinrich 226

wage earners 16
increasing remuneration after 1349 16–17, 24–6, 78, 120, 151–2, 161, 192, 222
legislation concerning 78, 116, 152
paid in grain 3
supply of 17, 84, 120, 151–2
vulnerability of 41
Wales 6, 217, 220, 228
Walker, Richard 208
Wallonia (Belgium) 162
war
effects of 32–3, 105, 125, 129–30, 149, 172, 205, 219–20
Warboys (Huntingdonshire) 29
Warmia (Poland) 163
Warwick, earls of 36
wax 96
wealth, distribution of, 82–3
weather 12, 15, 22, 34, 39, 74, 84, 88, 93, 126, 145, 168, 178, 220
Weardale 32
Wear, River 171
weights and measures 7, 64–5
Wenlock (Shropshire) 93
Wessex 88, 132–46
Westerton (Co. Durham) 166, 168, 171, *173*, *174*, 175, 176
Westminster Abbey 27, 28, 29, 30, 79
Westminster Chronicler 27

Westmoreland 55
Wharram Percy (East Riding, Yorkshire) 151
wheat 16, 24, 33–4, 67–8, 78, 100, 109, 137–9, 143–5, 171, 222
  prices 45–51, 58–63, 78
Whitworth (Co. Durham) 166, *173*
Wiltshire 33, 34, 135, 137–40, 142, 145–6, 225, 226
Winchester
  bishopric manors
    estate management 7
    grain production 29, 33, 141
    landholding 158, 166–7, 179–98
    livestock production 29, 34
    prices 42
    weather 145
  bishopric rectory *see* East Meon
  Cathedral Priory 137, 138
Winchester College 135, 136, 140, 142n, 145–6
wine production and trade 11, 18, 67, 75–6, 122, 154–5, 160, 220, 224
Winterbourne Stoke (Wiltshire) 142
Wisbech Barton (Cambridgeshire) 16, 34, *36*, *37*, 38, 39
Wistow (Huntingdonshire) 29
Wittelsbach, Ludwig von 152
Wodman, John, wife of 63
Wolviston (Co. Durham) 206n, 208, 209
women
  agricultural work by 84
  tithe–farming by 105, 108
  trading by 62–3, 65–6
Wood, John 195
Woodbury (Devon) 98
wool
  exports from England 23–4, 27, 31, 221, 224
  exports from Scotland 64, 67
  exports from Spain 156
  prices of 22, 26, 31–2, 35
  production of 5, 18–19, 23–4, 28, 31, 33, 36, 156, 224
  tithe of 95, 97–8, 100, 102, 107–9, 146
  trade in 5–6, 9, 109
Wootton (Hampshire) *133–4*, 138–9
Worcester, bishopric 36
Worcester Priory 27
Wormot, Robert 68
Wright, Thomas 168
Wrocław, duchy of 158, 163
Wykeham, William of, bishop of Winchester 140
Wynsour, John 109
Wyss', John, of Dornoch 63

York 24, 51, 54, 102, 109, 121
Yorkhouse (Co. Durham) 172, 176, 177
York, Roger of 172
Yorkshire 93